D1613656

Sports Turf

Sports Turf

Science, construction and maintenance

V. I. Stewart
Soil Science and Sports Turf Consultant

Published in association with the
National Playing Fields Association

E & FN SPON
An Imprint of Chapman & Hall
London · Glasgow · New York · Tokyo · Melbourne · Madras

Published by E & FN Spon, an imprint of Chapman & Hall,
2–6 Boundary Row, London SE1 8HN

Chapman & Hall, 2–6 Boundary Row, London SE1 8HN, UK

Blackie Academic & Professional, Wester Cleddens Road, Bishopbriggs,
Glasgow G64 2NZ, UK

Chapman & Hall Inc., 29 West 35th Street, New York NY10001, USA

Chapman & Hall Japan, Thomson Publishing Japan, Hirakawacho
Nemoto Building, 6F, 1–7–11 Hirakawa-cho, Chiyoda-ku, Tokyo 102,
Japan

Chapman & Hall Australia, Thomas Nelson Australia, 102 Dodds Street,
South Melbourne, Victoria 3205, Australia

Chapman & Hall India, R. Seshadri, 32 Second Main Road, CIT East,
Madras 600 035, India

First edition 1994

© 1994 V.I. Stewart

Typeset in 10½/12½ Sabon by Photoprint, Torquay, Devon
Printed in Great Britain by The Alden Press, Oxford

ISBN 0 419 14950 3

A catalogue record for this book is available from the British Library

Library of Congress Cataloging-in-Publication data

Stewart, V. I.
    Sports turf : science, construction, and maintenance /
V.I. Stewart.
        p.   cm.
    Includes index.
    ISBN 0–419–14950–3
    1. Athletic fields--Design and construction.   2. Athletic fields-
-Maintenance and repair.   3. Turf management.   I. title.
GV413.5.S74   1993
725.7--dc20   93–2377
                                                                  CIP

Printed on acid-free text paper, manufactured in accordance with
ANSI/NISO Z39.48–1992 and ANSI/NISO Z39.48–1984

Contents

Contents

Contents

Preface

This book has its origins in a pamphlet, produced for the National Playing Fields Association Conference for Local Authorities in 1971. In this an attempt was made to rationalize the new approaches to sports ground drainage which were then being explored. At that time these were fairly simply described as being either 'all sand' or 'sand slit' in character. These have now been much more fully researched and refinements developed, greatly improving efficiency. Engineers and contractors have also contributed, developing purpose-built machinery whose potential has now to be taken into account when determining how best to proceed.

This new publication aims to provide a rational, scientific appraisal of current practice and practical guidance to those with problems to solve. No attempt is made to describe patented or commercially packaged designs, or to specify particular machines and materials by their trade names. The purpose of the book is to establish general principles and to illustrate these by reference to worked examples. It is assumed that clubs and local authorities will wish to adapt the advice given to meet their own special circumstances, some utilizing design consultants and contractors; others proceeding stepwise on a do-it-yourself basis. Those involved in the training of groundsmen, greenkeepers, agronomists, horticulturalists, landscape architects, environmental scientists, soil scientists, ecologists, etc. may find the specifications for construction and maintenance a useful starting point for discussions where the aim is to stimulate constructive criticism.

The advice given in this publication is intended primarily for those working under moist temperate climatic conditions, where rainfall exceeds evapo-transpiration, at least seasonally, so that efficient soil drainage is a priority and irrigation no more than an occasional benefit. The special needs of those working to create and maintain sports surfaces under arid conditions are not given specific mention, although some aspects are covered indirectly.

Acknowledgements

R.B. Gooch, F.F.S. (Technical Director, N.P.F.A.) assisted as co-author until his death in 1987 and was largely responsible for Chapter 8 and portions of Chapters 1 and 2. J.C. Parker, BSc(Hort), A.L. (Chief Landscape Manager, Kent County Council) contributed Chapter 5. E.D. Stewart, MA, PhD (currently Research Fellow, Department of Physics, University of Kyoto, Japan), contributed Appendix E and portions of Chapters 4 and 13. D.R. Stewart, BA(Design), (currently Illustrator/Graphic Designer, Reprographic Services, University of St. Andrews) contributed all the figures and illustrations. Secretarial and editorial assistance was provided by R.B. Gooch until 1987, then by P.J. Heseltine (formerly General Manager, N.P.F.A. Playground Services Ltd.) until 1989, and finally by Wm.C. Runciman, LLB (formerly Director, N.P.F.A. Scotland) and my wife, Shirley Stewart who saw the project through to its conclusion.

Introduction

Although the history of artificial land drainage can be traced back to Roman times and possibly earlier, it was probably not until the latter part of the Middle Ages that any work of significance was carried out in Britain. This took the form of the still familiar system of ridge and furrow ploughing.

From around 1600 land was gradually enclosed and the field ditch system began to take shape. By about 1700 urban populations were on the increase and the resultant rise in demand for food led to the Enclosure Acts from which it has been said the origins of modern farming can be traced. A first effect was to show the need for more efficient methods of drainage as an alternative to the surface run-off system in general use at that time. There were a few examples of early experiments with underdrainage and this idea was followed by the use of such materials as brushwood (faggots), local stone and baked clay roofing tiles (hence the term 'tile drains') as a means of maintaining a free flow of water underground. Various designs of baked clay piping were later developed but it was not until 1845 that a machine was invented for the manufacture of round clayware pipes by the extrusion method. This led to a great reduction in price and it became possible, under the supervision of the Enclosure Commission, for owners to borrow money for drainage improvement against the security of their land. From this time on Government assistance by way of financial help and technical advice has consistently encouraged the improvement of farmland by artificial drainage.

Through the centuries the stimulus for the development of methods of artificial drainage has been provided mainly by the need to improve crop yields, the modus operandi for this being the installation of integrated systems of underdrains and/or open ditches.

From a study of the history of land drainage it is hard to discover any reference to the drainage of land for recreational purposes until after the First World War. The few text books published that refer to playing fields and sports grounds advocate methods of drainage similar to those employed for agriculture, regardless of the fact that the problem is seldom one of a high ground watertable but much more frequently a problem of getting superficial water off the grass playing surface. In consequence, many schemes of drainage for the improvement of recreational land, though carried out at considerable expense, have failed to achieve their purpose. This has generally arisen because of the failure to provide adequate means whereby surface water could be cleared to underdrains through a topsoil made impermeable by the heavy treading of players' feet in wet weather.

Research carried out since the mid-1960s in the USA, Britain and Europe, has improved our understanding of how best to use sand, either to improve permeability by ameliorating the whole of the topsoil, or confining the sand to a full, integrated, by-pass system of vertical slits linked through to underdrains. As a consequence the drainage designer can now adopt a more scientific approach to drainage problems and specify with greater accuracy the rate of drainage likely to be attained.

However, successful sports ground construction is not solely a matter of getting the drainage right. The end-product must promote healthy, vigorous grass growth, and meet the specific requirements of the games for which it is intended. This generally means that, while the nature of the construction will dictate major essential features of maintenance, so also will the specific requirements of the game and the equally characteristic features of wear that are the inevitable consequence of use. Nothing created in sports turf will remain for long as constructed unless maintained in a manner sensitive to the inherent trends towards change that have to be continually controlled. Like the pilot of a hovering helicopter, a groundsman has to work hard merely to stand still.

If full advantage is to be taken of the modern techniques explained in detail in the following pages, there is no substitute for a careful initial design and diligent advance planning. Rarely will amendments after installation be as economic as getting it right initially.

About the NPFA

The National Playing Fields Association is a charity devoted to sport as recreation, education and fun. It is not involved with sport for political purposes or to help professionals make money by creating spectacles for others to watch. The N.P.F.A. is interested both in those who want to develop their physical skills through sport and those whose only wish is to participate in a game safely and enjoyably. They are on the side of the little boy who everyday kicks a tennis ball across a park on his way to school, counting the kicks, never wanting his self-imposed task to be made easier or the challenge more predictable by the removal of any obstacle, the lowering of any bump or the draining of any puddle that may have appeared overnight. They would also understand why the same little boy would not see the point of cheering for a team if it was made up mainly of players brought in from elsewhere to represent his school.

Sport involves tests of skill developed to deal with the predictable, but those of us who are concerned with providing the facilities must appreciate that too great an emphasis on predictability and learned skills can lead to boredom. Out with the intense competitiveness of professional sport, games should also be fun. This vital, additional element is often a product of the intervention of chance, re-levelling the odds and demanding innovation, but too much unpredictability allows chance to take over so completely that no worthwhile challenge remains.

For good, competitive sport we must create conditions under foot that will allow the game to fairly represent the nature of the challenge intended, but that does not necessarily require that the playing conditions should be standardized. One of the great virtues of soil-based turf is its ability to vary in character according to location and weather conditions. This is of particular significance in games such as cricket, tennis and golf where the reaction of the ball off the surface is so very much part of the game. Even to standardize the length of the grass in a game such as football would be to eliminate the differences between the more intricate skills of those, like the Brazilians, who prefer to play their football on grass cut less short than is customary in England where traditionally we have favoured a more open game involving longer passes.

In our provision for sport we should resist administrative and commercial pressures that may tend to propel us in the direction of dull uniformity. To achieve this we need informed and independent advice, but such advice is only a small fraction of that on offer. In promoting this book the N.P.F.A. has been concerned to make available in print the principles upon which sports facilities can be economically and efficiently constructed, and effectively maintained, wherever possible making intelligent use of locally available, natural materials. It is these materials that have helped to preserve a measure of diversity to which local sport in Britain has been traditionally accustomed.

Part One

General Principles

Chapter one

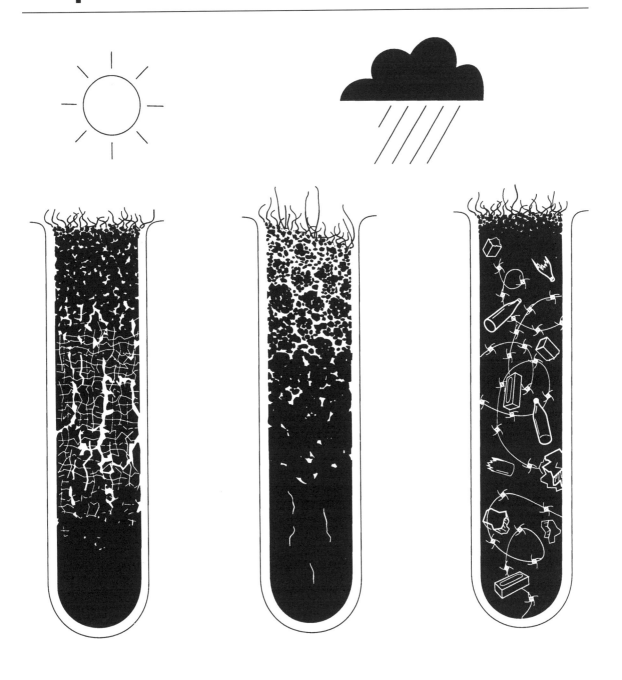

Identifying the problems

1.1 The needs of sport

Turf surfaces used for sport must be moist enough to sustain the grass, but not so moist as to affect adversely the quality of play. They will vary in character according to the special requirements of different games and the standard of provision that can be afforded. For instance, the artificial drainage system which a first-division soccer club might feel was essential to ensure play in all but the worst weather conditions could not normally be afforded or justified by the average sports club, or by a local authority responsible for the provision and maintenance of playing fields out of public funds.

Those involved in new constructions are very frequently asked to specify the usage that can be expected from the final turf surface. Such a request seems reasonable, especially from a club or educational establishment for which use has to be matched to a fixture list or integrated into a fixed timetable. In this respect, however, grass pitches can be a problem. Although grass is ideal as a playing surface when fit for play, it is not so reliably programmable as the more expensive synthetic surfaces.

An improvement in the quality of a surface, suiting it better to the skills of the game, can often be quite easy to assess. For example, the pace of a cricket pitch can be determined by the rebound of a cricket ball dropped dead onto the playing surface from a height of 4.88

m (16 ft). A bounce height of less than 508 mm (20 in) is slow, 508–635 mm (20–25 in) easy paced, 635–726 mm (25–30 in) fast, and so on. The time a perfectly weighted bowl will take to roll to a stop over a standard distance of 30 yards (27.42 m) can be used to assess objectively the pace of a bowling green. A slow green will require a weighty, robust delivery to achieve the distance but will rapidly decelerate as it reaches the mark, rolling to a halt in only 8–10 seconds after release. This compares with 14–18 seconds for a fast green where the bowl can be delivered with much less weight, or the 21 seconds that can be achieved on New Zealand's Cotula greens.

Improved performance in terms of the number of games a surface will take in a given period, though often asked for, is difficult to specify. Intensive use probably begins at two adult games a week and accumulative damage can become critical at three games a week, even if play is avoided when the surface is squelchy. One game played on a squelchy surface, at any time in the winter, may so damage the sward as to affect performance for the rest of the season.

If play is confined to the summer period or to children of 12 or under, these criteria change dramatically. Five games per week, avoiding squelchy conditions, might represent intensive use by children, but here the quality of play can be a problem, concentrating damage down the centre of the pitch and especially in the goal areas.

These conclusions on wear are supported by evidence of the following type.

1. A senior club playing first and second team games on their main home pitch may well average two games per week each season. By the end of the season most of these pitches are badly in need of far more renovation work than the average school or parks pitch would expect to get.

2. An extensive vegetation and soil survey of league soccer pitches at the end of one season revealed how frequently pitch deterioration was blamed by the groundsman on the one game that was played when it should not have been (Thornton, 1978). The trouble is that once the sward has been broken there is virtually no chance of recovery during the winter. Instead, bared areas tend to extend because of the low shear strength of the non-root-bound surface.

3. Tear wear begins when a stud or heel breaks into the surface. This is most likely to happen when the surface is wet. A well-drained soil, though moist, will often feel firm underfoot. Under these conditions the weight of a child is scarcely sufficient to cause studs to penetrate but, with adults, stud penetration may be readily achieved. This explains the big difference in the effect of child and adult use, a point not always taken into account by those who advocate the dual use of school playing fields by children and adults.

4. A qualitative scale used in agriculture to monitor surface wetness after drainage makes use of the following hierarchy of categories:
   (a) hard and cracked;
   (b) firm and dry but not cracked;
   (c) firm and moist;
   (d) moist and soft;
   (e) squelchy in patches;
   (f) squelchy all over;
   (g) pools of standing water;
   (h) surface awash.

If we could persuade referees, who are the only people officially sanctioned to cancel a game, to cancel all games when at least one third of the surface is squelchy, and to allow games only exceptionally, i.e. no more than one game in a week, when the surface remains moist and soft, the staying power of our swards would be greatly enhanced.

5. Even with the same soil and the same general intensity of use, effects determined by climate, shading and standard of maintenance may also modify performance, as in the following examples.
   (a) Features of climate such as rainfall and temperature vary significantly across Britain. Thus, in Wales, there is a risk of 'puddling' or 'poaching' because of excess soil moisture from September onwards, whereas in East Anglia, the same conditions are not to be expected until the beginning of December. In the north they have more frequently to face the dual hazards of rain and frost.
   (b) Shading by grandstands can weaken growth through reduction in light intensity, reduced evaporation and increased persistence of frost.
   (c) Height of cut, frequency of cutting, regular over-seeding with the stronger-growing grasses, proper fertilizing, pest control, special treatment and care of goal areas, the immediate treading back of turf torn out during play: all these features, in addition to good drainage, distinguish good maintenance from bad and affect the survival of a sward through the winter.
   (d) Park pitches or school pitches cannot always be patrolled out of hours to stop boys ruining the goal areas by 'kicking in'. Children would rather have the alternatives of mini-goals and a mini-

pitch of their own but too few of these are provided.

With so many factors contributing to the fate of a sward in use through the winter it would be foolhardy at present to predict the consequences of any particular pattern of usage defined solely in terms of hours of play. What can be said is that sound construction, good maintenance, a dry climate and discretion in use will all contribute favourably.

1.2 Effects of poor drainage

Poor drainage quickly becomes apparent as soon as too much play is permitted in wet weather. It may then be too late to remedy the situation until the winter is over and meantime, poor playing conditions, cancellations and disruption of fixture lists will probably be difficult to avoid. It is, however, the long-term effects which are likely to be most damaging. Excess surface moisture over a long period will generally lead to:

- greatly reduced aeration of the soil;
- reduced root development;
- less resistance to tear wear;
- less resistance to drought;
- inefficient use of plant nutrients;
- late and slow growth in the spring;
- increased susceptibility to disease.

The end result is a grass cover insufficiently durable to support the amount of use normally expected from a winter games pitch.

Most of our sports-field drainage problems are not to be attributed to the ill effects of too high a ground watertable. More typically, water from a shower of rain fails to penetrate below the immediate surface even though the soil beneath is quite dry. The problem, in fact, is one of free water perched over trapped air.

Though air appears to be empty space available for filling by water, air must be able to escape before water can move in to take over

the space that the air occupied. The problem becomes clear when water is poured too rapidly into a narrow-necked bottle. The water cannot get in if it blocks the only passage through which the air can get out. This is very similar to the situation in soil when a period of intense rain floods the surface and the infiltration of water is then impeded by water obstructing the upward escape routes for air. Thus drainage can become as much a matter of the movement of air as the movement of water.

The problem of the competition for pore space between water and air becomes worse the more uniform the pore size. Given a range of pore sizes the capillary forces will ensure that eventually the water is preferentially drawn into the smallest pores. This leaves the air to coalesce into progressively larger bubbles in the larger pore spaces, making escape even more difficult unless the large pores form part of a continuous channel linked through to the surface. Here is one benefit that earthworms, old root runs, cracks and soil granulation can confer to the mature soil, but this structure may be lost during disturbance and stockpiling. It explains why the click of air bubbles bursting can often be heard if one jumps to shudder the soil round a temporary pool of surface ponded water.

Only where the soil is well endowed with large pores and is closely underlaid by a drained gravel bed is air likely to be pushed down through the soil and cleared along with the drainage water. In all other circumstances it has probably to be cleared back up to the surface, a possibility more likely to occur in response to light rain that fails to flood the whole surface. The gentle fine rain that the farmer prefers can be safely absorbed by a well-structured soil into the small pores within soil aggregates, leaving the large pores between aggregates free for the simultaneous escape of the displaced air. However, on the 'poached', de-structured surface of an abused sports field the whole soil is small-pore in character and a false surface water table can be rapidly established over a drier layer of air-locked pores.

This is the classic situation that requires drainage water to be by-passed through specially installed, freely permeable, vertical slits, linking the surface directly though to the underdrains.

1.3 Climate

Climatic effects of importance to sports turf are not to be summarized simply by reference to temperature and rainfall considered separately. Frequently, it is an evaporative effect caused by the interaction of rainfall and temperature that more clearly distinguishes the nature of the climatic stress and the manner in which grass growth is affected in different parts of the country.

Because the range of climatic data available in published form for the whole of Great Britain and Northern Ireland is very limited, detailed consideration of climate, as it affects the construction and maintenance of sports turf, will be illustrated by reference to an analysis based only on the figures for England and Wales (Table 1.1). All the figures used are average values for the period 1941–70, and have been directly extracted from, or derived from, information available in Meteorological Office or Ministry of Agriculture publications. However, take note of the Meteorological Office warning: '. . . it is an unusual year that follows the average pattern.'

From the data on average monthly rainfall, quoted in Table 1, it is evident that rainfall in Britain is fairly uniformly distributed throughout the year with amounts generally higher in the north and west. The figures for potential transpiration in England and Wales quoted in Table 1.2 show that roughly 500 mm (20 in) of this is returned annually, direct to the atmosphere. This loss varies little throughout England and Wales because it is mainly determined by the input of solar energy, a feature of

latitude. However, the input of solar energy varies tenfold between midsummer and midwinter, hence the special significance of the figures for excess winter rainfall (Table 1.2).

Field capacity, in so far as it represents the normal drained state, three days after saturation, reflects the combined effect of site drainage and pore-size composition. It does not guarantee the ideal air/water balance of 70% of total pore space filled with water and 30% free for aeration that would benefit healthy root activity. If the site is poorly drained, e.g. an enclosed hollow, the soil within it may remain waterlogged for long after the three-day period has elapsed, continuing to receive water as it drains down from higher up the slope. But even if the site is not in a receiving location, or does not restrict water loss, the pores of the soil may be so small that they cannot be cleared of the water they hold by capillarity, against the force of gravity, but only in response to the much slower process of evaporation upwards. However, a well-structured soil (Figure 1(c)) in a free-draining site will lose water from the large, more than 30 μm diameter pores, between the water-stable, particle aggregations, and thereby will admit air. Meantime, the small pores, less than 30 μm in diameter, between the soil particles bound together within the aggregates, will retain their water, much of it released only in response to root absorption. A freely drained, well-structured soil, left undisturbed after saturation, may well, in three days or less, achieve an ideal, air/water state for healthy root activity, but it may also still be sufficiently wet to smear and poach into a compact, de-structured state, if animals, humans, or heavy machines are allowed to traffic across it. Only a frozen soil or a dry, clay-rich soil has sufficient structural cohesion to resist collapse in these circumstances. Thus, because even our free-draining, well-structured loam soils are liable to fill up and hover around or above field capacity from sometime in the autumn to sometime in the spring, throughout this period

TABLE 1.1 District values of total rainfall and number of rain-days* 1941–70 (Data abstracted from information supplied by Meteorological Office)

No.	District	Total rainfall (mm)												
		May	Jun	Jul	Aug	Sep	Oct	Nov	Dec	Jan	Feb	Mar	Apr	Total
	Scotland													
0	North	71	76	88	102	114	134	117	140	115	92	80	79	1208
1	East	67	59	77	91	78	80	86	85	78	61	53	52	867
6	West	84	85	105	118	144	151	138	157	138	97	91	88	1396
	(Average)	74	73	90	104	112	122	114	127	110	83	75	73	1157
	England and Wales													
2	E & NE	53	51	61	77	60	57	75	61	64	53	44	47	703
3	E Anglia	46	49	59	63	54	55	63	55	53	42	41	40	620
4	Midlands	61	54	63	78	66	64	78	70	69	54	51	51	759
5	C, S, SE	55	49	58	70	66	73	87	74	70	53	49	46	750
7	NW, N Wales, IOW	82	77	94	115	122	121	129	132	123	90	77	79	1241
8	S Wales, SW England	81	67	81	102	104	109	127	126	119	83	78	71	1148
	(Average)	63	58	69	84	79	80	93	86	83	62	57	56	870
	Northern Ireland	70	73	88	99	101	100	96	108	100	70	67	65	1037

No.	District	Number of rain-days												
		May	Jun	Jul	Aug	Sep	Oct	Nov	Dec	Jan	Feb	Mar	Apr	Total
	Scotland													
0	North	16	16	18	18	19	21	21	23	21	18	18	18	227
1	East	15	14	15	17	16	16	17	17	16	15	14	14	186
6	West	15	15	17	18	19	19	19	21	19	16	15	16	209
	(Average)	15	15	17	18	18	19	19	20	19	16	16	16	207
	England and Wales													
2	E & NE	13	12	13	15	13	14	18	17	16	14	13	14	172
3	E Anglia	12	11	12	13	12	13	16	16	16	14	12	13	160
4	Midlands	14	12	13	14	14	14	17	17	17	14	13	13	172
5	C, S, SE	13	11	11	14	13	13	16	17	16	13	12	12	161
7	NW, N Wales, IOW	14	14	15	16	16	16	18	19	17	15	14	14	188
8	S Wales, SW England	14	13	13	16	15	16	18	19	18	15	14	14	185
	(Average)	13	12	13	15	14	14	17	17	17	14	13	13	173
	Northern Ireland	17	17	19	19	20	19	20	22	21	18	17	17	226

* A rain-day is defined as a period of 24 hours commencing at 0900 GMT on which 0.2 mm or more of rainfall is recorded.

TABLE 1.2 Digest of agro-climatic data of special significance for sports turf

	Min	Av	Max	Rainfall (mm (in))	Potential transpiration (mm (in))	Growing season (days)	Grazing season (days)	Start growing season	End of capacity
Dyfed	0	123 (403)	389	1258 (50)	513 (20)	271	161	Mar 20	May 20
Norfolk	0	33 (108)	77	623 (24)	530 (21)	248	245	Mar 26	Apr 2
Hampshire	0	45 (148)	150	807 (32)	543 (21)	279	226	Mar 13	Apr 18
Lancashire	0	116 (380)	482	1133 (45)	484 (19)	238	154	Apr 2	May 13
Leicestershire	51	117 (384)	192	661 (26)	494 (19)	238	223	Mar 30	Apr 15

this period they will be liable to poach if used for rigorous games by adults when wet enough to feel soft.

Dates indicating the extent of this poaching risk in England and Wales are listed in Table 1.2 (wet growing days). The areas chosen as examples in England and Wales are all fairly low lying and are representative of the north (Lancashire), the south (Hampshire), the east (Norfolk), the west (Dyfed) and the centre (Leicestershire). These show that there is a risk of poaching damage throughout our winter playing season – early September to mid May – in the north and west. In the east and the south there is a good chance that this risk will not begin until well into the playing season – late November or early December – and will be over by the beginning of April.

When we take into account the risk of frost,

which can further aggravate the problem of surface water retention, the figures in Table 1.2 clearly indicate how the north of England is likely to lose out on both wetness and frost, indicating a special need for drainage and under-soil heating, whereas the south is the region most favoured.

By contrast, when the figures indicative of summer drought risk are considered (Table 1.2) these show that it is in the east, south and central regions of England that provision for irrigation might well be considered.

The start and the end of the growing season, as recorded in Table 1.2, is based on a threshold value for soil temperature of 6°C (43°F) at 300 mm (12 in) depth. Well below the surface the seasonal trends are more easily distinguished, uncomplicated by short-term effects of day-and-night or day-to-day fluctua-

TABLE 1.2 *continued*

End growing season	Return to capacity	Max summer SMD (mm (in))	Grass drought factor (days)	Excess winter rain (mm (in))	Winter degree-days below 0°C	Wet growing days*	Wet growing days as percentage of growing season*	Drainage design rate V (mm/hr (ins/ day)) for grassland/ arable/ horticulture
Dec 16	Sep 5	57 (2¼)	5	700 (27½)	85	162	60	1.3/1.5/2.0
Nov 29	Dec 1	113 (4½)	48	160 (6½)	140	6	2	0.7/0.8/1.2
Dec 17	Oct 30	103 (4)	35	310 (12¼)	75	84	30	1.0/1.2/1.5
Nov 26	Sept 11	58 (2¼)	<5	600 (23¾)	120	116	49	1.3/1.5/2.0
Nov 16	Nov 23	102 (4)	35	205 (8)	170	25	11	0.8/0.9/1.3

Abstracted or derived* from MAFF (1976, 1982).

tions. At 6°C on the surface, seeds will readily germinate. However, experience in West Wales suggests that the threshold value of 9–10°C (48–50°F) at the more easily reached depth of 250 mm (10 in) corresponds well with the onset of vigorous grass growth.

Soil temperature is well worthwhile monitoring weekly, from the end of February to the end of May, and again from the beginning of September to the middle of November, following the onset of growth in the spring and the cessation of growth in the autumn (Appendix 7). This can be done most easily under a uniform, fully exposed sward, each time using a metal spike to create a new hole for a metal-shielded soil thermometer to record the temperature at the required depth. Leave the thermometer in place for at least two minutes to equilibrate. Record the information in a diary, or on a graph, plotting temperature according to date. Also, at the same time, make notes on the weather, and any vegetation response such as grass starting to grow, daffodils starting to bloom, apple trees in blossom, tortoise stirring from its winter hibernation. All such events, both at the start and the end of the growing season, will be seen to be related to soil temperature, and the reasons for variations, one year to another, explained. In time, the pattern of soil temperature response for the locality will become evident and put to practical use for predicting when best to sow seed or apply fertilizer, with good prospects of achieving the desired response.

Using the growing season dates in Table 1.2 to indicate the period over which soil tempera-

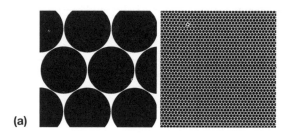

(a)

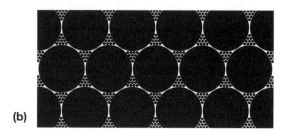

(b)

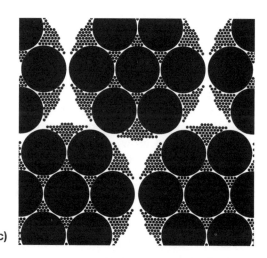

(c)

FIGURE 1.1 Particle packing and pore space. (a) Single particle, close packing: large particles – large pores; small particles – small pores. (b) Mixed particle, close packing: particles interpack – small pores throughout; problems! (c) Mixed particle, open packing: dual pore system – large pores between granules, small pores within; problems solved if granules water-stable.

ture is likely to favour growth, and the grazing season dates as indicating the soil moisture state, we can estimate the number of days in the spring and autumn when soil temperatures encourage growth but the roots supporting this growth have to function in a soil that is likely to be too wet for adequate aeration. Note the widely varying length of this period for the five regions of England and Wales being considered. These figures have been derived from the difference in days between the date given for the start of the growing season in spring and the end of the poaching risk, plus the days between the date given for the return of the poaching risk in autumn and the end of the growing season. These totals point to very clear regional differences in the growing conditions likely to be experienced by grass across England and Wales. It could well be this feature of climate that has most to do with the variable performance in Britain of 'continental' grass species such as *Poa pratensis* (smooth-stalked meadowgrass). This potentially highly desirable, sports turf species, that does so well in parts of the USA, is claimed to be successful in Norfolk, but the many varieties so far tested in Dyfed have all succumbed hopelessly to disease.

It would be interesting to know more about the performance of *Poa pratensis* in the other regions, intermediate between these two extremes – for example, is Leicestershire favourable but Lancashire not?

The purpose of this brief review of some of the direct and indirect effects of climate on soil conditions has been to show how variable this can be even within the relatively small area represented by the lowlands of England and Wales. The extent of this variation is such that it should not be ignored when interpreting the behaviour of existing pitches, or designing new, anywhere in Britain. For example, we should be less willing to compromise on an overall design rate of 50 mm (2 in) per 24 hours for drainage in the north and west of Britain than in the south-east; more inclined to include *Poa pratensis* in a seeds mixture for sports turf in the south and east of England and less so elsewhere in Britain; more inclined to consider undersoil heating for professional sport in the north, east and inland areas of Britain, and more inclined to make provision for irrigation in the south-east.

1.4 Soil texture and soil structure

In site preparation for playing fields the first step is to provide a true surface, relieved and protected by peripheral interception drainage. The next step is to make certain that the soil on the playing area will infilter the water required to sustain grass growth and clear excess so as to maintain an adequately aerated soil environment for healthy root development. The means by which any given soil will have to be managed to achieve the desired air/water balance will depend on its texture. The extent to which it is already appropriately organized will depend on its structure.

While the qualities of soil structure are those concerned with the shape and stability of the functional units, loose particles, granular aggregates, clods, etc. into which the raw materials are organized, and through which the nature of the living space is determined, qualities of soil texture are those reflecting the nature of the primary components, stones, sand, silt, clay and organic matter.

1.4.1 Soil texture

Where the organic matter content does not exceed about 10% by weight (25–35% by volume), soil texture will be determined mainly by the particle-size composition. A simple and commonly used classification of particle-size grades is given in Table 1.3.

The use of a single dimension to define these particles assumes their shape to be square or spherical, but in practice this defines the ranges of particles which behave on sieving or sedi-

TABLE 1.3 Classification of particle-size grades

Particle	Abbreviation	Size (mm)
Stones		larger than 8
Coarse gravel	CG	8–4
Fine gravel	FG	4–2
Very coarse sand	VCS	2–1
Coarse sand	CS	1–0.5
Medium sand	MS	0.5–0.25
Fine sand	FS	0.25–0.125
Very fine sand	VFS	0.125–0.060
Coarse silt	CZ	0.060–0.020
Fine silt	FZ	0.020–0.002
Clay	C	less than 0.002

mentation as if they were spheres of the given diameter, i.e. these are 'nominal' size categories. The gradings offered by sand and gravel suppliers usually refer to quantities of materials passing (or failing to pass) certain sieve sizes.

As mineral soils are made up of a mixture of particle-size grades, it is useful to recognize the simple distinctions between soils sufficiently sandy to be classed for practical purposes as sands (soils more than 70% sand), others sufficiently clay-rich to be regarded as clays (soils more than 40% clay), and the rest, loams, weak or strong according as the clay content is above or below about 15%.

Sands will drain freely and their open structure will not collapse with physical abuse but, unless fortified with organic matter, they are liable to be both hungry and thirsty.

Clays readily hold water. They swell and shrink very actively in response to wetting and drying. Hence, given the right sequence of weather conditions, they can break up into a fine, fracture tilth at the surface and free-draining, deep cracks below. Also, clay particles carry a charge which enables them to store important plant nutrients in a readily available state, thereby promoting fertility.

The wide range of particle sizes present in loams encourages inter-packing and hence fine-particle dominance of the pore system (Figure 1.1(b)). In their natural state loams have insufficient sand to avoid the need for structure development to facilitate drainage and insufficient clay to structure themselves by intensive cracking. They are dependent on biological processes to be physically conditioned into the water-stable, granular state which is typical of a loam in 'good heart'. This structure allows for water and nutrient retention within granules and free drainage between (Figure 1.1(c)) but is liable to collapse under physical abuse or decay of the organic binding agents.

If a system of granular aggregation disintegrates, the open structure will readily collapse to a compact arrangement of individual particles, very liable to hold water to the exclusion of air. Only clay-textured soils have sufficient clay to develop the binding strength necessary to resist collapse in the absence of any assistance from organic binding agents. A loam, therefore, is potentially a problem soil. It is dependent on assistance from organic agents and biological processes for both the development and retention of the open structure that it, like any other soil, requires to meet the demands of normal plants for easy root access, through well-aerated channels to adequate reserves of water. But both the biology and the open structure are liable to be adversely affected by human activity, e.g. failure to return organic residues, elimination of the vital soil organisms and physical abuse leading directly to soil recompaction, much of which would appear to be inevitable under the management considered to be appropriate for sports turf.

The soil texture classes distinguished on a triangle of texture (Figure 7.1(a)) make no reference to stones or organic matter content, but no classification of soil texture is complete without some further, qualifying reference to these components – details are given in Appendix A, section A.5.2, pages 219–222.

Simple tests enabling soil texture and soil structure to be assessed are also described in Appendix A.

1.4.2 Soil structure and drainage

The extent to which water will either accumulate on the surface of the soil, or infilter, will depend on the intensity of the rainfall and the nature of the soil's pore system, i.e. its structure. Pore sizes required for rapid infiltration and air release are large enough to be seen by the naked eye (macro-pores), the smallest correspond to those that would be formed by close-packed, very fine sand. Most soils in Britain have sufficient silt and clay in their make-up for these very fine particles to fill all the potential macro-pore space between any sand particles present, creating a structure entirely dominated by water-holding micropores (Figure 1.1). Thus for most soils in Britain, soil compaction must be avoided if the rapid infiltration of surface water is to be satisfactorily achieved.

Though sands and loamy sands, being more than 70% sand, may avoid becoming micropore dominated even when compact, and some soils that are adequately clay-rich may periodically regenerate an open structure by intensive cracking, for the great majority of soils, the loams, an open, free-draining structure can only be developed by a combination of cracking, root activity, worm tunnelling and worm aggregation. However, this favourable, water-stable structure can be dispersed during storage and will fail to regenerate if earthworm activity is discouraged (Stewart and Scullion, 1989). It can be churned out of existence by foot traffic if the surface is wet. It is at most risk when our winter games season is at its peak and most cattle farmers would have their animals corralled on concrete. It is surprising, therefore, that any of our recreational areas escape long periods of waterlogging during the winter.

The best hope for intensively used grass surfaces is to utilize adequately sandy surfaces linked to some system of sand-stabilized, vertical drainage. The aim should be to by-pass any compaction within the indigenous soil, clearing excess water laterally to a linked system of under-drains for final discharge off site.

The only alternative to sand or sand-modified soils for recreational use is to select a well-granulated, worm-worked, naturally free-draining soil and a site requiring minimal regrading so as to avoid the major soil disturbance of cut-and-fill. Use should then be controlled to give absolute priority to the well-being of the soil and the biological components responsible for its conditioning – see Tables 6.1 and 6.2.

1.5 Soil texture amelioration

For the satisfactory drainage of structureless soil it may be expedient to amend the texture to provide an adequate infiltration rate. To achieve this, sufficient sand must be added to bring the percentage of medium plus fine sand particles to at least 70%. Depending upon the range of particle sizes present in the particular sand selected, the total proportion of sand to silt and clay may have to be anything up to 90% to ensure a sufficient content of sand in the medium-plus-fine range. Thus, in practice, the ratio of sand to topsoil could vary from 2:1 to as much as 5:1. A method of calculating the amount of a specific sand required for the textural amelioration of a particular topsoil is described in Appendix 3.

1.6 Gradients and undulations

Although level grass surfaces are capable of being drained artificially, a slight slope is desirable as a means of encouraging surface run-off following intense rainfall. Depending on the standard of play anticipated, for team games a uniform gradient of between 1:50 and 1:100 should be aimed at. Whenever possible, pitches should be sited so that they are as level as possible along their length with the crossfall occurring over their width.

To prevent ponding, particularly where

major grading is involved, it is of the utmost importance that the final consolidation of both the subsoil and the playing surface is very carefully carried out to avoid any chance of subsequent, differential settlement. Even a hollow left in a clay subsoil could retain water infiltrating through the topsoil and result in that part of the pitch becoming wetter than the rest. It is worth noting that a general slope of 1:50, on the surface, will not be sufficient to ensure the complete emptying of a surface depression 5 m (16 ft) in diameter, if the dip in the depth of the hollow exceeds 50 mm (2 in).

1.7 Use and design rate

The extent to which artificial drainage is likely to be required depends not only on the natural drainage capacity of the land and the rainfall expectancy, but also on the type and amount of use to which the playing surface may be subjected. Use factors which should be taken into account include:

- the games to be catered for;
- the standard of play;
- the number of games and training sessions per pitch, weekly;
- the pattern of use, e.g. weekends only, or weekends and mid-week, or both;
- the age of the players, e.g. adults, school children, or both;
- cancellation repercussions, e.g. loss of gate money or problems over time-tabling;
- extent of any additional, casual use, e.g. for training or by local children kicking into a goal. Casual use leading to localized severe wear can become such a problem that it may be worthwhile providing a purpose-made alternative on land specifically set aside.

A knowledge of these factors is necessary to enable the designer to arrive at an appropriate rate of drainage sufficient to satisfy the requirements of a given set of circumstances. This may be anywhere between an agricultural rate of 12 mm (0.5 in) of rainfall a **day** (24 hours) for a public recreation ground in the south-east of England, and 12 mm (0.5 in) an **hour** for golf and bowling greens. For the average winter games pitch it is likely that a design rate of 50 mm (2 in) a day will be adequate.

This means that the only grounds likely to have a **natural** drainage rate good enough to meet the requirements of winter games are those with the right kind of sand content in the topsoil and a free-draining subsoil. However, most sports grounds in Britain are based on soils with a much lower sand content than the 70% which is required and, therefore, most demand the assistance of some form of supplementary artificial drainage.

Where a gradient has been improved by major grading operations, thereby disrupting the natural drainage channels, extra provision will have to be made for the interception of extraneous water encroaching through the subsoil or as surface run-off.

1.8 The site

A thorough diagnosis of a drainage problem takes time and can be expensive.

1.8.1 Type of information required

1. An accurate plan of the area showing the banks and other physical features with details of any existing rights of way, drainage runs, manhole, siltpits, outfalls, perimeter drains, ditches and public utilities conveying gas, water, electricity or sewage.
2. A grid survey of surface levels at a minimum of half-metre height intervals to provide for contours of the area to be drained. Also record outfall levels and related benchmark.
3. Evidence from soil pits of the nature and extent of soil variation across the site to a depth of at least 500 mm (20 in). For a natural, undisturbed site, use evidence of

variation in slope and vegetation to define areas likely to be uniform in character and dig trial holes in the centre of each of these. Then, confirm boundaries by auger examination of soil between the initial trial holes. On an existing pitch, which may well be on disturbed land, explore first within the four corner areas, in both goalmouths and at the centre, then supplement with auger examination. The evidence from the corner areas should indicate the general nature of the soil construction and the evidence from the goalmouths and the centre may well indicate any previous remedial action taken to cope with severe wear. The following features should be recorded:
   (a) the depth and character of both topsoil and subsoil;
   (b) the depth and type of other material such as rock, sand and buried rubbish that might affect the drainage layout;
   (c) whether ground water is present and, if so, the estimated level of the watertable at different seasons;
   (d) whether the stone content of the soil to drain depth is such that it could cause serious problems in trench excavation, subsoiling, etc.
4. Further examination of any existing drains and outfalls to ascertain their depth, capacity and condition, and the nature and extent of any backfill.
5. Notes on vegetation and any minor surface irregularities to be taken into account when soil sampling.
6. Location of representative soil samples taken for mechanical and/or chemical analysis. In some cases visual examination of auger borings may provide all the information required.
7. Information on the history of the field, especially information of any constructional work, drainage and maintenance that might previously have been carried out. Interviews with people familiar with past performance

to help establish why particular problems have arisen.

8. Copies of specifications, plans and relevant correspondence relating to previous work.

1.8.2 Interpretation of information obtained

1. If existing rights of way, water courses or public utilities traverse the area, the appropriate authorities will have to be approached to establish the nature of any restrictions they may wish to impose.

2. The existence or absence of perimeter catchment drains will help to determine whether water is reaching the site from surrounding areas either on the surface or along underlying strata. The absence of efficient perimeter interception is often a prime cause of waterlogging problems.

3. The colour of the soil profile can be a useful pointer to its condition. Tints of blue, dark grey, olive green or black usually indicate that aeration is poor because of permanent waterlogging. Rust-coloured mottling, usually localized to old root runs, suggests that the soil is prone to waterlogging only at certain times of the year. On the other hand a profile which is a uniform shade of brown or reddish brown generally signifies that aeration is good and that there are no serious drainage problems.

4. Where there is an existing drainage system, it is important that the flow from the outfall and through inspection chambers and silt-pits is checked during a wet period, ideally in winter. Lack of flow at these times does not necessarily mean that the pipe system is at fault. Lack of any substantial drain flow response to heavy rainfall, combined with persistent surface ponding, probably indicates that surface water is not able to infiltrate through the topsoil to reach the pipe drains below. This is perhaps the most common form of drainage failure and can

usually be demonstrated by the relative dryness of the soil below 50 mm (2 in).

5. Surface undulations and depressions, particularly on fine-textured soils, tend to nullify the advantages of having a slight gradient as they can effectively impede surface run-off. Even if examined during drought, the vegetation may provide clues to the normal state of affairs in these hollows. For example, infestation by sedges and rushes indicates waterlogging for long periods.

6. Both chemical and physical soil analysis is necessary to determine the important inherent characteristics of the soil, i.e. its potential fertility, its potential to drain and its potential to be changed.

1.9 Differences in drainage requirements of agricultural land and sports grounds

Land configuration, soil and the nature of use intended are the main factors governing the type and design of the artificial drainage required. Differences between the drainage requirements for farm land and sports turf have their origin in the very artificial and disturbed nature of many of our playing-field soils, and the extremes of wear to which they are often subjected.

1.9.1 Nature of site

For agricultural purposes the natural slope of the land and the natural texture of the soil must generally be accepted. For sport, on the other hand, it is sometimes possible, or even essential to import soil, or to modify texturally the indigenous soil, for example, by incorporation of sand.

Now that efficient earth-moving equipment is freely available, levelling by cut-and-fill and artificial grading are procedures commonly used to provide the uniform surfaces required for sport. Thus sports turf surfaces are frequently based on disturbed and biologically degraded soils.

However, while a farmer has to contend with a multitude of drainage situations varying in size, shape and slope, the person with playing surfaces to drain has more predictable situations to deal with. Every field on a farm may be different, but football pitches and bowling greens, for example, are each very much of a kind, wherever they are. This makes it reasonable to work towards fairly standardized designs to meet the individual needs of the different sports.

1.9.2 Nature of use

For successful farming it is necessary to have an open, water-stable structure, at least to plough depth. To preserve this ideal state, excessive and untimely cultivations must be avoided and caution exercised over grazing and the passage of vehicular traffic. The whole success of farming requires that the creation and preservation of an open, topsoil structure is continually kept in mind.

A true clay topsoil, appropriately structured, may infilter water at a rate as high as 250 mm (10 in) per hour and, if effectively mole-ploughed to drain across to an underground pipe system, may achieve an overall peak discharge rate of 50 mm (2 in) per day. Such a soil avoids ever becoming really waterlogged but, in practice, will maintain this level of performance only so long as the mole channels continue to function and the management of the land does nothing to degrade its structure.

Unfortunately, the farmer's open structure is neither strong nor long lasting. It can be dispersed by bad weather and damaged by machinery and the treading of animals. It can be dissipated if not continually regenerated from within by the appropriate soil biology. On a sports ground a similar open soil structure can be poached out of existence by players treading the surface while it is wet. This risk to

structure is greatest when the need for rapid infiltration of excess surface water is most urgent, at the very time of year when agriculturists would advise staying off. It can also be lost if the topsoil has been stockpiled prior to spreading and will threaten trouble for years after construction. A farmer is usually in the fortunate position of being able to exercise some control over the timing of his various farming operations and the grazing of stock. A groundsman, faced with pitches unfit for play, fixture lists prepared weeks or months in advance, and players with only limited free time available, has to accept the referee's arbitration based solely on whether play of a reasonable standard can proceed without risk to the players. If the surface cuts up, however, such indiscriminate use may initiate a trend in sward deterioration that cannot be arrested until grass growth resumes in the spring.

Because a farmer can control his pattern of field use he can preserve his soil structure or help to regenerate it periodically by cultivation. This generally takes care of the problem of surface infiltration and makes it possible to limit the height of the permeable fill over the pipe drains to that required to intercept mole drainage. However, because topsoil structure is unlikely to survive winter use we now realize that, for sport, methods must be devised to continue artificial drainage interception right through to the surface.

Until the mid-1960s the drainage of sports grounds followed very closely the principles and practices used for the drainage of agricultural land. When the cost of land for sports ground purposes began to increase substantially it became widely appreciated that, to improve the quality of the pitches and increase the number of games played each week, would require improved drainage, but the methods of drainage then practised were far from adequate for the task. Even expensive schemes of pipe drainage, thought by experts to be well designed and efficiently executed, were often found to be largely ineffective when used for play in winter. The sight of a muddy playing surface with relatively dry soil at 75 mm (3 in) and no significant flow in the pipe system is by no means an uncommon spectacle.

In the late 1960s and 1970s the author, amongst others, began to develop an interest in new methods by which the problems of topsoil impermeability on sports grounds could be overcome. One result was a paper given to the annual National Playing Fields Association Conference for Local Authorities and published in booklet form under the title *Drainage Problems on Playing Fields* (Stewart, 1971). The main recommendation that emerged from this research was to use sand to form a direct link to the underdrains, either in the form of a superimposed ameliorated sand topsoil, or confined to narrow vertical slits at close centres. The situation gradually finding acceptance today is that satisfactory drainage design rates can only be maintained by techniques which are not only more sophisticated than hitherto but also much more expensive.

1.10 Cost

Though soil drainage can now be organized with a reasonable expectation of achieving a specific design rate, the problem in practice is to bring the new techniques within reach of the client's financial resources.

Fortunately there are usually two or more different arrangements that will give approximately the same rate of drainage so that by juggling with such features as length, width and depth of slits, different grades of fill, spacing of underdrains, etc. it is possible to arrive at the most economical permutation. Key factors in the equation are often the cost of sand and gravel and the labour and machinery costs for excavating the trenches and slits. (Chapter 4 has detailed information on design criteria.)

1.10.1 Winter games pitches – soccer and rugby

Complete schemes

For the efficient drainage of sports grounds the importance of ensuring that surface water is able to find its way fairly rapidly through the topsoil to the pipe underdrains is now probably well understood. It is not always appreciated, however, that the extra cost of achieving this desirable state of affairs, e.g. by the inclusion of slit drains at 1 m spacing (Chapter 11), can be two to three times the cost of a conventional pipe drain layout for the same area. As an example of comparable costs (UK, 1988), if a senior-size soccer pitch cost £19 000 to drain satisfactorily to a design rate of 50 mm (2 in) a day, an approximate breakdown of this total might be:

Installation of outfall, manholes, main pipes and lateral underdrains	£3 000
Slit drainage	£12 000
Preparation and seeding of slits and damaged areas	£3 500
Minimum initial fine sand topdressing before allowing play	£500
Total	£19 000

The spacing of the lateral underdrains for the slit drainage system described above is likely to be of the order of 15–20 m (16–22 yards), whereas the old type conventional system without slit drains would probably have been designed with laterals at a much closer spacing of 6.5 m (7 yards). On this basis the capital costs in 1988 of a pipe laterals only scheme, plus manholes, main and outfall, would probably have been in the region of £8000, i.e. much less than half the cost of a slit drainage scheme for the same size of pitch.

With slit drainage the financial implications for maintenance have also to be borne in mind.

It will be found that unless steps are taken to repeat the initial application of fine sand top-dressing, at least once a year, the slits will gradually become so soil capped that they will no longer be able to perform their function of channelling water from the surface to the pipe underdrains. In addition, if the soil is at all clay-rich, there is always a tendency for depressions to form along the lines of the slits as an effect of soil shrinkage during the summer (Figure 6.1).

It is therefore of vital importance that, in addition to the capital cost of installation, there must also be included in maintenance budgets a sum sufficient to ensure that dressings of fine sand can be applied annually. A slit drainage scheme not protected in this way could eventually turn out to be a waste of money.

Further information on cost benefit implications for the drainage of winter games pitches is given in Chapter 5.

Staged schemes

Clubs and authorities may find that the cost of improving the drainage of their grounds in one go is beyond their means. However, it is often possible by phasing the work into stages that are financially manageable, or by adopting DIY methods, to achieve the necessary improvements over a period of time.

When upgrading an existing scheme a lot depends on the condition of the existing pipe laterals and the kind and depth of backfill used. If the pipe system is still in good order and the backfill is suitable for linking up with sand/gravel slits, the way ahead should be fairly straightforward. On a football pitch, for example, the worst parts are usually the central area and the goalmouths. These could be slit drained first, leaving the treatment of other bad areas to subsequent years.

If it is found that some, or all, of the laterals are no longer in working order through pipe damage or inadequacies in the backfill, these will have to be repaired or replaced before

slitting can proceed, but again, this could be part of a phased programme.

1.10.2 Hockey

Hockey is difficult, as the game requires a small ball to roll evenly along the surface and is played during the winter season, when the combined hazards of excess rainfall, frost and studded footwear make this particularly difficult to achieve.

If slit drainage is required it will be essential to avoid any risk of depressions forming along the lines of the slits. To achieve this a carpet, 100–125 mm (4–5 in) in depth, formed of suitably ameliorated sand topsoil, should be laid over the surface after slitting. If so designed at the outset the spacing of the slits can be marginally increased but should not exceed 1200 mm (4 ft). The total cost is likely to exceed that of a simple slit scheme by at least 70%.

Although the initial application of fine sand topdressing before any play is allowed will not be required, it will still be necessary, for the reasons explained in section 6.2, for fine sand top dressings to be applied annually thereafter.

1.10.3 Difficult sites

On tip sites, or where there are obstacles at depth, trenching with standard equipment is not likely to be possible. On such sites heavier machinery is usually necessary. This is expensive to operate and may leave a much wider trench than is actually necessary. Thus not only does more spoil have to be excavated and taken away, but an increased amount of backfill has to be brought in. It therefore becomes essential on economic grounds to keep the number of pipe laterals to an absolute minimum, installing them at the maximum effective spacing. To help with this an intermediate, linking tier of shallower gravel channels may be introduced between the pipe drains and the slits (Chapter

3, page 54 and Chapter 4, pages 71–74). Any extra cost will depend on the trenching difficulties, especially the deep trenching required for the installation of the third tier of pipe laterals.

1.10.4 Main use in summer

Where little heavy use takes place in the winter months and there is only light use such as cricket, athletics and casual play to contend with in the summer, it may be possible to use a shallow, single tier of close-spaced laterals. This might be achieved satisfactorily with a miniaturized, pipe-assisted, slit system, discharging directly into a main, off the playing area (Chapter 4, page 69). With no pipe laterals required and given appropriate installation machinery, the cost might be about the same as for an ordinary slit system, but again, special maintenance, including regular sand topdressing, will be necessary to maintain the permeable link through to the surface.

1.10.5 Fine turf areas

For facilities such as golf greens and bowling greens a very high rate of drainage is expected. It may be achieved by placing a carpet of ameliorated sand topsoil, 300–400 mm (12–16 in) in depth, over a gravel bed with pipe drains underneath (Chapter 10). This is an expensive form of construction, at least five times as much per square metre as a slit system, and very careful maintenance is essential, which is also expensive.

A much cheaper alternative for crown bowls or a golf green is to steeply grade both subsoil and topsoil so that they run parallel and shed all excess water to the periphery (Chapter 9, page 144 and Chapter 11, page 171). The final configuration of the surface, however, will have to conform to the requirements of the game and maintenance will still have to be of a very high standard.

1.10.6 Control of use

Unfortunately there is one cost factor over which there is little control. In section 1.1, reference is made to a soil survey of league grounds which disclosed that pitch deterioration was frequently blamed by the groundsman on the one game played when it should not have been. This is perhaps one of the most difficult situations that can confront a groundsman. No matter how unfit for play he may consider the pitch to be, the sole arbiter on whether play should proceed is the referee, but his remit covers only the safety of the players and the quality of the play that will be possible. The referee need not be concerned with the effect that play may have on the pitch or the cost of the remedial measures that will have to be taken to make good the damage.

The groundsman will also be aware that any move towards a general improvement in the playing surface brought about by better drainage can bring in its wake a clamour for greater intensity of use. In these circumstances it is possible to sympathize with the groundsman who feels that unless decisions over use are left in his hands, he is on a hiding to nothing.

1.11 The importance of a clear, concise and comprehensive specification

For contractors and direct labour departments of public authorities to have a clear understanding of drainage work requirements, it is essential to prepare a sound and properly detailed specification. This should include appropriate drawings and a bill of quantities suitable as a basis for tendering.

Not only is a well drawn up specification essential for best results, it is also necessary to enable contractors to tender on a common basis. A loosely worded specification, or no specification at all, makes it impossible for tenders to be fairly compared.

If a contractor finds himself obliged to submit a specification with his quotation, he often words it in such a vague and equivocal manner that it is virtually impossible to arrive at any precise conception of what is to be provided for the money. Where it is the usual practice for the lowest tender to be accepted a situation may arise where a contractor, either through lack of the required experience, or because of uncertainty about the authority's requirements, quotes an unrealistically low price. He may then finish up doing a bad job to avoid losing money, or may himself lose money trying to do a good job. Either way it is unsatisfactory and all concerned are likely to suffer, including reputable firms which may find themselves at a disadvantage through trying to maintain good standards.

An increasingly serious problem is that those involved in soil disturbance, i.e. architects, surveyors, engineers, consultants, contractors, etc. are not always well informed on the biological basis of soil fertility and its significance for drainage. The scientific content of this work has of late tended to change faster than the personnel concerned. It is vital, therefore, that all are properly trained and keep abreast of developments. It is a sad state of affairs when only the most recent recruit is conversant with the latest developments and the boss is isolated from enlightenment by his defensive adherence to tradition. One aim of this book is to help senior personnel to update themselves, beyond rigid recipes to a more scientific understanding of general principles that will give them the confidence, not just to follow but to lead.

Where knowledge is lacking there is often a tendency to pass the buck to the contractors in the sometimes mistaken assumption that they are the experts. The practice of simply defining the end-product in terms of function, drainage design rate, or minimum time to playability after rain can lead in the end to expensive remedial measures and possible litigation.

A contractor is in business to make money and he can only do this if he is competitive. In the real world of commerce the sharp practice often necessary to achieve a competitive advantage can only be avoided by the employing authority setting out its requirements in sufficient detail to ensure that they are fully understood. Only then can the specification and terms of contract be effectively enforced by the employer while the work is in progress.

There is a good moral reason for insisting on the employing authority itself preparing a detailed specification: it is manifestly unfair to put this time-consuming task onto the contractors when only one will get the contract. One practical consequence of this practice is that all the necessary preliminary investigational work on levels, soil samples, materials and design data may not be properly carried out by the contractor submitting the lowest tender. These limitations will then only emerge after both parties are irrevocably committed to a cost ceiling that is quite inadequate.

The right of contractors to be given proper specifications when invited to tender, including the guidance inherent in the bills of quantities, should be more generally recognized. It is with this in mind that the following recommendations are made.

1. Those authorities responsible for carrying out drainage work on sports grounds should always have ready access to staff or consultants adequately qualified in the up-to-date techniques of land drainage.
2. Tenders for the drainage of sports grounds should not be invited except on the basis of properly prepared specifications.
3. The subject of field drainage should be given increasing priority in the courses organized by professional bodies whose members are likely to be engaged in the provision and maintenance of sports grounds and playing fields.
4. Staff of public authorities and private firms (consultants and contractors), either propos-

ing to, or already practising in the field of land drainage, should be encouraged to attend refresher courses to keep them abreast of modern practice.

1.12 Site supervision and checking of materials

1.12.1 Supervision

Today the scientific nature of drainage design is such that as little as possible should be left to chance. From the information given in Chapter 4 on design criteria it is clear that if a given rate of drainage is to be achieved all the specification requirements – design and materials – must be complied with explicitly. No deviation from the specification should be permitted without the express consent of the drainage designer, in writing.

It follows from this that the client organization must exercise very close supervision of the work. It is strongly advised, therefore, that the drainage designer or a specialist consultant be retained to approve materials before use and check the various stages of the work as it proceeds. In addition, it is an advantage if there is a groundsman on the spot who can act as an observer. Ideally, everyone concerned with supervision should be briefed on the specification in the presence of the contractor's site agent and foreman so as to provide an opportunity for misunderstandings to be cleared up before work begins. Thereafter, the job of anyone acting in the role of clerk of works is to have close liaison with the contractor. He should be present when each new phase of the work is due to begin and should confirm the suitability of the materials delivered on site, the procedures to be adopted and the standard of work expected. He should also be present to approve each phase of the work as it is completed. In the event of disputes he should briefly record his observations in writing, leav-

TABLE 1.4 *Stewart zones* defining sand and gravels of particular value for the construction, drainage and maintenance involved in sports-turf provision

Sieve size (mm)	Percentage by weight passing the specified sieve		
	Topsoil sand	Blinding sand	Trench gravel
	Coarse–Fine	Coarse–Fine	Coarse–Fine
14.00	–	–	100
10.00	–	100	82–100
5.00	–	95–100	0–100
2.36	100	80–100	0–10
1.18	98–100	46–89	0
0.60	83–100	21–59	–
0.30	10–100	5–30	–
0.15	0–22	0–11	–
0.075	0	0	–

Sieve size (mm)	Percentage by weight in each particle-size category		
	Topsoil sand	Blinding sand	Trench gravel
	Coarse–Fine	Coarse–Fine	Coarse–Fine
8–16	–	–	73–100
4–8	–	8–0	27–50
2–4	–	20–0	0–44
1–2	5–0	33–17	0–6
0.5–1	23–0	23–33	–
0.25–0.5	69–0	14–26	–
0.125–0.25	3–90	2–17	–
0.060–0.125	0–10	0–7	–

ing a copy with the foreman and passing the original to the consultant or the client.

If drainage work is put out to contract, and forms part of a main contract, it should be made quite clear to the main contractor that on no account should any work be sub-let to another firm without the client's expressed agreement in writing. The client should satisfy himself that the sub-contractor chosen has adequate practical experience of the type of drainage work to be carried out and is fully conversant with the requirements of the specification.

1.12.2 Precise specification checks of sands and gravels used in sports field construction and maintenance

Because existing systems of classification used in Britain for specifying sands and gravels are intended primarily to serve the needs of the concrete industry, it has been found necessary to develop an alternative system for sports turf. This is summarized in Table 1.4 and is discussed more fully in Chapter 7. It is these materials to which reference will be made from Chapter 2 onwards. They will be referred to as *Stewart zone* **trench gravels**, **blinding sands** or **topsoil sands** or, more commonly, just *trench gravels*, *blinding sands* or *topsoil sands* without reference to their *Stewart zone* origin. The limits of these zones are described analytically in Tables 1.4 and 7.1, and graphically in Figure 7.6.

Although the designs featured in this book have been matched to a closely specified range of materials that are commonly available, it does not mean that materials outside this range are necessarily useless. A locally available material may have a distinct cost benefit and, by some modification of the general design, may well be utilized to advantage by someone adequately trained to calculate the necessary adjustments. Experience suggests, however, that not all contractors or technicians are aware of what may be available outside that provided by a narrow range of suppliers whose primary purpose is to meet the needs of the building and concrete industry. The advice is to shop around yourself before accepting pronouncements, favourable or unfavourable.

Chapter two

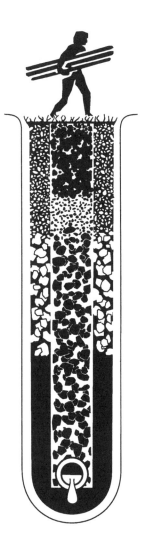

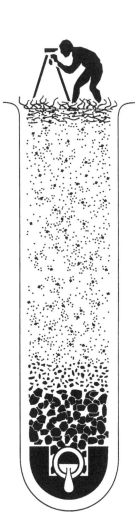

Chapter two

Components of a drainage scheme – function and installation

2.1 Field drainage

2.1.1 Peripheral, cut-off or interception drainage

It is important to ensure that the field to be drained is protected against the influx of water from surrounding land. Within-field drainage then needs to be designed to cope only with the excess rain falling onto the field itself. In some cases it may be found that a good system of perimeter drainage will obviate the need for anything more.

If there is the slightest risk of extraneous water reaching the area to be drained, either on the surface or below ground, its interception must be assured by the installation of appropriately sited drains before work on the within-field drainage system is allowed to proceed. Without this protection the drainage designer cannot specify accurately a drainage system to a given design rate.

Interceptor drains may be in the form of 'French' or catchment drains, or open ditches leading to outfalls capable of taking the full amount of water likely to be collected under peak conditions. Ideally, any peripheral interceptor drain should be monitored as an open

trench for a year to assess the efficiency of interception and the amount of flow, before piping and backfilling.

'French' or catchment drains

These are often fairly wide, tapering trenches, perhaps 300–450 mm (12–18 in) at the top, filled with clean, 12–38 mm (½–1½ in) stone, or 6–10 mm (¼–⅜ in) gravel, to within 25–50 mm (1–2 in) of the ground surface. The depth is usually between 600–900 mm (2–3 ft) but may be more where there are deep underground flows requiring interception. There should be a good fall towards the outfall. If the accumulation of water at peak periods of rainfall is likely to be high, the rate of flow will be greatly improved if drain pipes of adequate capacity are laid along the bottom of the trench for at least the lower part of its length. This type of drain is widely used for interception along boundaries and at the foot of banks; also as a main where it can be sited clear of the playing and spectator areas.

In certain situations, for example, as a catchment drain around a football pitch, or within banks where a continuous grass surface is required, a narrower trench, some 250 mm

(10 in) wide, may suffice. This should be piped if necessary and backfilled with *trench gravel* to within 100 mm (4 in) of the surface, then topped with *blinding sand* to ground level without a fine soil capping.

Open ditches

Ditches that are regularly cleaned out and maintained are the most effective water carriers as they are generally of large capacity with little or no impediment to the flow of water. On play areas, where they are in the way but have a drainage use, they must be piped before filling in. Elsewhere, such as along side boundaries, it is usually advantageous to keep them open but they will then require proper maintenance. Open ditches are the best solution for the interception of surface run-off but, for the interception of underground water only, they need not be kept open. Whether open or piped, however, they should be made deep enough to ensure that all potentially troublesome flows are properly intercepted.

2.1.2 Within-field, pipe underdrainage

Mains and laterals

The function of a lateral is to intercept water moving towards it through the soil or over the surface. It should be looked upon as the combined system of perforated pipe and permeable backfill, all contained within the same trench. The purpose of the permeable fill is to improve the efficiency of interception and direct the captured water down to a pipe, perforated to accept it throughout its length, then convey it onwards to a main.

The function of a main is to collect drainage water gathered by the laterals and convey it without loss to the intended outfall. In a grid system, where slit drainage is proposed, the mains pipe should not normally be perforated and there is no need for the trench backfill to be other than soil. From the cost point of view this is an advantage, as to backfill with gravel what is often a wide and progressively deepening trench, could be very expensive.

Where a lateral pipe is perforated and surrounded by gravel, there is every chance that water will enter and flow laterally through the gravel as well as the pipe. At the junction with the main, therefore, there could be a problem because of water from the gravel accumulating in the soil above and around the closed main. For this reason some large pipes are made to the design illustrated in Figure 2.1. The bottom half is unperforated and intended to be bedded within a purpose-made trough in the soil so that it can act as the main channel for water flow. The top half is perforated and intended to be enveloped in a shallow depth of gravel, linked to the gravel at the base of the laterals. Thus the main need no longer lie in a water-logged trench, acting as a sump for water not confined to the pipe system. But such a pipe is relatively expensive and may not be locally available.

Banks

Where natural banks exist, or major grading is proposed, it will almost certainly be necessary to install interceptor drains to prevent water flowing down banks onto the playing areas. If only one is to be installed it is best placed along the foot of the bank but, if the bank itself is to be kept dry and stable, an interceptor drain may also be necessary at the top of the bank, or within the slope. For example, in the course of excavations during grading operations water-bearing strata may be exposed or old land drains disturbed. Special attention will then have to be given to intercepting any outflow, diverting it to a safe outfall before further work proceeds.

Outfalls

No drainage system can function unless there is an adequate escape route for the water. This is the first thing to check when planning a

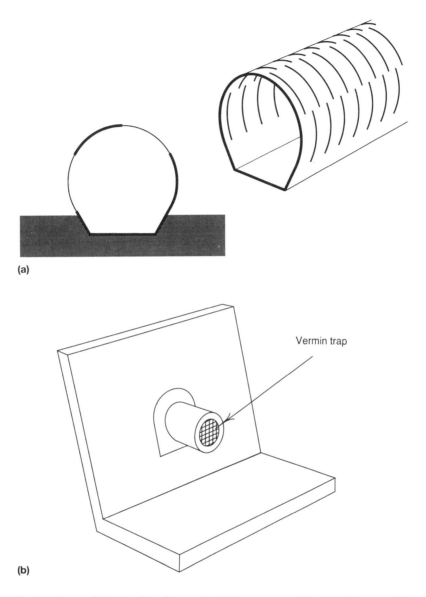

(a)

(b)

FIGURE 2.1 (a) Plastic pipe, well designed and properly laid so as to achieve both interception and discharge. (b) Headwall and splash surface.

drainage scheme. Usually there is an existing ditch, stream or even a nearby storm-water drain that is suitable, although use may have to be negotiated with the rightful authority. Failing any of these the use of boreholes, soakaways or even a pump may have to be considered. Boreholes and soakaways, however, seldom provide a satisfactory solution unless somewhere below they can be positively linked through to a permeable stratum with a consistently low watertable.

Pumps, either electric or diesel, are used

mostly for the drainage of agricultural land but are also available for use on small areas such as sports grounds. They are generally capable of operating automatically when water in a sump reaches a given height. A solution on these lines, however, is not recommended, except in very special circumstances, as such equipment, with its ancillary housing, is expensive to install and requires periodic attention to ensure that it is always in satisfactory working order. Useful information on pumping systems is given in the MAFF leaflet, No. 14 *Pumped Field Drainage*.

All outfalls into ditches should be above peak high water wherever possible and at least 150 mm (6 in) above normal water level. The outfall pipe should discharge through a properly built headwall and be fitted with a flap valve or vermin trap (Figure 2.1(b)). At least the last 1.5 m (5 ft) of buried pipe should be of a rigid type, held firm by being closely packed around with soil.

Differential settlement of the pipe and the headwall can lead to pipe displacement or fracture where the two meet. It would be wise, therefore, to check on the continuing efficiency of these junctions a year or so after construction.

As a general principle, to avoid a situation where intercepted water cannot easily be cleared, work on drain installations should proceed backwards from outlet to inlet.

Drain falls

Pipe drains should not be laid to a fall of less than 1:200 as it is difficult to lay a drain to such a small fall uniformly; steeper falls are preferred. Mains should generally be laid to a slightly steeper gradient than laterals. This will ensure that there is no check to flow water at the junction.

Drain falls should be kept as uniform as possible. Any reduction in fall along a drain run may slow down the rate of flow to the extent that silt disposition will occur and the pipe eventually becomes blocked. Sharp bends should also be avoided unless an inspection chamber with silt trap can be provided at the change of direction.

Distance between laterals

The spacing between laterals depends on:

- climate, pattern of use and budgetary constraint;
- the expected efficiency of other parts of the system – the slope and trueness of the surface, the nature of the soil, and the capacity of any auxiliary system installed to intercept surface water and pass it on.

In practice the rate of drainage that is adequate for most clubs is likely to be between 25 mm and 50 mm (1 and 2 in) per day depending on geographical location and nature of use. To achieve this most soils in Britain require a two-tier system of artificial drainage consisting of a lower tier of pipe drain laterals crossed at right angles by an upper tier of closely spaced sand/gravel slits (Chapter 3, page 49 *et seq* provides a full discussion of 'tier systems'). Details of spacings, depths, etc. are worked out on the basis of a simplified version of Hooghoudt's drain spacing equation (Chapter 4, page 57 *et seq*), much depending on the characteristics of the backfill materials used in the slits. For this type of design the spacing of the laterals commonly works out at around 10–20 m (11–22 yards).

Schemes aiming to avoid the need for some form of artificial, auxiliary system to intensify surface interception cannot expect to approach a satisfactory design for winter use, even under favourable conditions of slope, soil and discriminate use, without laterals spaced less than a maximum of 4 m (4½ yards) apart. However, reducing pipe spacing below 4 m (4½ yards) is unlikely to be economical compared to the cost of a two-tier system, unless the pipes and trenches are miniaturized.

Depths of drains and width of trenches

Extreme depth can add greatly to the cost, generally for no useful purpose. Extreme shallowness, on the other hand, may considerably reduce the efficiency of interception and court damage when the trenches are crossed by heavy equipment. For laterals the depth to the surface of the pipe should exceed the depth of the freely permeable topsoil and should exceed, by a margin of at least 150 mm (6 in), the depth to which equipment will later be operating to install ancillary drainage such as sand/gravel slits or mole channels. Even then it is always worth checking, by means of an initial demonstration on site, that the technique which the contractor proposes to use for the installation of ancillary drainage will not risk indirect pressure on the pipe system. The gravel backfill used in pipe trenches is loose, uniform in size and somewhat rounded, and will readily transfer pressure downwards. This may lead to pipe damage when the rotating tines on the excavating arm of a mechanical trencher exert downward pressure as they circle round the far end of the boom (section 11.4, pages 177–179). Where heavy, wheeled equipment is used, it may be necessary to adopt the precaution of using temporary bridging planks over each pipe trench to take the weight of the installation machinery as it crosses.

In practice laterals generally should be laid in trenches not less than 450 mm (18 in) nor more than 750 mm (2 ft 6 in) deep, although as much as 900 mm (3 ft) or more, may be necessary where the drain has to be deepened along its run to obtain the necessary fall. Where there is to be mole drainage or subsoiling the depth should not normally be less than 650 mm (2 ft 2 in) nor more than 750 mm (2 ft 6 in), the distance between the top of the pipe and invert of the mole channel being not less than 100 mm (4 in), preferably 200 mm (8 in).

It must be remembered that the deeper the trench, the greater will be the cost of excavat-ing and carting away soil and then replacing it with permeable fill. For this reason also it is important to ensure that the width of trenches is kept as narrow as possible, consistent with ease of pipe installation; generally around twice the pipe diameter.

The difference in the outside diameter of perforated plastic piping and the clay tile equivalent should always be borne in mind when specifying depths and widths of excavations.

The depths of main drains must depend upon the layout and design of the system as a whole – for example, the depths of the laterals or the level of the outfall. For this reason, when designing, it is always wiser to work back from the final outlet so that any limitations on depth and fall are immediately apparent.

In tight situations it is the depths of the peripheral, interceptor drains and ditches that can be a problem. To be effective along the downhill margin of a site they have to be deep enough to help control any ground watertable and deep enough to allow for unrestricted discharge from any field drains.

Pipe junctions

To avoid any obstructions to the flow of water from branch drains, purpose-made angle junctions should always be used. Manufacturers offer a range of such junctions but all too frequently they are not available on site. The flash discharge, characteristic of modern sports field drainage, will not benefit from a sudden check to flow in a lateral main through an indirect gravel bridge; and neither will a flow in a main benefit from being checked by the end of a lateral protruding into it. Such checks will encourage silting and a progressive deterioration in efficiency.

Pipe size, flow rates and overall design

Choice of pipe

There are a large number of pipes on the market that can be used for land drainage purposes but, for the majority of sports ground schemes, the types most generally favoured are the clay tile pipe and the flexible plastic pipe.

Sports fields are fairly restricted in their pipe drainage requirements:

- they seldom exceed 6 ha (15 acres);
- gradients normally lie between 1:200 and 1:40;
- design rates are generally adequate at a maximum of 50 mm (2 in) per day.

For an overall design rate of 50 mm per day and a gradient of 1:100, maximum pipe sizes normally do not have to exceed 150 mm (6 in) internal diameter, and this maximum size is required only for the main running to the final outfall of a 2 ha (5 acre) field. For an area the size of a football pitch the maximum requirement for the pipe at the outfall may well not need to exceed 100 mm (4 in).

Table 2.1 has been prepared to provide guidance on a selected range of pipe sizes currently in use for sports field drainage projects. Rates of flow and areas served are also given but, because type of pipe and availability are bound to vary with time, these are offered merely as general guidance.

Flow rates are of value for indicating the capacity required in the final outfall. A speed of flow in excess of 30 cm (1 ft) per second is likely to be adequate to carry fine sediment out of a pipe drain line and this should be exceeded for all the examples listed, but only when the drain is running full. Hence there is some virtue in not being over generous in pipe size provision. Joints on mains need to be sealed where there is a risk of speeds of flow in excess of 150 cm (5 ft) per second but this applies only to those examples bracketed.

To calculate speeds of flow, measured in centimetres per second, from information on flow rates, in litres per minute, and internal pipe diameter, in millimetres, use the formula

speed of flow (cm/s)

$$= \frac{\text{flow rate (l/min} \times 2121}{(\text{pipe diam in mm})^2}$$

The recommendations in Table 2.1 include an allowance to limit the risk of surcharging in the mains but no allowance for silt deposition limiting effective pipe diameter in either main or laterals. In addition they assume an overall drainage rate of 50 mm (2 in) per day to be cleared through the installed drainage system. The reasons behind these choices need to be discussed as there are circumstances in which some further modifications may be justified.

Surcharging and silt deposition

The absence of any safety margin built in to avoid surcharging in laterals is acceptable, particularly under sports field conditions, because of the freedom for water to escape as well as enter throughout their length. The runs are relatively short (less than 100 m) and gradients generally low (less than 1% when installed diagonally across slope) so that water can readily back up along the length of the pipe without developing sufficient head to raise it onto the surface. Also, in a modern sports field drainage installation, there is an abundance of easily accessible and stable storage space for excess water in the gravel fill around and above the pipes, and in the base of the slit systems to which they are linked. Occasional surcharging under these conditions need not be a problem and may be an advantage. The enhanced scouring effect when pipes are running full will help to clear small accumulations of sediment along to the silt traps.

By contrast, though mains may be open (perforated) throughout their length, as when acting also as part of a peripheral catchment system, many are closed (unperforated) with access only where they link to laterals. In either case, however, they tend to run fuller than laterals throughout their length and, in sports fields, run for longer distances and at steeper

TABLE 2.1 Pipe performance[a]. Area served at overall design rate of 50mm/day[b]

Type	Pipe diameter (mm)		Used as	Gradient 0.5% (1:200)				Gradient 1% (1:100)				Gradient 2% (1:50)			
	Outside	Inside				Max area served[d]				Max area served[d]				Max area served[d]	
				cm/s	l/min	m²	Examples (m)	cm/s	l/min	m²	Examples (m)	cm/s	l/min	m²	Examples (m)
Clayware	95	75	Lateral	68	180	5 184	65×75 / 110×45	88	234	6 739	65×100 / 110×60	120	318	9 158	65×140 / 110×80
	120	100	Main[c]	57	270	7 776	65×110	84	396	11 405	65×175	122	576	16 589	125×125
	175	150	Main[c]	76	810	23 328	150×150	112	1 188	34 214	180×180	(163)[e]	1 728	49 766	220×220
	250	225	Main[c]	98	2 340	67 392	250×250	145	3 450	99 360	310×310	(214)[e]	5 100	146 880	380×380
Smooth (plastic with longitudinal slits)	50	45	Lateral	57	54	1 555	65×20 / 110×14	75	72	2 074	65×30 / 110×18	101	96	2 765	65×40 / 110×25
	70	65	Lateral	72	144	4 147	65×60 / 110×35	96	192	5 530	65×85 / 110×50	130	258	7 430	65×110
	90	85	Main[c]	60	204	5 875	65×90	88	300	8 640	65×130	130	444	12 787	110×110
Corrugated (plastic with transverse slits)	35	30	Piped slit	33	14	403	400×1 / 65×6	45	19	547	540×1 / 65×8	59	25	720	700×1 / 65×10
	60	53	Lateral	41	54	1 555	65×20 / 110×14	54	72	2 074	65×30 / 110×18	72	96	2 765	65×40 / 110×25
	80	72	Lateral	49	120	3 456	65×53 / 110×30	64	156	4 493	65×65 / 110×40	88	216	6 221	65×90 / 110×55
	110	100	Main[c]	51	240	5 875	65×90	57	720	7 776	65×115	81	384	11 059	65×170
	165	150	Main[c]	51	540	15 552	120×120	74	780	22 464	145×145	102	1 080	31 104	175×175

[a] For safety margin to be allowed for different soil conditions see page 28 et seq.

[b] 50 mm/day = 0.03472 l/min/m².

[c] Main intercepts laterals.

[d] Examples only approximate. Laterals related to pitch dimensions 110 m×65 m.

[e] Bracketed values – pipe joints require to be sealed if speed of flow exceeds 150 cm/sec.

Flow rates abstracted from MAFF (1982).

gradients than the laterals feeding to them. They must be protected, therefore, from surcharging or they will transfer their problem back along the laterals, particularly those entering lowest down slope. It is for this reason that the recommendations quoted for mains in Table 2.1 include a safety margin to protect against surcharging. This is particularly important with the 'flash discharge' potential of modern slit systems. It also justifies the further precaution of always erring on the generous side when faced with a choice between two reasonably close, pipe size options.

Mole drainage systems work best in cohesive soils, e.g. soils such as clays. In such cases mole drainage is unlikely to increase the risk of siltation in the laterals, because moles should never be installed in other than cohesive soils. However, any risk of surcharging within the laterals into which they empty should be avoided. The unstabilized mole drainage crack and tunnel system is very liable to collapse if allowed to remain full of water. In an effort to extend the effective life of such systems care should be taken to keep the top of the pipe at least 20 cm (8 in) below the normal 450–525 mm (18–24 in) moling depth and an additional 10% margin of safety should be included in the carrying capacity of the pipe system throughout.

When corrugated pipes are used, either for mains or laterals, the recommendations in Table 2.1 may have to be modified to take account of extremes in the pitch of the pipe corrugation. The value shown will underestimate by 10% the carrying capacity of a corrugated pipe where the pitch of the corrugation is less than $\frac{1}{20}$th of the diameter of the pipe, or over-estimate by 10% where it begins to exceed $\frac{1}{5}$th.

Because sports fields generally are fairly flat, small irregularities in the surface can make it difficult to install pipes to an even gradient and deposition of silt in the low spots may ensue. In addition, the supply of silt may be enhanced by

the open nature of the permeable fill, the narrowness of the trenches and the weak structural state of the soil. As no allowance is made for effects of siltation in the recommendations listed in Table 2.1 the recommendations given are most appropriate for cohesive soils, over 35% clay.

For very unstable soils, mostly very fine sand and silt with less than 15% clay, it would be advisable to design the pipe layout with numerous silt traps allowing easy access to pipes for clearance. Alternatively, trenches may be lined and pipes wrapped in appropriate synthetic filter fabrics. A small increase in pipe size alone will not be sufficient.

For all other soils (i.e. soils 15–35% clay) it would be advisable to make a standard allowance of an additional 10% in pipe capacity as a safety margin against the consequences of a small amount of siltation restricting flow. This applies particularly to open mains where there is unlikely to be free access to an under-bedding of gravel into which any initial flush of silt in a new construction might otherwise escape.

Significance of overall design rate
The advice on safety margins so far given is aimed primarily at ensuring the internal integrity of the drainage system, avoiding troublesome bottlenecks so that once free water has been intercepted it can flow smoothly right through to the final outfall. However, the scale of the whole operation is conditioned from the start by the efficiency with which the overall design rate meets the problems posed by the incident rainfall. In Table 2.1 the assumption is made that the objective is to be able to clear up to 50 mm (2 in) per day through the installed drainage system. In effect this could amount to at least 60 mm cleared in total if a pessimistic view is taken of the contribution likely to be added by natural seepage which bypasses the installed system. The significance of the 50 mm per day target is that it comes very close to the maximum which agro-meterologists assume to

be appropriate, in England and Wales, for mole-drainage assisted schemes, designed to meet the needs of all-the-year-round productive horticulture, the nearest equivalent we have to the demanding requirements of sports turf (last column, Table 1.2). This target is reduced in the drier south-east of England to something close to 30 mm (1½ in) and rises to over 60 mm (2½ in) in hilly districts in the west.

However, the importance of this range of variation for sports turf should not be exaggerated as it need amount to no more than selecting the less generous or more generous option, according to circumstances. The cost difference will be a relatively small item in the overall cost of the drainage installation.

Short periods of intense rainfall may occur at anytime, but amounts of the order of 5 mm (⅕ in) can usually be accommodated within the temporary storage space immediately available in the topsoil, the pipes, and the abundance of gravel fill in a modern slit drainage system. Storm conditions are probably best provided for by grading the surface so as to clear surface water off the playing area, to storm channels around the periphery.

Filling material over pipe drains

All lateral pipe drains should be covered with permeable fill to help achieve their function of interception. The grade, nature and depth of the fill layers will be dependent upon the type of drainage system to be installed. Where clay pipes are used the fill immediately over and around them must be large enough to ensure that it cannot enter the pipes at joints where gaps may occur as a result of differential settlement. A suitable specification for use with clay pipes might be

Backfill to 100 mm (4 in) over the pipe with 20–30 mm (¾–1¼ in) 'beach' or clean stone, followed by a layer of 5–10 mm (³⁄₁₆–⅜ in) clean *trench gravel* (e.g. SN7 in Table 7.1) up to within 150 mm (6 in) of the surface. . . .

Where plastic pipes are used the 'beach' or stone should be omitted and the *trench gravel* layer taken right down to the pipe. This reduces the number of backfilling operations and allows a small saving in cost. In addition, the tradition of using 95 mm (3¾ in) clay tiles as laterals where the smaller 60 mm (2⅜ in) plastic pipes would do should be discouraged as the wider trench required must necessarily involve an additional cost for extra excavation and backfill.

Unless serving also as a peripheral catchment drain, the main need function only as a collector for the laterals to which it is linked. As such, it need not be perforated or the trench backfilled with gravel. However, as some mains may also act as peripheral interceptors of extraneous site water, the pipe used in these instances will have to be perforated and the backfill organized as for pipe laterals.

With laterals it is necessary to determine whether the gravel backfill should be topped to the surface with topsoil or with sand. If the laterals are to be fed by a closely spaced system of slits, topping the laterals with sand becomes superfluous. Putting back neatly cut, carefully preserved, 50 mm (2 in) thick turfs on 50 mm (2 in) of good topsoil, supplemented with a phosphate-rich fertilizer, should not noticeably affect the efficiency of the system and will make sward restoration easier. However, to avoid any risk of the soil weeping down into the gravel, a 50 mm (2 in) layer of *blinding sand* (SN10 in Table 7.1) should be inserted between the soil and the gravel (Figures 4.2 and 11.1). This is particularly so where lateral trenches are excessively wide, as may well be the case when dug by a hydraulic excavator in stony ground.

On the other hand, laterals in narrow trenches at fairly close spacing and not augmented with any slit drainage, should always be topped with sand in order to retain the capability of infiltering surface water. The sand used should be a coarse-to-medium *blinding sand* (SN10 in Table 7.1), extended to 50 mm (2 in) above surface level with a *topsoil sand compost* (SN16 in Table 7.1) to allow for initial settlement and provide a reasonable seed bed. For further information and more detailed advice on establishing grass on sand-filled trenches, see Chapter 2, page 41.

On new grounds, the need to preserve the sand topping of the laterals uncontaminated by soil presents difficulties when there is a need for a measure of surface cultivation prior to seeding. The only way to avoid this completely is to defer the installation of pipe drains until after the new sward has been established and the soil firmed into place. This is not always practical, however, and the establishment of the initial sward, with no drains in place, may be adversely affected by surface waterlogging. The aim, therefore, must be to prevent too intimate a mix of soil and sand by cultivating parallel to the laterals rather than across them.

If sand, or sand/gravel, slit drainage is intended, or is a future possibility, it is essential that the backfill of the pipe drain is not so coarse that the sand or gravel within the slit will run into the backfill of the drain, impeding flow and causing the level of the fill in the slit to drop.

Due priority must be given from the start to ensuring the compatibility of all the materials likely to be used to achieve a fully integrated construction that will drain efficiently, whether or not all stages of the construction are to be implemented immediately. The task of upgrading an existing construction is all too often hampered by lack of forethought on the part of those responsible for the initial design. Because of this, special consideration is given in Chapter 7 to the specification of appropriate materials, in particular, soils, sands and gravels.

Installing pipe drains

Normal trenching

As explained in the section on filling material over pipe drains, the details of this operation vary according to whether the gravel backfill is extended to the surface with topsoil or sand.

The initial procedure for trenching in laterals normally involves excavating and carting away the soil as work proceeds. If the gravel backfill is to be covered by topsoil and turf, these should be excavated separately and placed beside the trench, ready for replacement. Excavating machinery which transfers the soil directly onto a trailer by appropriately screened conveyer belting should leave a clear surface free of loose soil and stones.

Every effort should be made to ensure that subsoil from the trenches does not become mixed into topsoil. If this occurs it may have harmful effects on permeability and nutrition.

The trenching procedure for a main will be similar to that for a lateral if its function is not only to collect water from laterals but also to act as a catchment drain in its own right, e.g. along the perimeter of a site. Because in this case the pipe will have to be perforated, soil from the trench will have to be removed off-site and replaced with permeable fill. However, a main whose purpose is solely to collect water from laterals and convey this onward to an appropriate outfall will not be perforated, entry being restricted to the purpose-made junctions with laterals. In this case, the need for permeable fill does not arise and subsoil as well as topsoil should each be preserved separately for replacement to appropriate levels after the pipes have been laid.

It is most important that all piping is laid accurately to correct lines and falls. Clayware drains should be closely butted together and the top end of each run sealed by a broken tile. Plastic drain runs should be sealed by plugging with the appropriate end-stop accessory. All drain runs should be checked for accuracy of line and gradient before being buried under backfill.

The order of installation is: the outfall, followed by inspection chamber and silt pit; then the main, complete with purpose-made

Field drainage

pipe junctions for linking up with the laterals; the laterals; finally, the sand or sand/gravel slits. Following this sequence ensures that any water invading the workings during construction can be cleared without difficulty.

Sophisticated techniques such as laser beam projection are increasingly employed to ensure that levels and falls are consistently true and uniform.

As PVC pipes are liable to become brittle at low temperatures, they should not be installed, nor permeable fill placed over them, when the air temperature is less than 0°C.

Trenchless drainage
On sites where good lengths of drain run are possible and the work is reasonably straightforward, the 'trenchless' system, as commonly used for agricultural drainage, is sometimes a more economical system to employ. This type of drainer lays flexible plastic piping with a mole plough pattern slitter, and back-fills the slit with small stone or gravel in one operation, without the need for excavating and removing any soil. The employment of the trenchless drainer is generally confined to the installation of drains prior to the preparation of a seed bed. This requirement is dictated by the fact that the machine causes a considerable amount of unwanted surface heave that may have to be trimmed off level.

On grounds where major regrading is necessary, trenchless drainage should be installed before the topsoil is replaced and the gravel backfill brought right up to the exposed subsoil surface. Slit drainage can be organized through the topsoil later.

A trenchless drainer can be tractor drawn or winch operated, the latter method reducing the risk of wheel rutting. Either way, it is necessary to dig a hole or enlarge the mains trench at the beginning of each drain run so that the plough can be eased down to begin its run at the correct depth.

Silt pits and inspection chambers

Silt pits (sometimes known as silt traps or settling chambers) are required wherever there is a marked change in the direction of a main drain, or a reduction in fall: that is, where a slowing down of flow may lead to an accumulation of silt and perhaps the eventual blockage of the drain run. They are required particularly at mains junctions and at the final junction to the outfall. Where water from an open ditch enters into a pipe drain there should be a silt trap as well as a grating.

Internal dimensions of silt pits should be not less than 900 mm × 600 mm (3 ft × 2 ft) and the floor should be at least 300 mm (1 ft) below the outlet pipe (Figure 2.2).

Inspection chambers (without silt pits), are smaller and less expensive than silt pits. They are useful for augmenting silt pit provisions where there are minor changes in direction or fall in long mains which might otherwise be difficult to inspect.

Internal dimensions for inspection chambers should be not less than 600 × 600 mm (2 ft × 2 ft) and the floor should be at the same depth as the invert of the outlet pipe, i.e. where the base of the pipe turns inwards.

It must be emphasized that silt pits and inspection chambers are an essential provision for the proper maintenance of a drainage system. In addition to routine work, such as periodic removal of silt and the rodding of mains, flow at the vital points can be regularly monitored and unusual changes investigated. Because of their cost, however, they are not always provided on sports grounds to the extent they should be. There is no doubt that without at least a minimal provision, the task of checking the efficiency of the various sections of the system and of locating and repairing defective lengths of drain, is likely to be much more difficult and time consuming.

For ease of access, manholes should be sited outside the main playing areas. If this is not

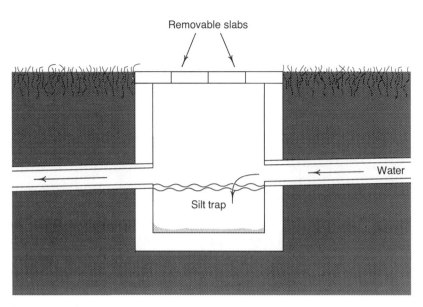

FIGURE 2.2 Silt trap.

practicable, or there is likely to be unauthorized interference, the covers should be sunk 150 mm (6 in) below the level of the finished surface and covered with soil and turf. Sunken manhole covers should be of thick reinforced concrete, sufficiently strong to withstand the passage of tractors, rollers, mowers, etc. but capable of being manhandled. The thickness of the covers should be 75–100 mm (3–4 in) according to span, and countersunk lifting rings should be fitted. If exposed at surface level, heavy duty covers can be used and should be sited slightly below the surrounding turf so as not to interfere with mowing operations. Their positions, particularly if below ground, should be carefully measured and recorded. Inlet and outlet pipes should be salt-glazed or unperforated plastic.

Ancillary items

Important features of a drainage scheme such as purpose-made junctions, silt pits, inspection chambers, end-stops, headwalls, flap valves and vermin traps are often either inadequately provided or omitted altogether. They have their purpose and should always be included in a quality construction.

2.1.3 Iron ochre – a special problem

Silt pits and inspection chambers assume particular importance in areas where the environment is conducive to the formation of iron ochre (hydrated ferric oxide). It is not a common problem, but tends to occur in proximity to waterlogged places where iron in the soil forms iron sulphides (pyrites). Under certain conditions, such as when air is admitted to the system, the sulphides are oxidized to ferrous sulphate by sulphur bacteria. This ferrous iron may then be further oxidized, either chemically or by iron bacteria such as *Thiobacillus ferroxidans*, to a soft, often gelatinous orange/yellow material which, on drying, becomes powdery, fibroid or a solid deposit of iron oxide (rust). Such deposits are often found in the vicinity of shale rock and coal seams where there has been disturbance for mining but are generally far more associated with peaty soils, or very acid soils close to peat deposits. Ochre deposition, often accompanied by an oily film, may show up along the banks of ditches, in isolated pools of water or where spring water emerges.

By introducing oxygen into the soil, a drainage system may set in motion a chain of events which might not otherwise have occurred. Iron ochre deposits, in manholes or at the outfall, may be the first indication of the presence of an ochre problem which, on further investigation, may be seen to affect the pipes, the permeable fill in the trenches and the adjacent soil. Hitherto, the measures most likely to be employed to dislodge ochre deposits have been mainly pressure jetting and/or rodding of the pipes. Recently experiments with weathered conifer bark in field trials at the Macauley Institute of Soil Research (Vaughan *et al.*, 1984) have shown encouraging initial results in absorbing ferrous iron from solution before it is oxidized to the ochre form. These investigations are still continuing.

Where the problem of iron ochre contamination is occurring, or is anticipated, it is suggested that, as a first step, water reaching the site from springs or underground seepage should be intercepted before it reaches the pitch areas, diverting it into a ditch system. The layout for the drains should then be designed to ensure that water from the open ditch or trench system discharges into an inspection chamber before passing on into a pipe drain. In severe ochre cases, chambers should be positioned at 30–35 m (33–40 yards) intervals along the main until the outfall is reached. In each chamber (1 m diameter) four or five loose-weave polypropylene sacks containing a total of approximately 80 kg (dry weight) of weathered conifer bark should be placed, the sacks being arranged in the chamber sump in such a way that inlet water passes through them

before reaching the outlet. The bark should last at least six months before requiring replacement. In less severe ochre cases, the drainage pipes should be surrounded by a 1:1 mixture of conifer bark and gravel during installation.

2.2 Auxiliary soil drainage – assisting water movement through the soil

2.2.1 Soil by-pass systems (slit drainage)

Slitting can be looked upon as the sports field equivalent of agricultural mole drainage. Both procedures aim to improve surface infiltration and, by a direct continuous route, move the excess water rapidly sideways into the backfill over pipe under-drains. It is the continuity of the route for free water flow, right through from the surface to the assured outfall, that is so important and must be maintained. With mole drainage the route is simply the crack and tunnel system formed by the special plough drawn through the soil. With slits, the route, once excavated, is stabilized against collapse by freely permeable backfill. Unlike surface spiking, these systems are intended to aid infiltration and discharge without relying on much help from the fine pore system in the soil itself.

Mole drainage

Moling and subsoiling
Mole ploughing and subsoiling are similar procedures involving a robust, sharp-edged blade being sliced vertically through the soil, drawn downwards to its working depth by the action of a chisel toe protruding forwards from the base of the blade (Figure 2.3).

Subsoiling is primarily aimed at breaking up soil compaction and improving surface infiltration by the creation of a series of cracks spreading obliquely upwards from either side of the chisel end of the plough blade. To encourage extensive cracking this procedure is best

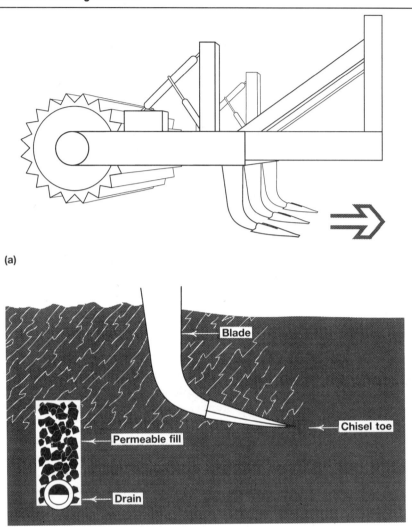

(a)

(b)

FIGURE 2.3 (a) Multi-tined, vibrating subsoiler and roller. (b) Subsoiling action viewed from one side. Used to lift the topsoil and create cracks, allowing surface water to enter and excess to clear slowly in the general direction of the underdrains. Rooting should benefit, at least temporarily, from the improved air/water balance. (c) Subsoiling action viewed from behind.

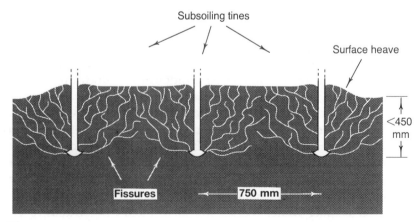

(c)

carried out when the full depth of the soil being treated is dry.

Various modifications have been developed to improve upon the basic subsoiling equipment. Wings have been added to the subsoiler shoe increasing the area of soil disturbance by as much as two to three times. Miniaturizing the equipment, linking several subsoiling tines together on a rigid or vibrating frame, sloping the tine legs back at an angle of 45°: all these are approaches aimed at improving the effect or minimizing surface disruption when working at shallow depths.

Moling aims to provide both for infiltration and discharge and involves pulling through a bullet-shaped expander behind the toe of the subsoiling plough so as to squeeze out a continuous, well-formed tunnel along the line of origin of each set of outwardly diverging subsoiling cracks. Moling, therefore, is best carried out in the spring or early summer when the topsoil has dried out enough to crack, but the subsoil at moling depth is still moist enough to shape into a well-formed tunnel (Figure 2.4).

Moling and subsoiling are both used in agriculture but even on favourable soils and after satisfactory installation, their efficiency can be limited by the panning effects of subsequent cultivation and wet-weather poaching by animals. Their passage through established grass can lead to a degree of surface disturbance requiring special attention if the means of restoration is not to hazard the long-term objectives of the initial moling operation. For example, ploughing, harrowing and seeding may immediately restore a flat surface but the shearing effect of a plough share as it is drawn horizontally through the soil, aggravated further by tractor wheel compression, can interrupt the continuity of the vertical cracking system installed by the initial mole-draining procedure. Where possible, therefore, it is more effective to mole after ploughing, thereafter merely harrowing to true.

Depths
The preferred depth for moles is 600 mm (2 ft); they should never be less than 450 mm (18 in), commonly 525 mm (21 in). The pipe drains into which they discharge should be at a sufficient depth to ensure that when the moles are drawn through the backfill their invert is at least 150–200 mm (6–8 in) above the top of the pipe. There should be enough distance between the pipe drain and the boundary of the field, usually between 10 and 15 m (11–17 yards) to allow the mole plough to reach working depth before crossing the first of the pipe trenches.

Mole size and spacing
The standard mole is 75 mm (3 in) in diameter but can be fitted with an expander to increase the diameter of the channel to 90 mm (3½ in) or 100 mm (4 in). When conditions are sufficiently dry, fissures caused by the action of the mole extend upwards at an angle of about 45°. The spacing of the moles depends on the depth of the mole invert and should normally equal four to five times this figure. Thus, at a minimum depth to invert of 450 mm (18 in) the spacing ideally should be 2 m (6½ ft) and certainly should not exceed 2.7 m (9 ft).

Gradients
A gradient of 1:200, or less, may result in a flow that is so sluggish that the mole channel fills with water, causing the roof to collapse. On the other hand, with too fast a flow, excessive scouring takes place and again blockage may occur. These extremes should be avoided, either by keeping the runs as short as possible or, in the case of a steep slope of 1:40 or more, by drawing the moles diagonally across it.

As mole ploughs are not normally equipped with a grading device for ensuring an even fall on the mole drain they cannot be operated successfully on undulating land. Generally the most that manufacturers provide is a long and heavy beam that slides along the ground to

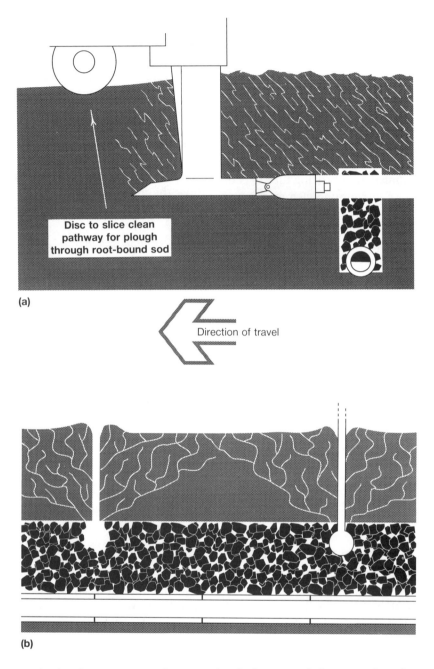

FIGURE 2.4 (a) Mole ploughing across piped system of underdrainage. Blade, toe, mole and expander of chisel plough producing subterranean tunnel, at approximately 500 mm (20 in) depth. (b) Mechanically induced crack system improves interception and links mole tunnel through to the surface. Intercepted drainage water cleared through mole tunnel to permeable fill over pipe in drain trenches. Ideally tunnel system formed in moist soil; cracks induced by mechanical disruption of dry soil, therefore timing critical. Use tractor wheel or roller along line of disturbance to re-true the surface. Worm action will then be required to keep the surface open.

prevent minor irregularities from affecting the general grade of the mole. However, laser control is now available as a more efficient alternative.

Practical constrains liable to limit the effectiveness of mole drainage

To maintain a beneficial effect it must be possible to repeat the moling operation at regular intervals, something to which a farmer can adjust, but much less so a groundsman.

Factors tending to promote crack and mole channel collapse are as follows.

1. Soil inadequately clay-rich – less than 35% clay and especially soils less than 15% clay.
2. Poor installation because of inappropriate soil moisture state at the time of installation.
3. Wet rather than dry weather immediately following installation, preventing maturation of the newly exposed soil surfaces.
4. Inadequate slope and imperfect grading of the mole channel leading to water ponding within the channel and increasing the risk that the adjacent, saturated soil will slump.
5. Excessive slope or excessive length of run increasing the risk of disruption by scour.
6. Boulders and other obstacles in the soil repeatedly impeding progress.

Mole drainage and subsoiling in sports fields

Though, at first thought, moling would appear to be an ideal method of improving soil drainage it is generally much less useful in sports fields than in agriculture. When dealing with a compact soil it is impossible to introduce extra pore space without displacing the soil upwards. The consequent surface disruption may well require so much renovation that such an operation could not be contemplated annually. It is only when the soil is already maintained open by earthworm activity that moling can complete the task of re-aligning some of the available space to effect rapid lateral discharge without undue surface disruption. This is likely

to be the case only on a new site taken over in good condition from agriculture and maintained biologically active thereafter.

With discretion in use, however, mole drainage is a relatively cheap operation and can be made to work on a suitable site with a suitable soil texture and an adequate level of earthworm activity. For example, on a clay-rich, worm-worked soil, sloping uniformly at a gradient of 1:60, moles should be drawn diagonally down slope to cross pipe laterals running in parallel succession at 30 m intervals down the other diagonal. To help leave a level surface, spacing of the mole runs should be reduced to approximately twice working depth, e.g. 1 m (1 yard), so that the whole surface is loosened and lifted uniformly. To avoid tearing the grass sward unevenly, a disc should be run ahead of the blade of the mole plough, ensuring that the sward will be neatly slit apart and as neatly restored by immediate rolling. There is much to be said for working at half the spacing of the tractor wheels. This will allow one tractor wheel to roll back any surface disruption along the previous run as the next run is installed.

Subsoiling, which is essentially a soil-cracking operation, is useful as part of a soil-deepening procedure at the cut end of a cut-and-fill operation, or for the relief of compaction caused by heavy machinery during construction. Like moling, it may also be used to good effect on a potentially good soil to co-operate with earthworms in the relief of surface compaction prior to sward restoration in spring. However, such a soil-opening operation will not necessarily benefit grass growth unless the soil structure restored is adequately water-stable and the extra water infiltered can be cleared before it adversely affects soil aeration.

Both moling and subsoiling will tend to bring obstacles impeding progress up onto the surface. On bouldery soils and tip sites this can be disastrous and may require the abandonment of the whole operation. Prior to starting on any such operation, therefore, examine the soil to the full working depth of your equipment. Water is more acceptable on the surface than stones, glass or scrap-iron!

Where a system of sand-and-gravel stabilized slits has been introduced soil drainage may have been greatly improved without necessarily improving the soil's structural state between the slits. This may lead to a sward very sensitive to drought because its roots cannot fully exploit the soil in depth. Subsoiling to relieve compaction at this stage, however, will hazard the stability of the slit drainage system by creating horizontal cracks into which sand fill may weep away sideways. Only subsoil through a slit system where, prior to subsoiling, the whole surface has been carpeted with a thick covering of sand to preserve sand continuity from the slit through to the surface. When time and resources allow, it is better, on a bad site, to first install the pipe underdrains, then improve the physical condition of the soil by subsoiling before going on to install slit drainage.

In the hands of a conscientious, skilled groundsman, suitably equipped and familiar with both the technical procedure and the need for correct timing according to soil condition, moling and subsoiling can be used effectively on sports fields to aid soil drainage. These are not techniques that lend themselves to effective use by a busy contractor, however, as correct timing is of the essence.

Sand and sand/gravel slits

The basic requirement for ensuring satisfactory drainage for winter games on a non-sandy soil is a sand or sand/gravel slit system linked below to pipe underdrains. The actual efficiency of such a system depends on the type of slits installed, their spacing, length of run and the continued effectiveness of their permeable link through to the surface.

All the main design features of a slit system, except slit spacing, can be resolved by calculation. Once surface run-off has entered a slit system much can be done to design and choose suitable materials that will ensure that a certain design discharge rate can be maintained through the slits to the pipe underdrains and final outfall. Slit spacing was initially determined by reference to the spacing used in agricultural mole drainage and by practical experience of the extent to which a benefit could be felt underfoot immediately after rain, either side of a lateral pipe drain. Both of these pointed to spacings of no more than one pace. Subsequent unhappy experiences with schemes utilizing wider spacing have tended to confirm the practical value of a 1 m (1 yard) limit. However, this feature of design will continue to be a subject for debate as so much depends in practice on the smoothness and slope of the surface, the extent to which access to the slit is preserved and protected by a surface covering of sand, and the standard of efficiency demanded. A typical scheme, evolved and tested by trial and error over the past 20 years, is illustrated in Figure 11.1.

The slits are normally formed by machine and vary in width from 25 to 75 mm (1 to 3 in). Often the width is determined by the type of trench excavator employed. Slits greater than 38 mm (1½ in) are usually formed by excavation, therefore it is necessary to remove and cart away the surplus soil. In this operation great care must be taken to ensure that the excavated soil is not accidentally scattered and left lying on the grass surface for any length of time before being cleared away. With slits less than 38 mm (1½ in) in width, the cut is usually formed by pressure from the blade of a subsoiling plough leaving no soil to be removed. Ground heave from this operation may be unavoidable, however, and any attempt to re-true the surface by rolling afterwards requires care to avoid capping the slit surface with soil.

Where slits are formed by excavation it may be found that the actual width of the slit dug out is greater than the rating for the machine. For example, a slit taken out by a trencher with a 50 mm (2 in) cutter may be found to measure as much as 75 mm (3 in) across in places, particularly on difficult, stony ground. If this is likely to happen, special care must be taken when calculating and costing the amount of backfill required.

The depth of slits will depend upon the drainage rate, the nature of the backfill materials, and the length of run between the relieving underdrains. Normally, depths range between 250 and 360 mm (10 and 14 in). However, soil impediments to trenching, or features of an existing pipe system may impose constraints necessitating a measure of compromise. There will then be a need for a compensating adjustment in some other feature of the scheme, such as slit width, slit spacing or the nature of the permeable fill.

Ideally, slits should run across the slope and be as near as possible to an angle of 90° to the pipe drain laterals into which they discharge. This will ensure maximum efficiency in surface water interception and minimum slit length before discharge.

Backfill for slits can be sand only or sand over gravel. If sand only is used the lateral discharge along which water will flow to satisfy sports ground drainage requirements is limited to less than 5 m (5½ yards). In practice, therefore, the use of sand-only slits tends to be restricted to the improvement of existing schemes where there are already closely spaced pipe drains with backfill suitable for satisfactory sand slit linkage.

Where drainage schemes are designed from the start with slit drainage discharging into pipe laterals, it is desirable for reasons of economy to space the pipe drains as widely apart as possible. To achieve this the slits are backfilled first with clean 6–8 mm (¼–⅜ in) *trench gravel* to at least half slit depth, followed by 5 mm (³⁄₁₆ in) concreting sand (typically a *blinding sand*) to just above surface level. In this way the surface water infiltrates vertically through the sand and then flows laterally along the gravel

layer to discharge into the gravel fill in the pipe-drain laterals. The spacings of the laterals are normally anywhere between 10 and 20 m (11 and 22 yards) according to the width, depth and spacing of the slits and the nature of their backfill materials.

There are calculations involved in all these design features which are described in Chapter 4. Schemes utilizing standard Stewart zone materials can make use of the simple relationship between the depth of the gravel layer in the sand/gravel slit and the acceptable length of run between laterals (Chapter 7, page 117).

For slits less than 50 mm (2 in) in width, a satisfactory grass cover can usually be established in a fairly short time by over-seeding with ryegrass and relying also on grass growth spreading in from the adjacent sward. The strong growth required can be encouraged by periodic, light applications of a nitrogenous fertilizer, plus irrigation if conditions threaten to become dry enough to halt growth. Where slit width is 50 mm (2 in) or wider, special surface preparation and seeding will probably be necessary to compete with the desiccating influence of the adjacent soil, weeds often succeeding where grass fails. The challenge is to achieve germination and establishment of grass on a sandy surface that is very liable to dry out and become impoverished of nutrients. Weather conditions are crucial, spring and autumn being the most favourable seasons. The following type of procedure is required.

1. Apply a pre-seeding fertilizer.
2. Sow a ryegrass/fescue seeds mixture and bury by rolling or treading and covering with a topdressing of damp, amorphous, sedge peat or grass clippings.
3. After germination apply small doses of general-purpose fertilizer, in liquid form, at fortnightly intervals, until the new grass has rooted sideways and become fully established. Irrigate if seedlings are caught by a period of drought.

Under no circumstances should play be permitted until grass cover over the slits has been fully re-established and the whole surface topdressed with a fine *topsoil sand* at a minimum rate of 80 tonne/hectare (30 tons/acre), i.e. a covering of 5 mm (⅕ in) overall. For general advice on sward establishment and immediate aftercare see Chapter 6.

Transverse and longitudinal sub-surface gravel channels

Gravel channels, without pipes, are sometimes employed as one element of a drainage scheme where soil conditions are difficult for slit trenching below 200 mm (8 in) or thereabouts. As they are likely to have to be dug by the narrow bucket of a hydraulic excavator the width will be around 150–200 mm (6–8 in). The backfill should be gravel (e.g. *trench gravel*) from a depth of around 400 mm (16 in) to within 150 mm (6 in) of the surface and, thereafter, a blinding layer of sand (e.g. *blinding sand*) followed by replaced topsoil and turf.

A system of gravel channels will normally be best aligned so as to intersect both the gravel layer in the sand/gravel slits and the gravel fill in the pipe trenches at right angles. Ideally, pipes and slits should be aligned parallel to each other, on one diagonal across slope, and the gravel channels, intercepting the slits and delivering to the pipe underdrains, along the opposite diagonal.

Spacings will depend on the circumstances that condition the type and capacity of the slits but will normally be less than 5 m (5½ yards). At these relatively narrow intervals the gravel channels could be designed to run for distances of the order of 20–25 m (22–27 yards) before themselves discharging into pipe underdrains.

A gravel channel link in a tiered system of drainage may be useful when a stony sub-surface layer makes narrow trenching difficult for the full depth of a normal sand/gravel slit. It can also form the basis of a scheme designed to work on a soakaway principle. This may be necessary where there are difficulties over organizing an acceptable, final outfall for discharge off site. Such a construction has to be designed flat so as to stop drainage water surging about. The aim should be to hold any temporary excess in the slits and gravel channels below ground until it can leak away by natural seepage.

Mini-slitting

This is sometimes a preferred alternative to ordinary slitting where surface trueness is of particular importance, e.g. for hockey or a cricket outfield (see also section 11.2).

Mini-slits are formed by blade pressure, not excavation, and any slight heave can be settled by rolling along the line of the slits. The slitting machine is usually equipped with a sand hopper.

Mini-slit widths can vary from 15 to 30 mm (⅜ to 1¼ in) and depths from 200 to 300 mm (8 to 12 in) according to the type of machine used. Spacing ranges from 200 to 400 mm (8 to 16 in). The backfill should be 5 mm (³⁄₁₆ in) concreting sand (i.e. a *blinding sand*).

As for the system involving gravel channels in the previous section, the mini-slits are probably best aligned diagonally across the slope, parallel to the pipe underdrains. They can then discharge into sand/gravel channels, running at 4 m (4½ yards) intervals across the slope on the other diagonal, and the gravel layer in the sand/gravel channels can discharge into the gravel in the pipe trenches.

Piped mini-slits

Pipe-based, mini-slits, spaced about 1 m (1 yard) apart, are a recent development. They are liable to be more expensive and less efficient than a slit/pipe drain combination where each separate tier of drainage can be oriented to perform at maximum efficiency according to function. However, they represent a useful compromise where the nature of the topsoil favours narrow trenching but the subsoil below 300 mm (12 in) would make deep trenching for pipe under-drains very difficult. As the orientation of the one trench determines both the angle of inter-ception and the gradient for flow, the piped mini-slits should compromise on an oblique orientation across the slope. The precise angle chosen should give precedence to the need to assist discharge through the long runs of very narrow, 35 mm, corrugated pipe used to convey water all the way to the peripheral outfall. These very long runs of narrow pipe are not in themselves a specially commendable feature of the system, but they have to be made to function efficiently if the introduction of a pipe into each slit is to be justified.

This system certainly has merit where the subsoil does not favour deep trenching but elsewhere, though it may work, threatens to be expensive because it requires specialist machin-ery to install and is unnecessarily extravagant in the use of pipe.

Micro-slitting

Micro-slitting is an ancillary or remedial pro-cedure involving the cutting of continuous, thin slits along the surface. The aim is either to enhance the directional flow of surface water towards a previously installed, standard, slit-drainage system, or to improve the vertical infiltration of surface water to a sand drainage layer immediately beneath an impeding soil cap. To extend their effectiveness they can be sand-filled, and where expense is no problem, can be used overall to replace or supplement a topdressing of sand.

On a small area the job can be done manually with a spade but there are now machines available that cut and fill several slits in one pass. The slits are of the order of 13 mm (½ in) wide, 100 mm (4 in) deep and spaced about 200 mm (8 in) apart. They may be sand-packed simultaneously, or topdressed with a dry, free-pouring, medium *topsoil sand* (e.g. SN12, Table 7.1), well brushed in. At the end

of the operation, sand should be left, piled along each slit to compensate for any subse-quent settlement, then rolled and maintained moist to encourage the grass to grow through. Interruption to play need be minimal.

2.2.2 Whole soil constructions

A shallow, ameliorated sand top, over a slit system and pipe underdrains

This is probably the most efficient system of drainage for winter games pitches but, being a two-tier system plus a 100–125 mm (4–5 in) thick ameliorated sand carpet, is significantly more expensive. If designed as such from the start, a slightly wider spacing of the slits than 1 m (1 yard) is permissible but should certainly not exceed 1200 mm (4 ft). The surface carpet can either be an imported and suitably amelior-ated sand, or a loamy sand topsoil. Because the slits are well covered, this type of construction can provide the sort of true surface that is desirable for hockey.

Restricting the depth of the ameliorated sand carpet to around 100 mm (4 in) allows the grass to root down to the moisture and nutrient reserves in the soil below. Thus the sward will be protected from drought as well as waterlog-ging so long as the roots achieve and maintain contact with the soil below. Critical to success is the quick establishment of the sward (Chapter 11, page 168), the quality of the original buried topsoil (Chapter 11, page 167), and the appropriateness of the maintenance programme (section 11.3).

Irrigation should be available to assist during the initial stages of sand placement and during sward establishment. It may be required to help stabilize the loose sand surface against wind-blow or to safeguard the seedling sward against desiccation prior to roots reaching through to the buried soil beneath the sand carpet.

A deep, ameliorated sand top, over a gravel drainage bed

The deeper sand carpet supporting the sward in this system is mainly required for the finest turf surfaces used for golf and bowls. Because of the high cost of construction and maintenance this approach can seldom be justified for the construction of large areas of playing surface. The depth of imported and suitably ameliorated sand topsoil required is between 300 and 400 mm (12 and 16 in). This is laid over a blinded gravel bed with pipe underdrainage. Because the resistance of the sward to wear is minimal, great care and expertise is required in its establishment and maintenance (Chapter 10).

The gravel bed provides for the clearance of excess water filtering through from above but, when clear of water, it acts like an air lock to create a perched watertable in the over-lying soil. Contradictory though this may seem, a gravel bed assists both drainage and water retention in the topsoil. However, the water reserve available to the sward is strictly limited to that in the topsoil and, as this could be exhausted in two to three weeks of dry summer weather, irrigation must always be on hand to avoid desiccation.

To provide the desired rate of drainage the ameliorated topsoil must contain at least 75% of the right kind of sand, e.g. a *topsoil sand* (Table 7.1, SN12–15). This in turn determines its depth and is critical for aeration, tractive efficiency, drought risk, seed germination, rooting and choice of grass species (section 4.2).

The bed should be 5–10 mm ($\frac{3}{16}$–$\frac{3}{8}$ in) gravel (e.g. *trench gravel* SN7, Table 7.1) topped by 50 mm (2 in) of concreting sand (e.g. *blinding sand* SN10, Table 7.1). The rate of drainage through the sandy topsoil layer should be taken into account when deciding on the thickness and the composition of the bed, and hence also, the spacing of the underlying pipe drains. Using 125 mm (5 in) of *trench gravel* to form the

gravel raft under a bowling green will allow the pipe underdrainage system to be reduced to a single ring system under the peripheral ditch.

Full details of such a construction are given in section 10.3.

2.3 Timing of drainage work on established grounds

Drainage work on existing sports grounds often has to be carried out at a time most convenient to the users. However, in a country such as Britain, where weather conditions are so inherently variable, day to day, and only very approximately predictable according to season, the benefits to be derived from soil operations can depend very much on timing. For example, pipe drainage should be installed, ideally, in late spring or early autumn. Working in dry summer conditions is hard on trenching equipment and can also result in loss of turf, desiccated after disruption of the root system. Working in wet conditions creates unacceptable damage to the soil structure and to the grass. As has already been said, mole drainage is best carried out in the spring when the topsoil is dry enough to crack but the subsoil is still sufficiently moist to mould, and when there is every chance that the newly exposed soil faces will have a chance to be stabilized by summer desiccation. Sand slitting for winter games pitches should preferably be undertaken during the spring or summer months so that sward recovery can be achieved before winter sets in.

2.4 Sequence and timing of drainage operations on new grounds

On a site requiring major regrading, prior to the installation of pipe underdrains, there is no doubt that the topsoil will have to be removed to allow for redistribution of subsoil. However, there is then a choice to be made between installing the underdrainage prior to replacing the topsoil, or vice versa. The same choice arises when a new playing field surface is to be formed by spreading a shallow sand carpet.

There are two good reasons against laying pipe drains prior to topsoil placement:

1. machinery may smear subsoil into the gravel or sand backfill, topping the drain trenches, thus hazarding the freely permeable link through into the topsoil;
2. if, after using earthmoving equipment to regrade the subsoil, this equipment has to be retained to replace the topsoil after other equipment has been used to install the drains, on-site costs may increase enormously. The temporary removal of plant and equipment involves the doubling of haulage charges and possible delays in getting the machinery back again. Allowing the machinery to lie idle on site may incur the normal two-thirds standing hire rate.

Good reasons for installing drainage prior to topsoil placement are:

1. elimination of any risk of subsoil contaminating the topsoil during the trenching operation;
2. pipe drains can more satisfactorily be installed by the trenchless method. The subsoil presents a firmer surface than newly placed topsoil to work over and the ridges, heaved up either side of the trench, can be satisfactorily trued off prior to topsoil replacement.

When topsoil is replaced, unless it consists of sand, it should never by worked wet or its structure will suffer to the detriment of efficient drainage and vigorous grass growth.

In our climate, where heavy rain may occur at any time of the year, it is wise always to work uphill from an established outfall, avoiding any risk of the open trenches becoming flooded. Correct timing of operations during major construction work is very much a matter of judgement, often involving a measure of calculated risk.

2.5 Recording the position of pipe drains and slits

A record plan of a drainage scheme is a valuable document which should be carefully preserved for future reference. Not only is this information important for ensuring that the system is properly maintained but, without it, any extension in the future is difficult to plan and may lead to unnecessary duplication of drains, manholes, etc. Unfortunately, the detailed recording of drainage layouts in the past seems to have been badly neglected or, if it has been done, the plans seem generally to have been mislaid.

It is worth noting that where a scheme was grant-aided by the Ministry of Agriculture, Fisheries and Food, details of the work carried out will have been recorded and should be available from the Ministry's Divisional Office for a period of at least 20 years from when the grant was paid.

As soon as the installation of a drainage system is complete, the position of all branch, main and slit drains, silt pits, inspection chambers, outfalls, etc. should be accurately checked against the prepared plan and any alterations carefully recorded. Details as to depths, sizes and types should also be noted. The practice of marking important features, e.g. outfalls and hidden manholes, on nearby permanent surfaces, such as walls, can help with subsequent location.

Chapter three

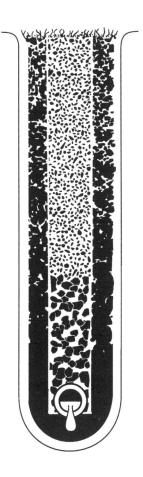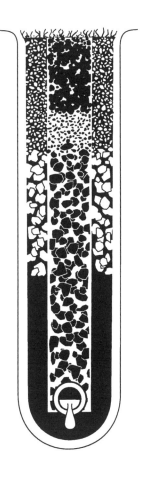

Alternative layouts

3.1 Options using existing topsoil

3.1.1 Assessment of priorities

When assessing a new site for sports turf development, or an existing facility for improvement, the designer at some point will require to know the finance available. In practice it frequently happens that the client turns the question back to the designer, requesting some idea of the costs to be associated with all the possible options. This is the point at which real discussion begins on priorities.

The first priority is to isolate the site from extraneous surface and ground-water influences by the installation of peripheral, interception drainage. Thereafter, the least sophisticated option would be:

1. grade the surface to an even slope of at least 1:60 so as to allow for substantial run-off at times of intense rainfall;
2. lime and encourage what drainage and structural improvements can be achieved by promoting earthworm activity;
3. control use to ensure that no play is allowed when the surface is soft.

This represents the minimum likely to be reasonably effective for general use on a natural site with a satisfactory soil profile. Unfortunately, in the majority of situations in Britain the natural soil is unlikely to provide drainage to a standard sufficient to sustain a full programme of winter use, unaided.

If it is the intention to provide facilities for a high standard of play, then early consideration may have to be given to the desirability of modifying the existing slope, recognizing that the soil disturbance involved will make sophisticated supplementary drainage inevitable. If the area is large enough for several pitches, major grading into terraces may be necessary and this will in turn affect the layout of any general system of drainage installed.

3.1.2 Technical considerations

Herringbone and grid systems of pipe underdrains

A herringbone system of pipe drainage involves a series of laterals linking into a main drain, alternately from either side. The main in the middle runs directly down slope; the laterals cross the slope diagonally.

A grid system consists of laterals, arranged in parallel succession, generally crossing the slope diagonally (Figure 3.1), discharging into a main drain on one side only, usually off the pitch or along the site boundary.

A grid system of drainage can be upgraded without difficulty by the addition of slit or mole drainage, either system being uniformly oriented at right angles to the laterals. In a herringbone system, because laterals come in from opposing

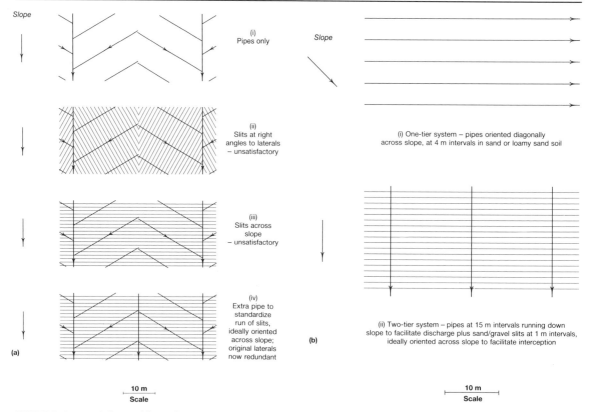

FIGURE 3.1 (a) The problem of superimposing a slit system on a herringbone layout of pipe underdrains. (b) Pipe layouts generally more suitable for sport.

diagonals, this makes it impossible for slits or moles to be effectively orientated across the laterals without the direction having to be changed whenever a main is crossed. Orientation at right angles to the mains leads to the problem of variable slit length. This dilemma is illustrated in Figure 3.1.

Situations where a standard or slightly modified herringbone system is likely to be preferred are as follows.

1. Situations where the sand content of the soil is sufficient to provide a degree of natural drainage through the bulk of the soil, obviating any need for augmentation by slits.

2. A site where opposing slopes meet, to form a shallow valley, leaving the main to follow the lowest contour.

Soil depth

In all cases the minimum depth of easily trenchable soil for the installation of pipe-drain laterals should not be less than 450 mm (18 in) and, ideally, should be at least 600 mm (24 in).

If deep trenching is likely to be difficult, the problem may be overcome in one of two ways:

1. inserting an intermediate system of transverse gravel channels between the surface slits and pipe underdrains to allow a marked reduction in the pipe required within the

inhospitable sub-stratum – a three-tier system;
2. employing perforated plastic mini-pipes at the bottom of the surface slits – a one-tier system (Chapter 2, page 42).

3.1.3 Theoretical considerations affecting the design of grid systems

Pipe and slit efficiency

1. Pipes are generally laid on a gradient to direct discharge one way. Rather than attempting to impose an even gradient on the trench base, which implies an ever deepening trench with increasing cost both for excavation and backfill, it is usually best to give the pipes the benefit of any general, site slope. This allows the trench to be maintained throughout at a constant depth from the surface.
2. On sports fields, slits and gravel channels are most efficient for surface interception when laid flat across slope and, as such, are free to discharge equally at either end.
3. As indicated by the relationships in equations (4.4) and (4.6), pp 67–68, halving the length of run between outlets, S, or doubling the depth of the slit, H, will result in a four-fold (2^2) benefit to the discharge rate, i.e. the overall design rate V. Similarly, as the data in Table 7.2, page 119 indicate that hydraulic conductivity K is improved roughly three-fold for a doubling of D_K (the effective particle size of the permeable fill), this is the order of benefit that will accrue to the overall design rate, V. However, a doubling of the slit width, or a halving of the interval between slits, will only increase the overall design rate two-fold.
4. If slits or gravel channels are oriented downslope and flow is redirected all one way, this will have two effects.
   (a) Efficiency will be reduced, by the path

length to discharge point having been extended.
   (b) Though the extra push given by the gradient will tend to increase the rate of flow, this effect will not produce a net benefit until the slope exceeds a gradient that would be unacceptable on most playing surfaces (see also section 4.1.2, page 66).

Which tier system of layout?

Depending on circumstances there are, broadly speaking, three grid systems of artificial drainage to choose from. These may be thought of as consisting of one, two or three tiers of artificially organized, horizontal flow and are summarized in Table 3.1.

One-tier systems
In a one-tier system the dual functions of surface interception and pipe discharge are carried out within one set of trenches, all of uniform depth, oriented in parallel succession, diagonally across the slope. The permeable backfill over the pipe, if brought through to the surface, will intercept free water moving downhill, either over the surface or through the topsoil, letting this down to the pipe for discharge. The ideal orientation for interception would be for the trench system to run directly across slope, but then the pipe would have no gradient to assist its discharge unless the expensive and cumbersome expedient were adopted of imposing a gradient on the base of each trench.

Running the trench system directly downhill, to give priority to discharge, would obviate the need for a graded fall to be artificially imposed on the trench but would adversely affect the efficiency of free water interception. The diagonal orientation is thus a logical compromise. It gives half the benefit of the slope to each of the two separate functions which, in a one-tier system, have both to be accomplished in a single trench.

TABLE 3.1 Drainage options

(A) Summary of options for new constructions

Layout	Comments	Immediate aftercare and annual maintenance
One-tier systems		
(1) Subsoil pipe drains only, with permeable backfill topped to surface level.	When widely spaced this represents minimum drainage, minimum cost and minimum maintenance, but is seldom satisfactory on its own. It serves mainly as a basis for future slit drainage. If this cannot be contemplated, soil should be worm-worked, or made very sandy, and spacing of pipe drains should not exceed 4 m (13 ft). Orientation necessarily a compromise.	Occasional application of fine sand topdressing along pipe trenches to maintain surface level and avoid soil capping of pipe trenches.
(2) A miniaturized, pipe-assisted, slit system consisting of 35 mm, corrugated and perforated, plastic mini-pipes in slits 300–350 mm (12–14 in) deep, spaced at intervals of 1 m or less, backfilled with grit or fine gravel to the surface and discharging directly into the main, off the pitch. Orient pipes to fall diagonally across slope.	This system is particularly useful when finance and/or the trenchable depth is strictly limited, and where use is mainly in the summer, e.g. for cricket. However, very long runs of such a small-bore pipe make it vulnerable to silting. Orientation is necessarily a compromise.	Before any play is allowed, apply fine sand topdressing to the whole area at a minimum rate of 80 t/ha (32 tons/acre), followed by annual topdressings at 40 t/ha (16 tons/acre). *Or* Micro-slit immediately using a medium sand fill. Slits approx. 13 mm (½ in) wide, 100 mm (4 in) deep, at 200 mm (8 in) intervals. Overfill slits to allow for settlement. Topdress with fine sand annually but repeat micro-slitting if the pipe slits become soil-capped.
Two-tier systems		
(3) A deep, imported and suitably ameliorated sand or loamy sand topsoil, 300–400 mm (12–16 in) in depth, over a gravel drainage bed with pipe underdrains.	Liable to be expensive. Used mainly for golf and bowling greens with artificial watering. Not so suitable for rigorous winter games with studded footwear as, without worm activity, the grass will tend to become surface-rooting.	No topdressing necessary before play is allowed but annual topdressings, matched to the topsoil, essential. Maintenance must emphasize measures necessary to continually combat the tendency to accumulate thatch.
(4) Sand/gravel slits into pipe underdrains.	Generally very satisfactory and usually essential where construction has involved considerable soil disturbance, e.g. for levelling. Slits and pipe drains can both be optimally oriented.	Before any play is allowed, apply fine sand topdressing to the whole area at a minimum rate of 80 t/ha (32 tons/acre). Follow by annual topdressings at 40 t/ha (16 tons/acre).

TABLE 3.1 *continued*

Layout	Comments	*Immediate aftercare and annual maintenance*
(5) A shallow, 100–125 mm (4–5 in) carpet of ameliorated fine sand, 100–125 mm thick, over a pipe drained and sand/gravel slit, fertile soil surface. Slits, ideally at 1 m intervals.	Provides for very efficient drainage and drought resistance. Slits and pipe drains can both be optimally oriented. Cost likely to be 50% more than for (4) above. True surface, suitable for hockey.	No topdressing necessary before play is allowed but annual topdressings of fine sand essential as in (4) above.
Three-tier systems		
(6) Sand/gravel slits into an intermediate tier of gravel channels and then into widely spaced pipe drains.	An economical system for dealing with a site which is difficult to trench, e.g. a tip site. By linking the slits into fairly broad, e.g. 200 mm (8 in) wide, gravel channels at an intermediate depth, the pipe drains can be installed at much wider intervals, reducing the amount of deep trenching required. Orientation of tiers necessarily a compromise.	As for (4) above.
(7) Mini sand slits, 20 mm (¾ in) wide, 200–300 mm (8–12 in) deep, at 300–400 mm (12–16 in) intervals, linked across an intermediate tier of gravel channels discharging into widely spaced, pipe underdrains.	Useful where surface trueness is vital and option (5) is considered too expensive. Orientation of tiers necessarily a compromise.	As for (4) above.

(B) Modifications evolved to upgrade constructions previously found to be unsatisfactory

Initial construction	Design weakness	Remedy
(8) Slow draining, loam topsoil built over a freely permeable coarse-textured, natural or artificial substratum, pipe drained or capable of acting as an effective soakaway.	Topsoil holding water and persistently wet throughout the winter. Micro-pored topsoil failing to shunt water through to potentially free-draining layer beneath until the topsoil is itself saturated.	Take steps to increase macro-pore content of topsoil by encouraging worm action. Meantime, by means of sand/gravel slits, provide alternative routes for easy infiltration directly through to the drainage bed. This will bypass the soil and eliminate any risk of severe ponding. Any temporary waterlogging in the slit sand will be relieved by transfer into the micro-pore system of the adjacent soil. Topdress and maintain as in (4).

TABLE 3.1 *continued*

Initial construction	Design weakness	Remedy
(9) Slow-draining topsoil and relatively impermeable subsoil, pipe-drained only, the backfill being either: clean, assorted stone over pipe to within 150 mm (6 in) of the surface, or assorted stone stopping more than 300 mm (12 in) from the surface and/or blocked by intruded soil.	Inadequate provision for excess rainwater to reach pipe trenches. Pipe trench backfill unreliable as stable link for standard slits.	Organize surface interception and lateral transfer to pipe trenches via stable system of sand/gravel slits. Details will depend on inherited spacing of drain trenches and the modifications required to form an efficient link through to the permeable fill in the pipe trenches. Topdress and maintain as in (4).
(10) As (9) but with pipe under-drainage organized in two-sided herringbone fashion. Mains running directly downslope at 40–60 m (44–66 yards) intervals. Laterals branching off at a 45°–60° angle and at some 10 m (11 yards) intervals, alternately to either side of each main. Laterals cross slope diagonally, but in two different directions.	Inadequate provision for excess rainfall to reach pipe trenches. Further complication of herringbone layout of pipes allowing no one direction for slits to intercept across slope and run for standard intervals between laterals.	Upgrade the backfill of the existing mains, if necessary, and add additional mains so as to reduce main spacing to about 25 m (27 yards). Organize for surface interception as in (9), orienting the sand/gravel slits directly across slope, at right angles to the mains. There being a reasonable chance that all slits will somewhere intersect an unmodified lateral as well as a main, slit depth need not be increased over the normal 300 mm (12 in) depth to compensate for the wide spacing of the mains (Figure 3.1(a)).

Notes
1. In all cases the layouts assume that appropriate, peripheral drainage has isolated the site from extraneous surface or underground water.
2. The tier nomenclature applies only to those layers where drainage water movement is effectively oriented in one direction, i.e. moving either way, in the one direction, along slits, gravel channels, a drainage bed or pipes.
3. The layout itself will not determine a particular rate of drainage. As explained in Chapter 4, this can be calculated for flow through a uniform, sand soil, or through the permeable fill in slits, channels or a drainage bed, or through a pipe of given dimensions, but the rate at which surface water will actually enter the soil bypass system has generally to be an assumption.
4. No slit drainage or imported, sandy topsoil, drainage scheme should be started without the client being made fully aware of the maintenance implications, particularly the need for topdressing annually with an approved sand.
5. For information on materials see Chapter 7.

Another system of one-tier drainage has been made possible by successful miniaturization of the much more massive, trenchless drainage equipment used by agricultural drainage contractors. It is now possible to insert continuous, corrugated, 35 mm, perforated plastic pipe, spaced at 1 m (1 yard) intervals or less, in slits 300–350 mm (12–14 in) deep. The slits should be just wide enough – 40 mm (1½ in) – to take the pipe and should be simultaneously back-filled to the surface with a free-flowing, fine grade of *trench gravel*, or a grit such as SN8 in Table 7.1 However, such a narrow slit and coarse backfill is very vulnerable to capping. Measures to counteract will inevitably involve the further expense of either an efficient and continuous programme of sand topdressing, or periodic recovery by cross-hatching with a system of micro-slits.

The main advantage of the main-pipe

approach is that it allows for the whole process of interception and discharge off pitch to be achieved within a total depth of 350 mm (14 in). It has the built-in disadvantages of having to intercept and discharge while oriented diagonally across the slope and re-quires a budget that will stretch to allow the mini-pipe trenches to be close-spaced and main-tained in freely permeable contact with the surface. The long runs of small-bore pipe, the coarse backfill and the narrowness of the slits, render the system particularly vulnerable to deterioration by silting (Chapter 4, page 69).

Two-tier systems

Only in a two-tier, grid system, where the two tiers cross at right-angles can we hope to achieve maximum efficiency. If the top tier consists of slit trenches, these can be oriented in parallel succession, directly across the slope, so as to intercept with maximum efficiency. The pipes, running directly down the slope, are at their best orientation for discharge and the trenches can all be installed at a uniform fixed depth from the surface. Slit length between the pipes will then be the shortest possible.

In a trenched two-tier system the relatively wide pipe trenches are not required for surface interception and so can be finished off at the surface by replacing the original turf. This eases the task of re-establishing the grass and main-taining a uniform appearance.

Because of budget constraints, or reluctance to risk prolonged loss of use, it may be necessary to phase the work, first installing the pipe drains, then following with the installation of slits sometime later. Installation of the pipe system need not be an unduly expensive operation and need not involve any loss of use if backfilling with gravel, sand and turf goes simultaneously with trench excavation and pipe laying. However, as the pipes run directly downslope this first phase will not confer much benefit on its own but, when funds and time are available to complete the job another year, the sand/gravel slits can then be rapidly installed on a stable surface, starting early in the spring. This early start will allow ample time to re-establish the sward and apply a protective topdressing of fine sand before winter use resumes.

Three-tier systems

Generally, three-tier systems arise when there are special conditions to cope with, either at the surface, or at the depth of the pipe drains. For example, when trenching and artificial grading of the pipe system is likely to be particularly difficult because of the intractable nature of the substratum, a second tier of gravel channels is introduced between the pipe underdrains and the surface slits. This allows the number of pipe underdrains required to be kept to a minimum.

In such a three-tier, intersecting, grid system it is inevitable that there will have to be compromises in efficiency unless the top tier is not a system of trenches but a substantial sand carpet. A top tier of slit trenches, oriented across the slope, would require the middle tier of intersecting gravel channels to run down the slope, and they, therefore, would discharge mainly one way. As explained later (page 66), providing the gravel channels are free to dis-charge either way, a slight slope on the trench will confer a small benefit on the rate of water clearance to the underdrains. The orientation with slope, however, will adversely affect their interception efficiency, except where drainage water is delivered directly to them by the top tier of sand/gravel slits. Also, as the third tier of pipe trenches would require to run across slope, any grading required for discharge would have to be achieved artificially. Alternatively, if priority is given to the third tier of pipe trenches, giving them the benefit of any natural slope, this would enable the second tier, repre-sented here by the gravel channels, a chance to achieve their maximum efficiency for intercep-tion by being oriented directly across slope. However, the top tier of sand/gravel slits would then be at a disadvantage for their main function of free water interception, because they would have to run in parallel succession down slope. The compromise of skewing all tiers to run alternately on one-or-other diagonal would incorporate some element of inefficiency in each tier. Inherited elements of the drainage system, or constraints imposed by the site will normally dictate which alternative to choose.

Example 3.1
On many tip sites the assortment of rubble, domestic debris and blinding material forming the substratum is not only difficult to trench and of uncertain permeability, it is often covered by less than the minimum 450 mm (18 in) of easily trenchable soil normally required for pipe drain installation. It may then be advisable to plan from the start for minimum deep trenching. Thus, though we install from the bottom up, it is often useful to plan from the top down; in this case planning first for surface interception into sand/gravel slits. These can run at 1 m intervals in parallel succession across the slope, and beneath these an intermediate tier of gravel channels, 200 mm (8 in) wide, 350 mm (14 in) deep, at 4 m (13 ft) intervals, running downslope. The gravel channels will then be able to leak away into the tip blinding layer wherever they can, allowing a minimal pipe system to be installed within the rubble, at right-angles beneath the gravel channels, in trenches artificially graded to ensure discharge.

Example 3.2
Where surface trueness is vital, as for hockey, but there is insufficient money available to plan for a slit system covered by a 100–125 mm (4–5 in) deep, ameliorated sand carpet, a reasonable alternative is to plan for surface interception into a mini-slit system. For this, thin slits, 20 mm (¾ in) wide, 200 mm (8 in) deep, filled with a medium sand (e.g. SN12 in

Table 7.1) and spaced 300 mm (12 in) apart, should run in parallel succession, at right-angles across the slope. Beneath these there can be an intermediate tier of grit or fine gravel channels, and at right-angles, beneath the gravel channels, an artificially graded final tier of pipes, or a stone soakaway.

In three-tier schemes neither the trenches forming the gravel channels nor the pipe trenches need be backfilled with freely permeable material right through to the surface. They can be finished off with a soil-based turf that will rapidly marry in with the rest of the sward. This leaves only the two-part, sand/gravel slit system, or the mini-slit system to be directly re-seeded, or to grass itself over by re-invasion from the side.

Example 3.3
A temporary, three-tier system may arise by accident when a two-tier slit system is allowed to become soil-capped through maintenance neglect. Shallow micro-slits, aligned at right angles to the original slits, are used to re-establish surface interception.

Practical considerations arising on site

1. Whichever system is used, the layout should be so arranged that, as far as possible, main drains avoid the actual pitch areas. In particular, they should not pass under cricket tables.

2. It is desirable that space should be available for the side-or-end-shifting of winter games pitches so that worn areas can be given a chance to recover between seasons. About 10 m (11 yards) is normally allowed for movement either way and it is essential that, where these areas are provided, they should be fully covered by the drainage system.

3. To prevent displacement or penetration of pipe drains by roots, drain lines should be kept well away from trees and bushes. Where such contact is unavoidable, special precautions should be taken to prevent

blockage of pipes, e.g. by using, for mains, glazed pipes with sealed joints.

3.2 Options where there is also a need for the importation of new topsoil

If the soil is very shallow, or thoroughly degraded and subsoil in character, it may be necessary to consider creating a new topsoil by importing appropriate soil-forming materials. This is a procedure that will inevitably lead to a major escalation in cost unless the materials to be imported are available at artificially low prices.

The only other alternative is to allow time for the degraded soil to be reconditioned biologically before further developing the site for sports use. This does not mean merely abandoning it to nature for a number of years as nature, unassisted, may take 50 years or more to achieve what well directed, purposeful management can achieve in 5–10 years (Stewart and Scullion, 1989).

Essentially, the aim must be to rapidly introduce an adequate and appropriate earthworm population to a mechanically opened surface, encouraging the earthworms to thrive and remain active by the prior installation of an underdrainage scheme that will allow for full drainage benefit from regular subsoiling. Maintain under grass with soil pH above 6. Avoid high concentrations of freely soluble fertilizer, and steer clear of pesticides, many of which are harmful to earthworms though not specifically targeted against them. Return all organic residues by allowing clippings to fly, or carefully grazing with sheep. An inoculum of earthworms, simply scattered onto the surface, will merely feed the birds.

A new semi-artificial surface can be formed of *topsoil sand* plus appropriate ameliorants. This should be laid over one of two very different systems of underdrainage:

1. a slit system, bypassing excess, infiltered, surface water directly through the buried, problem layer;
2. a drained gravel bed protected from infiltration of fine sand from above and soil from below by shallow layers of a blinding sand or by sheets of a synthetic fabric filter.

Choice will involve considerations of cost and the type of playing surface required.

3.2.1 Cost

The gravel-bed approach involves two or three times the amount of imported material compared with that required for the slit-based alternative. On the other hand, although slit systems require much less imported material, they require special equipment to cut and backfill the extensive system of narrow drain trenches.

3.2.2 Character

For winter games, a sward established on an ameliorated sand topsoil, and shallow enough at 100–125 mm (4–5 in) depth to ensure that the roots reach through to the water and nutrient reserves retained by the slit-drained soil beneath, will be well buffered against waterlogging, drought and hunger. Under these conditions a strong-growing grass, such as ryegrass, can dominate and form an excellent, wear-tolerant sward for rigorous games such as soccer, rugby and hockey.

However, a sward established in a deeper layer 300–400 mm (12–16 in) of *topsoil sand* perched over a blinded and drained gravel bed will have to be well adapted to cope with the dual threats of periodic waterlogging and periodic drought. The drought risk is an inevitable consequence of the severely limited depth of the soil layer. The waterlogging, which particularly affects the lower half of the soil, arises from the break in capillary continuity caused by the air that is locked within the gravel. In such a construction, water can be rapidly shunted through the sandy topsoil to clear the surface, but even sand cannot then complete the job of drainage through to emptying enough of the pore space to allow for satisfactory aeration. Ryegrass yellows badly under these conditions and also, being ill-adapted to cope with drought, gives way to the finer grasses which, though better adapted to cope with drought, are ill-adapted to cope with wear. The result is a construction that is only

appropriate for the smooth, worm-free, close-cropped surfaces required for golf and bowling greens. They look well if protected from wear but they are the most demanding and expensive of all swards to construct and maintain.

Thus, to plan construction we need to know the type of use and the standard of maintenance that can be anticipated, and then, taking the character of the site into consideration, progress stepwise through the possibilities until the client finds the best match between the budget available and the standard of performance considered acceptable.

Chapter four

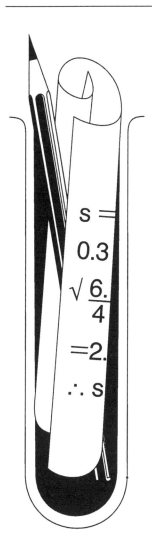

D
E
S
I
G
N

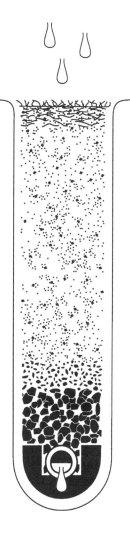

Design criteria – theory and practice

4.1 Transmission of water

Calculations are described in Chapters 4, 5, 7 and 13 that should be part of the stock-in-trade of any professional designer, but not everyone involved in sports-turf provision will feel that their concern obliges them to immediately get so deeply involved. Others, though wishing to make the effort, may initially experience difficulty because the practical objectives are not yet sufficiently clear in their minds. Anyone thus deterred might do well to move on first to page 62 of this chapter, chapter 7, pages 114–117 and then to Part 2, returning to the more detailed calculations when the need seems more clearly to justify the effort. Those with special skills in mathematics are referred to Appendix 5 where the subject is considered at the fundamental level necessary to generate the equations used for design purposes in the main text of the book.

4.1.1 Theoretical considerations affecting design calculations

Darcy's Law

Darcy's law is the fundamental law which describes the flow of water through porous media. It is very similar to other fundamental laws of physics that describe the flow of electricity and the flow of heat. These state that, in the first instance, the flow is a charac- teristic of the medium, some media being inherently better conductors than others. Thereafter, for water, the flow is directly proportional to the hydraulic head providing the push, and inversely proportional to the resistance as determined by the nature of the pore system and the path length through it. Thus Darcy's law may be written

$$Q = K\frac{H}{L}A,$$

where Q is the quantity of water flowing per unit time, K is the hydraulic conductivity of the medium, A is the cross-sectional area through which water flow is limited, H/L is the hydraulic gradient, H being the hydraulic head, i.e. the height of the continuous water column of free standing water within the medium and above it, and L the length of the path through the medium controlling flow.

Hooghoudt's drain-spacing equation

Dr Hooghoudt (1940) of the Netherlands pub- lished an equation which, on a level site, describes the interrelationships of all the factors controlling the lateral discharge of drainage water through soil to drainage trenches when input is balanced by output. The conditions envisaged are illustrated in Figure 4.1 (a). At equilibrium the watertable is held at a fixed height H above the level of the water in the drainage ditches. In these circumstances Hoog- houdt's equation states

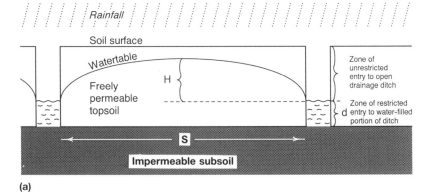

(a)

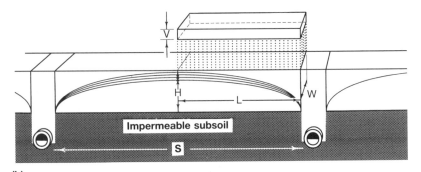

(b)

FIGURE 4.1 Drainage dia-grams. (a) Agricultural con-ditions for which Hooghoudt's original drain-spacing equa-tion typically applies. Water-table held at a fixed height in equilibrium with rainfall. (b) Sports-turf constructions for which the simplified form of Hooghoudt's drain-spacing equation has been used. Con-struction typical of general amenity grass areas where pipe placed within trench, cut into impermeable subsoil and linked through to surface by permeable fill. (c) Construc-tion for intensifying used sports turf where a gravel drainage bed underlies a sand-dominated topsoil, or where surface water is channelled through the topsoil into a sand/gravel slit system, linked across pipe, drain trenches. (d) Model used for the heuris-tic purpose of illustrating how the simplified version of Hooghoudt's equation may be conceived as quantitatively de-scribing the discharge of water through a saturated soil to a drainage trench (pages 59–62).

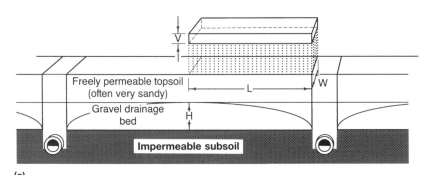

(c)

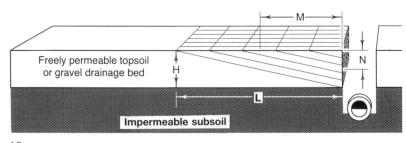

(d)

$$S^2 = \frac{4KH}{V}(2d + H),$$

where S is the drain spacing, K is the hydraulic conductivity of the free-draining soil, H is the maximum height of the watertable over the level of the water in the drainage ditches, V is the rainfall in equilibrium with drain discharge, d is the depth of free-draining soil from the surface of the water in the ditches to the surface of the next layer below which can be considered to be impermeable.

This equation is in fact a special case dealing with horizontal discharge, in two directions, across a level site, with unimpeded discharge through the entire exposed face of each of the outfall ditches. This follows upon the more general, fundamental work of the Russian Kamenskii (1938). For consideration of the case where there is some impedence to discharge in the ditch walls, see pages 61–62; for consideration of the effect of slope and for discharge in four directions see page 66.

Hooghoudt's equation applied to sports-field drainage

Theory

I. G. Daniells, who was researching on sports-field drainage in Aberystwyth during the period 1972–75, pointed out that in most sports-field situations where intensive drainage is required the pipe, with permeable fill above it, is placed in a trench cut into relatively impermeable subsoil (refer to Thornton, 1978, pp. 36–40). Drainage water is then directed to the drain trenches in one of the following ways:

1. through a special layer of very free-draining soil on top of the impermeable subsoil, as in Figure 4.1(b);
2. down through a very free-draining topsoil and then laterally though a specially constructed gravel bed to the drain trenches, as in Figure 4.1(c);
3. through special channels cut into the existing relatively impermeable topsoil and made

permanent by filling with sand overlying gravel; very similar to Figure 4.1(c) so far as the slits are concerned.

In all these circumstances the variable d in Hooghoudt's equation has no value so long as the pipe can clear all water reaching it without excess accumulating in the trench. This then allows the further simplification to

$$S^2 = \frac{4KH^2}{V}.$$

When comparing Figure 4.1(a) with Figures 4.1 (b) and 4.1 (c) it is important to note that in (b) and (c) the water cleared sideways falls into the drain trench from above. The pipe is installed at a depth that keeps it well clear of damage from construction work carried out over it, and the drainage link with the surface is maintained by permeable fill. Water tumbling discontinuously down through the gravel in the pipe trench will contribute no extra pull and should not feature, therefore, in any assessment of hydraulic head. H should only take account of the height of the watertable perched above the surface of the impermeable subsoil and should not include any additional allowance for the depth of the pipe.

When choosing an overall design rate for drainage the aim should be to avoid surface ponding caused by the watertable breaking through the surface. Any water infiltered should be cleared without this happening. Surface ponding resulting from soil conditions impeding infiltration should be treated separately. In the circumstances depicted in Figure 4.1 (b) it might sometimes be more reasonable to design for the maximum height of the watertable H to be held just below the surface at peak capacity, for example 75 mm (3 in) down.

When utilizing a gravel bed (Figure 4.1(c)), as for golf and bowling greens, it can be assumed that lateral flow will take place through the gravel bed as if it existed in isolation from the overlying topsoil, its full depth being considered the maximum height available for any watertable perched within it. This leaves the sand soil above to be designed solely with regard to efficient infiltration, vertical drainage, plant growth and playing character. In the similar circumstances of sand/gravel slits, lateral discharge is also best considered to be determined only by conditions within the gravel layer. The sand above is, to the gravel layer, merely the conduit through which the water to be cleared arrives.

To pursue the subject of water movement through soil, quantitatively, requires advanced mathematics. This is the purpose of Appendix 5. However, for those who are not mathematicians a heuristic approach based on the model illustrated in Figure 4.1(d) will serve as an adequate starting point from which to proceed to the intelligent use of Hooghoudt's equation and its extensions.

In Figure 4.1(d) flow is conceived as taking place across the drainage layer in a tightly packed arrangement of small, square tubes, all sloping down diagonally from the surface towards the nearest outlet end of the free-draining layer. The total amount of water moving laterally increases progressively as further increments enter from above and, in the model, probably unlike reality, the soil beneath the main diagonal is virtually redundant.

When in equilibrium at peak capacity the rainfall which the model is designed to accept just matches the water discharged through the pipe-trench face. For this shunting through of water to be simultaneous it must take place when the tubes are full, i.e. the soil is saturated.

Consider the situation in just one of the tubes, starting at distance M from the drain trench and discharging at the trench face, a distance N from the surface. The flow through this one tube can be quantitatively described by Darcy's Law

$$q = K \frac{N}{M} a,$$

where q is the infiltration required at the inlet end of the tube, K is the hydraulic conductivity of the medium in the tube, a is the cross-sectional area of the tube, N/M is a reasonable approximation to the hydraulic gradient, M being very close to the path length through the tube when N (normally 100–200 mm) is very small compared with M (normally 100 000–200 000 mm).

Or, as all the tubes are conceived as grading uniformly, and N and M are proportional in length to H and L,

$$q = K \frac{H}{L} a$$

and the total flow through all the imagined tubes, to all intents and purposes, aggregates to

$$Q = K \frac{H}{L} A$$

where, referring also to Figures 4.1(b) and (c), Q is the total amount of rain, represented by the volume VLW, which must be cleared through the topsoil to achieve the desired design rate, and A is the approximate cross-sectional area of all the tubes discharging drainage water through the trench face with area HW. Substituting VLW for Q and HW for A,

$$VLW = K \frac{H}{L} HW,$$

which can be simplified and re-arranged to

$$L^2 = \frac{H^2 K}{V}.$$

Since $L = S/2$, i.e. L is half the drain spacing, we have

$$\frac{S^2}{4} = \frac{H^2 K}{V},$$

which re-arranges to

$$S^2 = \frac{H^2 4K}{V} = \sqrt{\left(\frac{H^2 4K}{V} \right)} = 2H \sqrt{\left(\frac{K}{V} \right)}.$$

All these are forms of the simplified Hooghoudt drain-spacing equation and may be used as they best fit the type of calculator available. The dimensions must all be expressed in the same units, e.g. S and H millimetres (inches), K and V in millimetres (inches) per hour.

In reality, flow is not constrained within tubes and does not traverse the drainage layer in straight lines, but the result from the heuristic model, where approximations of this kind have been used to simplify the mathematics, appears to be identical to that reached by Hooghoudt's more rigorous approach. The fact is that the relationship summarized in Hooghoudt's standard equation holds only over the normal range of conditions encountered in constructions for sport. However, as shown in Appendix 5, Hooghoudt's drain-spacing equation tends to slightly exaggerate performance. The error increases in significance as S becomes progressively smaller compared with H but, even at spacings only of the order of 1 m and H values of the order of 300 mm, the error is unlikely to exceed 1%.

Practical considerations affecting design for drain interception of slits
If the area through which water is free to discharge through the trench face is restricted, e.g. where the intersection between the gravel layer in a sand/gravel slit incompletely intersects the gravel fill in a pipe trench or gravel channel, the heuristic model suggests this may reduce the rate of discharge significantly. The effect will be seen in the adjustment required in the H^2 factor of the standard Hooghoudt drain-spacing equation. One of the two Hs involved should be reduced to represent the actual height of the window through which the drainage water can discharge at the trench face, i.e. the intersection link. The other H, representing the maximum height of the watertable over the level of the water in the drainage ditches, is unaffected. The message here is that, for maximum efficiency in a linked, tier system of drainage channels, the main discharge routes – normally the gravel layers – should intersect to the full depth of the gravel layer in the discharging tier.

In Figure 4.1(c), however, which is probably closer to reality, it is assumed that water accumulation in the freely permeable layer will reach a peak midway between the pipe trench outfalls, while clearance needs only take place through the base of the vertical, discharge face.

When it comes to effecting links of this nature in the field, e.g. between sand/gravel slits and pipe underdrains, these conflicting assumptions lead to two different conclusions on the most effective way to organize the junctions. Theoretically, Figure 4.1 suggests that in Figure 11.1, the layout for a standard slit system, the gravel layer in the slit trenches needs only a minimal depth of intersection with the top of the gravel layer in each of the pipe trenches. What is illustrated is intersection to the full depth of the gravel layer in the slit trenches: hence the range of alternative depths indicated for the soil and gravel layers in the pipe trenches.

However, since it would be possible for the watertable at the mid-point between the drain outfalls to rise further, into the layer of *blinding sand* above, and even on to the surface temporarily, there needs for this reason alone to be some generosity in the design of the outlet from the slit into the pipe trench, as the heuristic model allows. At the same time, the gravel drainage layers must be protected as much as possible from soil invasion by placing them as deep as possible, away from the topsoil where most of the lateral tunnelling of earthworms takes place. Thus the option to avoid any unnecessarily deep intersection between the slits and the pipe trenches should not be at the expense of overall slit depth. Figure 4.1(c) suggests that it would be theoretically acceptable to reduce the gravel layer in the pipe trenches to the absolute minimum required for a clean, horizontal link between the gravel at the base of the slits and the surface of the gravel in the pipe trenches. This would work, however, only if the flow through the horizontal interface was adequate, because there would be no option for any substantial additional discharge sideways, along the pipe trench.

In the field we must expect to encounter practical difficulties over ensuring so critical a link without allowing a large margin for error. Should the normal differential settlement between the trenches and the soil lead to a drop in the relative height of the gravel at the top of the drain trenches and the gravel at the bottom of the slits, or should additional drains be required after slitting, there will then be a risk, with a tight design, that the vertical, outfall face of the slits themselves will be unduly restricted to allow for peak flow. Thus, for practical reasons, the design of the vital link between the slits and the pipe trenches should err on generosity in a new construction. But there is some margin for adjustment when the specification has to be tight, or when installing slits to upgrade the drainage provided by an existing pipe system, if soil conditions do not favour deep trenching.

Preliminary note on the *Stewart zone* approach to design

When designing a drainage system involving superimposed sandy topsoils, or artificial, vertical drainage, bypassing the soil *en route* to the pipe system, the aim should be first to evaluate the flow required through each separate part of the integrated system then, secondly, to select materials that will meet these requirements, avoiding bottlenecks, and getting maximum benefit for minimum cost.

In Chapter 7, pages 114–117, the *Stewart zone* system is described. This develops the idea of working with a limited range of the most commonly available materials, chosen to make efficient design and specification much easier by eliminating the need for elaborate calculations. This approach will be demonstrated through-out the remainder of this chapter, after examples have been worked through by the more rigorous procedure of precise calculation. See first example, page 71.

Fitting values to factors *K* and *V* in the simplified Hooghoudt equation

Hydraulic conductivity K available for lateral discharge through materials considered uniform

Whatever the drainage medium through which water must pass to reach the pipe drains, whether it be soil, sand, gravel, or some special mixture, it is necessary to know the rate of flow through the material in question. This will be at a peak when saturated. It is this value, the saturated hydraulic conductivity, that we determine in the laboratory and use to determine from theory the nature of the backfill and the width, depth and spacing of the drainage channels required to achieve any target design rate.

As indicated in Table 4.1 a granular loam may have something like the hydraulic conductivity of dune sand, 200–400 mm/h (8–16 in/h), when in 'good heart', i.e. when the granulation is water stable. The same soil, destructured and compact, as it may well be on the abused surface of a soccer pitch, can drop down in hydraulic conductivity to 0.05 mm/h (1/500 in/h), a value more typical of subsoil. Casagrande and Fadum (1940) give values of 360 mm/h (14 in/h) for well-structured topsoil (a value equivalent to that for dune sand), 3.6 mm/h (1/7 in/h) for the beginning of poor drainage, and 0.003 mm/h (1/7000 in/h) for a soil that is practically impervious (compare SN21 and SN22 in Table 7.1)

For many British soils the change from ploughed topsoil to unploughed subsoil indicates a hundred or thousand-fold drop in hydraulic conductivity. This means that, in effect, the lateral discharge of excess surface water to pipe systems is mainly confined to flow over the surface or through the topsoil.

TABLE 4.1 Permeability and drainage characteristics of soils (adapted from Casagrande and Fadum, 1940)

Hydraulic conductivity K (mm/h and in/day)	360 000	36 000	3600	360	36	3.6	0.36	0.036	0.0036	0.00036
Drainage	Good					Poor		Practically impervious		
Soil types	Clean gravel	Clean sands, clean sand and gravel mixtures			Very fine sands, organic and inorganic silts, mixtures of sand, silt and clay, glacial till, stratified clay deposits, etc.				'Impervious' soils, e.g. homogeneous clays below zone of weathering	
			'Impervious' soils modified by effects of vegetation and weathering							

In most calculations concerned with rapid drainage, any slow discharge through the subsoil can be considered no more than a gratuitous bonus.

It is this dominating influence of the topsoil in lateral flow that must be taken into account when deciding to what height the permeable fill over pipes should be brought. If the surface becomes structurally degraded and infiltration so slow that the surface is frequently ponded, this can only be relieved by arranging for effective surface interception into purpose-made vertical channels, bypassing the soil and linking directly through to pipe underdrainage. Similarly, if the space available for water storage below ground has been filled it is hydraulic conductivity in the horizontal direction that is crucial for the discharge of any further excess. In worm-worked soil, for example, vertical infiltration of water down earthworm burrows may be very rapid, but the eventual benefit to drainage will depend on the general rate of dispersion through the surrounding soil and the frequency with which the temporary storage capacity of the burrow system is exceeded.

Values for the hydraulic conductivity of isolated, disturbed samples of soil in the laboratory are unlikely to relate very well to performance in the field. For uniform materials, such as the sands and gravels installed as horizontal layers in special constructions, or in the vertical channels of a drainage scheme, packing is uniform and water movement is potentially the same in all directions. Therefore, in these circumstances hydraulic conductivity determined in the laboratory can be assumed to relate closely to that which can be expected to assist drainage in the field. However, the hydraulic conductivity of a material determined under ideal conditions of saturation in the laboratory is likely to be an exaggerated version of that which occurs *in situ*. In the field the pore space is liable to become partially blocked by trapped air, especially when water filters down from above. Compensatory effects working in the opposite direction are: (a) the care taken to achieve maximum packing density when loose materials are tested in the laboratory, whereas less perfect packing is likely to prevail in the field; (b) channels, assumed in a calculation to be of the precise width shown on the plans, frequently are to some degree wider; (c) the soil, usually assumed to contribute nothing to rapid drainage, may in fact make some contribution. Theory and practice will therefore diverge but still much can be done by calculation to locate possible bottlenecks so that materials or dimensions that could not possibly achieve the target design rate can be eliminated.

Because the hydraulic conductivity K of the medium is the factor in the simplified Hooghoudt equation for which a reliable value is normally least readily available, actual values for typical materials are given in Table 7.1. In Part 2, where specific constructions are described, the outline specifications for typical schemes utilize only *Stewart zone* materials. Any modification involving the use of materials that fall outwith the prescribed *Stewart zones* will require the whole scheme to be reviewed and appropriate adjustments made by calculation.

Averaging hydraulic conductivities available for lateral discharge through layered systems
Where two freely permeable materials are to be laid in layers, one above the other, e.g. in a two-part, sand/gravel slit, it may be appropriate to assess their combined effect K_a for the lateral discharge of drainage water. This can be done by using the following formula to determine an average value, weighted to take account of the hydraulic conductivity and depth of each of the layers concerned. The average

$$K_a = \frac{(H_1 \times K_1) + (H_2 \times K_2)}{H_1 + H_2}.$$

However, the contribution of the sand layer in such a system is primarily to allow excess water down to the gravel layer below and it is in the gravel layer that lateral discharge predominantly takes place. This is why no allowance is made for the contribution to lateral discharge made by the sand layer in the simple, *Stewart zone* approach (Chapter 7, page 117).

Design rate V
The design rate is the rainfall in millimetres (inches) which it is desired to clear through the system in a given time. It is the factor V in Figure 4.1.

As explained in Chapter 1 (pages 13–14), a design rate for sport and recreation in Britain might vary anywhere between the two extremes of 12 mm (½ in) of rainfall a day and 12 mm (½ in) of rainfall an hour, depending on climate, the demands of the game and standard of play.

When specifying design rates it should be appreciated that 2 mm ($\frac{1}{10}$ in) per hour is about the minimum rate for hard porous surfaces (Chapter 13) and anything much in excess of this for turf is going to require vertical clearance of rainfall through a sand, or loamy sand topsoil to a gravel bed. Where lateral discharge has to take place through the topsoil itself – either the whole topsoil or sand slits – maximum design rates are unlikely to exceed 2 mm/h (2 in/day). A minimum rate normally considered to be reasonable for a sports ground in Britain is between 1 and 2 mm/h (1 and 2 in/day), according as rainfall ranges between 500 and 1250 mm (20 and 50 in) a year.

Where, for reasons of economy, the underdrainage is inadequate to cope with the consequences of short periods of intense rainfall, provision should be made to grade the surface to a fall of not less than 1:80. This should help to shed excess surface water to ditches or some form of catchment drain, around the periphery.

4.1.2 Practical application of theory to problems of transmission of water

Basic schemes

The simplified Hooghoudt equation

$$S = \sqrt{\left(\frac{H^2\, 4K}{V}\right)}$$

is a convenient formula to use for the design of any closed system through which the rapid transport of water is effectively confined, and for all parts of which the hydraulic conductivity can be predicted. It can seldom be used with the same confidence to predict the required spacing for drains, slits or gravel channels whose purpose is to intercept water flowing through the very heterogeneous pore system of a normal soil. This is because it is difficult to ascribe to such a soil a reliable value for K. However, it can reasonably be used for the following.

1. To determine the materials required, and the spacing for drain trenches designed to intercept excess water shed to them at a given rate through a defined, homogeneous, stable layer of freely permeable soil – one-tier systems.
2. To determine the materials required and the design of a sand, or a sand/gravel slit system, whose purpose is to convey surface-shed water at a given rate to a relieving system of underdrains, bypassing the intervening, relatively impermeable soil – a two-tier system.
3. To determine the materials required and the design of the sand, or sand/gravel slit system required to link to an intermediate system of deeper, transversely orientated gravel channels which, in turn, must be organized to discharge into a relieving system of pipe underdrains – a three-tier system.
4. To design gravel rafted schemes involving the vertical discharge of water through the whole of the sandy topsoil to an underlying gravel bed, and thence laterally through the bed to a pipe system of underdrains – a two-tier system.

Notation and dimensions for worked examples of basic schemes

One-tier systems
For a pipe-drained scheme, utilizing the entire topsoil as the route for water to drain laterally to the pipe trenches, the notation should read:

S = distance between pipes in mm;
H = depth of soil in mm forming the lateral conducting layer for which the K value is known;

K = hydraulic conductivity in mm/h for the lateral conducting soil layer;
V = overall design rate in mm/h.

Two-tier systems
For a pipe-drainage scheme, utilizing slits as the means of conducting surface water through the topsoil to the pipe trenches, the notation should read:

S_s = maximum effective length of slits in mm;
H_s = total depth of permeable fill within slits, in mm;
K_s = hydraulic conductivity of the permeable fill (sand, gravel or sand and gravel) within the slit in mm/h;
V_s = the overall design rate V in mm/r, modified according to the ratio of total surface to slit surface as it is only at the slit that infiltration effectively occurs, i.e.

$$V \times \frac{\text{slit spacing (mm)}}{\text{slit width (mm)}}.$$

This assumes that the surface is level and the slits are placed close enough to ensure that all surface-ponded water finds its way rapidly across the sward to the top of the slits.

Three-tier systems
For a drainage scheme, involving slits, gravel channels and pipes the notation should read:

S_s or S_c = maximum effective length of slits or channels between outfalls to next lower tier of underdrainage in mm;
H_s or H_c = total depth of permeable fill within slits or channels, both in mm;
K_s or K_c = hydraulic conductivity of the permeable fill (sand, gravel, or sand and gravel) within slits or channels in mm/h;

V_s or V_c = the overall design rate V in mm/h, modified according to the ratio of total surface to slit or channel surface.

Gravel-rafted schemes with clearance to pipe underdrains
In gravel-rafted schemes the hydraulic conductivity of the whole of the topsoil superimposed on the gravel bed (including any blinding layer) should in no part be less than the desired overall design rate. Thereafter, the calculation required for specifying the nature of the gravel, the thickness of the gravel bed and the spacing of the pipe underdrains is similar to that described for one-tier systems above, assuming that V is the overall design rate and that lateral flow takes place only within the gravel bed.

Gravel-rafted schemes clearing to four sides of a square
Where the design allows for pipe drainage to be restricted to a peripheral system around the four sides of a flat square, e.g. a bowling green draining freely down into a gravel drainage bed, lateral discharge through the gravel bed can take place in four directions, not just the two which up to now we have assumed. As explained in Appendix E, section E.21, the only modification this entails in the simplified Hooghoudt equation is a change in the constant from 4 to 6.79, i.e. equation (E.25) (page 240)

$$S \text{ (the side length)} = \sqrt{\left(\frac{H^2\,6.79\,K}{V}\right)}.$$

For rectangles other than squares see Appendix E, (E.24) (page 240).

Coping with the problem of slope
In sports-turf constructions a sloping surface may be part of the challenge required by the game, e.g. on golf and crown bowling greens, or may be incorporated in the surface configuration of the site to assist with surface drainage.

Drainage through the soil, however, will also be affected, and a basic assumption involved in Hooghoudt's standard formula used to describe this, may no longer apply. The lateral flow of drainage water through the soil may well not take place horizontally, discharging uniformly to underdrains in two, or more, directions.

In Appendix E, sections E.22 and E.23, this matter is explored mathematically. The results are applied in Chapter 13 where they have particular relevance to the design of the drainage carpet beneath the sloping surfaces advocated for hard porous pitches; the same would apply for grassed pitches similarly based on a drainage carpet. There will be gravitational enhancement of flow down slope, and with outfalls at both ends, there will remain some possibility of flow in the opposite direction. The result is that the extra distance which some of the drainage water has to travel to reach the down-slope outfall will be more than made good: by the extra gravitational head, and by the increment of flow to the up-slope outfall which occurs when the drainage layer is sufficiently saturated to provide the necessary head.

Though relevant also to the short-distance flow that is required under the irregularly sloped surfaces of golf greens, or the sloping trenches involved in three-tier drainage systems (Chapter 3, page 53), the need to take on the extra difficulty of the calculation, when slope is taken into account, may not be justified. On modest slopes, and over relatively short distances, the benefit of slope, though always positive, will be small and might well be treated as a prudent contribution to a safety factor.

When drainage through the soil is directed down slope there is much to be said for a built-in safety factor. Any failure to adequately clear water through the link into the next lower tier of drainage will carry the risk of drainage water re-appearing on the surface where it builds up by accumulation down slope. On a level surface such a build up would be more evenly spread, minimizing the risk of any artesian effect.

The example in Chapter 13 (page 201), deals with a gravel drainage bed beneath a hard porous surface, sloping uniformly at a slope of 1:90, for 64 m (70 yards) across the full width of the pitch. The aim is to calculate, for a particular gravel, the depth required when the only pipe outfalls run along either side of the pitch, i.e. at the top and bottom of the slope. When the procedure used takes account of the beneficial effect of slope, the estimate is for a depth of 216 mm (8½ in). This compares with 248 mm (9 in) when Hooghoudt's standard equation is used and no allowance is made for the beneficial effect of slope, i.e. a surplus of 13%. However, when an extra pipe outfall is introduced, halfway down the slope, reducing the flow path between outfalls by half to 32 m (35 yards), the estimate for depth of gravel by either method of calculation is also reduced by half, but the surplus which would be introduced by designing according to Hooghoudt's standard formula would remain at 13%. Thus, when the material requirements are small, as would be the case when just a few gravel channels were required to run with slope rather than an entire gravel bed, and the slope is quite modest, around 1:100, then the simpler procedure, using the standard Hooghoudt formula, will do. Otherwise, the more complicated calculation, described in Chapter 13 and explored more fully in Appendix 5, should be used, and any thoughts about a safety factor then considered separately.

Where there is only uni-directional flow to a single outfall, down slope, there will be no benefit from slope until the extra gravitational head exceeds three times the hydraulic head.

To adjust for uni-directional flow, down slope, Hooghoudt's standard equation can be used in the modified form

$$L = \sqrt{\left(\frac{H\,(H+G)\,K}{V}\right)},$$

where L is the length of the path through the medium controlling flow in one direction, downslope, and G is the extra, gravitational head resulting from slope. The need to use this modification of Hooghoudt's standard equation seldom arises, but when the conditions apply, it certainly should be used.

Using the simplified Hooghoudt equation to determine S, H, K and V

For drainage through the whole topsoil
Use the simplified Hooghoudt equation in the most appropriate of the following re-arranged forms:

$$S = \sqrt{\left(\frac{H^2\,4K}{V}\right)} \quad (4.1)$$

$$H = \sqrt{\left(\frac{S^2\,V}{4K}\right)} \quad (4.2)$$

$$K = \frac{S^2\,V}{4H^2} \quad (4.3)$$

$$V = \frac{H^2\,4K}{S^2}, \quad (4.4)$$

where S is the drain spacing in mm, H is the depth to impermeable layer in mm (usually depth of topsoil), K is the hydraulic conductivity in mm/hr for the soil layer through which excess water is free to drain laterally to the pipe system (usually just the topsoil).

For drainage through slit systems
The simplified Hooghoudt equation now takes the form:

$$S_s = \sqrt{\left(\frac{H_s^2 4K_s}{V_s}\right)}$$

$$= \sqrt{\left(\frac{H_s^2\,4K_s}{V \times \text{slit spacing/ slit width}}\right)}$$

Use an appropriate version of the above, or the same general equation re-arranged in one of the following forms:

$$H_s = \frac{S_s^2 V \times \text{slit spacing}}{4K_s \times \text{slit width}} \quad (4.5)$$

$$K_s = \frac{S_s^2 V \times \text{slit spacing}}{4H_s^2 \times \text{slit width}} \quad (4.6)$$

$$V = \frac{H_s^2 4K_s \times \text{slit width}}{S_s^2 \times \text{slit spacing}} \quad (4.7)$$

where S_s is the slit length between pipes in mm, H_s is the slit depth in mm, K_s is the hydraulic conductivity of slit fill in mm/h, V is the overall design rate in mm/h, V_s is the overall design rate modified for transmission only through slits.

Implications inherent in the simplified Hooghoudt equation

When seeking to upgrade a drainage scheme there is sometimes a choice between: shortening the interval between pipes, so shortening slit (or gravel channel) length; increasing slit (or gravel channel) depth; changing the particle-size grading of the backfill so as to increase its hydraulic conductivity; or increasing the capacity of the slits (or gravel channels) by increasing their width. From the form of the relationship between these variables, as shown in the simplified Hooghoudt equation, change in one does not necessarily ensure a directly proportional change in any of the others.

Thus, from the equation in the form

$$S_s = \sqrt{\left(\frac{H_s^2 4K_s \times \text{slit width}}{V \times \text{slit spacing}}\right)},$$

reducing the pipe spacing by half, i.e. halving the length of the slits S_s, will allow the possibility of halving slit depth H_s as this, though within the square root bracket, is itself a squared factor. However, if the change is to accommodate a change in any of the other,

unsquared factors – K_s, V, slit spacing or slit width – then halving S_s or doubling H_s will allow a four-fold reduction in K_s or slit width, or a four-fold increase in V. Slit spacing, however, is not so automatically amenable to adjustment. It has been arbitrarily fixed not to exceed 1m, by experience, not by calculation.

Similarly, halving V will allow a halving of K or slit width but only a reduction of $1/\sqrt{2}$ (i.e. 0.71) in H_s or S_s.

In practice it is important to recognize that it is modifications in S and H, or S_s and H_s, that have the greatest influence on the overall design rate V.

4.1.3 Worked examples of basic schemes

Calculations here do not include any adjustment for slope – see page 66 – and are based on metric values only.

Pipe drainage only (i.e. one-tier systems)

Example 4.1
Given the minimum acceptable spacing S for the pipe drain laterals is 4000 mm (4¼ yards), the depth of topsoil H is 300 mm (12 in) and the design rate V is 2 mm/h (¹⁄₁₂ in/h) what is the minimum hydraulic conductivity required of the topsoil if the watertable is not to breach the surface under the conditions specified? The site is flat and no slit drainage is intended. It may be assumed that the permeable backfill over the pipes will be *trench gravel* brought through to the surface as *blinding sand*.

By using the simplified Hooghoudt equation in the form

$$K = \frac{S^2 \times V}{4H^2}$$

we have

$$K = \frac{4000 \times 4000 \times 2}{4 \times 300 \times 300}$$

$$= 89 \text{ mm/hr } (3\frac{1}{2} \text{ in/h}).$$

A *K* value of the order of 75–100 mm/h is unlikely to be sustained by other than a pure sand medium, with all the difficulties this would imply for grass growth. The most that could be relied upon after settlement from either a 3:1 by volume sand/peat mixture (e.g. Table 7.1, SN16), or a loamy sand soil more than 75% medium plus fine sand (e.g. Table 7.1 SN18) would be of the order of 25 mm/h.

What then should be done in the circumstances envisaged in the example? The drain spacing *S* could be reduced by half to 2 m (6½ ft) or the topsoil depth *H* increased to 600 mm (24 in), but these alternatives would probably be unreasonably expensive. Another alternative is to accept a lower standard of efficiency, i.e. accept a design rate *V* of 1 mm/h, a standard of performance considered satisfactory for agriculture. This would probably be just acceptable for sport in areas of Britain with a relatively low rainfall, e.g. less than 700 mm (28 in) a year.

Changing the soil to a well-structured, granular loam (e.g. Table 7.1, SN21) could provide more than the required hydraulic conductivity *K* initially but the granulation might well not survive a winter of stud wear, and sand slitting would then be essential.

Generally, if drain spacings closer than 4 m (4¼ yards) are required, a two-tier system is more economical, using close-spaced sand or sand/gravel slits to intercept and then discharge excess surface water into the permeable fill of the trenches that carry the more widely spaced under drains (see Example 4.2 below).

Theoretically at least, there would appear to be scope for the alternative of a miniaturized, one-tier, pipe-drainage scheme. With trenchless machinery, suitably modified to bury small bore, perforated, plastic pipe into narrow 20–40 mm (1–1½ in) slits, and simultaneously backfill to the surface with appropriate fine gravel, clean grit or coarse sand, a type of pipe-assisted slit system could be created. However, the pipes would have to be very carefully installed so as to maintain flow for distances long enough to justify their inclusion. On a flat site this will involve very accurate grading of trenches to progressively greater depths. On an adequately sloping site, piped slits could be installed at a fixed, shallow depth of 250–350 mm (10–14 in) from the surface and, if oriented diagonally across slope, these will function for interception and discharge. But, in either case, the pipe being so small and the runs so relatively long, the very accurate grading required will make laser control of trench depth essential. The pipe performance data in Table 2.1 indicates that continuous runs of the order of a pitch length and more are possible. In these circumstances the permeable fill in the trench has only to allow the intercepted water down to the pipe. Virtually any clean sand could achieve this at an overall design rate of 2 mm/hr (½₂ in/h) and a slit spacing to slit width ratio of 36:1, or less.

Example 4.2
What permeable backfill would be appropriate for piped slits, 35 mm (1½ in) wide, spaced at 1 m (1 yard) intervals, and required to transfer water from the surface down to the pipe at an overall design rate of not less than 2 mm/h (½₂ in/h)?

The hydraulic conductivity required of the permeable fill is

$$2 \text{ mm/h} \times \frac{1000 \text{ mm}}{35 \text{ mm}}$$

$$= 57 \text{ mm/h} \ (2\tfrac{1}{4} \text{ in/h}).$$

This could be provided even by clean, very fine sand. However, such a sand could infilter the pipe perforations and would also be capable of ingestion by earthworms. It would be better, therefore, either to place *trench gravel* immediately over the pipe, followed by *blinding sand* through to the surface, or filter-wrap the pipe and then backfill with *blinding sand* only.

Pipe drainage augmented with slit drainage (i.e. two-tier systems)

Where the design of a drainage layout is planned to include surface interception by slit drainage, the drainage rate must be calculated separately for each tier of the system, working always from the surface downwards.

It should be recognized at the outset that it is not possible to put a firm figure on surface flow as this depends on surface conditions of smoothness, gradient and grass cover. However, experience suggests that slits should be spaced at intervals of the order of 1 m (1 yard) across slopes of the order of 1:100.

Note, it is only when the drainage water has entered the slit system that the calculations involving the simplified Hooghoudt equation really apply. As in Example 4.2, calculations for a slit system assume that the surface water arriving as rain over the whole playing surface will be concentrated at the slits, according to the ratio of total surface to slit surface.

Example 4.3
If required to cope with rainfall of 2 mm/h (¹⁄₁₂ in/h) what would be the maximum slit length between pipes for two-part, sand over gravel slits, spaced 1000 mm (39 in) apart, 50 mm (2 in) wide, 360 mm (14 in) deep, filled with 180 mm (7 in) of *blinding sand* (K = 500 mm/hr) over 180 mm (7 in) of *trench gravel* (K = 65 000 mm/h)?

Use the simplified Hooghoudt equation in the form

$$S_s = 2H_s \sqrt{\left(\frac{K_s}{V_s}\right)}.$$

In this case

$$2H_s \sqrt{\left(\frac{K_s}{V \times \text{slit spacing/slit width}}\right)}$$

Step 1: the average K_a for the two-part, sand over gravel slits

$$= \frac{(180 \times 500) + (180 \times 65\,000)}{180 + 180}$$

$$= 32\,750 \text{ mm/h.}$$

Note, the hydraulic conductivity value K_s used to represent the combined effect of the sand and gravel layers in the slit will be the average value K_a which has been weighted according to the depths and K values of the two materials concerned (see back to page 64).

Step 2: the overall design rate V, representing the rainfall the system as a whole is required to discharge, must be adjusted to take account of the fact that all runoff is assumed to be concentrated into the slits (see back to page 68).

$$V_s = \frac{V \times \text{slit spacing}}{\text{slit width}}$$

$$= 2 \times \frac{1000}{50}$$

$$= 40 \text{ mm/h.}$$

Step 3: to determine the safe slit length between pipe trench outfalls use

$$S_s = 2H_s \sqrt{\left(\frac{K_s}{V_s}\right)}$$

which gives

$$S_s = 2 \times 360 \sqrt{\left(\frac{32\,750}{40}\right)}$$

$$= 20\,602 \text{ mm or } 20.6 \text{ m (22 yards).}$$

Using *Stewart zone* materials (Chapter 4, page 62 and Chapter 7, pages 114–117) it is sufficient to take account only of the depth of the *trench gravel* layer. In a standard slit system, where slit spacing (e.g. 1000 mm) does not exceed more than 20 times slit width (e.g. 50 mm), every 1-cm depth of a *trench gravel* will safely provide for a minimum of a 1-m increment in the run of the slit between the intercepting pipe underdrains. In the above example, therefore, if the gravel used in the slit had fallen well within the finer half of the *trench gravel* zone, the 18-cm depth would have allowed the slits to run for a safe distance of 18 m between the relieving system of pipe underdrains at the 2 mm/hr design rate given.

This suggests a simple scheme of pipes at about 20 m intervals crossed at right-angles by sand/gravel slits at 1 m intervals.

Variations

1. If the slit is widened to 75 mm (3 in), V_s changes by a factor of 50/75 and S_s by $\sqrt{(75/50)}$. Hence the maximum slit length becomes

$$20.6 \sqrt{\left(\frac{75}{50}\right)} = 25 \text{ m (27 yards)}.$$

2. If the original slit is filled with 360 mm (14 in) of *blinding sand* only ($K_s = 500$ mm/h) the maximum slit length becomes

$$20.6 \sqrt{\left(\frac{500}{32\,750}\right)} = 2.5 \text{ m (2¾ yards)}.$$

This shows why slits most often are filled with two materials – sand over an appropriate gravel. The sand contributes little to the discharge capacity of the slit; none the less its presence is essential to allow the gravel to be placed well below the surface where it is less vulnerable to earthworm activity and other forms of soil disturbance. A purpose-made hopper, capable of backfilling simultaneously with two different materials, to two fixed depths, is an obvious practical asset.

3. If the overall depth of the 50 mm (2 in) wide slits is reduced to 250 mm (10 in) and each layer within it (sand over gravel) is reduced in depth to 125 mm (5 in) then the maximum slit length, which was 20.6 m, becomes

$$20.6 \times \frac{10}{14} = 14.7 \text{ m (16 yards)},$$

i.e. S_s is reduced directly in proportion to the change in slit depth.

By the *Stewart zone* approach, 12.5 cm of a *trench gravel* such as SN7 in Table 7.1 would allow a safe slit length of 12.5 m between pipe trench outfalls.

This example shows how a change in depth (being a squared factor) has a greater effect on maximum slit length (in this case drain spacing) than an equivalent change in slit width or the hydraulic conductivity of the permeable fill (refer back to page 68).

Pipe drainage augmented with gravel channels and surface slits (i.e. three-tier systems)

Under normal circumstances three-tier systems are not likely to be a first choice on a natural site. However, these may evolve, as in the following examples.

1. On an established site where a deep system of field drains already exists and contact with the permeable fill over the pipes may not be readily achieved by a simple system of sand/gravel slits. This could be because of the unsuitability of the fill over the pipes or the presence of obstacles to narrow slitting in the soil at 150–300 mm (6–12 in) from the surface.

2. On a tip site where the buried rubble has been covered by less than 250 mm (10 in) of stone-free topsoil and there is uncertainty over the extent to which the rubble fill will act as an effective soakaway. Because of the nature of the rubble fill it may well be necessary to use a large hydraulic excavator to dig out trenches and, if this cannot be done neatly or without great difficulty, it may be desirable to keep the number of pipe underdrains to a minimum.

In a three-tier system the extra tier, the gravel channels, is required to intercept the surface tier of slits at the limit of their effectiveness, and then link across to the pipe underdrains. Gravel channels of this type are likely to be at least 150 mm (6 in) wide, but their permeable fill need not be taken through to the surface as surface infiltration will already be adequately covered by the slit system.

If necessary, consideration can be given to increasing channel width to compensate for any limitation in depth. However, as H is a squared factor in the simplified Hooghoudt equation, a reduction by half in the depth of the gravel channel will involve a reduction by half in its hydraulic capacity and will require a fourfold (i.e. 2^2) increase in channel width to compensate.

Careful attention to the grading of the permeable fill will be necessary, above and below: above to avoid loss by infiltration into large cavities within the underlying rubble (or the backfill of the pipe drain); below, to prevent infiltration of soil used to cap the surface.

Example 4.4
Sand slits are required to clear surface water at 2 mm ($\frac{1}{12}$ in)/h through a level, slow-draining but easily trenched, stone-free topsoil, 200–250 mm (8–10 in) deep. However, the topsoil rests on a compact foundation of stony, tip waste which becomes progressively more difficult to trench with depth. What system of intercepting gravel channels and pipes could be organized to complete the job of drainage, keeping deep trenching to a minimum?

Step 1: the initial tier of surface slits might be, for example, 50 mm (2 in) wide, 225 mm (9 in) deep, at 1 m intervals, filled first with a 100 mm (4 in) layer of *trench gravel* ($K = 55$ 000 mm/h) and topped up to the surface with a 125 mm (5 in) layer of *blinding sand* ($K = 800$ mm/h).

To achieve a design rate of 2 mm ($\frac{1}{12}$ in)/h such a system of slits would require relieving into a second tier of drainage channels at intervals determined by the hydraulic conductivity K_s of the sand/gravel slits:

K_s (i.e. K_a)

$$= \frac{(125 \times 800) + (100 \times 55\,000)}{125 + 100}$$

$$= 24\,889 \text{ mm/h.}$$

We can then go on to determine slit length S_s which will also be the spacing of the gravel channels if they intersect at right-angles:

$$S_s = 2 \times 225 \sqrt{\left(\frac{24\,889 \times 50}{2 \times 1000}\right)}$$

$$= 11\,225$$

$$= 11 \text{ m (12 yards).}$$

Note, for the purpose of this example a particular 10 mm gravel, currently available in mid-Wales, has been cited because the particle-size composition and hydraulic conductivity are known. This material, precisely defined in accordance with the guidance given in Chapter 7, is 10 mm, rounded but somewhat platey gravel; $D_{15} = 2.8$ mm, $D_{85} = 8.9$ mm, i.e. 70% of the particles, excluding 15% at either extreme are $2.8 - 8.9$ mm in diameter; and K (the saturated hydraulic conductivity) $= 55\,000$ mm/h. However, had another 10 mm gravel, known to be available in the south of Scotland, been used, the slits could have been allowed to run 22 m (24 yards) between the gravel channels. This other material, precisely defined, is 10 mm, single-size rounded gravel; $D_{15} = 5.8$ mm, $D_{85} = 9.8$ mm, $K = 225\,000$ mm/h, i.e. a material with 70% of its particles within the range 5.8–9.8 mm. Clearly it is very important to define materials used in drainage work more precisely than simply to quote the sieve size through which all the material has passed (Chapter 7).

Using the *Stewart zone* approach, the incremental allowance per cm of gravel in the case of the first gravel used, a gravel wholly in the finer half of the *trench gravel* zone, would be 1 m. Hence the 100 mm (4 in) layer of gravel in the slit would be estimated to allow for slit runs to underdrain outfalls of the order of 10 m long (compare the 11 m by precise calculation). For the second gravel, a material wholly in the coarse half of the *trench gravel* zone, the increment per cm of gravel would be 2 m. This would allow an estimate for slit runs of 20 m (compare the 22 m indicated by precise calculation).

Step 2: the medium immediately beneath the layer of superimposed topsoil on a tip site may have to keep the topsoil from seeping down into the large rubble below. Such a layer may contain numerous small stones making it difficult to slit but readily dug out by the narrow, tapered bucket of a hydraulic excavator. Thus gravel channels may be installed through the intermediate, blinding layer of stony soil, say 200 mm (8 in) wide and as deep as the larger rubble will allow efficient excavation, say 375 mm (15 in) deep. The backfill will then have to take account of the nature of the exposed rubble and the need to form a clean link to the gravel layer at the base of the slits, say a backfill of *trench gravel* taken to within 125 mm (5 in) of the surface, then 25 mm (1 in) of *blinding sand* and the remainder, soil.

To maintain the overall design rate of 2 mm ($\frac{1}{12}$ in)/day, such a channel system, unless able to soak away efficiently into the rubble, will require relieving into a third tier of pipe underdrains. As the pipes will have to be inserted into the least hospitable part of the tip rubble, where trenching may be particularly difficult, the aim should be to maximize the length of the gravel channels so as to keep the requirement for pipes to a minimum.

In this example the gravel channels envisaged would require the pipe trenches to be spaced at no more than 11 m (12 yard) intervals:

$$S = 2 \times 250 \sqrt{\left(\frac{55\,000 \times 200}{2 \times 11\,000} \right)}$$

$$= 11\,180 \text{ mm}$$

$$= 11 \text{ m (12 yards).}$$

This of itself achieves no benefit over a two-tier system of slits delivering to pipe drains at 11 m (12 yard) intervals, except that the gravel channels are effective within their limits when laid flat, whereas the pipe runs have to be graded progressively deeper into tip rubble. To be economical on deep pipe trenching, therefore, the middle tier of pipeless channels must deliver at the required design rate over a much wider spacing than the 11 m calculated for the channels cited above.

To treble the spacing of the pipes the options are:

1. multiply the channel width by 3^2, to 1800 mm, but this would be ridiculous;
2. multiply channel depth by 3, to 750 mm, but this could be difficult if the bottom of the trench had to be cut through the tip rubble;
3. reduce the design rate by one-ninth, to 0.22 mm/hr, but this would then be inadequate for winter use;
4. multiply the hydraulic conductivity of the channel fill by 9 for the bottom 150 mm (6 in) of its depth, e.g. by changing this to a single size, 20 mm ($\frac{3}{4}$ in), small to medium stone (*K* of the order of 900 000 mm/h).

To verify option 4 calculate first the hydraulic conductivity of the two-part gravel/small stone fill in the channel:

$$K_a = \frac{(100 \times 55\,000) + (150 \times 900\,000)}{100 + 150}$$

$$= 562\,000 \text{ mm/h.}$$

Then, calculate the maximum length of run for the gravel/stone channels between pipe runs:

$$S = \sqrt{\left(\frac{250 \times 250 \times 4 \times 562\,000}{2 \times 11\,000/200} \right)}$$

$$= 35 \text{ m (38 yards).}$$

This reduces the requirement for deep trenching considerably, making option 4 a good proposi-

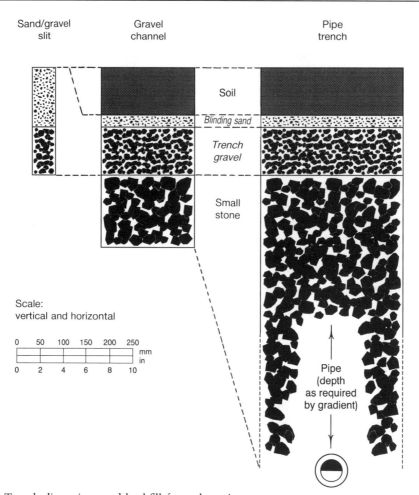

FIGURE 4.2 Trench dimensions and backfill for a three-tier system.

tion for meeting the requirements of this difficult site. Figure 4.2 summarizes the trench systems involved.

These calculations are inappropriate for the much simplified *Stewart zone* approach as (a) the main material in the channel, responsible for discharging water laterally is not a *trench gravel*, and (b) the trench width to channel spacing ratio is 1:55 which far exceeds the 1:20 ratio of a standard slit system.

If the tip is naturally or artificially drained at depth there may be no need for any third tier of pipes, but then either the slits or the gravel channels will have to be organized to discharge

at intervals into the underlying rubble. Blinding may be necessary to keep the channel fill from leaking away into the rubble.

Gravel-rafted schemes, generally for fine-turf surfaces

Where a freely permeable, sandy topsoil is laid over a drainage bed designed to do the entire job of lateral discharge to underdrains, the sandy topsoil has only to allow the incident rain water to drain vertically through to the gravel bed at the overall design rate V. However, in a layered construction it will be the hydraulic conductivity of the least efficient layer that will be the rate-limiting bottleneck, particularly a junction between layers where particles of different size are free to interpack. In time, also as the sward develops, organic matter, living, dead and decaying, both within and on top of the soil, will further modify performance. All this is difficult to predict theoretically, even for the initial, raw state.

Not only has the hydraulic conductivity of the different layers and layer boundaries to be considered however; we also need to know the extent of the effective head. At saturation this will not correspond just to the thickness of the layer itself but will extend both above and below into all layers that are effectively saturated.

Field checks on infiltration rates would seem to be the answer, but these are difficult to perform satisfactorily and, by the nature of things, can only be done after construction.

As general guidance, it would be worthwhile to assume that without worm activity to continually re-structure the soil for drainage, even a sand soil is unlikely to achieve an infiltration rate more than 25–50 mm (1–2 in)/h when maintained under grass. However, even a value of 2 mm/h (2 in/day) would be enough to achieve the minimum overall design rate normally found adequate in Britain for general sports turf, but is close to the rate required when the runoff is all concentrated into the sand at the top of sand slits.

For most sports we can make supplementary provision to cope with short bursts of intense rain by contouring the surface to clear excess surface water down slope to the periphery. By contrast, on a flat surface, we must work to maintain the initial infiltration of the raw surface by regular, sand topdressing, spiking and coring so as to make full use of the sand topsoil's own capacity for temporary storage.

To determine the hydraulic head likely to be effective at the surface in such a layered construction, account should be taken of the depth of the coarse sand forming the blinding layer as well as the depth of the fine sand forming the topsoil. However, only if the effective pore systems of the two materials are similar in size, or the pores in the blinding layer are smaller, will they behave as one when wetted from above. If the effective pores in the binding layer are large compared with those in the fine sand, then only after the fine sand has been more or less saturated will water be shunted through into the blinding layer. Similarly the blinding layer will have to be more or less saturated before it in turn will release water to drain away through the much larger pores in the underlying gravel drainage bed.

After any initial phase of relatively rapid soil water re-distribution and drainage through the bulk of the pore space itself, there is still the possibility of further adjustment by the much slower process of water movement through continuous films of water that creep over surfaces and cling tenaciously around individual particles. No doubt this also accounts for the slow rate of further drainage that can be observed to continue for many days after any initial phase of rapid drainage has ceased.

For the sake of cost the depth of the gravel bed should be kept to a minimum, but so also should the amount of pipe work. The balance struck will depend on the relative cost of the two features concerned.

Example 4.5
An organic-ameliorated, sand topsoil laid over a bed of *trench gravel* might have a K value between 2 and 20 mm/h. Suggest a suitable depth for the gravel bed to clear drainage water to pipe underdrains restricted to the periphery of a 40 m square, e.g. as for a bowling green. Assume the depth of the gravel bed is to be (a) restricted to 100 mm, (b) can exceed the 100 mm restriction. Compare for each case the effect of targeting overall design rates at the two extremes of 2 and 20 mm/h.

A suitable spacing for the pipe trenches can be determined by using the simplified version of Hooghoudt's drain-spacing equation

$$S = \sqrt{\left(\frac{H^2 4K}{V}\right)}.$$

Substituting 100 mm for H, 2 mm (or 20 mm) for V and 65 000 mm/h as the K value for the typical *trench gravel*:

$$S = \sqrt{\left(\frac{100 \times 100 \times 4 \times 65\ 000}{2}\right)}$$

$$= 36\ 050 \text{ mm}$$

$$= 36 \text{ m } (39\frac{1}{2} \text{ yards})$$

or

$$S = \sqrt{\left(\frac{100 \times 100 \times 4 \times 65\ 000}{20}\right)}$$

$$= 11\ 402 \text{ mm}$$

$$= 11 \text{ m } (12\frac{1}{2} \text{ yards}).$$

A suitable depth for the gravel bed when pipes are to be confined to the periphery of a square bowling green can be determined by using an appropriately rearranged version of the simplified Hooghoudt equation and a change in the constant from 4 to 6.79 (refer back to page 66). This will take account of the freedom in the situation for drainage water to clear in four directions instead of just two. Thus,

$$S = \sqrt{\left(\frac{H^2 6.79K}{V}\right)},$$

or

$$H = \sqrt{\left(\frac{VS^2}{6.79K}\right)}.$$

Substituting 2 mm (or 20 mm) for V, 40 000 mm for S and 65 000 mm/h for K,

$$H = \sqrt{\left(\frac{2 \times 40\ 000 \times 40\ 000}{6.79 \times 65\ 000}\right)}$$

$$= 85 \text{ mm } (3\frac{1}{2} \text{ in})$$

or

$$H = \sqrt{\left(\frac{20 \times 40\ 000 \times 40\ 000}{6.79 \times 65\ 000}\right)}$$

$$= 269 \text{ mm } (10\frac{1}{2} \text{ in}).$$

To achieve the 20 mm/hr design rate with a drainage bed only 100 mm deep would require the introduction of some stone. This will greatly increase transmission, but must do so without risk to the stability of the layers above, e.g. small to medium stone, $K = 900\ 000$ mm/h. (Chapter 7, pages 126–127 gives information on selecting materials likely to remain stable in a layered sequence.)

To calculate the effect of forming the drainage bed of 50 mm of small to medium stone covered by 50 mm of *trench gravel*, proceed as follows.

Step 1: for the averaged hydraulic conductivity required of the new drainage bed

$$K_a = \frac{S^2 V}{6.79 H^2}.$$

Substituting what we know,

$$K_a \text{ required} = \frac{40\ 000 \times 40\ 000 \times 20}{6.79 \times 100 \times 100}$$

$$= 471\ 281 \text{ mm/hr}.$$

Step 2: we also know that

$$K_a = \frac{(H_1 \times K_1) + (H_2 \times K_2)}{H_1 + H_2}.$$

Substituting what we know,

$$471\ 281 = \frac{(50 \times 65\ 000) + (50 \times K_2)}{50 + 50}.$$

Therefore the hydraulic conductivity K_2 required of the 50 mm layer of small to medium stone can now be calculated as $K_2 = 877\ 562$ mm/h.

This is a K value very close to the 900 000 mm/hr quoted for a small to medium stone referred to previously, page 73.

Note, it would not be wise to assume that if a particular small to medium stone is adequate to achieve the desired objective, an even bigger stone would be better. Too big a stone would allow the gravel above to interpack, dramatically reducing the effectiveness of the two materials organized as a stable, two-layered system.

The soil base of a gravel drainage bed might well slope slightly to assist the flow of water towards the pipe underdrains. A flat base would tend to lie wet and locally puddled. For designs of this nature, see those suggested for hard porous pitches (Chapter 13, section 13.3).

4.1.4 Two examples of practical circumstances justifying modification of standard schemes

Slope

Slope requires special consideration as the steeper the gradient the faster the runoff of surface water after rain. When the simplified Hooghoudt equation is applied to the slit situation it is assumed that excess surface water will mainly reach the slit by unimpeded flow over the surface. However, surface flow is bound to be much more effective on land with an appreciable slope. Hence there is a case for spacing the slits slightly more widely apart on slopes of the order of 1:50 or more, provided the slits run horizontally across the slope.

Availability of materials

A factor about which a designer must be particularly careful is the availability of materials. Theoretical calculations are of little value if the sand and gravel materials specified cannot be supplied, or are only obtainable at a cost far in excess of what the client can afford.

For efficient drainage we need to make use of materials that remain open, even when close-packed. Ideally, this means materials made up of rounded particles, all one size. However, the major users of sands and gravels are the construction industries and they are often looking for materials that will inter-pack to achieve maximum density. Before proceeding to calculations, therefore, it is important that the designer should first ascertain what is the range of materials at his disposal. Where, for tendering purposes, materials have to be specified in advance, the contractor should be made aware that use of a different material to that specified may necessitate a change of layout. (Chapter 7 gives further information on the selection and specification of sands and gravels used in the construction and drainage of sports turf facilities.)

4.2 Absorption and retention of water

4.2.1 Theoretical considerations affecting design calculations concerned with capillarity and critical tension

Demonstrations

To understand how water is absorbed, retained and cleared by a porous medium such as a soil, we need to have some understanding of the twin phenomena of capillary rise and critical tension. These are difficult to describe simply but can be demonstrated by the sequence of procedures illustrated in Figure 4.3.

For the experiments illustrated in Figure 4.3 (a.i–vii), the sand-filled glass tube is best made up initially of particles all of just one particle-size grade, e.g. all fine or all medium sand, and the base closed over with a small piece of finely woven, cotton cloth, secured with an elastic band. For fine sand the sand column should be approximately 400 mm (16 in) deep, and the tube some 200–300 mm (4–6 in) longer. For medium sand these dimensions could all be halved.

Lower the sand-filled tube into a reservoir of water, holding it upright and keeping the cloth-covered base just below the surface of the water. Observe how the water is drawn up through the sand column by capillarity, then proceed to explore the related phenomenon of critical tension.

For the experiments illustrated in Figure 4.3 (b.viii–xiv) it is necessary first to determine the critical tension of the foam sponge used so that the two strips required for the demonstrations that follow can be cut to the appropriate size and shape. Then explore how water can be retained or drained according as the two strips are organized.

A soil, saturated to the surface, may still allow additional water to infilter so long as an equivalent amount of water can be cleared out below to a drainage outfall. It is the rate of this saturated flow with which Hoogboudt's simplified equation is concerned (Chapter 4, section 4.1). However, having allowed additional water to be shunted through the water-filled pore space, the soil may not be able to complete the job of drainage by finally emptying the pores to admit air.

The transmission of water is only one aspect of drainage which, when it ends, may still leave the transmitting pore system completely water-filled. This can be demonstrated by the procedure illustrated in Figure 4.3 (a.v.4) and (a.vii.6). Note, the column of saturated sand will transmit additional water – one drop in being matched by one drop out – but there is no further drainage thereafter. Even spiking is ineffective unless, for some reason, particle segregation, organic accumulation, or in-appropriate topdressing has led to the creation of a fine-textured cap. (See Appendix 6 and Figure 4.3 (a.vii).).

The water held up in a perched watertable is under tension, unlike water within a ground watertable. As indicated in Figure 4.3 (b.ix, xii and xiv), however, it is this tension which provides the 'draw' that can be organized to assist drainage. Note the draw does not originate in any underlying pipe but in the perched watertable that can be organized in the trench fill above.

Theory

Wetting up from below is very effective – some might say too effective in that air will be readily displaced upwards, ahead of the rising water front – leaving the soil within the capillary fringe, virtually saturated to the exclusion of air. Unless water, wetting a soil from above, arrives in fine, dispersed droplets the surface will very rapidly flood over. This is because air bubbles have difficulty escaping upwards through a water-sealed surface, and cannot be displaced downwards through a compact sub-soil. As a result, because most soils in the field are wetted primarily from above, some air-filled pores are bypassed by the downward-moving water front. Thus topsoils tend only to become completely waterlogged when wetted from above if this trapped air is subsequently dislodged by the puddling action of wheeled traffic, or spiking treading.

Water is a polar liquid, i.e. the water molecules are charged both positive and negative, like little magnets, and thereby cohere to each other and adhere to the similarly charged surfaces of soil minerals such as quartz, or glass. This coherence also allows water to have a certain tensile strength when suspended as a drop or extended into a fine, capillary-sized thread. It is the attraction of water to glass that holds a raindrop to the vertical face of a glass window until it is unstabilized by vibration or increasing weight. It may then slip down over the surface but will still remain a coherent droplet, attached at one side.

Close examination of the surface of the water around the edge of a glass shows how the attraction of the glass raises the level of the water all around the rim. Now imagine the glass progressively reduced in diameter to a hair-like, capillary tube open at either end, the lower end immersed in a basin of water. The surrounding glass surface would then be large compared with the contained volume so that water, free to move, will be drawn some distance up the tube, like water into blotting paper. It is this process that enables water to be drawn up through sand from a free-water reservoir until the attractive force (the pull) is balanced by the weight of the suspended water column (Figure 4.3 (a. iv)). The finer the capillary system the stronger the influence of the particle surface over the water contained within it and, therefore, the higher the water can be raised. In section 4.2.2 this relationship is more fully explored by means of a formula which enables the extent of capillary rise to be predicted when the diameter of the capillary pathway is known.

In a capillary tube the length of the fine, water column that can be suspended is not affected by whether the water arrives from above or below, provided air can be displaced to make room for it. However, in a uniform particle-size sand, for example, though the surface to void ratio in the pore system may ensure some positive capillary effect, the pore system is not strictly tubular. The simplest such system would consist of closely packed uniform diameter spheres in which open cavities would be joined through funnel-like necks in a regular sequence, as illustrated in Figure 4.4.

The diameter of a spherical particle that could just fit into the cavities within such a system would be a little under half (0.42) particle diameter, and the diameter of spherical particles that could just fit the necks would be one-seventh (0.14) particle diameter. Water lifted by capillarity through such a system would be arrested ultimately by the position in which the attracting surface of the particles had their minimum effect, i.e. across the maximum diameter of the highest pore cavities invaded. Water cleared downwards from above, however, would tend ultimately to be suspended from a neck, which is the place where the retaining hold of the mineral surface on the water column is likely to be most effective. Thus, as comparison of Figure 4.3 (a. iv) and (a. vi) indicates, a water front lifted by capillarity from below will rise to approximately half the height to which water will be held up after drainage has ceased following flooding, i.e. capillary rise will always be less than critical tension.

In a natural sand, complications may arise, not only because of air entrapment, but also because the geometrical relationships described above will be modified by variations in particle-size, shape and packing. In Figure 4.3 (c) note how the variations in pore size which are liable to occur in a heterogeneously packed, narrow mixture of particle sizes results in the degree of saturation steadily falling off with increasing height. Also, the strength of the attraction between the mineral particles and the water may be modified by impurities in the water and coatings on the particles affecting wettability (Thornton, 1978, p. 501). Hence, predictions based on the simple relationships in the calculations that follow (section 4.2.2) are probably exaggerated, and should never be considered more than approximate.

As in a sand, the amount of water retained in a normal soil after drainage has ceased will depend on the initial state, and which way the soil has been watered. A dry soil, with a water-stable granular structure, when wetted quickly from above, will tend to allow much of the water to fall freely under gravity. This will descend rapidly through the inter-connected system of very large pores between the soil granules, air being simultaneously displaced upwards. Thereafter, re-distribution will take place under the control of capillary forces into the fine pores within the granules, but again, only if air can be displaced. However, if mechanical smearing creates a cap of de-structured soil at the surface, this fine-pored

Preparations

i) Materials & equipment

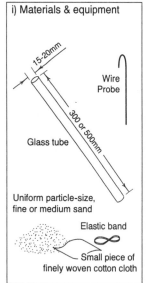

15-20mm

Wire Probe

Glass tube

300 or 500mm

Uniform particle-size, fine or medium sand

Elastic band

Small piece of finely woven cotton cloth

ii) Ready for action

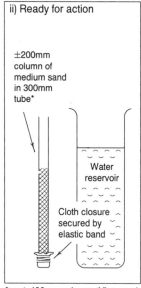

±200mm column of medium sand in 300mm tube*

Water reservoir

Cloth closure secured by elastic band

* or ± 400mm column of fine sand in 500mm tube

iii) KEY

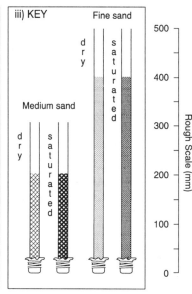

Fine sand

dry   saturated

Medium sand

dry   saturated

Rough Scale (mm)

500 — 400 — 300 — 200 — 100 — 0

Wetting up from below

iv) Capillary Rise (medium sand)

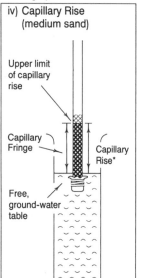

Upper limit of capillary rise

Capillary Fringe

Capillary Rise*

Free, ground-water table

* Medium sand ± 100 mm
(Fine sand ± 200 mm)

Draining down from above

v) Medium sand column transmits but fails to empty

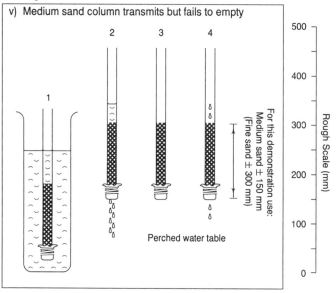

1   2   3   4

For this demonstration use:
Medium sand ± 150 mm
(Fine sand ± 300 mm)

Perched water table

Rough Scale (mm)

500 — 400 — 300 — 200 — 100 — 0

Fig 4.3 (a)

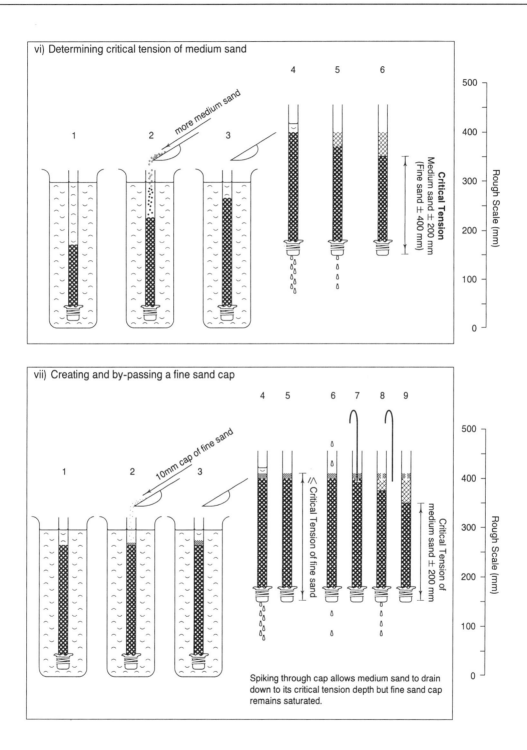

Fig 4.3 (a) continued

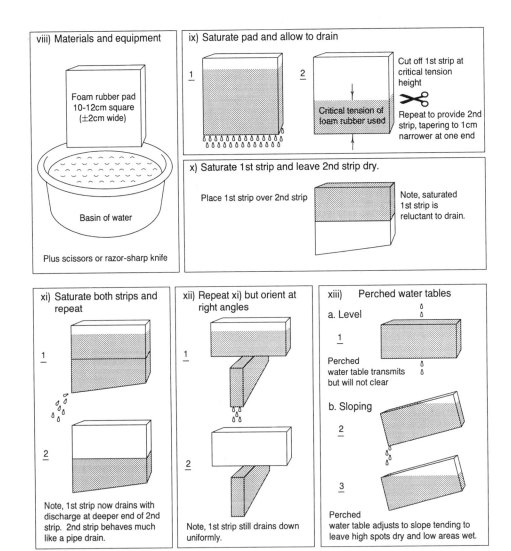

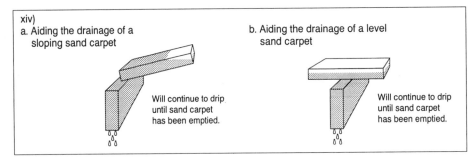

Fig 4.3 (b)

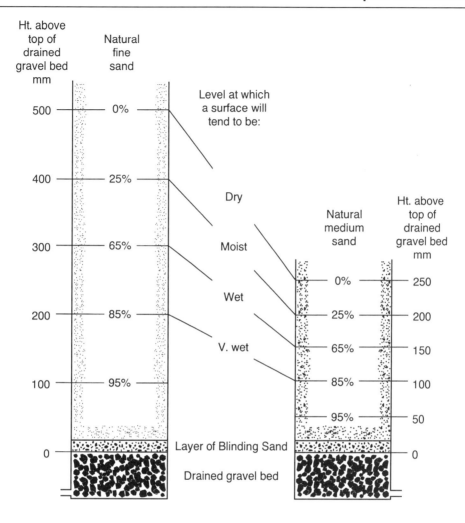

Soil columns dominated by either fine sand or medium sand, each with a BLINDING SAND base of similar DK value,placed over a drained bed of TRENCH GRAVEL. Sand layers each heterogeneously packed.

Moisture profiles recorded after leaving to drain for two days following complete saturation. Moisture states expressed as percent of saturation.

Note how the height of the construction above the gravel bed will change the moisture state to which the surface will tend to adjust whenever re-wetted by rainfall.

FIGURE 4.3 Demonstrating capillary rise and critical tension. (a) Using columns of uniform, artificially graded sands. (b) Using foam-rubber sponges to simulate soil. Moisture profiles for (c) natural sand soils rafted over gravel. Soil columns dominated by either fine sand or medium sand, each with a blinding sand base of similar D_K value, placed over a drained bed of trench gravel. Sand layers each heterogeneously packed. Moisture profiles recorded after leaving to drain for two days following complete saturation. Moisture states expressed as percentage saturation. Note how the height of the construction above the gravel bed will change the moisture state to which the surface will tend to adjust whenever re-wetted by rainfall.

**Pore system created by
single-sized spheres in
closest packing**

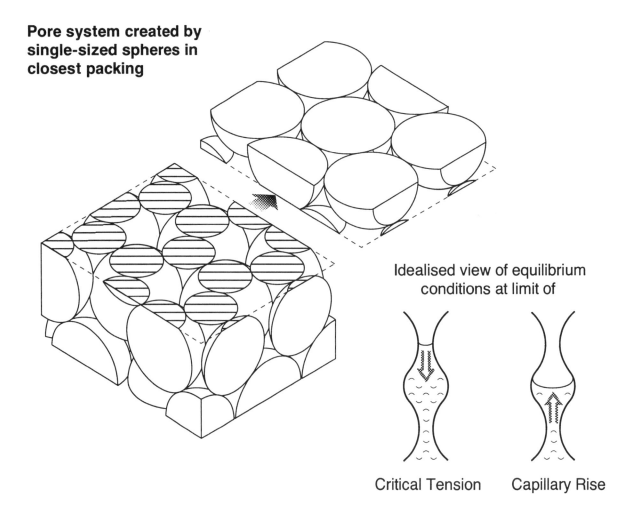

Idealised view of equilibrium
conditions at limit of

Critical Tension   Capillary Rise

FIGURE 4.4 (a) Three-dimensional drawing to show pore system created by single -sized spheres in closest packing. Note the continuous hexagonal formation. (b) Idealized view of equilibrium conditions within the pore system at critical tension and at the limit of capillary rise.

barrier will hold on to the water it absorbs, and will impede further infiltration by obstructing the release of the trapped air.

Only an uncapped, worm-worked soil will maintain the wide range of pore sizes, that allow for the air release required to ensure the rapid infiltration and re-distribution of rain-water necessary for an efficient moisture regime. All soil reacts best to the farmer's fine, wetting rain, rather than the same amount of rain in intense, short bursts. Heavy rain may physically degrade a mechanically formed structure and immediately flood the surface, trapping air below. This impedes infiltration so that water accumulates above ground while run-off over the surface threatens to cause erosion.

4.2.2 Calculating critical tension from information on particle size

Critical tension can be determined practically but it is probably more convenient to make an estimate based on the formula used to estimate the capillary rise of water in uniform diameter capillary tubes. This process is described by the equation

$$h = \frac{2T}{gDr},$$

where h is the height of the water column in cm, T is the surface tension of the water (75 dynes/cm), g is the acceleration due to gravity (approximately 1000 cm/s/s), D is the density of water (1 g/cm^3) and r is the radius of the water-containing pore in cm.

As T, g and D can all be considered constant, and with all measurements expressed in centimetres, the equation reduces to

$$h = \frac{0.15}{r}.$$

But, as the initial information which we want to use is concerned with particle size, not pore size, the equation must be adjusted to take this into account. We can do this by using the information that, for a uniform set of spheres in closest packing, pore radius is approximately 0.21 times particle diameter. Thus, assuming that silt and sand particles attract water similarly to glass and are roughly spherical in shape, the equation, expressed in millimetres, becomes

$$\text{critical tension (mm)}$$
$$= \frac{71.4}{\text{effective particle diameter (mm)}}.$$

The form of this equation suggests that critical tension is inversely proportional to particle diameter so that doubling the particle size will halve the critical tension. Thus, the critical tension for fine sand of uniform, 0.2 mm particle diameter, should be approximately

71.4/0.2 = 357 mm (14 in); a medium sand of 0.4 mm particle diameter would be expected to have half the critical tension of fine sand, i.e. 178 mm (7 in).

As critical tension is controlled more by the necks of the pore outlets than the pore itself these values could be looked upon as likely to under-estimate the true value. However, because of particle surface limitations on the efficiency of wetting, and the state of closest packing being seldom fully achieved in the field, theoretical values may well exaggerate the field response.

Very few commercially available sands are likely to be of single particle size, but when adequately mixed, can be assumed to behave in accordance with the particle size of the finest group of particles that come to dominate the pore space by interpacking. As this is true also for hydraulic conductivity we can hope to develop a system for predicting both, based on the idea of the dominating, or effective particle diameter (D_{15}, D_{25} or D_{35}). Such a system is described in section 7.1.8, and has been used in Table 7.1 to predict values for hydraulic conductivity and critical tension (refer also to Figures 7.7 and 7.8).

4.2.3 Practical application of theory to problems of the absorption and retention of water

Combining rapid drainage with adequate water retention

A fine pore system will tend to abstract water from a large pore system. For this reason, a sand layer blown over a freely drained, fine-textured soil will tend not only to lose excess water by drainage to the soil below but, as the fine soil itself drains, so it will tend to draw out capillary-held water from the coarser-pored sand.

However, the ability of a sand to hold on to a store of water, at least to the extent of its effective critical tension, can be induced by establishing a horizontal capillary break between the sand top and the fine soil below. This can take the form of an air lock created by draining an underlying, coarser pore system, e.g. a drained gravel bed. Thus a 300 mm (12 in) layer of fine sand can be organized to store 90 mm (3½ in) of water, i.e. a fortnight's supply of water for vigorous grass growth in mid-summer or a 3–4 week buffer against death by desiccation. Note, this perched watertable will clear downhill if the interface forming the capillary break is inclined on a slope (Figure 4.3 b. xiii and b. xiv).

Because of capillarity a soil can be watered from below without raising the watertable to the surface, e.g. by using a sub-irrigated bed of gravel to maintain a free water source in continuous contact with the base of the soil. But if the base of the soil is compact and very fine in texture, as would necessarily have to be the case on a cricket square, the rate of wetting up through the capillary pore system could be frustratingly slow. A sand soil is nothing like as slow to wet up by sub-irrigation and is also effective for surface irrigation, discharging excess water through the gravel bed only after replenishing the reserve capacity of the sand layer.

For a sand soil constructed over a gravel drainage bed there appears to be a range of soil depths over which grass may perform satisfactorily after successful establishment. Thornton (1978, pp. 526–527) concluded, after careful monitoring of similar sets of differently constructed field plots located at four main centres in England and Wales, that construction down to a depth of sand, approximately half the laboratory-determined value for critical tension, was justified. However, he also found that grass performance was no less good at the full critical tension depth. To explain the absence of poor aeration in the top 100 mm (4 in) of the soil, even at the shallower soil depth, he draws attention to the possibility that variations in the efficiency of air displacement could arise from variations in wettability, according as the sand particles are coated, e.g. with a film of iron oxide or protein. Alternatively, it could be that re-distribution of water under capillary forces following any initial wetting (as discussed in section 4.2.1, page 85), may lead to an equilibrium moisture profile more in line with expectations based on capillary rise rather than critical tension.

However this may be, the practical evidence seems to support the idea that the construction depth for a sand soil, perched over a gravel drainage bed, should neither be more than the critical tension nor less than half. Any blinding layer required beneath the sand soil should be included within this depth if the D_K values are similar, indicating that the pore systems present in both layers are likely to be compatible, i.e. similar in diameter (page 119). At the full critical tension extreme, the surface may tend to dry out so rapidly that it will require repeated irrigation to remain sufficiently moist for seed germination but, thereafter, should encourage deeper rooting unless transformed by thatch development. At the shallowest extreme of half the critical tension, the surface should more readily remain moist enough to encourage rapid seed germination but, thereafter, the grass may tend not to root as deeply, and there may be a greater risk of invasion by weeds, moss and disease. For a fine sand soil this points to an optimum range of between 250 and 300 mm (10 and 14 in) for the consolidated sand soil over the top of the gravel drainage bed.

At the low concentrations of organic matter or mineral soil amelioration used in sand soils we can assume heterogeneous packing and that the top as a whole will behave in a manner controlled by the sand. Any localized concentrations of organic matter, or fine particles of soil, will exert their own greater tendency to hold on to water, acting as local reservoirs outwith the general situation dictated by the sand. However, should the different materials segregate with agitation during placement, some form of layering may develop subsequently through downward migration and redeposition of silt and clay. It will then be the fine pore system in the deposition layers that will control the downward clearance of water and provide localized, potentially anaerobic barriers to root penetration.

Counteracting risks of desiccation

When sand rests directly on soil, as in the case of a construction involving a surface carpet of sand, it should be appreciated that a freely drained soil at field capacity behaves as if it is equilibrated at a tension of the order of 1000 mm (40 in). The soil under the sand, therefore, will tend to withdraw water from the surface layer of sand. This means that the grass should be encouraged to root through into the underlying soil to acquire an assured water supply. For this reason, the sand carpet should not exceed 150 mm (6 in) in depth and due regard

should be paid to the fertility of the buried soil before covering it. It also explains why subsequent maintenance should aim to avoid any surface accumulation of organic debris or applied phosphate, both of which will encourage surface rooting.

For a similar reason, sand in slits will lose water to the soil with which it is in contact and the establishment of grass along the slit may well be difficult. To minimize this problem consideration should be given to the following features:

1. watering the surface by artificial means until germination and establishment has been achieved;
2. seeding only in the autumn when weather conditions are likely to be most favourable;
3. avoiding unnecessarily wide slits so that the grass can root sideways into the soil;
4. topdressing materials, such as grass clippings, moist peat, or seaweed to help retain water near the surface.

Chapter five

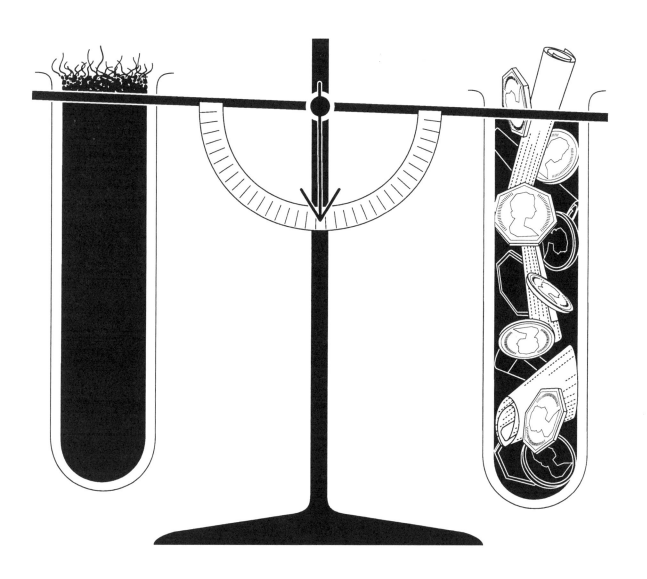

Cost benefit implications

5.1 Assessing the value of drainage

The economic value of drainage on any plot of land is usually difficult to quantify in precise terms. Even in agriculture where crop yields can be accurately measured, it is still not possible to predict with any certainty what would be the most economic level of artificial drainage in terms of return on the capital involved. This does not mean that the advantages of drainage are not discernible but it does mean that it is very difficult to estimate the optimum level of capital investment.

In sports-field drainage the advantages are even more difficult to assess in economic terms. At best the capital costs can only be compared with matches played or not played, or the number of days on which the surface is fit for use. Nevertheless, the costs of drainage can be considerable and it is important to at least try to predict what advantages could accrue from the installation of various alternative systems. This is particularly so when the performance of a drainage system can be accurately designed, as shown elsewhere in this book.

The advantages of playing-field drainage are mainly that surface water (rainfall) is cleared more rapidly and that the soil provides a better

This chapter was contributed by J.C. Parker, B.Sc. Hort., A.L.I., Chief Landscape Manager, Kent County Council, based on a section originally included in *Landscape Management and Maintenance – A Guide to its Costing and Organisation*, published by Gower Technical, 1989.

playing surface and a better growing medium for the turf. The latter advantage is often the most important in agriculture and promotes:

- earlier warming of the soil in spring because any substitution of air for water means lower specific heat;
- earlier spring regeneration of worn turf because of the beneficial effect on soil temperature;
- improved drought resistance because of deeper, more efficient rooting.

These improvements during the growing season can be considerable but during the winter months the more important effect of drainage is that rainfall is removed faster from the surface so that play can take place on a reasonably firm surface and without unduly damaging the soil structure. This increased availability for play is the factor on which most players would base their judgement on the value or otherwise of a drainage system.

5.2 How much drainage is needed?

The optimum drainage rate that a designer should try to achieve depends on:

- the rainfall that can be expected;
- the proportion of lost playing days that the client is prepared to accept;
- the anticipated pattern of use.

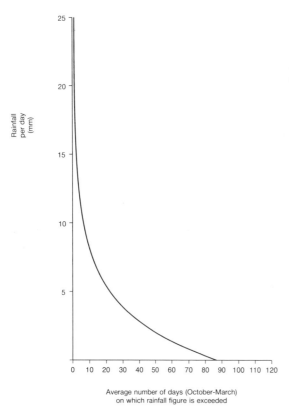

FIGURE 5.1 Average winter rainfall distribution.

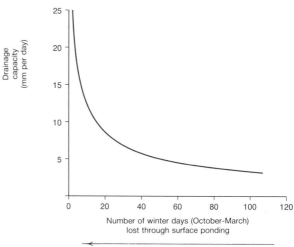

FIGURE 5.2 Theoretical relationship of days lost and drainage rate.

Looking first at rainfall, Figure 5.1 shows, as an example, how rainfall is likely to be distributed throughout the winter months. The graph is based on a ten-year period at a recording station in the south-east of England. It shows that for half the days there was very little or no rain at all and only on about 20 days (11%) in the whole winter was there more than 5 mm of rain. (Graphs from wetter parts of the country would show higher rainfalls but are likely to show a similar distribution pattern.)

This rainfall evidence suggests that even a modest drainage rate would probably make a pitch playable for the majority of the time. However, with a low drainage rate it is likely that the heavy rain, from the few really wet days, would flood the surface for several days afterwards. Taking this last factor into account Figure 5.2 has been constructed to show the likely number of lost days that can be expected with various levels of drainage capacity.

This again shows that for most of the time a relatively low drainage rate would be likely to keep the pitch clear and high drainage rates may only be needed for a very small number of days in any one year. Therefore, if the users can afford to be flexible in the way they use the pitches in winter, and only use them when weather conditions are favourable, a relatively low drainage rate would be adequate. If, however, there is strong user pressure to play on pitches whatever the weather, the drainage rate needs to be very much higher so that it will deal with most intensities of rain as it falls. A professional football club ground, for instance, probably comes within the second category. Here, the necessary capital expenditure and maintenance of a high-intensity drainage system can usually be justified by fewer matches having to be cancelled.

Figures 5.1 and 5.2 both refer to theoretical drainage requirements but in practice much higher rates are likely to be needed to take account of:

- local ponding in dips and hollows;
- gradual deterioration of the drainage system (silting up etc.);
- higher rainfall in wetter parts of the country;
- year-to-year variations (when rainfall is above average).

Therefore, as a general guide, a drainage rate of at least 25 mm (1 in) per day is probably needed for even a lightly used winter pitch and, at the other end of the scale, a professional football pitch might require as much as 25 mm (1 in) per hour to be reasonably confident of staging matches, whatever the weather. However, such a very high drainage rate could only be achieved by a sand soil perched over a drained, gravel bed and such a soil needs special maintenance and shielding from too frequent use.

5.3 Effect of drainage system design on capital cost

When sports-field drainage systems are being designed there are often several different ways of achieving the same or similar results but the costs of the alternatives can sometimes be very different. In each situation the designer has to work out the likely cost difference and, for instance, decide between either a system of substantial surface slits and few underdrains or simple slits with many closely spaced interceptors.

The final solution will depend on many factors, including the local availability of suitable materials, machinery and contractors, but the general principles given below should help as a guide towards achieving the lowest capital cost.

5.4 Spacing of underground laterals or interceptor drains

Underground laterals, with or without pipes, are nearly always more expensive to construct per metre than surface slits. For this reason alone it would appear more sensible to use as few as possible. However, extra capital spent on underground laterals is usually more than amply repaid in drainage capacity and, as a general rule, a doubling of the number of underdrains will give the potential for a four-fold increase in drainage rate.

Example 5.1
If laterals are laid 10 m (11 yards) apart in a uniformly draining soil, 500 mm (20 in) deep with hydraulic conductivity of 10 mm/h ($\frac{4}{10}$ in/h), then, using equation (4.4) on page 67

$$V = \frac{H^2 4K}{S^2}$$

the drainage rate V will be

$$V = \frac{500 \times 500 \times 4 \times 10}{10\,000 \times 10\,000}$$

$$= 0.1 \text{ mm/h.}$$

If, however, the laterals are laid at 5-m (5½-yard) centres the drainage rate will be

$$V = \frac{500 \times 500 \times 4 \times 10}{5000 \times 5000}$$

$$= 0.4 \text{ mm/h.}$$

This example shows the advantages of extra underground laterals and illustrates that a misguided attempt to save capital costs by halving the number of laterals would reduce the drainage to a quarter of the original design rate.

This same principle will apply to the lower levels of any two- or three-tier system of underground drains connecting with surface sand slits. However, it does not apply to the top layer of slits that collect rain water directly from the surface.

Cost benefit implications

TABLE 5.1 Costed schemes – examples of slit drainage systems with a design rate of 48 mm/day (2 mm/hr)

| | Surface slits | | | | Approx. cost per hectare* (£) | | |
| | Dimensions (mm) | | Spacing (m) | Backfill | | | |
Spacing of laterals	Width	Depth			Laterals	Slits	Total
'Ideal' schemes							
A, 22 metres	60	300	1.0	Sand over gravel	2 050	18 000	20 050
B, 4.7 metres	60	300	1.0	Medium sand	9 570	10 000	19 570
C, 6.6 metres	60	300	0.5	Medium sand	6 820	20 000	26 820
'Cost cutting' schemes							
D, 18 metres	60	300	1.5	Sand over gravel	2 500	12 000	14 500
E, 3.8 metres	60	300	1.5	Medium sand	11 840	6 670	18 510

* Estimated 1989 prices, excluding mains, outlets, junctions, etc.: laterals at £4.50/m; sand/gravel slits at £1.80/m; sand-only slits at £1.00/m.

5.5 Spacing of surface slits

Surface slits are usually relatively cheap per metre run but, because they are close together and many metres have to be laid, their total cost is a major part of the capital outlay. It is therefore often tempting to space them as widely apart as possible.

The scope for such saving is severely limited as surface slits only have an effective influence over a very narrow band, simply because rain water can travel only very slowly across the grassed surface. Footmarks and the like will slow down the surface flow even on a surface that has a gentle slope. In practice, therefore, a surface slit will drain a band only about 1.50 m (5 ft) wide. Thus, even if slits are placed at 2 m (6½ ft) apart there is a considerable risk of surface ponding or sogginess between the runs.

For this purely technical reason it is usually best to space surface slits about 1 m (1 yard) apart. Closer spacing will improve the efficiency of surface interception still further but the costs will increase pro rata.

Savings on surface slits can sometimes be made by only slitting the heavily used or badly drained parts of a pitch or field. Alternatively a whole pitch can be slit at 1.5-m (5-ft) centres with additional slits put between to give 0.75 m (2½ ft) spacing of the wet or heavily used areas. (Note that this only gives a cost saving, compared with 1 m spacing overall, if wet areas are less than half the total area.)

5.6 Cost comparisons of alternative systems

Some examples of possible costs of alternative systems are shown in Table 5.1. The figures (based on 1989 prices) have been deliberately simplified in order to illustrate the comparisons and must only be used in that context. The availability of different materials and machinery could well alter the conclusions and in each case the designer must work out the costs that are likely to apply to the specific site. Some comments on the data in Table 5.1 now follow.

1. There is little to choose between schemes A and B but B has the advantage that even underground laterals would give a fair measure of drainage if the permeable fill in the pipe trenches was brought through to the surface as sand, especially if the field was lightly used and retained a good surface structure. Scheme A might be preferred if

ground conditions were difficult for deep trenching.

2. Scheme C has the same advantages as but the extra cost of the close-spaced slits is unlikely to be justified except on very heavily used areas – goalmouths, etc.

3. Scheme D is significantly cheaper than all the other options considered, but wider slit spacing would be less effective under heavy use, particularly where the ground is level.

4. Scheme E has only a slight cost advantage over A, B or C and would normally not be worth considering.

5. Schemes A and D could be upgraded to a design rate of 8 mm per hour by doubling the number of underground laterals at an extra capital cost of only around £4.50 per metre.

5.7 Effect of drainage on total use

All the above have been concerned with the effect of drainage rates on the chances of pitches being waterlogged at any one time and do not take account of the total hours of use once drainage problems have been eliminated. This total use is normally limited by the amount of wear that the actual surface carpet of turf is able to bear. Improved drainage will influence this to the extent that it encourages better growth and also that a drier surface discourages the players from sliding and damaging the turf by a shearing action. However, the more important effect of adequate drainage is to make a pitch playable throughout the season and allow considerably more play in the wettest months of the winter. Without drainage the pitch could be completely unplayable for weeks on end.

5.8 Cost-saving strategy for a new playing field

Artificial drainage is only necessary when the natural drainage is inadequate. When a new playing field is being planned it is extremely difficult to assess, in advance, what the natural drainage rate will be. Soil structure can easily be destroyed by adverse weather conditions during levelling and grading, or merely by the time the topsoil stays in a stockpile.

Once a field is sown down to grass the natural soil structure may regenerate again within a year or two on heavy clays by the natural expansion and contraction of the clay particles through the seasons. On silty soils however, the natural structure will always be weak and, once lost, may not reform for very many years. Therefore, depending on soil type an elaborate and expensive drainage system could be of only temporary value or an absolute necessity, essential in the long term.

In order to minimize the risks of either extreme it would be wise to install only a basic underdrainage system during the construction stage. Subsequently a slit drainage system could be added if it is found to be necessary. This could be laid out across the whole field or just across goalmouths and any especially wet areas. Alternatively in scheme A, Table 5.1, the major capital cost could at least be delayed until experience proves that a full slit system is needed.

In these and other ways capital costs can be kept to a minimum, but there are often administrative difficulties with obtaining an additional capital sum for sand slitting several years after the main part of the construction has been completed. It is therefore essential to ensure that the promoters of the construction scheme are aware of the possible need for extra works as the new playing field becomes established.

Finally, it cannot be over-emphasized that any drainage system will be largely wasted if it is not backed up by regular maintenance, not only to prevent pipe blockage and smearing of sand slits, but also to retain as open a soil structure as possible.

Chapter six

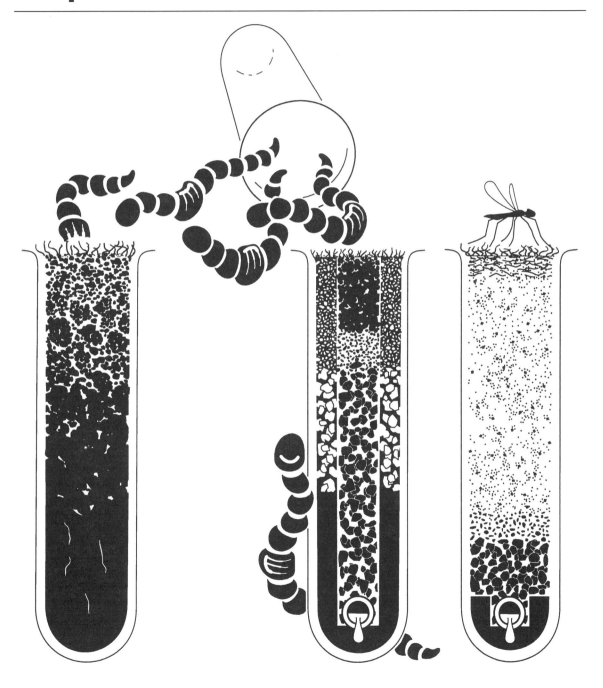

Interrelationships of sward biology, construction, maintenance and use

6.1 Establishment and immediate after-care prior to allowing play

While the soil is still relatively loose the juvenile roots of the grass may be encouragingly long, but the sward will not be firmly established until the root system develops into a fibrous, much-branched, intertwined tangle.

The introduction of sand or sand/gravel slits, to complete the job of surface water interception, may well be delayed until a sward has been established. This will make it easier to excavate narrow, stable-sided trenches. Thus establishment of a sward may have to proceed in two stages: first by an initial seeding prior to slitting, and then by over-seeding to repair damage following slitting. This can provide the opportunity to establish, at the initial phase, a sward of the slower-germinating, lower-growing, bottom grasses, such as the browntops and smooth-stalked meadow grasses. The more easily established, more vigorous growing rye-

For detailed instructions on specific maintenance programmes refer to sections 10.5 and 11.13, and Appendix 6.

grasses can be introduced later, e.g. by slit seeding.

Immediate after-care usually involves cleaning up, re-truing and firming down the soil surface, over-seeding to repair damage and fill gaps in the original sward; also fertilizing, irrigating and sand topdressing, nursing the sward through to a firmly anchored, dense, uniform covering of vigorously growing grass.

6.1.1 The soil surface

It is assumed that the bulk of the work required to achieve a true surface will have been carried out before grassing up. However, if more drainage operations are carried out through the initial grassed surface, this may require further time to be spent on more stone picking, surface truing and light rolling. After this final construction stage further surface truing will have to be by repeated cycles of sand topdressing, co-ordinated with over-seeding.

6.1.2 The sward

Sward maintenance in the early stages of establishment should aim at vigorous growth and deep rooting. This is largely a matter of adequate moisture, good aeration, proper fertilizing, and correct frequency and height of cut.

No play should be allowed until the whole surface is grass covered, including the sandy surfaces of pipe trenches and/or slits.

6.1.3 Fertilizing

Compensating for accelerated leaching losses

Constructions giving priority to drainage must inevitably risk continuous loss of readily soluble nutrients by leaching. This can be further aggravated by the fact that improved drainage is usually dependent on the liberal use of sand which is a poor medium for nutrient retention. The approach to nutrition should aim, therefore, either at slow release, or little-and-often application. Slow release is inevitable with phosphate fertilizers as phosphate is so insoluble. The problem materials are the nitrate, ammonium and potassium fertilizers which are generally highly soluble.

Sward establishment on the sand surface of slits or pipe trenches is bound to be difficult. Successful germination and establishment requires frequent re-wetting and this increases the risk of nitrogen and potassium loss by leaching. Therefore, special attention must be given to the regular replenishment of these nutrients until sideways rooting can be established into the adjacent soil. This is a factor to be considered when contemplating the installation of trenches more than 50 mm (2 in) in width. It also stresses the importance of the effort to try and include some nutrient and moisture-retaining organic component in the top 150 mm (6 in) of the sand backfill.

Any yellowing of the grass along the line of the slits and pipe trenches should be taken as a warning of a need for nitrogen, and possibly also potassium.

Stimulation of root branching

It has been known for years that root density is very much influenced by the distribution of organic matter. If the organic matter accumulates on the surface we have what might be described in soil terms as the 'Mor' condition, referred to in Table 8.1. Here, rooting is also concentrated at the surface, whereas with organic matter deeply incorporated, as in the 'Mull' condition, roots are distributed throughout the soil. The reason for this relationship has been explained by experimental evidence (Drew, 1975) showing that root branching is a response to the presence in solution of available forms of nitrogen and phosphorus. This does not affect the behaviour of the primary, exploring roots; they seem to be adapted to explore the soil in depth, controlled only by their need for adequate aeration. Thus a medium providing for satisfactory rooting must allow for the exploitation of a large volume of soil by branch root proliferation in response to incorporated sources of available nitrogen and phosphorus. If the primary root can carry this process deep into the soil then the plant will not only be well equipped to secure its nutrient requirement, but also well anchored and buffered against drought.

All sources of phosphate applied to a soil are rapidly immobilized by association with calcium, iron or aluminium, whereas ammonium and nitrate sources of nitrogen remain freely soluble. It must frequently be the location of the applied phosphatic fertilizer, therefore, that will effectively control the distribution of the mass of plant feeding roots. With this in mind we should take advantage of the opportunity during construction to build sources of phosphate into the soil within rooting depth and, during subsequent maintenance, take steps to only apply phosphate when it can be fed down into spike holes or incorporated by a subsequent topdressing of sand or loam.

6.1.4 Fine sand topdressing

Topdressing with fine sand (e.g. a *topsoil sand* such as SN 12–15 in Table 7.1) is an important feature of the maintenance of any sward used for sport but, with new constructions involving surface slitting, it is particularly important to topdress generously before the first season of winter play. This general topdressing is necessary to help true the whole surface and protect the slits from being capped by soil. The minimum cover that should be achieved before allowing play is of the order of 80 tonne/hectare (30 tons/acre), i.e. a covering of 5 mm ($\frac{1}{5}$ in) overall. To avoid any risk of smothering the sward this should be applied in two increments, allowing adequate time for sward recovery after each application has been thoroughly worked into the base of the sward. Purpose-made machinery is now available to ensure an even spread at a rate that will achieve the necessary application in each pass. Provided the sand can be kept dry, an alternative, DIY procedure involving a tractor-drawn, rigid, metal lute, some 2 m wide, can be used to spread the sand from pre-placed heaps or regularly spaced bands, levelling the surface simultaneously. If the grass is not to be smothered, both the sand and the surface must be dry enough for the sand to fall freely into the base of the sward, exposing the leaf tips to sunlight.

In order that all the foregoing operations can be performed in the right conditions, eg. fertilizing and seeding when conditions are likely to remain moist and topdressing with fine sand when the surface is dry, it is essential to make adequate preparations in advance.

6.2 Considerations for the long-term maintenance of new constructions

6.2.1 Surface sanding

A sand-slit top cannot hope to retain its trueness and drainage efficiency permanently without continuous, careful maintenance. The differential response of sand and soil to the swelling and shrinking effects of wetting and drying leads to the slit surface sinking relative to the surrounding soil (Figure 6.1). The resulting washboard effect can be off-putting and dangerous for the players. If allowed to persist, or if corrected by heavy rolling in wet conditions, the end result will be drainage deterioration because of soil capping the slits.

This trend must be anticipated and counteracted by an annual topdressing of fine sand (*topsoil sand*) applied during a dry spell in the late summer before the playing season starts. The method of application must ensure that the sand can be drag-brushed or luted into depressions, particularly the depressions along the line of the slits. After a 5 mm ($\frac{1}{5}$ in) application of sand before the first season of play, the minimum annual rate of application thereafter should be of the order of 40 t/ha, or 2.5 mm overall (16 tons/acre or $\frac{1}{10}$ in).

More than one such topdressing annually could well be beneficial but cost, and the practical possibilities of achieving this, make it very unlikely. The other alternative of increasing the amount of sand applied in a single topdressing carries with it the risk of sward damage by smothering. However, a single application of 25 mm (1 in) was successfully applied in a single application onto a vigorous ryegrass sward at Cardiff Arms Park in the summer of 1972.

6.2.2 Surface response

Choice of sand for construction or topdressing affects not only drainage but some of the

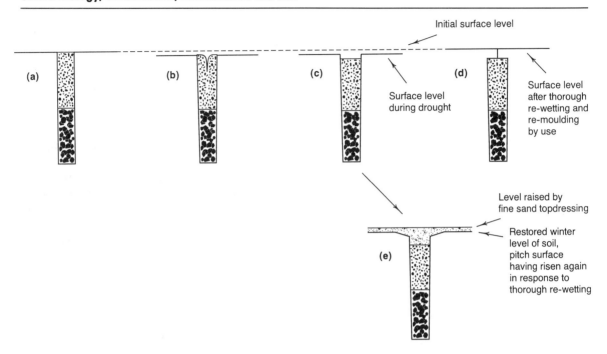

FIGURE 6.1 Essential maintenance to overcome the problem of progressive settlement within slits. (a), (b), (c), and (d) illustrate how slits may be affected by seasonal variations in soil moisture conditions because the soil and sand/gravel fill will respond differently. Whereas the sand and gravel will neither shrink nor swell significantly they will readily settle down into any extra volume made available within the slit. The soil, however will shrink in depth and contract horizontally in response to desiccation (a–c), then swell back to its former volume, though not necessarily its former shape, in response to thorough re-wetting (d). (e) Topdressing and re-truing the surface with sand, when the soil is fully desiccated, cases (b) and (c), will avoid any adverse effect on the efficiency of the slit system by ensuring that surface water continues to have free access into the slits.

playing characteristics of the surface and its tractive efficiency.

For the bounce-deadening response of golf greens we need uniform, rounded particles that will 'hold' by yielding rather than becoming dense, rigid and potentially 'fiery'.

On a bowling green there is no need to make provision for bounce. Priority instead can be given to trueness and the pace of the roll of the bowl. For these qualities to be achieved with a quick-draining sand soil, roundness and uniformity of particle size have not the same priority.

For vigorous winter games tractive efficiency depends on the dryness of the surface and the grip achieved by a studded boot. Players require the surface to give sufficiently to allow the studs to penetrate, but not to shear. To 'give a stud' without having to be wet, the sand forming the surface should have the same uniform roundness that is required on a golf green, but no sand of this type will provide any significant tractive strength when dry. This means that, for the most part, the tractive efficiency of such a surface, when dry, depends primarily on the root-binding strength of the sward.

However, such surfaces are seldom dust dry in winter and any moisture present can contribute significantly to tractive efficiency, even without the assistance of grass. With the addition of water, tractive strength increases as particle size decreases, reaching a satisfactory level for play when water-bound, like fine sand in the inter-tidal zone of a beach.

To have maximum effect for the improvement of soil permeability a sand topdressing should be carefully chosen. It should not only work on its own to readily transmit water, but when worked into the soil, should rapidly ameliorate the particle-size spectrum to peak at over 75% in the medium-to-fine sand categories. Using a sand of a wide, particle-size range tends to lead to a hard, dense, slow-draining soil because of the inter-packing possibilities presented.

In practice this means: (a) we should top-dress with a very narrow particle-size-range sand, like dune sand which has 95% of its particles in the medium-fine sand range (*topsoil sands* like SN12, 14 and 15 in Table 7.1); (b) we should aim to match the dominant particle size in the top-dressing sand to the dominant particle size in the medium-to-fine sand categories in the soil (Appendix C).

The soil brought to the top by burrowing earthworms may not be identical in texture to the original topsoil. There seems to be a limit of about 0.5 mm to the diameter of particles ingested by worms so that, in time, their activities can effect a small shift in soil texture at the surface. One practical application of this knowledge is to use sand with a coarse sand matrix in slits and pipe trenches where worm activity might be expected to threaten the survival of the permeable link through the topsoil to the surface.

6.2.3 Deciding a policy about earthworms

The decision that should not be deferred

To base one's thoughts on construction and maintenance on the consequences that flow naturally from earthworms being present or absent may appear to be too abstruse and theoretical to have practical significance. However, in pasture, earthworms may number some 2 500 000 per hectare (1 000 000 per acre or 200 per square yard), weighing around 5 t/ha (2 tons/acre or 1 lb/sq yd) fresh weight. They turn over some 50 t/ha (20 tons/acre or 9 lb/sq yd) of fine soil annually, corresponding to some 25 mm (1 in) of fine soil placed onto the surface in the course of 10 years. They are well able to consume and bury all the grass clippings from a well-maintained sward in the course of a year. The influence of earthworms on soil is so fundamental that to fail to take their presence or absence into account would be like ignoring the influence of man when viewing the environment around us.

On sports turf a long-term decision has to be made on whether maintenance should encourage or discourage earthworms. It is particularly important that this subject is brought up for consideration early, ideally prior to construction. As farmers who have inherited land disturbed for opencast mining have good reason to lament, once lost, an earthworm population can take a generation or more to recover by natural colonization (Stewart *et al.*, 1988).

To assist in the preservation of an existing earthworm population thought should be given to how any stockpiling of topsoil can be avoided. The aim should be to achieve transfer without any intervening period of temporary storage. Once in its new location, the topsoil should be worked through mechanically as little as possible because earthworms can be maimed and suffocated when their living space collapses around them. It is one thing to re-populate a soil from a viable residual population, but quite another to recover from complete annihilation.

Thus, unless prior thought has been given to this problem at the construction stage, a groundsman may find that the decision whether to work with or without earthworms has

TABLE 6.1 Plant adaptation to the soil development dichotomy, conditioned by the presence or absence of burrowing earthworms

High, pH typically above 6 – **Lime** – Low, pH typically below 5
Succulent, palatable, plentiful – **Organic matter** – Fibrous, unpalatable, insufficient
Physically and chemical benign – **Human intervention** – Physically and chemically hazardous

Effects of earthworm presence	*Effects of earthworm absence*
Soils	
Profile tending to be uniform	Profile tending to become layered
Organic matter incorporated	Organic matter unincorporated
Mineral soil aggregated ('Mull' condition, typical of brown earth soils)	Mineral soil compact ('Mor' condition, typical of podzol soils)
Freely drained and well aerated if site drainage satisfactory	Drainage impeded and aeration poor unless mineral soil very sandy
Plants	
Deep rooted	Surface rooted
Ill-adapted for drought and waterlogging	Well adapted to cope with periodic drought and temporary waterlogging
Nutrition mediated through free-living bacteria in rhizosphere	Many conditioned to 'special' feeding mechanisms mediated by symbiotic relationships with fungi
Intolerant of drought, waterlogging and acidity, leading to problems of aluminium and iron toxicity	Intolerant of earthworms and disturbance, alkalinity leading to problems of low availability of iron
Vegetation	
Floristically diverse, tending to be **calcicole** in character	Floristically restricted, tending to be **calcifuge** in character

Adapted from Stewart and Scullion, 1989.

already been taken for him. If he does take over a soil with a viable earthworm population then he should review his proposed maintenance procedures for their likely impact on the population and the consequences for the playing surface should they be eliminated.

Encouraging the right worms

The importance of worm burrowing as an aid to infiltration, drainage, air circulation and rooting is now generally recognized but less so their beneficial effects in counteracting the build-up of thatch and in initiating the development of a granular soil structure (Stewart and Salih, 1981; Stewart, 1985).

As Table 6.1 suggests, there is much more that could be said about the possible evolutionary significance of the important dichotomous relationship between soils and vegetation developed in the presence or absence of burrowing earthworms. The general consequences for sports turf are summarized in Table 6.2.

However, not all earthworms are equally effective for soil conditioning. Of the 25–30 species of earthworm found in Britain only five are of any great importance for their beneficial effects on the incorporation of organic residues and the natural drainage of soils under grass. These are generally the worms that grow to a size longer than 75–100 mm (3–4 in) when mature. Unfortunately, the relatively large worm species most commonly available to fishermen, the Brandling (*Elsenia foetida*) is not an effective soil burrower. It breeds readily in wet compost and sewage, but will ingest very little mineral matter and does not survive long if introduced to a normal field soil.

TABLE 6.2 Construction options and maintenance requirements conditioned by the presence or absence of burrowing earthworms.

$+$ ← *Increasing earthworm presence*   *Decreasing earthworm presence* → $-$

Soil undisturbed; pH 5.5–8.0; clippings returned	*Indiscriminate use – surface muddy and tending to poach* / *Loams, inherently compact and liable to pond on the surface*	Soil disturbed and stockpiled; pH below 5; chemicals antagonistic to earthworms; clippings removed
PIPE UNDERDRAINS supplemented by periodic mole drainage. Mole drainage especially effective in clays.	PIPE UNDERDRAINS linked above to SAND/GRAVEL SLITS and surface of soil SAND CAPPED*	SAND SOIL rafted over drained GRAVEL BED, or surface configuration organized to ensure effective runoff.
Coarse turf, suitable e.g. for football and soccer.	Suitable for all winter activities requiring good quality, coarse turf.	Suitable for good quality, fine turf, e.g. for bowling and golf greens
Used with discretion; drains, wears but recovers.	Essential where assistance is required to bypass surface water through topsoil to underdrains.	Infiltered-water drains rapidly but only if soil of sand or loamy sand texture.
Clippings rapidly incorporated. Soil of good structure, encouraging deep rooting to assist with nutrition and water supply. Few pests and diseases.	Surface water and wear damage markedly reduced. Progressive soil improvement now possible.	Uniform soil depth and character will contribute to uniform response of sward. Few weeds unless damaged areas left bare.
Main problems Surface soft, uneven and weedy, requiring brushing, rolling and regular over-seeding.	*Main problems* Weather must be adequately moist to achieve even seed germination along sand surface of slits.	*Main problems* Even grading of surface essential to avoid scalping when mowing close.
Because of soft top and relatively slow drainage, must be used with utmost discretion.	Progressive settlement of slits requiring annual, fine sand top dressing to rectify.	Though clippings removed, organic debris and roots liable to accumulate at the surface.
		Verticutting to encourage vertical growth, scarification to remove debris and topdressing to true surface and re-bury roots all routinely essential.
		Vulnerable to excessive wear. When sward damaged may need immediate repair by turf patching.
		Nutrition – needs feeding little and often.
		Water reserve limited by soil depth to approx 2 weeks mid-summer, therefore requires provision for efficient irrigation.
		Vulnerable to pests and disease. Moss invades where grass cover is thin.

Notes
See page 145 for special cases: hockey, cricket, tennis and horse racing.
* See page 144 for the pros and cons of progressive sand accumulation by annual topdressing as against immediate sand carpeting.
Adapted from Stewart and Scullion, 1989.

All that can be done at present to preserve and prosper an indigenous population of burrowing earthworms under grass is to let the clippings lie, maintain the pH above 6 and avoid the adverse effects of pesticides. Many pesticides which are sold for the control of insects, nematodes, fungi and other organisms considered to be pests, also have lethal side-effects on earthworms.

Problems that the right worms bring with them

If earthworms are encouraged for the benefits they confer, it must be recognized that the surface they create will tend to be weedy and soft. They bring buried, viable, weed seeds to the surface in their casts and, at the same time, their casts provide open sites for aerially dispersed weed seeds to invade. Casts need to be dispersed by brushing when dry and the surface periodically rolled to reconsolidate. If the rolling closes the burrow openings the earthworms will soon open them again but the surface should never be rolled when the soil is wet enough to smear and pan. The fine soil brought to the surface in casts, yearly, can amount overall to a layer 2–3 mm (¹⁄₁₀ in) thick, enough to cap an originally sandy surface unless diluted by the addition of further topdressings of sand.

Managing without the assistance of earthworms

On fine turf areas used for ball games such as lawn tennis, bowls, putting and croquet, where surface trueness is absolutely vital, worms cannot be tolerated and positive measures may have to be taken to discourage their presence. However, that should not be considered the end of the matter. In loamy soils the elimination of worms by wormicide or acidity leads to progressive soil compaction and associated problems with drainage. On the surface, organic residues accumulate leading to surface rooting, susceptibility to drought and an increased requirement for fertilizer which, if satisfied, can lead in turn to the lush growth that encourages insect and fungal pests.

All this has implications for construction and maintenance. The soil will either have to be constructed of sand or the surface sloped to disperse accumulating water. Maintenance will have to be of a very high order, incorporating tasks that earthworms would otherwise accomplish: removal of clippings and residual organic debris, top-dressing to bury exposed roots, extra fertilizing to compensate for the organic residues removed, greater vigilance over disease, pests and drought. It would be very negligent to wait until actual problems arise as all these consequences should be predictable to anyone aware of the dynamic nature of a grassland eco-system (Appendix 6).

Practical conclusions and the search for a compromise

The decision to encourage or not to encourage earthworms varies for different games and, therefore, may vary within a single sports complex offering a range of specialist facilities. For example:

1. the beneficial effects of earthworms on drainage, soil structure and rooting are advantages that may tip the scales in their favour on areas in use throughout the winter;
2. assuming adequate provision for special maintenance, earthworms can be eliminated on small areas such as ornamental lawns, golf and crown bowling greens provided that slopes can be organized to achieve adequate surface runoff;
3. on large areas used for hockey or cricket, where a smooth surface is desirable, the situation is not so clear cut. Except for special venues these areas are too large to get the maintenance required, should earthworms be eliminated, and yet they could probably benefit from earthworm assistance with drainage.

What most groundsmen would like is a means of putting an earthworm population to sleep for the duration of a playing season, allowing them to return to full vigour for the rest of the year. This seems a tall order but recent research by Salih (1978) and Al-Bakri (1984) suggests an approach which might be developed in this direction. Their research has shown that the well-known tendency for the deep-burrowing species to retreat from the surface during drought may be part of a general reaction to anything which threatens their well-being. The sense organs of earthworms are chemo-receptors, very sensitive to changes in the chemistry of the soil solution. This probably explains why both Salih and Al-Bakri found that earthworms tend to avoid the surface of the soil when it has been treated recently with even relatively innocuous chemicals such as lime and ammonium-rich fertilizers, if these are applied in highly soluble and concentrated form. Eventually they will return but only after the concentrations have been significantly reduced by leaching. It could well be that the agro-chemical industry will take this up and develop purpose-made chemicals of this type to provide short-term relief from surface casting.

Fortunately, it is not easy to eliminate an established earthworm population completely by one treatment of a wormicide. Much will depend on whether the worms have a chance to take avoiding action. Though the adults are particularly vulnerable, recovery can be achieved within a year from any residual stock of viable cocoons. However, three treatments over a year to eighteen months should thwart natural recovery from juveniles and cocoons.

6.3 Construction options and maintenance implications

6.3.1 Options for the maintenance of a sufficiently sandy surface

Sand capping

Throughout this book a recurrent theme within maintenance is the need to apply regular top-dressings of fine sand. This has been mentioned in respect of surface truing, maintenance of effective surface infiltration into slits, burial of organic debris and surface roots when earthworms are absent, and the dilution of soil brought to the surface in earthworm casts.

An alternative to an annually topdressed, slit scheme is an ameliorated fine sand carpet, 100–125 mm (4–5 in) deep, over slits placed between one and two metres apart. The large quantity of sand used in such a sand-carpeted scheme allows ample scope for heavy rain to be absorbed and temporarily stored within the sand carpet. This avoids any risk of even slight surface ponding, and the exposed sand surfaces of the underlying slits are very well protected against soil capping.

However, on a sand carpet skill has to be used in establishing a new sward from seed. The immediate surface dries quickly and young roots need nursing through to the underlying soil. As a seedling will have no difficulty pushing its way through loose sand to the surface, germination will be improved if the seed is well buried to a centimetre or more and firmed into place by rolling. It is only pro-longed drought and the attendant risk of sand loss by windblow that is liable to cause anxiety, prompting some thought of provision for sur-face irrigation. For this reason there is much to be said for the sand-carpeting operation being delayed until the autumn when seeding can take place in a season not normally associated with drought.

As described in Chapter 6, the dynamic nature of a grass eco-system carries with it implications for maintenance that should be appreciated before decisions are taken on choice of construction. If earthworms are still present in the buried soil under a sand-carpeted surface they will bring fine soil through to the new surface. This need cause no anxiety in the first few years, but will require monitoring by soil testing to determine when annual, sand topdressing should begin. If a complete soil cap is allowed to develop it may be necessary to undertake some form of surface cultivation or hollow-tine spiking to achieve the required amelioration with sand. And even if worms are absent, there will still be a need to monitor the condition of the surface, in this case to look for signs of superficial accumulation of organic residues. If this occurs and is not treated by periodic scarification and annual sand topdressing it may lead to reduced wear tolerance because of excessive surface rooting, and damage from disease and pests.

In fact, after many years of appropriate maintenance, the sand slit and sand-carpet approaches should converge to a similar end product. A simple slit system normally starts with the original sward established in the existing topsoil, then, by substantial initial topdressing and annual repetition, a sand-ameliorated carpet is built up and the sward keeps pace by growing through. The sand carpet approach also begins with a scarcely less intensive slit-drained surface leading to piped underdrains. But what might be described as a vast amount of sand is required to form the sand carpet, and this means that an entirely new sward has to be established under what can be drought-threatening circumstances until the young grass has rooted through to the soil beneath. In due course the sand carpet becomes progressively modified by the incorporation of soil from below and organic residues from above so that again we can have a deep, sand-ameliorated surface overlying the original soil, and all the maintenance necessary to hold this physically viable.

Micro-slitting

This form of shallow, close-centred, sand slitting, aligned at right-angles to the main slits, can be used as an alternative to topdressing, but it is more expensive. If so used it can be carried out as the final constructional operation before play is permitted and then repeated at regular intervals thereafter. Alternatively, it

may be used to re-establish efficient surface interception where the original slit system has become soil capped through maintenance neglect.

6.3.2 Improving permeability of the whole soil

As explained in section 1.4, any lasting improvement in the permeability of moisture-retentive soils used for winter games can only be achieved by altering their texture. Structural improvement achieved by mechanical means is seldom likely to be more than temporary.

Improving permeability at time of construction

Subsoil and topsoil cultivation

Severe compaction of the subsoil by heavy machinery during grading operations can be minimized by the avoidance of working when wet. Structural damage to fine-textured soils resulting from wet working can be difficult to remedy. If the ground is stony, subsoil cultivation to alleviate compaction should be carried out before topsoil replacement, then again to counteract effects of equipment used to return and spread the topsoil. The subsoiling involved should always be carried out under dry conditions to ensure maximum cracking and to avoid undue wheel damage.

Where a pipe drainage system is installed, further subsoil cultivation, or mole ploughing across drains, can be beneficial as a stop-gap until biological structuring processes have had time to develop, or some sort of stabilized slit system installed. However, subsoil cultivation would have to be repeated annually and this would only be possible if the damage to the sward was tolerable.

Topsoil inversion is no longer essential to clear the surface of weeds prior to seeding; chemicals can now do this job just as effectively. However, some light soil cultivation may be necessary to re-true the surface and prepare a seed bed, e.g. by shallow chisel ploughing, spring-tine harrowing or spike-tine, rotary cultivation. Here again the benefits to surface drainage will be temporary at best but can help through the phase of seed germination and sward establishment. There is a risk, however, that merely replacing the water-shedding efficiency of a compact surface by greatly improved surface infiltration may simply result in a soft, waterlogged topsoil unless there is also an adequate link to some form of effective underdrainage.

Addition of soil ameliorants

Whether earthworms are present or not there are good reasons in the dynamic nature of a grass eco-system why a sand top-dressing should feature in maintenance annually. It will either be necessary to dilute a capping of fine soil brought to the surface by earthworm casting, or to incorporate any residual surface accumulation of organic matter and roots. However, this also provides an opportunity for re-truing the surface, helping not only the run of a ball, but also the efficiency of water movement by surface flow to slits and, on fine turf in particular, the efficiency of close mowing. Nothing is worse than the alternation of lush growth in the low spots and moss struggling to green up the scalped surfaces of high spots, clear evidence of the need for surface regrading.

There is good reason to consider how any annual increment of sand should be applied, i.e. little and often or in one large application. Guidance on this is given in the general instructions on maintenance, sections 10.5 and 11.3. In any event, the minimum amount to be applied annually should be of the order of 40 tonne/hectare or 4 kg/m^2 (16 tons/acre or 7½ lb/sq yd). The sand should be of a type with a narrow, particle-size range (0.125–0.500 mm, e.g. a *topsoil sand* like SN 12, 14 and 15 in Table 7.1), biased towards the medium or fine sand end according to whichever of these particle sizes can be most easily reinforced to achieve dominance in the existing soil. To avoid loss of particles by solution it should not be lime rich, but where earthworm activity is to be encouraged, as on a general grass area used for winter games, a 5% lime content would help keep soil pH above 6. On acid, fine turf the sand should be lime-free or the sudden rise in pH may allow the opportunist fungal disease *Ophiobolus graminis* (now re-named *Gaeumannamyees graminis*) to invade, albeit temporarily. On the other hand, if a sward has long been established on a lime-rich soil, then further additions of a lime-containing sand will leave undisturbed the established biological equilibrium that in keeping *Ophiobolus* at bay.

If the necessity arises for the importation of topsoil, the opportunity should never be missed of selecting soil in which the medium plus fine sand content exceeds 75%. This provides a soil with good traction potential and a useful measure of rapid drainage, even when compacted by use (Appendix C).

Techniques of routine maintenance aimed at preserving or improving surface drainage after constructional work has been completed

If no thought has been given to the problem of maintaining topsoil impermeability at the time of construction, it may be extremely difficult to deal with this satisfactorily without incurring considerable extra expenditure on new drainage and the inconvenience of pitches being out of use while work is in progress. A variety of expedients are used by groundsmen in an effort to allow play to continue, but all too frequently this involves a great deal of work for a temporary benefit and in the long run, may only further aggravate a fundamentally unsound condition.

Spiking

Spiking is a procedure which groundsmen employ with varying degrees of enthusiasm. At first glance it would appear to be an obvious means of improving aeration and surface infiltration. Unfortunately this will only be successful where the soil condition being treated is a compact surface cap over an otherwise free-draining soil. However, spiking is often pursued as if it were a universal remedy for all conditions of surface waterlogging, whether or not there is a free-draining outlet at the end of the spike hole.

Forcing a metal spike down into the soil will not create any extra pore space unless there is a coincidental rise in the general level of the soil. There must be extra volume before there can be extra space. All that spiking will do, without any change in overall soil volume, is squeeze out a hole at the expense of pore space elsewhere, smearing the sides of the new hole in the process. The result can be a reservoir for infiltered water that may then be poached into the soil by treading.

If a real enthusiast for spiking is let loose on a field there is a risk that the whole process will have the same effect as the rodding of concrete. It is a useful experience to rod saturated sand in a bucket and feel how the sand compacts from the bottom up, requiring the limit of rodding to be progressively raised. No wonder that layers of compaction can often be found at depths corresponding to the limit of spiking.

If spike holes are to be inserted into a water-logging surface this should only be considered as an occasional remedial treatment in situations where contact can be made with free-draining material beneath. Otherwise, any insertion procedure should aim to create a continuous slit, linked across to the permeable fill of an artificial drainage outlet such as a sand slit.

Hollow-tine spiking followed by removal of cores is a useful remedial treatment for the control of thatch, the deep placement of fertilizer or the progressive lowering of troublesome high spots. But again, when the hole is used to insert a column of sand this will only benefit drainage if the sand links through to a freely permeable medium below. On desiccating high spots, in a sandy medium, the holes can be used to insert a plug of loam that may help in the retention of moisture.

Sand filling of cracks in clay soils

In clay soils the deep cracks that appear during periods of drought can be converted to a form of natural slit drainage by filling with a free flowing, medium or fine sand (e.g. SN12, 14 and 15 in Table 7.1).

This sand infiltration procedure will only be successful if carried out under very dry conditions with the surface smooth, the grass cut short, and the sand powder dry; easier still on a bare, panned surface as might occur in the early stages of construction. The procedure can be repeated annually as part of a general, fine sand, topdressing procedure, compensating for the progressive fall of the sand level as the surrounding clay soil swells and shrinks in response to changes in moisture content. So long as the cracks remain sand-filled to the surface they will improve the infiltration of water and, when linked to a system of mole drainage or stabilized slits, should also function for lateral discharge.

As this treatment is likely to be effective only for strong clay soils, here is one good reason for learning how to distinguish such soils by the method described in Appendix A.

Subsoiling

As described in Chapter 2, page 39, subsoiling can be an effective means of relieving compaction at topsoil and subsoil levels, even after the work of construction has been completed. However, it is a procedure which must be approached with caution. The nearer to the surface soil displacement takes place, the greater the risk of severe surface disruption. Under good conditions the heave can be organized to coalesce into an even elevation of the surface overall, but major horizontal cracking can provide space into which sand can leak away sideways from a slit system, hazarding the link with the surface. If the soil is bouldery or, worse still, incorporates debris such as glass or scrap metal, the playing surface may be rendered unsafe and any potential improvement in drainage may not compensate for the cost of reinstatement after hazard removal.

Rolling

Dry, loose surfaces or surfaces made soft by earthworm activity may become easily disrupted and scored by play, making reconsolidation and re-levelling necessary. If rolling is used it should never be attempted when the soil is in a soft, squelchy condition, and should not be used to carry out what should really be a grading operation. Injudicious rolling may achieve a temporary improvement in appearance, but if in the process the surface becomes panned or slits sealed over with soil, the long-term effect may be harmful.

Rolling is best carried out when the soil surface is moist but firm, a condition under which the soil will adjust to pressure by crumbling. Large stones and potentially hazardous objects exposed by surface disruption should be removed, not rolled back in. The circumstance in which rolling is most obviously beneficial is the consolidation of loose, sandy soil around seed. With loam and clay-textured soils, beware of panning the surface and excluding air from the sealed-in seed.

On balance, treat rolling with caution unless money is available to pay for the remedial treatment that may eventually become necessary. Re-truing by luting out *topsoil sand* will often be a better option.

Finally, because of the importance of appropriate maintenance, it cannot be reiterated too frequently that money spent on scientifically designed schemes of construction may be wasted if the subsequent standard of maintenance is not appropriate.

Chapter seven

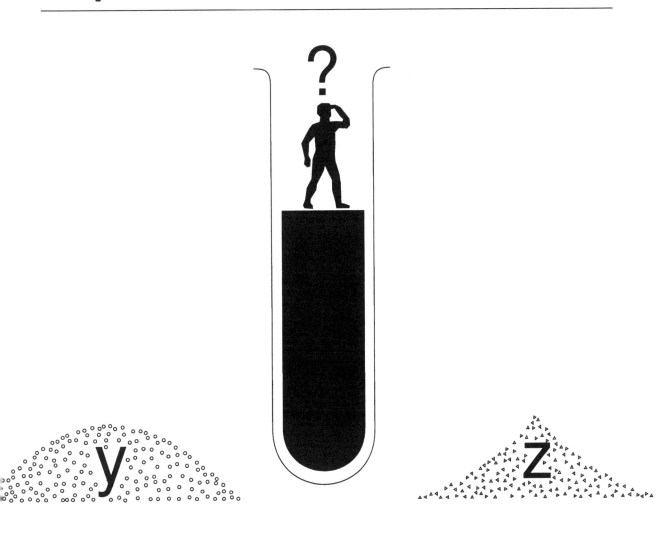

Specification of materials – soil, sand and gravel

7.1 Methods of specifying particle-size composition

7.1.1 The need for precision

Choosing the best materials from those on offer locally can make all the difference to the efficiency of construction. Cost and availability can be misleading as the market tends to be geared more to the needs of the civil engineer and the builder than to those concerned with sports turf. The increasing density that comes with the progressive interpacking of smaller and smaller particles within the pore space formed by larger particles is a virtue for making concrete. It is not a virtue when seeking maximum pore volume for water movement and easy root penetration.

The commonly available 10 mm ($\frac{3}{8}$ in) gravels (SN7 in Table 7.1) and the 5 mm ($\frac{3}{16}$ in) concreting sands (SN10 in Table 7.1) are often loosely defined only by the upper limit of the particle sizes present, but for sport turf we need to be more precise. At the very least we need to know both the upper and lower limits of the particle-size range and may even require a full particle-size grading so that other properties, such as hydraulic conductivity, can be estimated with sufficient precision for design purposes.

7.1.2 Particle-size grades

For the classification of particle-size grades used in this publication see Tables 1.3 and 7.1. Tabulated information of this type can be used for identification and to assist in specification. However, the evidence revealed by graphical representation can often be more useful as it makes comparisons easier. Two such methods of display are described: a triangular graph explained in section 7.1.3, and a summation graph explained in section 7.1.5.

A triangular graph (the *Triangle of Texture*) is used to indicate general differences based on percentage composition expressed as sand, silt or clay. It is of particular value for comparing soils likely to reflect properties associated with these three very broad particle-size categories. For comparisons within a narrow range of particle-size grades, e.g. the categories spanning the sand and gravel grades at the coarse end of the particle-size spectrum, a summation graph is often more appropriate.

7.1.3 Triangle of Texture

For the mineral skeleton of a soil, texture classes have been traditionally defined by reference to a *Triangle of Texture* such as that currently used by soil surveyors (Figure 7.1(a)).

TABLE 7.1 Drainage and soil materials for sports turf

Serial number used in text		*1*	*2*	*3*	*4*	*5*	*6*	*7*	*8*
		Stewart zone materials for sports turf							
Standards and examples		*Trench gravel*		*Blinding sand*		*Topsoil sand*		10 mm (⅜ in) gravel	Fine grit
		Coarse	Fine	Coarse	Fine	Coarse	Fine		
Organic matter	% dry weight								
Stones	over 8.000	73						72	10
Coarse gravel	4.000–8.000	27	50	8				26	67
Fine gravel	2.000–4.000		44	20				2	22
Very coarse sand	1.000–2.000		6	33	17	5			1
Coarse sand	0.500–1.000			23	33	23			
Medium sand	0.250–0.500			14	26	69			
Fine sand	0.125–0.250			2	17	3	90		
Very fine sand	0.060–0.125				7		10		
Silt	0.002–0.060								
Clay	less than 0.002								
20.000 mm aperture									
14.000 mm aperture		100							
10.000 mm aperture		82		100				100	
5.000 mm aperture		0	100	95				60	100
2.360 mm aperture			10	80	100	100		5	23
1.180 mm aperture			0	46	89	98		0	3
0.600 mm aperture				21	59	83			0
0.300 mm aperture				5	30	10	100		
0.150 mm aperture				0	11	0	22		
0.075 mm aperture					0		0		
Gradation Index	D_{90}/D_{10}	2	2	8	8	2	2	2	2
	(Maximum acceptable)	(6)		(24)		(5)			
Summation % used to predict D_K	(%)	35	35	15	15	15	35	35	25
D_K value	(μm)	8200	3600	480	180	310	165	4200	2020
	(mm)	8.200	3.600	0.480	0.180	0.310	0.165	4.200	2.020
D_K minimum based on materials with maximum gradation index and summation % of 15	(μm)	(2650)		(170)		(140)			
	(mm)	(2.620)		(0.170)		(0.140)			
Hydraulic conductivity (K) by direct measurement (falling head, saturated)	(mm/h)	Theoretical only						108 000	38 000
	(in/h)							4252	1496
K estimate using D_K and graph, Figure 7.7 (minimum values in brackets)	(mm/h)	320 000	76 000	2300	430	1400	350	102 00	41 000
			(43000)		(380)		(270)		
	(in/h)	12 598	2992	91	17	55	14	4016	1614
			(1693)		(15)		(10½)		
Pipe spacing/cm when used in slits, $\dfrac{\text{slit spacing}}{\text{slit width}}=20$, overall design rate V = 2 mm/hr (minimum values in brackets)	(m)	1.8	0.9					1.0	0.6
			(0.7)						
	(ft)	6	3					3½	2
			(2½)						
Pipe spacing/cm when used to form level drainage bed, overall design rate V = 20 mm/hr (minimum values in brackets)	(m)	2.5	1.2	Unsuitable				1.4	0.9
			(1.0)						
	(ft)	8	4					4½	3
			(3)						
Critical tension using D_K and graph, Figure 7.8 (maximum values in brackets)	(mm)	9	20	149	397	230	433	17	35
			(27)		(430)		(510)		
	(in)	½	1	6	16	9	17	½	1½
			(1)		(17)		(20)		

9	10	11	12	13	14	15	16	17	18	19	20	21	22	23	24
Examples of materials used in construction and maintenance							*Examples of sports-field soils encountered in Britain*								
Example of crushed rock used for hard porous surfaces	5 mm (³/₁₆ in) concreting sand	Bunker sand	Filter sand	USA golf-green sand (1975)	Building, plaster, or foundry sand	Dune sand	Loamless, fine sand compost, 3:1 by vol., sand/sedge peat	Humose, fine sand compost, 2:1 by vol., sand/sedge peat	Loamy, fine sand (Swansea)	Sandy loam (Gower)	Silt loam (Crowborough)	Clay loam with excellent, water-stable, granular structure (Cribyn)	Cribyn soil completely de-structured by poaching	Silty clay loam (Surrey Loam)	Clay (London Clay, Sudbury)
							5	8	6	4	4	9	9	7	11
2										2		5	5		
38	15									2	1	3	3	1	
11	24	3								1	0	4	4	1	
12	24	46	5	10	2				1	3	2	4	4	1	1
7	21	47	63	51	62	15	15	15	31	15	1	4	4	2	1
6	13	4	32	33	34	82	82	82	43	21	0	3	3	4	1
7	3			6	2	3	3	3	13	18	1	3	3	4	3
14									6	25	82	45	45	52	44
3									6	13	13	30	30	35	50
100	100						Not suitable for analysis by sieving alone because of the need to separate silt, clay and organic matter, as well as the various sands and gravels							
67	90	100													
51	68	99	100	100											
40	43	75	98	95	100	100									
32	22	6	60	57	61	95									
26	6	0	0	12	6	15									
19	0			0	0	0									
154	13	3	2	4	3	2	Inappropriate for prediction from D_K alone because of the need to take account of the complicating effects of soil organic matter and structure							
15	15	25	35	15	25	35									
45	240	380	255	170	220	180									
0.045	0.240	0.380	0.255	0.170	0.220	0.180									
30	560		710			400	200	25	190	34	<1	227	<1	<1	<1
1	22		28			15½	8	1	7½	1½		9	Poor to impervious		
40	660	1600	760	390	610	410	Inappropriate							
1½	26	63	30	15½	24	16									
							Unsuitable								
1587	298	188	280	420	325	397	Inappropriate							
62	12	7½	11	16½	13	15½									

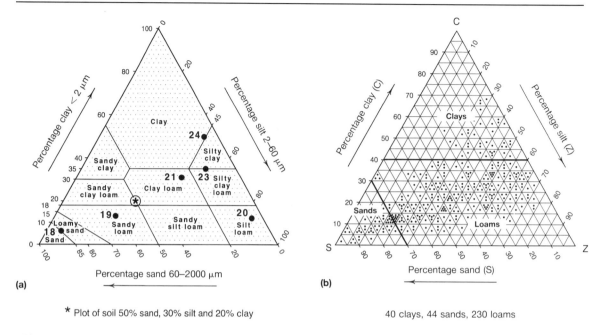

(a)

* Plot of soil 50% sand, 30% silt and 20% clay

(b)

40 clays, 44 sands, 230 loams

FIGURE 7.1 Determining soil texture class. (a) Soils SN18–24 from Figure 7.3 and Table 7.1 plotted on a *Triangle of Texture*. (b) Plots representative of the texture of English and Welsh soils, based on a systematic sampling of information in soil survey records, Nos 1–56, and the soil memoirs for Leeds, Cardiganshire, Aylesbury and Hemel Hempstead.

This is merely a triangular graph with values for percentage sand (nominally 2.0–0.060 mm in diameter), silt (0.060–0.002 mm) and clay (less than 0.002 mm), read off on each axis. A line for each value is then projected into the triangular diagram, parallel to the side directly opposite the 100% value for the category concerned. As an example, the plot for a soil, 50% sand, 30% silt and 20% clay is shown on Figure 7.1(a) as an asterisk. The other plots are for the soils numbered SN18–24 in Table 7.1.

The areas delineated within the main triangle are the different texture classes. These are subjective in origin, reflecting handling properties of value for identification in the field, and behaviour characteristics of significance for agricultural management.

The second *Triangle of Texture*, Figure 7.1(b), shows the distribution of plots derived from a systematic sampling of data available

for the soils of England and Wales in 1979 (Stewart *et al.*, 1980). This is included to indicate the relative proportion of soils within the broad texture classes – *sands*, *loams* or *clays* – and the extent to which the soils in series SN18–24 (Table 7.1) are typical.

7.1.4 Specifications based on sieve size gradings

Because of the inefficiency of sieving as a procedure for fine particle fractionation at the level of silt and clay, this approach is used only for the characterization of materials, predominantly sand, gravel or stone. Normally the results are tabulated, or plotted on summation graphs.

The least precise method of defining particle size by sieving is to use only the smallest sieve size through which all the material has passed, e.g. 10 mm (⅜ in) gravel. Such a material could

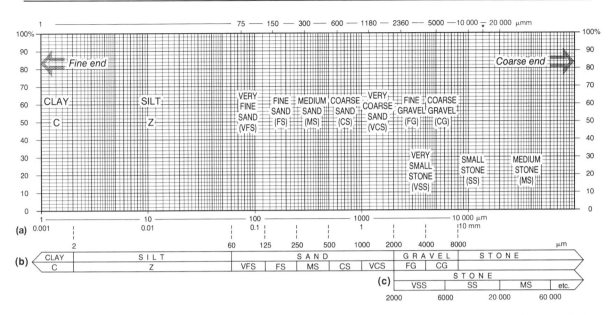

FIGURE 7.2 Summation graph. (a) Engineers' values expressed as the percentage passing sieves of progressively smaller mesh size; therefore, plot downwards from coarse to fine. * = 14 000 μm sieve also used. (b) Soil scientists' categories separated by sieving or sedimentation, each expressed as a percentage of the whole range of particle-size categories to be included in the total. Enter the progressively accumulated values, starting from the fine end of the particle-size spectrum. (c) Alternative categories for the coarser particles outwith the fine earth range (Appendix A, Table A.3).

consist of particles ranging widely in size or, for example, particles ranging only between 10 and 5 mm. The true nature of the material will depend very much on the nature of the deposit being worked and the extent to which it has been cleaned of fine particles by washing.

7.1.5 Summation graphs

Materials are sorted by sieving into their particle-size composition and then the various categories plotted cumulatively as percentages. A zone, as defined on a summation graph, delimits the range of tolerance allowed for particular materials.

The summation graph used for this purpose indicates the particle sizes on a logarithmic scale (Figure 7.2). This allows fine particles, such as clay and silt, to be included in a graph that also allows for special attention to be given to details of grading within the much larger but less widely spaced categories of sand and gravel. The vertical axis is a straightforward linear scale from 0 to 100 representing the sum of the percentages for the individual particle-size fractions. The plot representing the composition of any particular material can be built up by plotting individual particle-size percentages cumulatively, starting at the fine end. Alternatively, data in the form normally supplied by the sand and gravel industry, i.e. percentages passing each sieve in a bank of progressively smaller sieve sizes, can be used by starting to plot at the coarse end. The steeper the line on the graph the narrower the range of particle sizes present.

Figure 7.3 shows:

1. the plots of individual materials listed in Table 7.1 for comparison with *Stewart zones* (see also section 7.1.6);

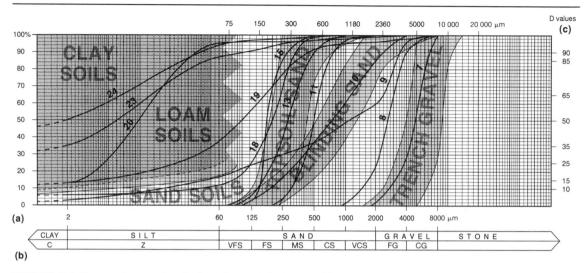

FIGURE 7.3 Summation graph of selected materials from Table 7.1. (a) Sieve-size categories used by engineers. (b) Particle-size categories used by soil scientists. (c) D values, i.e. summation totals used to indicate particle diameters of special interest. See also general key, Figure 7.6.

2. the region within which the fine end of the loams and clays plot out. These are the soils which have to depend on cracks, old root runs, worm channels and particle aggregation for drainage. They are the prime candidates for supplementary, artificial drainage when subject to intensive use (section 2.2);

3. the region between the *topsoil sands* and the loams and clays where the sand and loamy sand soils plot out. This region, like that of the loams and clays, can only be precisely defined at the fine end of the texture spectrum. Though not pure sands these soils are likely to continue to drain freely so long as the small amount of silt and clay present remains heterogeneously distributed or trapped within water-stable granules.

7.1.6 Grading zones

British Standards Specifications for aggregates and sands

The system used by suppliers of aggregates to the building industry is based on British Standards Specification BS 882 1201: Part 2, 1973 and the later amended version, BS 882: 1983 (see particle-size zones plotted on summation graphs, Figures 7.4 and 7.5). These define fine aggregate material from natural sources as used for making concrete, but lacking anything better, these standards have also been used in specifications relating to the construction and maintenance of soil-based facilities used for sport. Unfortunately, the objectives of those using fine aggregate to make concrete are not the same as those aiming to assist soil drainage and promote the growth of grass (section 7.1.1). Though the BS categories do include materials suitable for sports-field use the boundaries are not sufficiently well drawn to serve without need for additional, qualifying statements (compare Figures 7.4 and 7.5 with 7.6).

Stewart zones

To facilitate greater precision in the specification of materials required for sports-turf construction and maintenance it has been necessary to define new particle-size zones. This has involved research based not only on technical

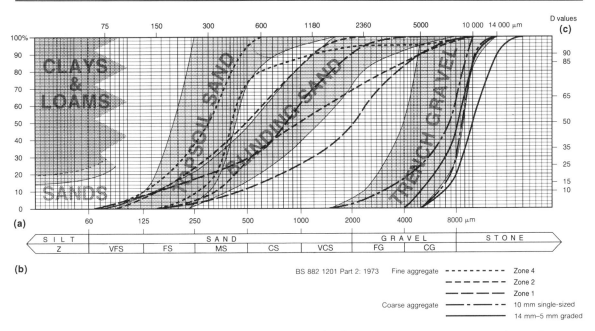

FIGURE 7.4 Summation graph illustrating BS (1973) zones for fine and coarse aggregate materials. (a) Sieve-size categories used by engineers. (b) Particle-size categories used by soil scientists. (c) *D* values, i.e. summation totals used to indicate particle diameters of special interest. See also general key, Figure 7.6.

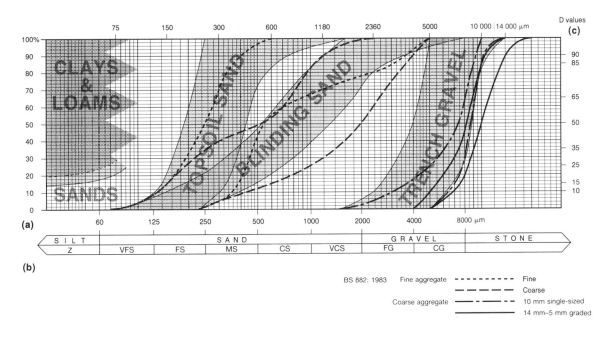

FIGURE 7.5 Summation graph illustrating BS (1983) zones for fine and coarse aggregate materials. (a) Sieve-size categories used by engineers. (b) Particle-size categories used by soil scientists. (c) *D* values, i.e. summation totals used to indicate particle diameters of special interest. See also general key, Figure 7.6.

115

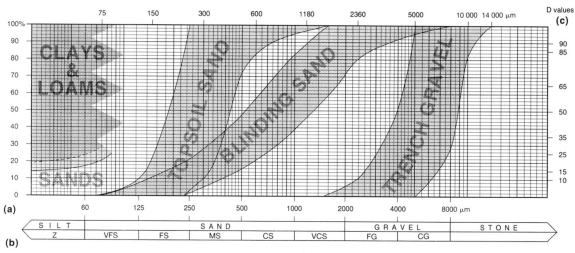

FIGURE 7.6 Summation graph defining *Stewart zone* materials for sports-turf constructions, drainage and maintenance. (a) Sieve-size categories used by engineers. (b) Particle-size categories used by soil scientists. (c) D values, i.e. summation totals used to indicate particle diameters of special interest.

Clays and Loams – Soils dependent on cracks, worm channels and particle aggregation ': assist drainage. Unreliable for winter use unless pipe drained **and** slit.
Sands – Texture target for clays and loams ameliorated with *topsoil sand*. Note the broad boundary between the loams and sands. Within the upper and lower limits of this boundary zone there are some mixtures that can provide a useful measure of free drainage, but others may not because of the way the sand particles themselves interpack.

Topsoil sand – Used for soil construction, soil amelioration and topdressing.
Blinding sand – Used as intermediate, blinding layer between soil or *topsoil sand* and *trench gravel*. Preferred to *topsoil sand* where earthworm ingestion is to be discouraged
Trench gravel – Used as backfill in the lower half of drain trenches and slits. Laid directly over and around perforated plastic pipes, or as an intermediate layer over small stone where clay tiles have been preferred. Also used as the main, water transmission layer in a drainage bed.

requirements but also on availability. The result is the summation graph zones in Figure 7.6 and the particle-size categories defined in Tables 7.1 and 1.4. To avoid confusion with the previously used British Standards, developed primarily for the making of concrete, these new zones are identified in this book as *Stewart zones* and the materials they characterize designated *topsoil sands*, *blinding sands* and *trench gravels*. If these become generally accepted they will encourage the standardization of efficient designs and assist in precise specification.

Topsoil sands are suitable for top-dressing and topsoil construction. *Blinding sands* are for bringing permeable backfill through to the surface over gravel or for use as an intermediate layer between a fine-textured topsoil and an underlying gravel bed, preventing the soil from infiltrating the gravel. *Trench gravels* are suitable: for the gravel element in a two-part sand/gravel slit; as permeable fill in a trench over a perforated plastic pipe; for use as the gravel bed in a rafted construction.

The advantages of these categories are listed below.

1. They are safe because any material falling within them will not infilter the material of the zone immediately adjacent. For example, a *Stewart zone topsoil sand* will not infilter a compact *Stewart zone blinding sand*, nor will a *Stewart zone blinding sand* infilter a compact *Stewart zone trench gravel*.

2. A compact *Stewart zone topsoil sand* will blind out most soils and a *Stewart zone blinding sand* will be too coarse for earthworms to eat their way through.

3. A *Stewart zone trench gravel* will not pass through the perforations of a plastic pipe and yet, when compact, will be small enough to avoid being infiltrated by a

Stewart zone blinding sand placed above it. Hence, only two of these materials are required to form a stable, permeable link between a perforated plastic pipe and the soil surface.

4. The *Stewart zone trench gravels*, though small, have a sufficient hydraulic conductivity for every centimetre used in the bottom layer of a two-part slit to add a safe minimum of 1 m to the interval between the intercepting pipe system. This assumes that the overall design rate does not exceed 50 mm (2 in) per day and slit spacing does not exceed 20 times slit width. The standard schemes described in this book all comply with these requirements.

In fact, these incremental allowances may be applied to any trench system filled with a *Stewart zone trench gravel* running flat to the next relieving tier of underdrainge: for example, gravel channels 150 mm (6 in) wide, spaced in parallel succession at 3 m (10 ft) intervals. Here a 30 cm (12 in) depth of a *Stewart zone trench gravel* would allow for the relieving pipe system to be spaced at a safe minimum of 30 m (33 yards). This could be increased to 45 m for a *trench gravel* plotting wholly within the coarser half of the *trench gravel* zone, but for *trench gravels* whose particle size distribution spans most of the *trench gravel* zone, or in case of doubt, use the safest and simplest, 1 cm:1 m relationship (Table 7.1).

5. The *zone* limits are not based only on theoretical considerations but reflect, both in their form and in their range, materials that are currently widely available.

7.1.7 *D* values and gradation indices

To make full use of a summation graph, a form of shorthand is used to indicate the particle diameter D reached at any specified cumulative total: for example, a *topsoil sand* with D_{85}–D_{15} consists of particles within the range 600–140 µm in diameter. These values can be read off a summation graph where D_{85} represents the particle diameter D at 85% of the cumulative total, and D_{15} is the same at 15% of the cumulative total. This would allow for a maximum of 15% of particles larger than 600 microns and a further 15% smaller than 140 microns. Of the actual materials listed in Table 7.1 only SNS 12–15 would comply with this requirement.

This approach can also be used to define a 'gradation index', i.e. a number indicating a degree to which any normal, fairly symmetrically graded material peaks around the average particle size. For this purpose we generally ignore the small percentage of particles at the largest and smallest extremes and concentrate on the ratio of the upper and lower limits of the particle-size range spanned by the bulk of the material. Thus we can describe the dune sand, SN15 in Figure 7.3, as having a D_{90}/D_{10} gradation index of 270/140 = 1.9. The 270 represents the particle size in µm at the 90% cumulative total and the 140, the particle size in µm at the 10% cumulative total. By contrast, the concreting sand, SN10 in Figure 7.3, has a D_{90}/D_{10} gradation index of 2500/190 = 13.2, this relatively large value reflecting the much wider range of particle sizes present. SN7, the 10-mm ⅜ in gravel in Figure 7.3, has a D_{90}/D_{10} gradation index of 6600/2750 = 2.4. This again is a small value, typical of a single-sized aggregate.

In fact the gradation index (often quoted as G.I. for short) reflects the slope of the middle portion of the summation curve. A small value (less than 3) corresponds to a steep slope between the particle-size limits chosen and, as the value increases from 6 to 20 or more, so the slope represented is more obliquely inclined.

For typical, quartz-dominated sands and gravels we can assume that a material with a D_{90}/D_{10} gradation index of the order of 2 will have a bulk density of the order of 1.5–1.6 g/cm^3 and a pore volume approaching the theoretical maximum, for an unstructured material, of 40%. As D_{90}/D_{10} gradation indices increase beyond 6 and up to 20, so bulk densities are liable to increase towards a maximum of around 1.75–1.80 g/cm³ with pore volumes decreasing to 33%. However, it should be noted that shelly or very angular materials, or materials with very high G.I. values (e.g. SN9 in Figure 7.3, a crushed rock material used for hard porous surfaces) do not conform very well in the field with these predictions as they tend not to pack homogeneously. With soils there are additional complications introduced by organic matter and structure so that, outside the normal run of sands and gravels, the gradation index approach loses much of its significance and tends not to be used.

7.1.8 Using D_K to predict hydraulic conductivity, critical tension and pore-size compatibility

When selecting the best sand and gravel from locally available materials, or when using drainage schemes that do not conform in their dimensions to those assumed in the *Stewart zone* approach (page 117), it may be necessary to get some idea of the hydraulic conductivity or critical tension of the materials on offer. The practical procedures for doing this precisely are probably best left to the specialist, but experience suggests that a reasonable estimate can be made, within a 20% margin of error, by reference to the particle-size composition.

Predicting hydraulic conductivity

This prediction can be achieved in two steps.

1. Determine D_K, the particle diameter that effectively represents the dominant influence on the hydraulic behaviour of the material under consideration. The K in this context refers to the symbol K used to signify hydraulic conductivity, but hydraulic conductivity is only one of the values which the D_K particle size can now be used to predict.

Thus, it might have been more usefully designated the D_E value, the effective particle diameter, for it can also be used to predict critical tension, capillary rise and pore-size compatability with other materials. It remains as D_K however, reflecting its original use.

To determine D_K, one of the following procedures will be appropriate.

(a) For materials with four or more particle-size categories (as defined in Table 7.1) greater than 5%, or a D_{90}/D_{10} G.I. over 4, use D_{15} as the D_K value. For example, this would apply to SN10 in Table 7.1, indicating from its summation curve (Figure 7.3) a D_K value of 240 μm.

(b) For materials with three or less particle-size categories of 1%+, or a D_{90}/D_{10} G.I. less than 3, use D_{35} as the D_K value. For example, this would apply to SN15 in Table 7.1, indicating from its summation curve (Figure 7.3) a D_K value of 180 μm.

(c) For all other materials use D_{25} as the D_K value. For example, this would apply to SN8 in Table 7.1, indicating from its summation curve, a D_K value of 2020 μm.

(d) Check with the general formula suggested by Thornton (1978, p. 503):

$$D_K = 25 \times \frac{2.5}{\text{G.I.}}$$

$$= 62.5 \times \frac{D_{10}}{D_{90}}.$$

2. Use the data in Table 7.2 or the graph, Figure 7.7, both of which relate D_K to an estimated value for the saturated hydraulic conductivity K.

Thus, for the examples cited in (a), (b) and (c) above, we can arrive at the estimated

TABLE 7.2 Saturated hydraulic conductivity K predicted from particle-size composition D_K

D_K (µm)	K/h (mm)	(in)	D_K (µm)	K/h (mm)	(in)	D_K (µm)	K/h (mm)	(in)
10	3	0.1	100	150	6	1 000	8 300	327
20	9	0.4	200	500	20	2 000	27 700	1 090
30	19	0.7	300	1 020	40	3 000	56 100	2 210
40	31	1.2	400	1 680	66	4 000	92 600	3 650
50	45	1.8	500	2 480	98	5 000	137 000	5 370
60	62	2.4	600	3 410	134	6 000	187 000	7 380
70	81	3.2	700	4 460	176	7 000	245 000	9 650
80	102	4.0	800	5 630	222	8 000	309 000	12 200
90	126	4.9	900	6 910	272	9 000	380 000	14 900
100	151	5.9	1 000	8 300	327	10 000	456 000	18 000

values listed below. These and other results listed in Table 7.1 compare satisfactorily with the values determined by direct measurement.

Material	D_K value	K estimated from D_K		K determined by direct measurement	
	(µm)	(mm/h)	(in/h)	(mm/h)	(in/h)
SN10	240	660	26	560	22
SN15	180	380	15	400	16
SN8	2020	41 000	1614	38 000	1496

Predicted, approximate values for hydraulic conductivity are probably all that is required for normal design purposes, but it must be appreciated that supplies from quarries will vary to some degree from the sub-samples analysed, and that the procedure for the direct measurement of hydraulic conductivity is itself subject to error. A major problem with direct measurement is that the laboratory conditions under which K is measured – homogeneity of packing and degree of saturation – are very unlikely to be exactly replicated in the field. It would help greatly, therefore, if all sand and gravel suppliers provided data on particle-size composition when offering materials for sale so that K can then be estimated by the procedure given above.

Predicting critical tension

For critical tension it is necessary to start by following through the procedure described above for determining D_K from particle-size composition. An approximate value for critical tension can then be estimated by substituting D_K for particle diameter in the equation developed for this purpose in section 4.2.2:

$$\text{critical tension (mm)} = \frac{71.4}{\text{particle diameter (mm)}}.$$

Thus, for a typical dune sand (SN15 in Table 7.1),

$$\text{critical tension} = \frac{71.4}{0.180}$$

$$= 397 \text{ mm } (15\tfrac{1}{2} \text{ in}).$$

Alternatively, read value directly off graph, Figure 7.8.

Predicting pore-size compatibility

D_K may be said to define the particle diameter most likely to dominate the pore system of a mixed particle-size sand or gravel. As such it provides a useful basis upon which to decide if two otherwise unlike materials, laid one above the other, will blend hydraulically or behave as separate layers, tending to create a perched watertable above the junction.

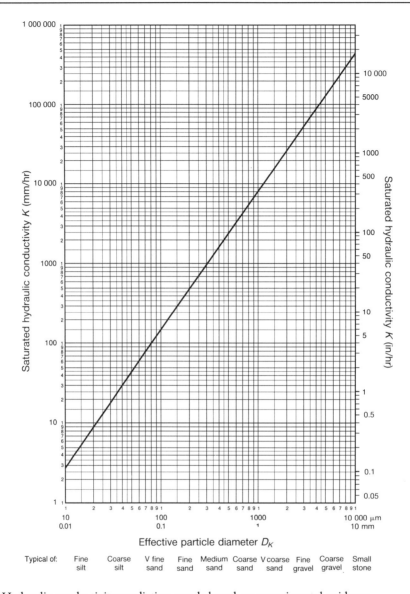

FIGURE 7.7 Hydraulic conductivity prediction graph based on experimental evidence.

1. When a relatively coarse sand is introduced between a topsoil dominated by fine sand and a gravel drainage bed, the primary objective may be to keep the three layers separate, but will the pore system controlling water movement between the two sand layers effectively merge, or will the two layers remain hydrologically separate?

If the D_K values of the two sands are very similar then it can be assumed that they will merge hydrologically. Therefore, when designing with critical tension in mind, the depth of the blinding-sand layer should be included with the depth of the fine sand topsoil to define the total height of the construction above the gravel drainage bed.

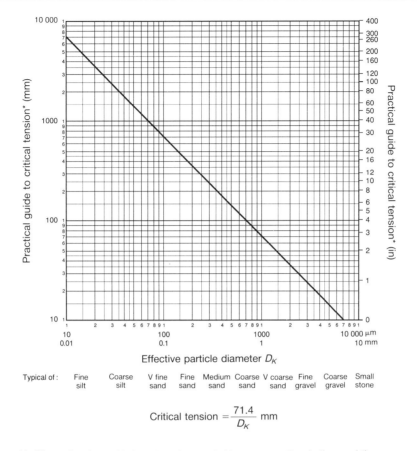

$$\text{Critical tension} = \frac{71.4}{D_K} \text{ mm}$$

*1. When using these critical tension values to decide on construction depth, regard them as maxima. In practice trapped air will prevent some pore space within the water-retention zone becoming water-filled (section 4.2.1).

2. To estimate capillary rise, assume that it is unlikely to be much more than half the critical tension value (section 4.2.1).

FIGURE 7.8 Critical tension prediction graph based on experimental evidence.

2. Except when trying to germinate seed we normally want water to work itself well down into the soil in the hope that the roots will follow. What will be the effect of changing from a coarse to a fine sand top-dressing? Will the change encourage undue water retention at the surface, adversely affecting aeration?

Only if the D_K values of the two materials in a layered sequence are very similar, or the D_K of the lower material is smaller, will the two materials combine to keep water moving freely across the junction. However, if the D_K value of the next layer below is significantly larger than the layer above then the downward migration of water will be held up at the interface until the top layer is saturated. Therefore, avoid unnecessary layering of hydrologically incompatible materials unless, as with a very coarse sand, blinding layer, or a gravel drainage bed, this is what is intended to help retain some water within reach of the surface.

Do not gratuitously introduce complications by

unnecessarily varying your topdressing materials or you may introduce unwanted layering effects.

7.2 Choosing the correct materials according to function

7.2.1 Introduction

Though several methods developed for the precise specification of soil-forming materials make use of data on particle-size composition, experience suggests that the easiest to implement is likely to be one based on zones defined on a particle-size, summation graph or in a table of sieve-grading limits. The following review of features likely to influence choice of material according to function will therefore be based mainly on materials defined in Figure 7.6, or Tables A1.3 and A1.4 in Appendix A.

7.2.2 Choosing the correct soil

In situ or imported topsoil should be free of glass and other potentially dangerous material as well as being in a structurally water-stable state, i.e. in 'good heart' (section A.7). As such it will probably have a pH in the region 5.5–7.5 and an organic matter content between 4 and 10%. Thereafter, the performance of the soil will depend very much on its particle-size composition. It is impossible to predict from a knowledge of particle-size composition alone whether any particular soil will drain badly. However, if the soil when compact has the potential to drain badly because of its content of fine particles, it should be considered a likely candidate for intensive, supplementary drainage.

Sand, silt and clay content of the 'fine earth'

Soils with less than 75% of the fine earth (particles less than 2 mm in diameter) consist-

ing of sand, or more than 25% silt + clay are the loams and the clays (e.g. Table 7.1, SNs 19–24). They are soils dependent on worm channels and particle aggregation to maintain a structure favourable to the rapid infiltration of surface water. They are unreliable for winter use unless pipe-drained and slit.

By contrast, soils classified as loamy sands or sands (e.g. Table 7.1, SN18) have so little silt and clay that only when this fine material is concentrated into a layer will there be a risk of developing a problem of drainage impedance. Loamy sands or sands are soils with less than 25% silt plus clay and, as such, are good prospects for sports turf, generally requiring underdrainage only. (See note on Sands, Figure 7.6.)

If a sand soil is to be ameliorated by addition of a strongly granulated loam, no effort should be made to break down the granulation and homogenize the two materials or the drainage efficiency of the sand will immediately be compromised. The aim should be to achieve a 'spotted dog' effect, i.e. granules of soil set in a matrix of sand. This is best done by careful mixing when dry.

Soils dominated by very fine sand and silt (e.g. Table 7.1, SN20) are particularly difficult to deal with because they are water-holding, structurally very unstable and liable to wind-blow when left bare during construction. They may well benefit from steep grading (e.g. 2.5% or 1 in 40) to ensure that excess water will be shed off the surface.

Topsoil quality

Soil from a stockpile may well be structurally unstable in water, readily capping when rained upon. This would be typical of subsoil but could also be topsoil that has deteriorated during storage. No matter how good the original quality of a topsoil, it will rapidly deteriorate in storage during the course of a single growing season, especially if soil temperature, soil aeration and soil moisture are adequate for biological activity to continue.

Storage under dry, cold, well-aerated conditions, or grassed over in a heap no more than 60 mm (2 ft) high, would be much less harmful. In the normal large stockpile, biological activity goes on but, because aeration below the surface is restricted, the supply of oxygen is greatly reduced and the nature of the microbial activity changes. This results in the dissipation of organic matter and production of noxious end-products. The structure deterioration that follows may require many years of special management to rectify.

Soil degradation is a problem far more widespread than is generally recognized. It probably stems from the skills of our engineers in earth moving having gone beyond their knowledge of soil as a dynamic, biological system. Before the advent of modern heavy equipment, earth-moving projects were achieved by manpower and a system of skips and rails; a procedure which probably limited the extent of such operations and the degree of compaction caused.

By careful selection of site we should aim at minimum disturbance and only very minor grading within the topsoil, preserving soil structure and the organisms responsible for it. Time should be allowed for re-consolidation and root-binding after the loosening consequent upon the disturbance involved in grading. It is important to realize that unless the topsoil is fresh and not structurally degraded by stockpiling, it may prove quite unsuitable for the satisfactory establishment of a sports-turf sward. Note the adverse effect of structural collapse on hydraulic conductivity in the clay loam soil, SN22, Table 7.1.

In summary, if non-sandy soils are to have a satisfactory air/water balance for root development, they must be selected for their desirable structural state and then handled so as to preserve it. When using such soils the aims should be as follows.

1. Avoid disturbance if at all possible so that full benefit can be derived from existing worm channels and well-established, subsoil cracking systems.
2. If the soil has to be disturbed, work it only when it is dry enough to be brittle. Take every precaution to avoid either dusting or panning by injudicious and over-zealous use of machinery.
3. Avoid storage; if at all possible, arrange for direct transfer. If storage is necessary, then recognize that rapid structural deterioration will take place in a time span to be measured in months rather than years.

Stones and boulders

Stones and boulders should not be so large or so numerous as to interfere with the smooth progress of a slit trencher machine. This means that stones larger than 75 mm (3 in) in any dimension are liable to be unwelcome in the top 300–450 mm (12–18 in) of soil.

Total stone content should not exceed 15% by weight, 8% by volume, as even at this moderate level of stoniness all the soil agitation inherent in harrowing, raking and frost action will tend to leave them concentrated on the surface where they are least acceptable. To merely roll them back in is like forcing marbles into porridge with predictable, adverse effect on surface infiltration.

In time, surface casting by earthworms will bury stones, but a made-up or severely disturbed soil is not likely to be well endowed with earthworms initially, and the rate of re-burial by this means is, in any case, bound to take years. In practice, therefore, any adverse concentration of stones at the surface should be dealt with by some process of mechanical removal before grassing up; particularly so if the stones are sharply angular fragments that could cause injury. Far better to avoid these problems by careful soil selection in the first place.

Peat

To be described as 'peaty' a soil needs to contain more than 25% dry weight of organic matter, about two-thirds organic matter by volume. A true peat is made up of more than 35% dry weight of organic matter, more than three-quarters organic matter by volume (Figure A1.3, Appendix A).

Deep peat, once adequately drained, can provide a satisfactory grass surface for sport, especially for controlled use by juveniles, but there are special problems, unique to peat, that have to be taken into account.

1. Peats vary, most typically, according to their origin. Deep, fen-type peat is formed in the hollow of a natural catchment and, because of the stable nature of the ground water-table and the natural sequence of vegetation through which it has been built up, it may have a fibrous, reed-residue layer at the base. This can be utilized for the efficient, lateral discharge of drainage water once a satisfactory outfall has been established. Bog peats accumulate as a blanket in very high rainfall areas but are liable to dry out seasonally. This means they may be quite well humified and compact throughout, requiring a system of underdrains to assist with lateral discharge.

2. If the watertable is lowered, particularly in a fen-type peat, there will be considerable subsidence. Initially this will be as a result of the de-watering process but will then continue, albeit at a slower pace, because the peat itself will decompose in response to the improved aeration. These two processes can lead to falls equivalent to one third of the fall in the watertable height.

   Though initially a saturated, fibrous peat may have a hydraulic conductivity comparable with that of fine sand, the combined effect of shrinkage and decomposition can reduce this to a value more comparable with silt. This may not yet make it unduly limiting for vertical infiltration down to the watertable but it would be very slow for clearance laterally.

   It is important, therefore, that we should recognize not only the initial differences that may occur between peats but also the changes in performance that are likely to occur with time, especially if the site is completely de-watered. For example, there may be no benefit to be gained from attempting to de-water a basal layer of fibrous peat. This could be left waterlogged so that it could maintain, by efficient lateral flow, the water level in a peripheral ditch forming part of a pump drainage scheme, or a height-controlled outfall.

3. Improved aeration on sites showing the visual warning signs of 'oily' sheens on the surface of ditch water, or of red ochre staining around springs and drain outfalls, can lead to major problems caused by a build up of iron ochre deposition (section 2.1.3). If iron ochre deposition does occur it will be particularly devastating in the aerated channel system of slits and pipe under-drains.

4. There may be some difficulty over organizing a satisfactory outfall to allow the watertable to be lowered and maintained at an appropriate level. This may entail clearing a passage through a natural drainage barrier or turning instead to some form of pump assistance. In either event this problem should be thoroughly explored with professional help from the local drainage authority.

5. Because of the low density of drained, moist peat (about a quarter of the drained, moist density of a loam or a sand) and the risk of shallow rooting, any grass sward established may not be sufficiently anchored to resist the tear-wearing stress of studded footwear. As already pointed out in section 1.10.6, this would be much more of a problem with adults than juveniles.

6. The virtual necessity of an open ditch approach to ground-water control requires serious thought being given to the frequency with which balls will require to be recovered from this location. Though recovery poles may be made available for this purpose the menace of vandalism may result in their not being available to casual users. In these circumstances the task of ball recovery from open, slippery-sided, water-filled ditches will at best be a nuisance and, at worst, may constitute a serious child hazard.

With the above problems in mind, a peat project is best tackled in stages, first concentrating on lowering the ground watertable to no more than 1 m (1 yard) below the playing surface. This is probably best done initially by a well-maintained system of ditches around individual pitches, linked up to an effective, controlled outfall.

Once de-watering has stabilized the surface enough to take the necessary light weight, load-spreading machinery, progress can be made with weed killing, removal of trash and regrading by minimal re-distribution of peat. Then the surface can be fertilized and firmed up by pushing out a carpet of topsoil sand, 50 mm (2 in) – 100 mm (4 in) thick, according to resources. Finally the surface can be grassed and maintained as advocated in Section 6.1. Only if, after 2–3 years of use this fails to satisfy should any consideration be given to the possible benefits of pipe and/or slit drain supplementation.

Tip sites

It may be found that the existing surface on a tip site is seriously contaminated with dubious or potentially harmful materials such as glass and noxious chemicals, or half-buried obstacles such as large stones and boulders, concrete, metal, refuse, etc. It is normally unwise to attempt to clear such objects by trawling through the soil with a subsoiling device; far better to aim at safe burial.

After clearance of all loose debris and obstacles standing proud of the surface, burial may involve importation of 450 mm (18 in) of good soil, sufficient to avoid any adverse effect of frost heave, and to allow adequate clearance for soil cultivation and drain trenching. Since this should be regarded as a minimum safe depth, an additional allowance of one-sixth of the final desired depth should be made to take account of long-term settlement.

If noxious chemicals are suspected, and these cannot be entirely removed by excavation, the surface to be buried should first be chemically screened by a 50–75 mm (2–3 in) layer of at least 25 mm (1 in) of lime, and then 25 mm (1 in) of peat. The lime will tend to inactivate by precipitation, and the peat will tend to trap by chelation. These layers should be firmed into place by rolling and thereafter should not be disturbed.

Should there be any doubt over the stability of the tip surface or the height to which the new surface can be raised, then the tip surface should be trued off with a freely permeable, blinding layer of coarse sand, fine gravel or grit (unless already screened with peat and lime) and covered by an appropriate, synthetic filter membrane prior to topsoiling. Where the drainage scheme to be adopted requires pipes to be installed under the filter membrane these will have to be linked by permeable fill through the filter membrane. If the imported topsoil is a free-draining sand, or loamy sand, this may suffice, but if the imported soil will require slit drainage, provision may have to be made to continue the permeable fill in the pipe trenches well above the filter membrane. This can be done by piling the required *trench gravel* in ridges on the membrane surface, along the line of the pipe trenches. Alternatively, by marking the line of each pipe run with duct tracer tape (or equivalent), connection can be made later by trenching the link down from the new surface.

Obviously it would be advantageous to start with a stable tip, suitably trued off and blinded, and then to take time to find an adequate amount of good topsoil to build up to the desired 450 mm (18 in). However, if only a shallow depth of topsoil is to be used over a synthetic filter membrane, a great effort should be made to secure a sufficiently sandy soil so as to obviate any need for further amendment by slitting. In either case, the details of the design need to be carefully worked out as any later up-grading that requires trenching into the buried pit material could be very disruptive.

7.2.3 Choosing the correct sand and gravel

Because of the great importance of choosing the correct materials this subject has already been considered in Chapter 1 and the concept of the *topsoil sands*, *blinding sands* and *trench gravels* introduced on page 114 to simplify precise specification.

Sands for topdressing, soil amelioration and whole soil construction

These are typically the *Stewart zone topsoil sands*: the dune, filter, plaster and foundry sands listed as SN12, 14 and 15 in Table 7.1 and Figure 7.3. They have D_{50} values between 0.18 and 0.40 mm and D_{90}/D_{10} typically between 2 and 3.

When choosing a sand to ameliorate a soil, or for topdressing, the particle-size grading should be matched to the dominant, medium-to-fine particle-size category in the topsoil already in place. This will discourage any tendency to develop the sort of layering and interpacking that inhibits the free movement of water in a vertical direction. Additionally, for golf and bowling greens, where the topsoil has already become biologically stabilized under acid conditions, the sand should be lime-free. To verify, check for the absence of vigorous fizzing when the sand is treated with a 10% solution of hydrochloric acid. However, where the *in-situ* topsoil has become biologically stable at an alkaline pH then top-dressing with a sand that is slightly calcareous will not harm. It will not upset the established biological equilibrium and, therefore, will not allow ephemeral disease organisms the opportunity to invade. Sand for use as the primary ingredient in a specially constructed, sports-field topsoil should be in the finer half of the *topsoil sands*, with D_{50} in the region of 0.18–0.22 mm, like SN15 in Figure 7.3. This will help to develop the tractive efficiency required for vigorous games. On bowling greens, where drainage can be given priority over traction, a medium particle-size sand with D_{50} more in the region of 0.27–0.31 mm (SN12–14 in Table 7.1) would be preferable if locally available at an acceptable price.

Sands for use in layered constructions, and in slit and pipe trenches

These are typically the *Stewart zone blinding sands* found amongst the concreting sands (SN10 in Table 7.1, Figure 7.3) with D_{50} between 0.5 and 1.3 mm and D_{90}/D_{10} between 8 and 23.

Blinding layer sands have to be looked at from several points of view.

1. Because they are relatively wide-ranging in their particle-size composition they will tend to interpack and form a relatively stable surface to work over.
2. For most *blinding sands* the D_{15} particle-size grade will tend to determine the effective pore size and, if this matches the D_K particle-size grade in any sand layer immediately above, the effective pore size will tend to be continuous through the two layers. This will then allow the two layers to function more or less as one with regard to the vertical infiltration of water, e.g. SN14 in Table 7.1 laid over SN10.
3. As blinding layers are frequently the layer sandwiched between fine sand above and

gravel or small stone below, their particle-size grading should be specified so as to ensure that they will hold out the fine material above and not themselves infilter the gravel or stones beneath. To maintain a stable, layered system, and erring on the side of caution, the D_{15} of the blinding layer should generally not exceed four times the D_{85} of the fine material above. That is, the main range of larger-sized particles in the fine material above should be large enough not to filter through the necks of the pores formed by the main range of smaller-sized particles in the blinding layer below. Similarly, the D_{15} of the underlying gravel or stone must not exceed four times the D_{85} of the blinding layer.

Generally, for symmetrically graded sands and gravels made up of sub-angular and rounded particles, the procedure for determining the effective upper and lower particle-sizes can take into account the narrowness of the particle-size grading. Thus, D_{15} and D_{85} would be appropriate parameters for a wide particle-size grading, D_{35} and D_{65} for a narrow particle-size grading, and D_{25} and D_{75} for something intermediate between these two extremes. An important feature of the *Stewart zone* materials is that any *Stewart zone topsoil sand* will remain stable over any *Stewart zone blinding sand*, and this in turn will remain stable over any *Stewart zone trench gravel* (Figure 7.3 shows plots of typical materials with their D_{15}, D_{25}, D_{35}, D_{65}, D_{75} and D_{85} values indicated)

4. Where appropriate, because of the local supply situation, advantage can be taken of the reliably small perforations in plastic drainage pipes to allow the use of a suitable, washed grit, or washed concreting sand, immediately over the pipe. For this the appropriate D_{85}, D_{75} or D_{65} of the backfill material should exceed 4 mm ($^5/_{32}$ in), i.e. twice the maximum width of the pipe perforations. However, because of the tendency for the particles in loose grits and concreting sands to segregate during handling, a good deal of the fine material may weep through into the pipe before a stable, coarse-particle envelope is established around the pipe. In practice, therefore, it is usually more expedient to search widely for a *Stewart zone trench gravel* for this purpose, especially as this type of material is also likely to be required on site for any associated system of sand/gravel slits.

5. For clay tiles the problem is the possibility of pipe misalignment, and for this reason only, the normal practice of using 20–32 mm ($^3/_4$–1$^1/_4$ in) stone can be justified, but an additional blinding layer of *trench gravel* will then be required to allow a *blinding sand* to continue the permeable link through to the topsoil.

6. Where sand is intended to form a permeable link through the topsoil, the sustained permeability of this link may be threatened by the activity of earthworms consuming the sand and mixing it with the adjacent soil. In this position, however, we should also avoid too open a material, such as a 10–15 mm ($^3/_8$–$^5/_8$ in) gravel which earthworms can squeeze through, plugging the pores with fine soil as they go. In this situation a *blinding sand* has the advantage of being dominated by pores too small for earthworms to squeeze through yet it is mainly made up of particles larger than 0.5–0.7 mm which are too large for most earthworms to consume.

Gravels for use as permeable fill in slit and pipe trenches and drainage beds

These are typically the *Stewart zone trench gravels*, single sized 10-mm ($^3/_8$-in) aggregate with D_{50} between 4 and 9 mm and D_{90}/D_{10} less than 6 (e.g. SN16 in Table 7.1 and Figure 7.3). In sports-turf drainage there is seldom a need to contemplate the use of anything larger. To do so is to invite problems of infiltration by soil and the need for extra blinding layers.

Such gravels are used under sports turf for several purposes:

- as a drainage bed beneath a specially constructed topsoil;
- as backfill immediately over perforated plastic drainage pipes;
- as the gravel fill in pipeless drainage channels;
- as the gravel layer in two-part sand/gravel slits.

A useful feature of the *Stewart zone trench gravels* already pointed out (page 117) is that every centimetre depth of gravel used at the bottom of a normal two-part slit allows for an additional one metre run between interception pipe laterals.

Soil, bound by grass roots, seems generally to remain stable except where there is active redistribution by earthworms. However, where soil is liable to lie wet, as beneath a gravel bed,

some regard should be paid to the extent to which the D_{85} of the soil is less than a quarter of the D_{15} of the adjacent gravel. If this indicates the likelihood of soil infiltration it may be necessary to blind the soil with an appropriate *blinding sand*, or a synthetic filter fabric which has similar blinding properties. Only where there is a real risk of ground water surging up from below, as on a flood plain or a lowland coastal site, is it sometimes necessary to contemplate extending the use of synthetic filter fabrics to lining the walls of drainage trenches.

Soils will increase in stability according to clay content and degree of water-stable granulation. However, where silt (SN20 in Table 7.1) or fine sand forms the bulk of the soil, a check should be made on the nature of the backfill over the pipe and in the other drainage trenches to ensure that the soil will not infilter laterally. For this, check that the D_{15} of the adjacent backfill is not more than four times the D_{85} of the soil.

Chapter eight

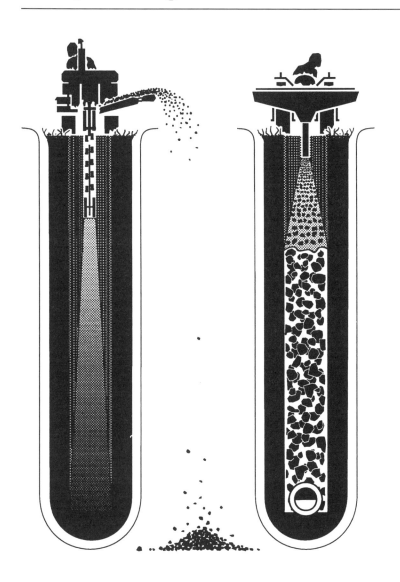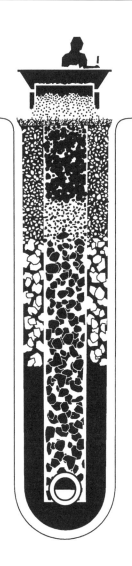

Machinery, special equipment and DIY drainage

8.1 Operations involved

The purpose of this chapter is to describe the kinds of machinery and equipment required for the various operations essential for the installation and efficient functioning of modern drainage systems. No attempt has been made to list or review the diversity of machines and equipment currently in use nor to comment on the attributes or otherwise of individual designs. The many possible design alternatives for achieving specified results are bound to lead to the development of new and better machines as time goes by so that any review based on present performance will soon become dated. What is of importance, however, is the understanding of the requirement of each operation. This is explained as fully as possible so that the capability of a particular machine can be checked against the desired end result.

The following is a summary of the various operations involved in the installation of drainage systems:

- cutting narrow trenches for pipe drain laterals, and sub-surface gravel drains without pipes, on soils that are relatively obstacle free;
- trenching for main and outfall drains;
- trenching for piped laterals in very stony or difficult ground;

- trenching for interceptor drains, catchwater drains and open ditches;
- installing pipes without soil excavation – trenchless drainage;
- trenching for slit drainage;
- ensuring uniformity of fall along the bottom of pipe trenches;
- providing motive power;
- disposing of soil from excavations;
- backfilling, consolidating and re-truing the surface;
- subsoiling;
- applying sand topdressing;
- spreading a sand carpet.

8.1.1 Cutting narrow trenches for pipe drain laterals, and sub-surface gravel drains without pipes, on soils that are relatively obstacle free

The most commonly used external pipe diameter for perforated plastic, lateral drains is either 60 or 80 mm (2 or 3 in); the clayware equivalents being 95 or 120 mm (4 or 5 in). This suggests minimum trench widths for installation of 100–200 mm (4–8 in) so long as the pipes can be handled within a comfortable working depth from the surface of the order of 750 mm (30 in).

It is always advisable to allow a small gap between the trench wall and the side of the pipe so that the backfill can surround as much of the pipe as possible, minimizing soil entry into the pipe drain through perforations or gaps. However, it is also important to keep the width of the trench no wider than is absolutely necessary for the size and kind of pipe used. Too great a width will not only involve the removal and disposal of an excessive amount of soil, but also more expense for backfilling material and additional costs for grassing over. The trencher should be capable of cutting to a depth of at least 1220 mm (4 ft), though trench depths for laterals seldom exceed 600–900 mm (2–3 ft).

If the purpose of the pipe drain is merely that of a conveyor, a closed pipe may be used with purpose-made junctions for lateral access. Soil may be substituted as backfill in place of gravel and sand.

8.1.2 Trenching for main and outfall drains

For mains and outfall drains the width of the trench has to be enough to take pipes of at least 120 mm (5 in) or 175 mm (7 in) external diameter. Where a slope has to be imposed on the base of the trench the depth of cut may have to exceed 1000 mm (3 ft). At such depths obstacles and difficulties over pipe installation may well require much wider trenching but, the pipes being closed, the extracted soil can be used again for backfilling.

8.1.3 Trenching for piped laterals on very stony or difficult ground

Where there are difficult ground conditions, such as on tipped land or where large stones abound, and trenching by chain cutter would be either uneconomic or impractical, there may be no alternative but to use a more robust machine such as a hydraulic excavator with a dipper arm and bucket. Under the worst conditions the extra effort involved in installing the

pipe drains, let alone the expectation of meeting similar problems in the installation of sand/gravel slits, may make the cost of the whole scheme prohibitive. However, before abandoning the project, it may be worth considering the advisability of importing enough stone-free soil to raise the general level of the area sufficiently to enable at least the slits to be trenched in without difficulty. In these circumstances any pipe underdrainage should be installed, and trenches appropriately backfilled, before the new stone-free topsoil is superimposed. As mentioned already, in Chapter 7, page 125, further trenching may well be required to extend the permeable fill of the pipe trenches into the lower half of the superimposed topsoil. It will help, therefore, if coloured tape is used to mark the surface of each run before burial.

8.1.4 Trenching for interceptor drains, catchment drains and open ditches

Drainage of this type is often required to intercept water encroaching from off site, either as surface runoff or as lateral seepage along impermeable sub-strata. Where surface flow is the problem, the width of the top of the trench should be adequate to ensure efficient interception of all surface flow. An open ditch would be the most desirable option. However, to avoid creating an obstacle to play, the trench is usually piped and then backfilled to just proud of the surface with a graded series of freely permeable layers of aggregate. No soil capping should be used to benefit grass growth as this will only impede surface infiltration.

The interception of moving ground water, seeping laterally over a relatively impermeable layer within the soil, requires only a narrow stone-filled trench, oriented across slope, and the trench extended below the seepage layer into the surface of the impermeable stratum.

A safe compromise on a site located at the bottom of a natural or man-made slope is to create a tapering trench, 300–450 mm (12–18 in) wide at the top and 125–150 mm (5–6 in) wide at the bottom. It should be deep enough to intercept the lateral flow of ground water, and organized at the top to capture all surface flow.

A suitable machine for excavation under difficult conditions of slope, surface wetness and substrata is likely to be an hydraulic excavator with dipper arm and bucket. Buckets are available in various widths, the smallest about 200 mm (8 in) tapering to 125 mm (5 in). Machines of this type are the stock in trade of most local contractors.

8.1.5 Trenchless drainage

This involves the use of machines which slit open the soil and put pipe and backfill in place all in one pass.

The use of the trenchless drainer on sports grounds is limited by the fact that to squeeze out even a narrow, 50–70 mm (2–3 in) wide slit without the extraction of soil is bound to cause considerable localized surface heave. Though these machines are robust enough to displace solid obstacles this can only be achieved at the expense of much soil disruption and may well lead to the lifting onto the surface of unwanted, potentially dangerous objects. Furthermore, the simultaneous insertion of pipe and backfill prevents any check on the nature of the base on which the pipe is laid. However, in new constructions, there should be no difficulty over the clearance and re-truing of the surface prior to grassing up.

Apart from the motive power, the main requirements of a trenchless drainer are a sturdy slitter, an efficient device for guiding flexible plastic piping into the slit and, ideally, a two-part hopper capable of feeding in gravel to a fixed height, followed by a blinding sand.

Because of the narrowness of the slit trench it is particularly important to use a small particle-size gravel as backfill to discourage soil invasion, e.g. a *Stewart zone trench gravel*.

8.1.6 Trenching for slit drainage

Objectives

As interest in the sand/gravel slit method of drainage did not receive serious attention in the UK until the late 1960s, the development of special drainage equipment for this purpose is still of comparatively recent origin. The greater sophistication evident in the design of machines now available is a welcome advance.

Our aim must be so to improve efficiency that the cost falls more easily within the range that the many hundreds of small clubs and local authorities could contemplate for the luxury of good outdoor playing conditions throughout the winter. However, even when costed solely on the basis of the materials required, these schemes can never be cheap. Probably the only scope for extending the market down to those with limited finances is to develop machinery for hire that will encourage the DIY approach. In such an open-market situation, manufacturers with existing equipment, developed primarily for the agricultural or civil engineering sector, may see possibilities for a useful extension of sales. In this there need be no harm so long as the design priorities for the sports-turf market are fully met.

The first priority of slit drainage is to install vertical channels, stabilized by permeable fill, at a spacing over which surface flow can be made effective, and along which discharge to a system of underdrains can be organized, with pipe interval as wide as possible. The narrower the slit width, the shorter the run and the more adverse the effect of soil contaminating the fill margin, but the less the problem of re-establishing a complete grass cover. The wider the slit, the greater the possibility for extending the run between pipes, but the more difficult the problem of re-establishing the sward along the line of the slit and, thereafter, maintaining growth uniformly over the whole playing surface. Though various modifications are possible, experience to date has tended to concentrate attention on 50 mm (2 in) wide slits, 300–350 mm (12–14 in) deep, spaced at 1 m (1 yard) intervals, backfilling typically with *trench gravel* in the lower half and *blinding sand* above. The slits are aligned across slope to maximize interception and discharge below to pipe underdrains, running down slope, at 15–20 m intervals (Figure 11.1).

Trenching for slits by excavation

The basic requirements for excavator-type, slitting machines are:

1. to neatly excavate trenches as close as possible to 50 mm (2 in) wide, for depths down to 400 mm (16 in);
2. to remove the excavated spoil cleanly so that it can be conveyed off site without any need for a subsequent clearing-up operation;
3. a hopper capable of delivering and compacting into the trench, gravel and/or sand, in one operation, to predetermined depths. Loose packing and voids should be eliminated so as to prevent subsequent shrinkage;
4. hopper compartments large enough to hold sufficient quantities of backfill to avoid too frequent stops for reloading. Ideally, the size of the hopper should require reloading to take place only at the end, or at some fixed point along each run. The aim should be to keep vehicular traffic crossing the playing area to a minimum;
5. an ability to cope with stones and to slice the existing sward cleanly;
6. co-ordination of the various operations to avoid open trenches remaining unfilled and vulnerable to collapse when rain intervenes;
7. speed, to allow this major task to be completed within the time span of fair-weather prediction.

All of these requirements have to be met either in a series of separate operations or by machines capable of carrying out all, or several of the required operations in a single pass.

Efficient machines capable of completing the whole operation in one pass are now on the market. Their advantages are that they will not leave trench runs in an unsafe, incomplete state, and, given good working conditions, they can slit an entire football pitch in no more than two days. But they have their drawbacks: (a) their weight and the motive power required to move them; (b) the time lost in extracting and re-positioning the machine when obstacles blocking progress have to be removed; (c) the length of the machine when space around the perimeter of the working area is limited. These are highly specialized and expensive machines, unlikely to be used by anyone other than a major, sports-field contractor.

To date the two main means of excavating narrow trenches, 50–75 mm (2–3 in) wide and 250–350 mm (10–14 in) deep have been either some form of circulating toothed chain or a toothed wheel, or a wide, subsoiling plough with a chisel foot angled to gouge out the soil in a continuous broad slice between two surface-stabilizing floats. To ensure clean excavation with the chisel type of trencher there needs to be a twin disc system ahead of the plough to slice through the turf along each margin of the trench to be slit.

Trenching for slits without excavation

Mini-slitting

Slits of this type can be created by slicing the soil apart, either with a disc, or a blade like a subsoiling tine. By comparison with the more open base formed by the toe of a subsoiling tine, a disc-formed slit will be distinctly V-shaped, effective for surface interception, but limited in capacity for discharge. As both achieve their effect by soil displacement the slit faces are bound to be smeared and compressed, and the surface of the soil is bound to be to some extent ridged up either side of the slit opening. This ridging has to be dispersed without adverse effect on the efficiency of surface-water interception.

In practice, slits formed in this way are generally restricted in width to something of the order of 25 mm (1 in). Mini-slits of this type can be installed fairly rapidly, but they have several potential disadvantages that require close attention by manufacturers and designers.

1. Because of their narrowness, backfilling with sand or gravel is difficult and to achieve the necessary compaction may require power assistance.
2. To have a discharge capacity equivalent to that of 50 mm (2 in) slits, spaced at 1 m (1 yard) intervals, 25 mm (1 in) wide slits have to be increased in number, or their interception by underdrains increased in frequency, all the more so if the backfill is changed from sand/gravel to coarse grit or *blinding sand* throughout.
3. Capping by soil, smeared over during play, will be difficult to avoid, and any sideways infiltration of soil from the slit walls into the backfill will immediately reduce their internal efficiency.
4. Because of the obvious tendency for a squeezed-out slit to close back rapidly once the blade has passed on, it is essential with this system that the backfilling and compaction operations be carried out simultaneously. One method utilizes a cavity maintained clear for this purpose immediately behind the solid part of the blade. If a vibrating mechanism can be fitted, this will not only help the smooth progress of the slitter through the soil but can also be used to improve the efficiency of the backfilling operation. The use of a winged, subsoiler shoe to relieve compaction in the same operation is tempting. It should be appreciated, however, that this may result in the backfill leaking away into the horizontal

cavities that the wing feature is also likely to create.

5. There is now the possibility of greatly extending the capacity for lateral discharge of the slits themselves by inserting perforated plastic mini-pipes along the base. If the extra cost is to be justified, by greatly extending the length of run before discharge, the trench base must be very carefully graded to avoid the narrow pipes silting up. On flat sites, where a steady gradient has to be imposed, this will entail great skill in the cutting, grading and backfilling of narrow trenches at depth.

Micro-slitting

Machines which will cut sets of narrow slits to shallow depths are now available and are used for enhancing the surface interception of standard slit systems. These micro-slits are of the order of 15 mm ($\frac{1}{2}$ in) wide, 100 mm (4 in) deep and spaced 150–225 mm (6–9 in) apart. In one pass they are drawn in at right-angles across the deeper, standard slits, simultaneously filled with closely packed sand and the surface trued off by rolling, ready for immediate use.

Micro-slits are an expensive but useful alternative to the annual sand topdressing procedure for maintaining sand continuity through to the surface. They are especially useful for restoring the efficiency of slit systems soil-capped by maintenance neglect. Initially the benefit is unlikely to last for more than one winter season but, if the sand injected is *topsoil sand* in character, in time, as the sand from successive treatments accumulates, it will favourably ameliorate the texture of the original topsoil. However, because a fine sand must be dry to flow satisfactorily there is a tendency to think only short term and use one of the readily available concreting sands that are freer flowing when moist. Unfortunately such a mixed particle-size sand may not favourably ameliorate the topsoil once both are thoroughly intermixed (Appendix C.1). It is important, therefore, that micro-slitting machines should be able to efficiently inject *topsoil sand* materials into the micro-slits they create, even when the sand is moist enough to be sticky. The alternative of purchasing specially dried sand can double the cost.

8.1.7 Ensuring uniformity of fall along the bottom of pipe trenches

Most land drainage machines have a sight rail or bar which will enable the operator to 'bone in' the cutting blades, using profile boards previously established along the trench line. For longer drainage runs, more sophisticated trenching machines can be laser guided, the digging depths being controlled automatically. For smaller machines, where these facilities are not available, it may be necessary to check the trench bottoms using a set of boning rods, rectifying any imperfections by hand. In any event, if localized silting is to be avoided, it is essential to ensure that pipe runs are true and even. This cannot be guaranteed merely by installing at a fixed depth below an existing surface which itself may be undulating.

8.1.8 Motive power

Excavation of pipe and slit trenches on relatively obstacle-free soil

To meet the demand for a wide range of trench widths and depths there are a large variety of power units available. On sports grounds the need to keep trench widths as narrow as possible permits the use of comparatively small, self-propelled units with economical running costs and a low weight to bearing-surface ratio. These are normally fitted with interchangeable chain cutters to give trench widths of 100–200 mm (4–8 in) and depths of 300–1220 mm (1–4 ft).

Where tractor power has to be supplied from a separate source, the aim should be to limit the risk of surface damage by spreading the load over more extensive bearing surfaces, e.g. by using balloon tyres, four-wheel drive or caterpillar tracks.

Trenchless operations

Slitters and mole drainers can be drawn by four-wheel-drive tractor, crawler tractor or by tractor and winch. Whichever method is chosen it must be capable of pulling the plough at full working depth, slowly, evenly and continously, so as to minimize the risk of excessive surface heave.

8.1.9 Disposing of soil from excavations

It is now common practice for most chain, wheel and chisel trenchers to have attachments capable of conveying spoil to an accompanying dumper, trailer or lorry. The alternative of immediate scattering on the pitch is not to be recommended at the slitting stage as it could compromise the need to maintain sand continuity right through to the surface.

8.1.10 Backfilling, consolidating and re-truing the surface

Hoppers may be towed separately or form an integral part of a trenching machine. They are generally available for backfilling with materials of most grades. Purpose-built, two-compartment hoppers, capable of backfilling gravel and sand in sequence to fixed heights, firming each layer and finishing to a smooth surface by rolling, are now more generally available. Without such purpose-made equipment, steps will have to be taken to limit the almost inevitable risk of surface undulations resulting from progressive settlement of trench fill. Loose materials will have to be tamped in by hand, or some mechanical equivalent, and then consolidated by a purpose-made, narrow roller or the wheel of a loaded vehicle running along (not across) the surface of the trench. This will squeeze back the soil to either side and leave a linear depression to be filled subsequently with *topsoil sand* ameliorated with peat, or lignite and seaweed, in which grass can be established from seed. The same approach can be used to disperse the heave created by a trenchless operation, but in all such situations, beware of crushing the pipes (section 11.4).

8.1.11 Subsoiling

As the aim is to relieve soil compaction it is inevitable that, when effective, the level of the surface will be raised. If this is to be achieved with minimum risk of an adverse effect on play, the lift must be general rather than localized to obvious lines.

It is because of these difficulties that the commonly available implements used for subsoiling in agriculture are considered too crude for use through established sports turf, though valuable at the early stages of construction. However, specially designed multi-tined compaction breakers are now coming onto the market. These have a shallow working depth, a clean cutting action and well-dispersed area of heave. All work on the same principle, using an upward sloping shoe or share, drawn through the ground at the bottom of an upright slitter, and progressing through a slit, cleanly pre-cut by a disc. Ideally, the motive power should be a crawler that will progress slowly and steadily so as to minimize the damage to the turf. Considerable power will be required to maintain a slow, even pace.

8.1.12 Applying sand topdressings

Because sand topdressings for grass surfaces that have been slit-trenched may have to be applied in single dressings of 50 tonnes/hectare (20 tons/acre), agricultural lime spreaders have sometimes been brought into use for this purpose but they are not entirely satisfactory, being heavy to use and irregular in distribution. However, there now are purpose-made, topdressing machines capable of providing a very uniform cover over the range of application rates required. Some can achieve this even with fine sand that is damp enough to be sticky.

Alternatively, given that sand can first be metered out dry into stockpiles or windrows throughout the area to be topdressed, the final task of spreading overall and levelling can readily be done by a large, purpose-made lute. Such a lute is essentially a robust, rectangular fabrication of metal struts, rear-mounted on the hydraulic, three-point linkage of a standard tractor. Pulled in one direction, the angle of the scraper bars will help in the spreading of the sand from the array of stockpiles. Pulled the other way, they will tend to smooth over the surface to complete the job of levelling. This is a most important item of equipment that should be readily available to every groundsman so that there is no excuse for a sand, topdressing procedure not being carried out annually.

A wide, rigid drag brush can be used to complement the action of a lute. The aim is to work dry sand down into the base of the sward so as to limit any risk of smothering the grass. Matting is mainly a smoothing operation best suited to a surface that is required to remain gently undulating, e.g. a golf green.

8.1.13 Spreading a sand carpet

In sand-carpeted constructions it is necessary for the slit-drained, soil surface to be covered with a uniform layer of ameliorated sand, 100–125 mm (4–5 in) deep. This should be pushed out from peripheral stockpiles by tracked, bulk spreading equipment. Wheeled vehicles are liable to founder in any deep layer of dry, rounded, uniform particle-size sand or gravel. When pushing out a sand carpet, therefore, wheeled vehicles should be kept off until the sand surface has been consolidated moist. The surface will need blade grading to the required profile and repeated harrowing and rolling to true and uniformly consolidated. A deep sand construction over a gravel bed will have similar problems.

The introduction of an organic ameliorant and phosphate-rich fertilizer reserve to the desired root zone beneath the surface can be done by pre-mixing off site or introduction on site. In either case it must be recognized that, when the mixture is dry, loose materials differing so much in particle size and density will continually tend to segregate on agitation so as to leave the larger and less dense, supplementary materials on top. It is better, therefore, that these materials should be buried at 75–100 mm (3–4 in) beneath the eventual surface so that the bulk of the agitation involved in truing off to a final level can take place in pure sand. Some of the buried organic matter and phosphate can then be worked up from below by just one or two slow passes of a shallow subsoiler, or spring tined harrow, set to a depth that will just avoid penetrating the underlying soil. A final pass across the line of the slit underdrains will encourage water movement in the right direction. Do not overdo cultivation as further upward migration of the ameliorants will be encouraged by the disturbance involved in the final operations associated with seeding.

To assist seed germination on such a quick-drying surface, equipment should be used that will place the seed at a depth of 5–10 mm (about ¼ in) beneath the surface. Reliance on raking is unlikely to be very successful but this is what the contractor who lacks the appropriate machinery will suggest.

8.2 DIY drainage

As suggested in section 8.1.6, the DIY approach to slit drainage may sometimes be the only way that smaller clubs and impecunious local authorities can finance a slit system of land drainage for their playing fields.

Firms that hire out specialized equipment for this purpose have now had many years of practical experience in working this way. With consultant advice and the guidance that these firms are able to give, most organizations, especially where there is a groundsman, should be able to achieve a satisfactory and worthwhile scheme of DIY drainage, carefully phasing the work as money becomes available.

8.2.1 Machinery and equipment for hire

A suitable excavator is a tracked trencher that will dig trench widths from at least as narrow as 60 mm (2⅜ in) for sand or sand/gravel slits, up to a minimum of 150 mm (6 in) for pipe laterals and mains.

Normally available for hire with the trencher are:

- a soil conveyor for raising the extracted soil to a height of at least 1.8 m (6 ft);
- a backhoe with 300 mm (12 in) bucket (for manholes and difficult ground).

Other equipment usually required but not necessarily available from the same firm includes:

- a dumper, tipping trailer or lorry, for the final carting away and disposing of excavated soil;
- a two-compartment hopper for simultaneous backfilling with gravel and sand, plus a dumper to fill the hopper;
- a clean-up chute and crumber to ensure that the trenches are free of loose soil and smooth at the base;
- a means of ensuring that the base of the trench is uniformly graded, even on undulating ground.

8.2.2 Conditions of hire

Typical conditions for the hire of trenching equipment are:

- a minimum period of hire, usually one or two weeks;
- hire rates inclusive of any spare parts specially subject to wear, but not fuel and oil, or delivery and collection charges;
- the fuels and lubricants used must be approved by the hire firm;
- training of operators to be carried out by hire firm on delivery;
- fitting of new tines or blades to maintain the digging chain in good order is the responsibility of the hirer;
- breakdowns are rectified by the firm and the hire period extended to cover the loss;
- damage to machines through misuse or accident rectified at the hirer's expense;
- the hirer is advised to insure against loss or damage to equipment hired and also to cover injury to persons and damage to property caused by, or arising out of, the use of the equipment.

8.2.3 Comments from a hire firm

Summarized below are some helpful comments from one of the main hire firms regarding their experiences with sports clubs and local authorities.

1. Local authorities seem to have sufficient technical knowledge, back-up and resources to carry out schemes to a high standard. Sports clubs tend to need further advice but, providing they have a caring, full-time groundsman, manage very well.
2. If satisfactory underdrains do not exist they must first be provided. To determine their direction the fall of the field must be accurately assessed and there must be a suitable outfall to which the drainage scheme can be connected.

3. If money is short it is recommended that the worst areas only are done, i.e. usually the goal mouth and the centre circle.
4. Some drainage improvement can sometimes be achieved by sand-slitting across the underdrains at 1.8 m (6 ft) centres. Further slitting can be done between these at a later date (but the client should be warned this will generally be necessary).
5. The best times for sports-field work are the end of May and all of June, July, September and October. Most other months are usually too wet or too dry, but allowances have to be made for variation in the normal weather cycle.
6. Most playing fields are quite well graded with a fall in at least one direction but, if there are undulation problems, advice may be required on boning rod or laser grading.
7. Common snags encountered are:

   - attempting to drain in the wrong weather and wrong soil conditions;
   - using the wrong type of backfill material;
   - tough ground conditions slowing down the work and so making it necessary to extend the hire period.

8.2.4 Other practical considerations

1. Before deciding to proceed with a drainage scheme as a DIY project it should be realized that the hiring arrangements, the selection, ordering and checking of materials, the programming and supervision of the work, all require careful organizing and this can be quite time-consuming for the person responsible.
2. To ensure that, once begun, the work proceeds smoothly and quickly, it is essential that a specification and layout drawing is prepared by a knowledgeable person, and agreed well in advance by all concerned. The hiring of the appropriate machinery and the ordering of materials can then proceed in good time. As the day

the machinery and equipment are delivered on site is the day the hire period commences, it is vital that all is ready, e.g. routes defined for the access of vehicles, lines of drains and manhole positions pegged out in advance, materials in nearby heaps, etc. The machinery can then be put to immediate and continuous use. Machines standing idle lead to mounting costs so that in the end there may be little saving over a contractor's price.

3. Always begin the excavation of trenches and the installation of pipes and manholes at the lowest point of the system, i.e. the outfall if it is a completely new scheme, otherwise start from the point where the new work links up with existing drains. If work starts at the top end and heavy rain follows, the trenches and manholes will flood and work will have to cease until the water clears and any damage has been made good.

4. If it is necessary to cross open trenches or slits with wheeled or tracked vehicles, planks should be laid at crossing points.

5. Try to plan operations so that, weather permitting, a given length of pipe drain or slit drain is completed each day, i.e. each length is excavated, piped and backfilled to the surface so that there are no open trenches standing empty overnight, or only partially infilled and at the mercy of the weather or any other disturbance. If work has to be left vulnerable overnight, any accumulation of water, collapse of trench walls or other damage should be rectified before further pipe laying or backfilling proceeds.

6. If 75 mm (3 in) clayware tiles are to be used for the pipe drain laterals, a trench width of 125–150 mm (5–6 in) will be needed to allow access for the individual placement of each short length of pipe. For 60 mm (2⅜ in) perforated plastic piping, trench width need only be 100 mm (4 in). This will affect both the amount of soil that will have to be carted away and the amount of extra backfill material required.

7. Care should be taken to ensure that there are no dips in the drain trenches that might cause silting in the pipes and eventual obstruction to the flow of water. Any such low spots should be made up to an even fall with gravel, firmed by treading.

8. Upper ends of pipe runs should be plugged to prevent entry of solids. Manufacturer's fittings should be used for junctions.

9. Before infilling the trenches always carefully check that the sand and gravel actually delivered is to the grading specified. As large quantities of materials may be required, continuity of supply may become a problem requiring approval of alternatives. Try and anticipate any such requirement so as to avoid being hustled into accepting the first alternative offered. Simple tests for sands and gravels are described in Appendix 2.

10. As a DIY, temporary expedient on small sites, much can be done to improve surface drainage by using a spade, opening up continuous, V-shaped slits, linked across the pipe drainage system and maintained open by infilling with *topsoil sand*. Where the slits actually cross the drain trenches, direct links to the permeable fill must be achieved, suitably blinded with *trench gravel* and/or *blinding sand* to prevent the slit fill leaking away.

Part Two

Specific Constructions

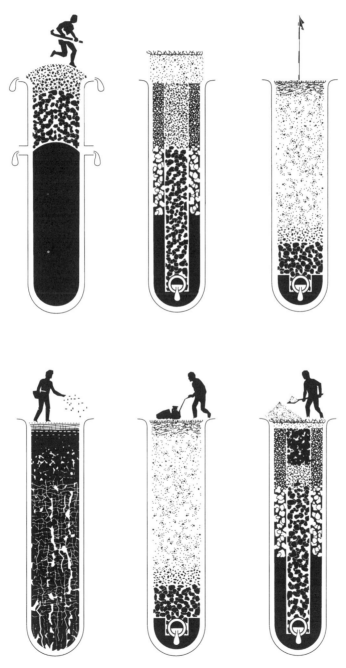

Chapter nine

Introduction to Part Two

The first step in creating an outdoor sports facility is to provide an acceptable playing surface, isolated, if necessary, by peripheral, interception drainage. The next step is to make certain that the soil on the playing area can infilter the water required to sustain grass growth and then discharge any excess in order to maintain an adequately aerated root environment and a tractively efficient surface. Finally, when an appropriate grass sward has been established, it must be used and maintained in a manner that will retain the virtues of the construction for the purpose intended.

9.1 Review of basic principles of construction

9.1.1 Surface configuration

Excess rainfall will tend to accumulate on the surface or within the soil and, given the chance, will run off downhill, more or less rapidly, according as the movement takes place over the surface or through the soil.

We may take advantage of surface flow as one means of rapidly coping with the sort of temporary excess that can arise at any time when rainfall intensity exceeds the infiltration capacity of the soil. However, the mere fact of surface flow carries with it the possibility of the moving water accumulating in local depressions unless the surface as a whole is at a

sufficient gradient to allow it to keep water moving downhill. This applies also to hard porous surfaces (Chapter 13) and synthetic surfaces. In fact, any sports surface will benefit from being constructed with either a uniform, cross slope, or some form of crowned profile to minimize the risk of ponding, at least within the playing area.

9.1.2 Peripheral interception

Encroachments of surface and/or ground water, originating from sources outwith the site, may have to be located, intercepted and diverted away before work can begin on the proposed playing area. Whether the problem originates from water discharging downhill, off land further up slope, or from the periodic backing up of a ground watercourse, interception is likely to be best achieved initially by peripheral ditching. Though this may be converted eventually to some form of catchwater drain (Chapter 2, page 23) the initial ditch system should be left open for as long as possible to confirm its effectiveness.

9.1.3 Soil structure and drainage

In British agriculture, the standard excess rainfall for which we make pipe underdrainage provision is of the order of 1 mm/hr; in sports turf we usually double this figure. In practice, discharge rates of this order can be achieved, through soil to pipes at 5–10 m intervals, only if the soil itself is a loamy sand (more than 75% sand), or has an adequate, water-stable, granular structure such as might occur naturally under worm-worked pasture.

The pore sizes required for rapid infiltration are those large enough to be seen by the naked eye. Pores of this size are formed by particles or aggregates similar in size to the fine sand in sand dunes, but most soils have sufficient silt and clay to fill the pore space within a close-packed arrangement of their coarser particle content. To avoid this a soil would have to be over 70% one grade of sand. Therefore, the rapid passage of excess water through most soils is dependent on avoiding a close-packed arrangement of the primary particles.

A clay topsoil that has been ploughed and allowed to crack down to a fine blocky tilth, or a loam, stably aggregated by worm casting, may transmit water at the rate of 250 mm per hour – a rate approaching that of dune sand (compare SN15 and SN21, Table 7.1). Such a soil, providing its structure holds up, and providing it can discharge excess water to an adequate subsoil soakaway, should never be waterlogged.

However, open structure, developed in loams by a combination of root activity, cracking and worm aggregation, is neither strong nor long lasting. It can disperse during storage and will fail to regenerate if the soil becomes acid and earthworms are thereby excluded. It can easily be damaged by wheel traffic and machinery used in construction. It can be poached out of existence by players treading the surface when wet. It cannot be preserved if the soil is abused at the very time of the year when most agriculturalists would advise staying off. It is surprising, in fact, that any of our pitches escape being waterlogged if they are used when wet in the winter.

In most situations, therefore, the only hope for intensively used grass surfaces is to link the surface directly through to the permeable fill above pipe underdrains by an adequate and reliable system of drainage routes. The aim must be to by-pass any impediment to drainage within the indigenous soil, utilizing an interconnecting system of vertical channels, stabilized by infilling with appropriate, freely permeable sands and gravels.

9.1.4 Precise specification of sands and gravels used in sports-field construction

Because existing systems of classification used in Britain for specifying sands and gravels are intended primarily to serve the needs of the building industry, it has been necessary to develop alternative systems for sports turf. One such is the *Stewart zone system*, summarized in Table 1.4 and, in greater detail, utilizing summation graphs, in section 7.1.6. It is to these materials that reference will be made in the constructions described in the chapters that follow.

In the *Stewart zone* system a *topsoil sand* is a material suitable for topdressing and topsoil construction. A *blinding sand* is suitable for bringing permeable backfill through to the surface over gravel, or for preventing a fine-textured topsoil from infiltering an underlying gravel bed. A *trench gravel* is suitable for use as the gravel element in a two-part, sand/gravel slit or pipe trench, or for use as the gravel bed in a rafted construction. These are new terms introduced to improve the precision of specifications and the efficiency of the end product.

9.2 Construction options for sports turf

The main alternative approaches now used for the construction and maintenance of sports-turf facilities are summarized in Table 6.2. Note the logical consequences that follow for construction and maintenance according as the eco-system established involves the presence or absence of burrowing earthworms. An important consequence of this relationship is that maintenance has to be tailored to the special needs of the type of construction chosen. All concerned should appreciate what this implies for equipment, manpower and long-term financial commitment, before construction begins.

9.2.1 Preliminaries

Preparatory site work

The initial circumstances of any site may well require some modification before the construction of the actual sports-turf facility can begin. The examples presented in subsequent chapters should progress only after the following conditions have been satisfied.

1. The land does not require any further major grading, and existing slopes are acceptable.
2. The soil, if required to form the topsoil or to accommodate slit trenching, is free of toxins and other noxious materials liable to endanger players or the healthy growth of grass. In addition, the soil is free of buried obstructions that might impede excavations by normal methods of trenching.
3. Full perimeter drainage has been installed to intercept extraneous water likely to reach the site from surrounding land, making the area to be used for playing-field construction an isolated catchment.

Records

As no two situations are alike, details of specifications will vary and may even have to be modified during the period of construction. Though during such negotiations verbal agreement may appear to have been reached it is important to keep written records, confirmed by both parties. The mere act of committing thoughts to paper can do wonders to clarify the mind and, in case of dispute, such records are often the only tangible evidence of what was intended. For personal reference it is also a

good idea to keep a note of all calculations until the work is completed and handed over.

9.2.2 Options

Apart from sites where a very low limit is placed on financial expenditure, sports-turf constructions nowadays tend to take one of two main alternative routes: a slit drainage system capped by a shallow or deep layer of sand, or a sand soil rafted over a drained, gravel bed. The former is more generally adopted for the coarser turf surfaces used for the more rigorous, winter games; the latter for the fine-turf surfaces on which the impact and roll of a small ball is a crucial part of the game.

With coarse turf, earthworm activity should be encouraged for its beneficial effect on the incorporation of organic residues, drainage, deep rooting and nutrition. With fine turf, surface casting of earthworms can be a problem, particularly on the specially groomed surfaces used for golf and bowls, but also, though to a lesser extent, cricket and hockey.

If the soil-conditioning activities of earthworms are excluded their beneficial effects must be achieved some other way. Much can be done by constructing the soil of sand and by very careful maintenance aimed at combating the inevitability of mat development which, in turn, will increase the risks of shallow rooting, desiccation, disease and insect pests. It is important for players as well as greenkeepers always to keep in mind that on a matted surface there may be nothing left from which natural regeneration can occur if a dislodged divot is not immediately heeled back into place.

Low-budget constructions

An expensive construction may not be necessary if a site is selected which has a naturally free-draining soil and the users are prepared both to adapt their requirements to what is available and make arrangements to avoid casual use. Thus a worm-worked pasture with a modest drainage scheme may be developed for use by juveniles, or by adults when dry enough not to cut up, and not be very demanding on maintenance. On the no-earthworm side, providing the area is not large and can be adequately sloped to clear excess water by surface run-off, a cheap but adequate playing surface can be created for crown bowls, or for putting greens on a low-budget golf course with modest ambitions. However, the standard of maintenance will still have to be high to counteract the inevitable tendency for the surface to become organically matted.

Good quality coarse-turf surfaces for winter activities

A soil surface, drained vertically through sand/gravel slits, linked for discharge to pipe underdrains, may acquire a progressively deeper sand cap by successive topdressings applied annually. Alternatively it may be carpeted initially by a deep (e.g. 100-mm (4-in)) layer of ameliorated sand. Crucial to the long-term success of a standard slit system is the maintenance of the permeable link right through to the surface. With the sand-carpeted alternative the permeable link is assured, but there is then a further problem of keeping the sward rooted through the sand carpet to benefit from the water and nutrient reserves in the underlying soil.

The sand carpet option provides such a reserve of readily available water storage capacity that the risk of surface ponding is virtually eliminated. However, the extra sand required greatly increases the cost and does not reduce the need for further increments of sand to be applied during maintenance (section 6.3.1). Where finance is limited, therefore, the 100-mm (4-in) depth of sand in the carpet might better be regarded as a 20-year reserve of sand to be used for progressively building a sand-dominated surface by sand topdressings applied annually.

Good quality, fine-turf surfaces for flat rink bowling greens, golf greens and croquet lawns

The sand soil rafted over a gravel drainage bed represents by far the most expensive approach to construction, and though it might benefit from earthworm activity when used for a large area such as a soccer pitch, it will normally have to manage without.

The required maintenance is bound to be very demanding. All steps will have to be taken to avoid surface accumulation of organic debris and the attendant problems of surface-rooting fungal disease and insect pests. Therefore, due priority will have to be given to continuous removal of organic debris and regular sand topdressing (Appendix F).

Any water reserve against drought is strictly limited to what can be stored within the fixed depth of the soil layer above the drained gravel bed, and even this can only be exploited to the effective rooting depth. In these circumstances there is no possibility of any replenishment from below by capillarity from a ground watertable.

A depth of 150 mm (6 in) of root-exploited soil will provide of the order of 25 mm (1 in) of available water reserve, starting from the drained state following saturation (field capacity). Water loss per day from a fully grassed surface in summer will range mostly between 2½ and 5 mm ($\frac{1}{10}$–$\frac{1}{5}$ in) according to weather conditions. A week of hot, dry weather in midsummer, therefore, is a significant drought and, in a sand soil, when desiccation threatens, any adverse effect is likely to be sudden. With a sand soil perched over gravel, it is not only necessary to make provision for irrigation, it is necessary also to plan ahead how best to use the water supplied. For more specific advice on this subject see Chapter 10, page 162.

This type of construction is forced upon those requiring a quick-draining, worm-free, close-mown and smooth surface but, outside the extravagances of professional sport, it can only be justified for the relatively small, specialized greens required for golf, bowls and croquet.

Special difficulties involved in providing grass surfaces for hockey, cricket, tennis and horse racing

Hockey, cricket, tennis and horse racing are particularly challenging sports for which to provide turf surfaces. They fall between the one extreme of soccer and rugby where the pitches can benefit greatly and suffer little from a soil continuously processed by earthworms, and the other extreme of the fine-turf surfaces required for golf and bowls where earthworms are unacceptable.

Hockey, cricket and tennis

The extensive, smooth surface required for hockey clashes with the fact that the game is played at a season of the year when a natural soil needs all the drainage benefit it can get from earthworm activity. No wonder that our hockey players turn increasingly to hard porous or synthetic surfaces, where these are available.

Similar conditions are required for cricket outfields as for hockey but, because cricket is a summer game, most County grounds try to get away without the assistance of earthworms for drainage. However, they are liable to become a sorry sight when the heavens open during a thunderstorm unless slit drained to bypass surface water through the compacted soil.

The pros and cons of earthworms on cricket squares are discussed at length in Chapter 12, page 188. The choice is by no means as clear cut as the prejudices of those on either side of the argument might suggest.

On cricket squares and tennis courts the conditions required are similar, particularly at top level. Both games need a surface that is uniform, smooth, non-slippery and strong enough to provide the special qualities of true bounce and pace. To achieve all this on a grassed, soil surface not only must the grass tolerate frequent close mowing and remain anchored effectively within a compact soil, the soil itself must have sufficient clay to strengthen the compact surface against deformation. Thus drainage through surfaces of this type can virtually be discounted when prepared for play.

Though the soil requirements for cricket and tennis are very demanding they do not preclude the retention of an earthworm population. Some groundsmen prefer on balance to keep them because of their beneficial effects on root distribution and in counteracting any tendency towards surface layering. They appreciate that surface casting is a potential problem, especially if the soil brought on to the surface is texturally unsuitable for the development of pace. However, both cricket and tennis require dry surfaces for play and these are the conditions when casting is minimal and any residual casts can be dispersed easily by brushing.

Because of the extreme hardness of the ball used for cricket the soil-binding strength required makes a clay content over 25–30% a major objective. If this is a feature of the local soil then the topdressing involved in surface renovation may well be left to the earthworms to provide in their peak phase of casting during the warm, moist conditions of autumn. But if the local soil is low in clay then a suitably clay-rich topdressing may have to be imported and problems may well arise over poor surface integration when incompatible materials are allowed to form layers, liable to crack apart on drying (Chapter 12).

These problems also occur on the special courts used for major lawn tennis tournaments but such courts provide an inappropriate model for others to try and emulate as they tend to be used for only two or three weeks each year. Elsewhere a compromise should be accepted between the occasional hazard of a bad bounce off an undispersed cast and the work done by earthworms to keep the soil in good condition below ground. As so much is involved in the preparation and maintenance of the special turf surfaces required for hockey, cricket and tennis, consideration should be given to the desirability of providing alternative, synthetic surfaces to protect the grass surfaces from excessive use.

Horse racing

A galloping horse puts tremendous strain on its own legs and on the shear strength of the turf. A soft, giving surface will cushion impact but may leave a hoof-print depression six inches or more deep. A firm surface will benefit forward movement but, if too hard, will jar joints severely on impact.

Judging from the extreme contrast seen in 1967 between the worm-worked soil profile at Newmarket and the worm deficient soil profile at The Curragh, there would appear to have been no consensus of view at that time in the horse racing world on which type of soil is best for horse racing. If the thick turf at Newmarket gave way it would expose a very well granulated soil underneath, excellent for drainage but possibly a little too soft to be ideal for traction. At The Curragh, the root-bound mat of unincorporated organic debris would have been like a cushioning layer of foam rubber over the compact mineral soil beneath. This may have become soggy after heavy rain descended but would have provided the house with a shock-free landing and a firm, though turf-shearing, take-off.

We still need to know which of these two very contrasting surfaces the horses prefer and how well they do if brought up and trained predominantly on one type of soil rather than the other. Only when we know this can we logically advise on the best way to construct and maintain a race course.

Chapter ten

The sand-over-gravel approach, typically for bowling greens and golf greens

10.1 Introduction

Where there is a need for rapid drainage, approaching 25 mm (1 in) per hour, and a true, uniform, fine-turf surface over which a ball will roll easily and predictably, this can be achieved only by a well-maintained sand soil, rafted over a drained gravel bed. Such a sand soil is unlikely to exceed 400 mm (16 in) in depth and will provide only a maximum of 14 days water supply to meet peak demand in summer. With this type of construction, therefore, it is essential to make provision for efficient irrigation.

Cheaper alternatives are described in section 11.2. It is appropriate only where a sloped or undulating surface is an acceptable feature of the game and combines limited infiltration and discharge to underdrains with efficient shedding of surface water to peripheral soakaways or ditches. The overall rate of discharge through the soil is unlikely to be more than a tenth of that of a gravel rafted construction, the rest being cleared, like storm water, over the surface. However, it is less dependent than a rafted construction on special provision for irrigation as the grass can root through any shallow carpet of sand to make use of the water stored in the underlying soil.

10.2 Sand-over-gravel approach for fine turf

A sand soil, rafted over a drained gravel bed, has special problems of its own as well as problems it shares with any other constructions in which the rooting medium is made up predominantly of sand.

10.2.1 General principles

Depth of sand soil

One effect of the layered nature of this construction is that the finer pore system of the sand will accumulate infiltered water to the full depth of its critical tension before shunting excess through to the air-filled pores of the gravel drainage bed. The gravel layer acts like an air lock, creating a perched watertable in the sand above. To obtain maximum benefit for

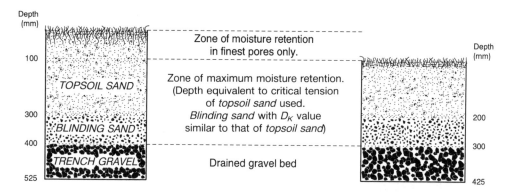

(a) Construction requiring moist weather conditions for seed germination but, thereafter, more favourable to deeper rooting and less favourable to moss.

(b) Construction encouraging moist surface favourable to seed germination but, thereafter, liable to discourage deep rooting and encourage moss.

FIGURE 10.1 Moisture profiles in sand soils, on level sites, rafted over gravel. (a) Deeper rooted, less matted turf. (b) Shallow, root-matted, turf. Initially, water applied to the surface of either soil will tend to accumulate to critical tension depth within the range of pore sizes present in the combined topsoil and blinding layers. Only as this layer is filled, to the extent that air entrapment and pore size allows, will excess then be shunted through the large-pore system of the gravel bed and onwards to underdrains. So long as the gravel bed remains sufficiently air-locked to form a capillary break at the sand/gravel interface, water within the critical tension zone of the sand layer will be retained after drainage from the gravel bed has ceased.

Where provision is to be made for sub-irrigation up through the gravel bed, there are advantages to be had from making provision for controlled air-venting from the top of the gravel.

water storage the sand soil should be built up to a height close to three-quarters of its critical tension (to predict, see Chapter 7, page 118). Under these circumstances the construction will combine the benefits of an even moisture profile with maximum water storage capacity and efficient clearance of excess (Figure 10.1). Too shallow a depth, i.e. half the critical tension of the sand used to form the topsoil or less, will encourage the persistence of surface wetness after rain, especially in winter, and will not increase the reserve of stored water with which to avoid the ill-effects of desiccation during drought. Though this tendency for surface wetness to persist will assist sward establishment, by encouraging rapid and uniform seed germination, it will do likewise for weeds and moss. Too great a depth of soil

over the gravel bed, i.e. a depth greater than the critical tension of the sand used to form the topsoil, will not increase the water storage capacity but merely place the stored water reserve further beneath the surface. The surface will then tend to dry off rapidly, becoming loose and difficult for the establishment of new grass from seed.

As no natural sand is likely to be formed of particles all exactly the same in size and shape, heterogeneous packing will ensure at least a two-fold range in pore size and a diffuse upper boundary to the water storage zone (see Figure 4.3c where the situation in columns of two different sands is quantitatively described). Soil depth to gravel surface, therefore, is bound to be a compromise, though the critical tension of the sand that dominates the topsoil will be the main consideration. Other factors will include the need to allow for long-term settlement, the need on some surfaces to incorporate slopes, and the need to allow for the balance likely to be struck between removals and additions in the course of maintenance.

Providing for slope

To construct the sloping surfaces required for golf greens and crown bowls there would appear to be two variations possible in the sand soil over gravel approach:

1. keep the surface of the gravel bed horizontal and vary both the depth and the character of the overlying soil;
2. incorporate the required undulations in the construction of the gravel bed and then make the overlying soil uniform in character and uniform in depth.

The first option requires the high spots to be created, either by an additional layer of finer textured sand, or by more of the initial fine sand suitably ameliorated with soil. In either case the effect will be to raise the level of the stored-water zone, coincident with the elevation of the surface.

The second option will require insertion of vertical barriers of polythene sheet around contours, e.g. at 100 mm (4 in) height intervals, to isolate the zones with potential for water storage in the elevated areas. Without such barriers water retained in the pore space would tend to be dragged away, downslope, leaving the high spots dry.

However, neither approach is likely to be entirely successful without further adjustments during maintenance: for example, local modification of the texture of the surface by careful choice of topdressing, especially when this can be incorporated after hollow-tine spiking.

Type of sand

As no element of bounce is favoured either in golf or bowls, the sand forming the mineral skeleton of the topsoil should be spherical and of uniform particle size so as to be yielding enough to deaden bounce on impact.

The grade of sand chosen to form the topsoil should fall well within the *topsoil sand* category in the *Stewart zone* system. If the D_K value (Chapter 7, page 118) is close to 0.170 mm, as might be the case for a fine *topsoil sand*, or 0.220 mm, as might be the case for a medium *topsoil sand*, then the surface should be built up to 350 mm (14 in) or 270 mm (10½ in) respectively. But note, within these overall construction depths the 100 mm (4 in) of *blinding sand* is likely to be included (Chapter 7, page 120). To allow for long-term settlement the initial depths might be increased by a further 10-20%, according as the initial soil is organic rich and/or unconsolidated.

Despite the old prejudice against using even slightly calcareous sands on fine turf, many fine greens have been created and subsequently topdressed with local dune sand of this type; those at Portrush in Northern Ireland and Newquay in Cornwall, being very good examples. The prejudice against calcareous sands has merit in so far as lime encourages earthworms, but a sudden change in pH upwards may also allow *Ophiobolus* patch disease to flourish temporarily. This disease seems to behave like an opportunist, flourishing temporarily in an immature soil, or when a sudden change in the chemistry of the soil environment upsets the existing microbial community and presents it with an opportunity to flourish. If it does manage to invade then it may give trouble for a few years before being subdued again by the longer-term, competitive efficiency of other micro-organisms.

There is much to be said for aiming at consistency in the sand used for construction and subsequent topdressing. This will avoid both the adverse effects of soil layering and also any risk of upsetting an established, healthy equilibrium in the biology of the soil. The aim should be to select, at time of construction, sands that are not only cheap and meet the necessary physical requirements but also afford the prospect of long-term availability; keeping in mind the years of topdressing that lie beyond the initial task of construction.

Consolidation during construction

To limit the risk of subsequent settlement upsetting the desired final levels, it is important to take care over the initial consolidation of the construction layers. This can best be achieved by wetting up from below (section 10.4), but where the necessary facilities for sub-irrigation are not available, settlement may well continue into the first year following construction. Saturated or completely dry sand settles well but moist sand is very sticky and needs a great deal of heeling and prodding to ease the sand particles into a stable, close-packed arrangement. Until this is achieved any surface application of water may lead to the soggy feel of a surface buoyed up by trapped air. It is for this reason that each 100–150 mm (4–6 in) layer of sand should be well consolidated before another layer is built on above.

Problems at the perimeter

If, around the periphery, the sand of the green abuts a vertical face of fine-textured soil there will be a tendency for the finer pores in the soil to abstract water from the coarser pores in the sand. To protect against any consequent risk of localized desiccation, consideration should be given to inserting a vertical plastic barrier between the soil and the sand. This need only extend from just below the surface to the full depth of the sand/soil junction (W in Figure 10.2), but if it extends to the whole depth of the excavation, it will also protect the gravel bed from the lateral incursion of soil.

Ameliorating the sand

Any soil or organic supplements should not be added in quantities likely to take over physical control of the medium, i.e. no more than 15% silt plus clay, or 10% organic matter, both estimated as percentage dry weight. Horticultural lignite can provide a durable, particulate, organic source which, unlike coal, its harder more fully carbonized relative, is not biologically inert and seems to release enough nitrogen and phosphate to encourage root branching in its vicinity. Seaweed meal, and other properly prepared organic residues, can provide a lush, biologically controlled, wide spectrum, slow release source of nutrients, valuable in a sandy medium which is not well endowed with mechanisms for soluble nutrient retention. A good topsoil might appear to be a cheaper alternative but it will be of value only so long as it retains its water-stable, granular structure. In the longer term the granular structure will collapse as the organic binding agents are dissipated by microbial decay and there are no earthworms to achieve the necessary restructuring. As a result the fine-particle components will then be free to migrate and may then block the free-draining pore space.

Grassing up

Choosing between direct seeding and turfing
For instant, visual effect, e.g. to discourage vandalism, turfing has much to commend it, but in the time taken to achieve a top quality playing surface, there is unlikely to be much difference between starting from direct seeding on site and starting from bought-in turf, provided conditions are ideal for establishment either way. The problem with seed is to get rapid, uniform germination, especially on a very sandy soil where there is always the added hazard of windblow, should the surface be allowed to dry out. Use of pre-germinated seed may shorten the period of anxiety but, having germinated, the seedling must not be left to desiccate. Part of the problem with turf is that not only must the species be appropriate but so must the soil that comes with it. A loam or organic-rich medium may be excellent for turf production but as a cap over the surface it may

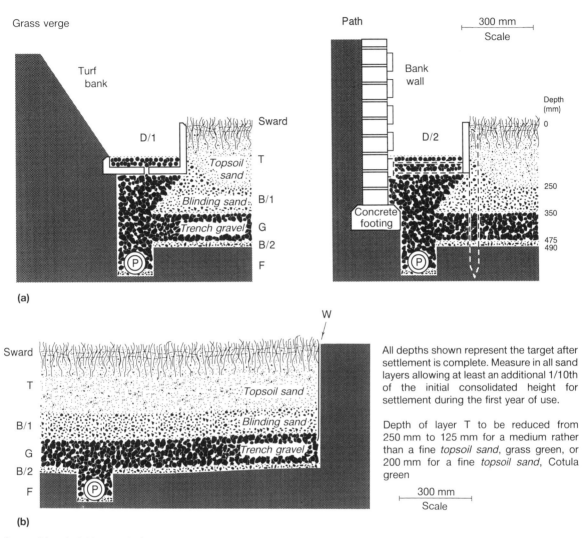

All depths shown represent the target after settlement is complete. Measure in all sand layers allowing at least an additional 1/10th of the initial consolidated height for settlement during the first year of use.

Depth of layer T to be reduced from 250 mm to 125 mm for a medium rather than a fine *topsoil sand*, grass green, or 200 mm for a fine *topsoil sand*, Cotula green

General key to letter symbols

For bowls, alternative designs for the banks are shown. Limitations on the height and slope of the turf bank and the arrangment of slats on the bank wall feature in the rules of the game but those illustrated are typical of what is acceptable.

D/1 and D/2 illustrate possible acceptable alternatives for ditch design and construction. D/1 utilizes precast, interlocking, concrete, channel units, provided with drainage holes. D/2 utilizes pre-treated, wooden, ditch boards, held in place, at 1.5 m (5 ft) intervals, by wooden pegs and cross-pieces.

W   Plastic liner to prevent surrounding soil withdrawing stored water from the sand topsoil of the green.

P   ±75 mm pipe bedded in *Stewart zone blinding sand*

B/2   15 mm layer of *Stewart zone blinding sand*, or synthetic fabric filter.

B/1   100 mm layer of *Stewart zone blinding sand*.

F   Formation soil.

G   ±125 mm layer of *Stewart zone trench gravel* continuous with gravel fill in drain trenches.

T   250 mm layer of *Stewart zone topsoil sand*, plus organic and mineral supplements.

FIGURE 10.2 Construction diagrams for putting and bowling greens: (a) bowls; (b) golf.

not benefit the performance of the soil already *in situ*. This is particularly important where the soil on site is necessarily very sandy to assist with drainage or, as for cricket (section 12.2), of a clay content appropriate for the development of pace.

The cost differential between direct seeding and turfing is considerable. Sward establishment from top quality turf can easily be ten times as expensive as direct establishment from seed, but this must be viewed as one part only of an overall construction budget. Loss of income from green fees because of delays in sward establishment will not help meet the interest payments on a loan. With turf, play may begin as soon as the sward has been stabilized in place by root anchorage, whether or not the playing characteristics are ideal. The only proviso is that the remedial action necessary to deal with any shortcomings in the playing surface can be carried out by the greenkeeping staff without undue interference with play: for example, core extraction followed by solid-tine spiking to lower high spots caused by uneven settlement, or hollow tine coring followed by sand topdressing to progressively remove an inappropriate capping of turf soil before it becomes buried, to persist as a drainage barrier under repeated increments of sand topdressing. There are no short cuts to sward use after establishment from seed but, since the character of the soil should be ideal, the initial maintenance can be concentrated solely on grooming the grass ready for play.

If the club can be persuaded that fine turf used for sport will require some provision for irrigation then it would be as well to install this at time of construction so as to have it available during the grassing-up period. It will be invaluable when seeding, not only to help initiate uniform and rapid germination and sustain subsequent growth, it will also be there to stabilize the surface against windblow in the event of drought. With turf, it will be there to wet up the soil surface before placement of the turves, encouraging root extension into the underlying soil. It will be there also to keep the turves moist until anchored against shrinkage. (Bounce variation arising from the shrinkage of new turves on a cricket square is discussed in Chapter 12, page 186.)

Turfing is an expensive option. Where economies are being sought, as with a DIY project, and seeding can be timed to take full advantage of warm, moist conditions, then seeding is a cheaper alternative. In Britain, after seeding in late August or early September a good sward can be established before winter and brought into use after thickening up in the following spring. (Further advice on seeding and working up a sward for use is given in section 10.3 and 10.5.)

Choice of species
The grass species chosen must be predominantly vertical in growth habit above ground, yet tolerant of frequent, close mowing. This could be achieved by a strongly rhizomatous, single grass species but, in Britain, is most commonly sought by seeding up with a mixture of suitable varieties of agrostis and fescue.

Recognizing and dealing with the problem of seed size
One problem with a fescue/agrostis mixture is that a single seed of fescue is some ten times larger than a single seed of agrostis so that such a mixture will readily segregate with agitation to leave the large fescue seed at the top and the fine agrostis at the bottom. This can happen in a seed hopper making it difficult to sow a mixture evenly. If possible, negotiate for the two species to be supplied separately, sowing them evenly in separate passes, crossing at right angles (page 159).

10.2.2 Management

Some practical aspects of management are also discussed in Appendix F.

Earthworms

Earthworms must be eliminated from bowling and golf greens as surface casts interfere with play. Therefore, if the soil is to drain rapidly it must consist primarily of sand. Also, without earthworms, there will be no natural agent present to incorporate organic residues off the surface. This means that organic debris will have to be removed physically or cliented and buried by regular topdressing, primarily with sand (Appendix F).

Topdressing

Frequent mowing, plus the surface accumulation of organic matter and fertilizer phosphate, will encourage surface rooting. If ignored this will in time make the sward sensitive to drought and intolerant of wear. The essential counter-measures will include scarification, hollow-tine spiking and again, regular application of very sandy topdressings.

Pest control

Any neglect of maintenance that leads to the surface development of a stable, root-bound mat of amorphous organic matter, or a loose accumulation of fibrous thatch, will favour the spread of the thread-like hyphae of fungal diseases and the root-eating larvae of insect pests.

10.3 Outline specifications for gravel-rafted golf and bowling greens

1. Excavate to form a foundation surface 125 mm deeper than the critical tension of the *topsoil sand*. For example, 125 mm + 350 mm = 475 mm (19 in) for a fairly fine *topsoil sand* intermediate between SN14 and SN15 in Table 7.1, or 125 mm + 225 mm = 350 mm (14 in) for a medium *topsoil sand* like SN12.
2. Blind the excavated, soil surface with a synthetic fabric filter, or excavate 30–40 mm deeper and use *blinding sand* in place of

a fabric filter. The aim is to prevent the movement of soil up into the base of the gravel bed.

3. (a) For a bowling green, install a pipe drain of not less than 75 mm (3 in) in diameter in a shallow trench, 150 mm (6 in) wide and 150 mm (6 in) deep, located beneath the perimeter ditch. This should be organized to intercept all water flowing off the surface of the green and out of the gravel drainage bed, Figure 10.2. The pipe should fall at a steady gradient of not less than 1:200, proceeding both ways round the periphery to an outfall pipe at the opposite diagonal. Backfill the trench with *trench gravel*, tucking the edge of the synthetic filter fabric (if used) down the inner wall of the trench and anchoring with the gravel backfill.

   (b) For a golf green, install one or more 150 mm (3 in minimum) pipe laterals in 150 mm (6 in) wide, 150 mm (6 in) deep trenches, linked through to a pipe main for discharge. This system of under-drains should be organized to intercept water according as it will flow through the gravel bed and discharge to a suitable outfall. If a synthetic filter fabric is to be used to blind the excavated soil surface, slit the fabric along the line of the drain trenches and tuck the spare fabric down, against the side walls, then put the pipes in place and backfill the trenches to the top with *trench gravel*. Again, a 10 mm layer of *blinding sand* can be used to blind the surface of the exposed soil in place of a fabric filter, Figure 10.2. Place plastic sheeting vertically around the side walls to prevent the surrounding soil from withdrawing stored water from the sand soil of the green.

4. Spread a 125 mm (5 in) deep carpet of a fine *trench gravel*, preferably somewhat angular

to aid stability, following with 100 mm (4 in) of a fine *blinding sand*. Firm each layer into place by treading, heeling, raking and making good to appropriate levels. For both materials assume a requirement of 160 kilograms per square metre of surface for a layer intended to be 100 mm deep after consolidation.

5. Spread the topsoil, consisting of *topsoil sand* plus supplements, to a firmed, uniform, consolidated depth of 250 mm (10 in) or 125 mm (5 in), according as the sand is the fine or the medium *topsoil* grade. Supplement below 100 mm (4 in) with 2% by weight of horticultural lignite. The top 100 mm (4 in) should contain the full range of supplements listed below under (a). For an approximate estimate of the materials required assume 150 kg of dry *topsoil sand* per square metre of surface, for a layer intended to be 100 mm deep after supplementation and initial consolidation. Adjust for actual depth and area, then use this total to estimate the weight of each supplement required. When ordering the sand, however, add 5% to allow for wastage. Any excess should be stored under cover and used subsequently for topdressing.

Use one of two methods to mix supplements into the *topsoil sand*:

(a) Pre-mix batches of sand with supplements off site, using the following weights of supplement per 150 kg dry weight (1 m^2) of *topsoil sand*:

3–4.5 kg low-fibre compost (i.e. C:N ratio less than 30) such as seaweed meal, worm compost, pelleted poultry manure, or composted farm yard manure

4.5 kg horticultural lignite

0.75 kg semi-organic, slow release or pre-seeding type of fertilizer, eg. 7% N: 10% P$_2$O$_5$: 7% K$_2$O.

Firm into place by repeated sequences of treading, heeling and raking to re-level,

then roll in at least two directions. Throughout the firming process, try to keep the topsoil mixture slightly moist and as little agitated as possible so as not to allow the lighter components of the mix to segregate and rise to the surface. Check that the consolidated depth allows for further long-term settlement, assuming an organic-rich sandy layer may eventually settle a further ⅛th of its depth, and sand alone, ¹⁄₁₀th. Make up with additional material, if necessary, and again firm into place before checking levels.

(b) Spread sufficient *topsoil sand* to raise the surface to a level 100 mm (4 in) short of the final height, and consolidate. Then, spread uniformly over this sand surface the total amount of supplements required to ameliorate the final increment of *topsoil sand*. If need be, dilute supplements with two to three times their volume of *topsoil sand* to make it easier to achieve a uniform distribution. Then cover with the amount of *topsoil sand* calculated to achieve the required final height after consolidation. Use a spring-tine harrow, or equivalent subsoiling tine system, to reach through to the buried layer of supplements. Proceeding slowly and with caution, work the supplements up through the sand. Aim at an even mixture, getting under the supplement layer so as to avoid leaving any concentration at depth. Again, do not agitate excessively, e.g. by rotary cultivation, or light materials will tend to accumulate at the surface. Finally, tread, heel, rake and make good to consolidated design level as described in (a) above.

When a stone-free, sterilized topsoil is available with a water-stable, granular structure, and known particle-size composition, this may be used to form the whole topsoil if suitably ameliorated with *topsoil sand* (Appendix 3). The seaweed and fertilizer supplementation will still be required for the top 100 mm but the lignite can be left out entirely. The sand content of the soil can be used to cut down on the requirement for *topsoil sand*. For example, if the soil is 25, 50, 75 or 100% silt plus clay this can be mixed in 1:1, 1:3, 1:5, or 1:7 dry-weight, soil:sand ratios, to form a free-draining, loamy-sand medium no more than 12½% silt plus clay, reducing the requirement for *topsoil sand* by one half, one quarter, one sixth or one eighth.

6. After the trued and consolidated surface has been thoroughly wetted to a depth of 100 mm (4 in) by rain or overhead irrigation, and when weather conditions look favourable for seed germination, topdress with a low-nitrogen, pre-seeding fertilizer, at about 70 g/m² (2 oz/sq yd). Seed with a fine-turf mixture consisting of about 80% fescue and 20% agrostis by weight, choosing modern varieties from the scored character list published by the Sports Turf Research Institute, Bingley. Sow a mixture at the rate of 34 g/m² (1 oz/sq yd). If the two species can be supplied ready for sowing separately, sow the fescue all in one direction at a rate of 27 g/m² (¾ oz/sq yd) and the agrostis at right angles, using 7 g/m² (⅕ oz sq yd). To ensure good soil contact and help the seed to acquire the water necessary for germination, it is better for the seed to be worked into the top centimetre of the sand surface and then firmed into place by rolling. Irrigate if drought threatens to kill off the seedlings after germination has been achieved.

7. When the sward reaches a height of 40 mm (1½ in), roll to firm the soil round the roots. After vertical growth has been restored, top with a sharp mower set to a cutting height of 25 mm (1 in). Continue mowing at 25 mm (1 in), twice a week during the first

eight weeks of growth, removing all clippings. After 2–3 cuts, fertilize as recommended for normal maintenance (section 10.5). Gradually lower the height of cut and mow correspondingly more frequently when preparing the surface for play.

10.4 Possibilities for further developments in the gravel bed approach

The gravel bed approach to construction is of special value under arid conditions where provision has to be made both for regular irrigation and the leaching away of salts. It can also find application in the construction of cricket tables, though the benefits of a gravel raft for drainage are much less likely to be required for a game played in summer-time on a heavily rolled, clay-rich topsoil.

The benefits of designs allowing for sub-irrigation through the basal gravel layer have yet to be fully explored. This approach has great potential to assist on critical occasions. For example:

1. to eliminate air for quick and effective consolidation of sand at construction time;
2. to more effectively saturate before leaching under arid conditions;
3. to ensure uniform seed germination and rapid establishment at time of construction or during pitch renovation;
4. to assist with cricket pitch preparation when the soil is deeply cracked and surface-applied water tends to trickle down past the bulk of the soil, instead of invading the clods to wet up evenly;
5. to maintain the exposed sand surface of a badly worn pitch stable for play.

Where provision for sub-irrigation through the gravel bed is contemplated, separate provision must be made for air-venting at the top of the gravel. Without this, trapped air will cause surface disruption if it is forced upwards in large bubbles through the topsoil. As an additional benefit, such an air-venting system will allow the gravel bed to be cleared separately after sub-irrigation, leaving the topsoil wet, e.g. to assist with sward establishment from seed.

10.5 Maintenance of fine, worm-free turf

Traditionally, autumn is the time for major renovation work and seeding. Spring is for boosting grass growth and removing weeds. However, completion of club tournaments often conflicts with the greenkeeper's need to begin major renovation work in good time to allow for a period of recuperative growth before all such work must cease for the winter. The alternative is to pursue a continuous renovation programme throughout the growing season, verti-cutting or lightly scarifying, spiking, over-seeding and topdressing a little every month, in harmony with the pattern of growth, rather than accumulating these tasks for one major effort in the autumn. Either way the players will be affected but, from the point of view of the sward, there is no doubt that the 'little-and-often' approach is preferable, unless arrangements can be made for play to be switched to alternative greens. Much can be done to limit the extent of any interference with play by making adequate provision for skilled manpower, efficient equipment, and the supply and safe storage of materials.

10.5.1 Maintenance that should be given priority in the autumn

Timing

As the autumn renovation work may well involve considerable damage to the sward it should be started early enough to allow for topdressed seed to germinate and establish before the onset of winter. In England and Wales the growing season, as dictated by temperature, normally continues at sea level until the end of November, but with increasing altitude, growth is liable to slow down progressively earlier, stopping before the end of October at 300 m (1000 ft). For topdressing with fine sand, however, dry sand and a dry surface are essential and generally this cannot be relied upon after September, except in the drier east. For these reasons autumn renovation work should be organized for completion during September. At an altitude of 300 m (1000 ft), or in Scotland, or the wetter northwest of England, a start should even be made as early as late August.

Scarification and spiking

Nitrate, ammonium and phosphate ions all stimulate root branching and even do so when present as constituents of decomposing organic matter. Thus, any soil allowed to accumulate organic debris at the surface will encourage shallow rooting, quite apart from fostering surface wetness, disease, insect pests, and slowness of pace in a rolling ball.

It is inevitable where earthworms are absent that organic matter will tend to accumulate on the surface of the soil. Initially this will form a loose thatch of leaf debris but will subsequently settle down to form a root-bound mat. Therefore, steps to counteract this inevitable trend are essential in the worm-free conditions that we have to live with in our bowling green and golf green soils.

It would be best to look upon the sward-grooming procedures, carried out during the main playing season to improve the playing performance, as also contributing to less thatch accumulation. These are combing, brushing, wire raking, verti-cutting and light scarification. Verti-cutting should be aimed primarily at cutting vertically through the living tissue that escapes horizontal mowing by sprawling and should be carried out routinely throughout the growing season, e.g. at least once/month. Light scarification should be considered at best, as a crude form of verti-cutting that can be used to scratch through into the skin of organic debris that clings close to the soil surface as the thatch settles down. Light scarification, to be effective, must reach through to disturb this water-proofing skin, just scoring the surface of the mat layer. Deep scarification, by contrast, should be confined to major renovation work carried out in the autumn and may involve up to four passes in different directions. (On a cricket square it is vital to remove all the year's accumulation of thatch so that the clay-loam topdressing, required for the promotion of pace, can integrate directly with a mineral surface. Thus scarification on a cricket square can involve up to eight passes in different directions and considerable sward damage requiring subsequent re-seeding to repair.)

Solid-tine spiking or slitting are procedures used mainly with the aim of relieving soil compaction but with very mixed consequences. Unaccompanied by surface heave they can do no more than re-distribute the existing pore space. Carried out repeatedly they are liable simply to transfer any problem of compaction one stage lower. These procedures should not be carried out routinely, but with discretion, primarily to help with the renovation of a matted surface or to help with the infiltration of irrigation water and the incorporation of phosphate-rich fertilizers, seed and sand. Gentle pricking of the surface with a spiked Sarel roller to disturb and bypass any developing skin of thatch can help with aeration and surface water infiltration.

Hollow-tine spiking is typically the autumn procedure used curatively for long-term and accumulating benefit below ground. Ideally, this should be carried out annually, including the early years immediately after construction. The aim is to progressively remove more of each year's increment of root-bound mat, allowing it to be diluted with sand as it sinks within the profile, keeping the subsoil free-draining. On any green, the extraction of cores

is necessary where a layer has been allowed to develop which is adversely affecting drainage. However, it can be effective only to the depth of tine penetration, and then much will depend on the nature of the soil beneath. At worst it will merely ensure that a buried, organic layer is helped to remain wet and anaerobic by having surface water diverted directly into it rather than through it. As with all other procedures, check to see that you have achieved what you intended. (See also Appendix G.)

Fertilizing

Spiking or slitting will open the surface to allow, first fertilizer, and then fine sand to penetrate. The autumn fertilizer should be low in nitrogen but high in phosphorus and potassium. Nitrogen (N) promotes lush growth, highly desirable in spring but too prone to frost damage and disease to be encouraged in the autumn. Potassium ions (K^+), though retained by clay-rich soils, are liable, like the ammonium (NH_4^+) and nitrate (NO_3^-) ionic forms of fertilizer nitrogen, to be lost by leaching through free-draining, sandy soils. It could well be added, little and often, throughout the growing season and is applied in the autumn because of its value for promoting a degree of frost tolerance. All forms of fertilizer phosphorus are so poorly soluble when added to soil that they persist where placed and can be applied in large annual or biennial increments. This should be done after the soil surface has been cleared by scarification and opened up by spiking to allow incorporation, and when subsequent sand top-dressing will ensure burial beneath the new surface.

A suitable, elemental, N:P:K ratio would be 4:7:7, **or** when expressed as $N:P_2O_5:K_2O$ (unfortunately also casually referred to as the NPK ratio) would be 4:16:8. There is no real advantage in every year using an organic carrier such as peat; most fine turf swards suffer from excess surface organic matter, not a deficiency. The aim during application should be to work this autumn fertilizer off the surface into the spike holes. Left on the surface, the insoluble forms of fertilizer phosphorus will stay there to stimulate surface rooting. Buried it will encourage root branching at depth; 35 g/m^2 (1 oz/sq yd) being sufficient.

Sand topdressing

Topdress the scarified, cleaned-up and fertilized surface with an approved sand, at something like 4 kg/m^2 (7 lbs/sq yd) if this is tackled only once a year. The purpose is to bury the fertilizer phosphorus, bury any residual organic debris, bury roots and re-true the surface. The sand, especially for the bounce-deadening character required of golf greens, should be fine and, normally, lime-free. It should be of a uniform particle size, like a plasterer's sand, and the particles should be rounded rather than the sharply angular and coarse material preferred by horticulturalists for potting composts. For bowls these requirements can be relaxed a little as a firm surface would not be unacceptable.

All of this will help to provide an open, yielding surface for rapid drainage and fast pace rather than a surface that may settle to become rigid and fiery, encouraging bounce. Choice of sand, therefore, is vital and doubtful samples should be sent for testing before application.

Pace is a matter of sward composition, vertical growth, mowing height, surface dryness and the absence of the spongy effect caused by a surface mat of thatch and superficial roots. The holding character required to stop a golf ball, that is pitched high on to the green, is better sought by proper maintenance and correct choice of sand than by the sogginess of a dampened mat. For application, the sand should be perfectly dry or, when brushed, it will smear over the sward instead of working into the base. Ideally it should be applied dry, onto a dry surface, systematically metered out in appropriate sized heaps and then luted into the base of the sward. The wider the lute the

better as it will act as a straight edge to scrape sand off the high spots and leave extra in the hollows, so smoothing out local irregularities. This will make close mowing possible without scalping, discouraging the spread of moss and truing the roll of the ball. A 3 m (10 ft) lute would not be unduly wide for a flat bowling green but a drag mat or smaller lute will be required to accommodate the gentle undulations that are a desirable feature of a golf, or crown bowling green. Roll to consolidate.

The emphasis on sand as a topdressing is deliberate. It may be modified occasionally by the inclusion of a low fibre compost, such as milled seaweed, or a durable, particulate form of organic matter, such as a fine (less than 2 mm) grade of crushed lignite. This will become necessary if the zeal of the greenkeeper in scarification and sand topdressing leads eventually to a topsoil so raw and sandy as to be organic deficient.

After topdressing, the green will appear to be a sea of sand, but a shower of fine rain or an equivalent irrigation, will settle the sand and allow the grass to show through. On no account should the sward be left buried under a complete covering of sand or it will be smothered. For this reason, topdressing with sand should never be left so late that soil conditions are too wet, and the temperature too low, for recuperative growth.

Disease, worms and insect pests

Where drainage is good, irrigation not overdone, appropriate grasses sown, thatch removed and luxury uptake of nitrogen avoided, as much as possible will have been done to avoid undue trouble from the competitive efforts of disease and pest organisms. Thereafter, specific, early, curative treatment should follow clear visual evidence of trouble, using spot treatments when the symptoms are well defined and localized.

For close mown, fine turf, earthworms, unfortunately, must be excluded. Normally this is an inevitable consequence of the removal of clippings limiting their food supply, and the acid conditions that develop in a non-calcareous, sand soil, leached by high rainfall and acidified by the application of fertilizers containing sulphur. In addition they will have been killed by many of the chemicals used against pests and diseases, e.g. benomyl (as in Benlate), thiophanate-methyl (as in Mildothane), and malathion (as in Malathion 60). In special circumstances, generally where lime in the sand keeps the soil pH up, some earthworms will persist and require elimination by repeated application of a proprietary wormicide.

Over-seeding

Do not expect too much from over-seeding into fine turf that is frequently close mown. Seedlings may well appear, borne aloft on the limited food reserves available within the seed. But will they be allowed time to become independent and build up the reserves required for re-growth following relentless close mowing? It would not be advisable to start mowing a newly sown lawn immediately growth exceeded 6 mm (¼ in)! With normal seeding, successful establishment requires delaying close mowing until at least two cuts have been taken at not less than 25 mm (1 in). This means that, if successful establishment is to follow on from seedling emergence, use must be suspended for at least 4–6 weeks during the growing season. Again, unless spare greens are available to switch to, the only alternative is to learn to live with the consequences of the relentless, self-seeding activities of *Poa annua*.

Over-seeding is necessary both to repair damage and keep abreast of the very efficient dispersal mechanisms of natural competitors. Well-managed, fine turf in Britain tends to be dominated by some combination of agrostis, fescue and the natural competitor, annual meadow-grass. The fescues used are fine, needle-leaved grasses, well-suited to cope

naturally with partial desiccation and burial. However, being a type of grass that regenerates vertically from near the surface, it is the lawn grass that is most punished by close mowing. Agrostis and annual meadow-grass tend to escape because they can be more prostrate in growth, regenerating laterally over the surface, or just within the soil. When close mowing is combined with frequent irrigation, fescue loses out to the greater vigour of the other two. The balance between agrostis and annual meadow-grass is shifted in favour of annual meadow-grass when luxurious supplies of water and nutrients are applied and the constant, natural dispersal of annual meadow-grass seeds is not challenged by regular over-seeding with desired species.

There is much to be said for keeping fescue and agrostis seed supplies apart, sowing each species separately. Alternatively, use a combination of two varieties of agrostis, complementary in their peak periods of performance.

When ordering and applying seed keep the following rough estimations in mind:

	Germination (days)	Seed (number per gram)	Weight/m² at 2 seeds/cm²	
			(g)	(oz)
Perennial ryegrass	4 – 7+	600	34	1¼
Creeping red fescue	7 – 14+	1 000	20	¾
Browntop bent	14 – 28+	20 000	1.3	¹⁄₂₀

The much larger seeds of fescue are probably best introduced in autumn, buried in coreholes or slits and under sand topdressing to ensure good seed/soil contact for the absorption of water. Agrostis seed, being very small and having a very limited food reserve, should not be buried deep, merely pressed into the surface at any time during the growing season when the soil can be maintained moist (e.g. by covering and/or irrigating) until germination is achieved.

As *Poa annua* seeds all the year round, even at close-mowing height, and does not require burial to germinate, it is exceptionally well equipped to invade any bare spots. The challenge, therefore, is to ensure that there is always some agrostis seed in place to compete. Hence, there is potentially some virtue in including at least some agrostis seed with all sand topdressings applied during the growing season.

A new development which promises to greatly assist sward repair and establishment from seed is the recent appearance of dry, pre-germinated seed. This offers the possibility of uniform germination in four days without the difficulties associated with handling wet, pre-germinated seed. The dry, pre-germinated seeds can be stored after treatment for many weeks, without loss of viability and, except for appearing to be at some risk from residual effects of herbicides such as paraquat, can be sown in the same way as ordinary seed. The extra cost of the pre-germination treatment can be off-set against the possibility of a reduced seeding rate because of the rapid, more uniform germination.

For equal numbers of seeds per unit area, the weight of fescue seed required is ten times that of agrostis. When uniformly spread, 1 g/m^2 of agrostis is equivalent in seeding rate to 10 g/m^2 of fescue, each providing six seeds per square inch (6.5 cm^2). Use this information to adjust seeding rate to visual evidence of need. For example, making a generous allowance for the practical difficulties of achieving a perfect distribution, try ½ g/m^2 of agrostis seed (approximately 1 oz for an area 4 yards by 4 yards) mixed into each sand topdressing applied during the growing season. Alternatively, apply separately each autumn 1 g/m^2 of agrostis and 10 g/m^2 of fescue (approximately 1 oz and 10 oz respectively for an area 6 yards by 6 yards.

Instant repair of localized sward damage

Fuel spillage, animal urination, mower scalping, weed removal, etc. may cause localized damage requiring instant repair by turf replace-ment. This points to the value of a small area of turf nursery on site, conveniently located where the soil, sward and maintenance can replicate that on the green. A neatly cut, 50–100 mm (2–4 in) deep, stable, turf patch can then be instantly inserted, using a turfing iron or, where a core 108 mm (4¼ in) in diameter will suffice, a golf hole cutter.

Summary

The normal autumn renovations should proceed in the following sequence: mowing, scarification, removal of debris; spiking or hollow-tining plus removal of cores; over-seeding and fertilizing; sanding, brushing and luting to level out and integrate; irrigating if necessary to finally settle in.

10.5.2 Priorities for maintenance in spring and summer

Timing

Soil temperature dictates the onset of growth in spring and, apart from maintaining good drainage, the greenkeeper can do little about this. In general, growth starts about the third week in March but may be a week earlier in the south of England and at least a week later in the north. However, altitude can have a marked local effect. At 1000 ft (300 m) the onset of growth may be delayed for an additional three weeks, until the middle of April. Therefore, there are special difficulties for maintenance at altitude, both in the autumn and in the spring, and due allowance should be made for this in the late recovery of the greens.

To enable some account to be taken of variations in season from year to year, it is worthwhile installing a soil temperature recording thermometer in an area of maintained sward free from vandalism. In general, a soil temperature of 8°C (46°F) at 25 cm (10 in) depth can be taken to indicate the start of the growing season. However, beware false springs and delay the application of seed and fertilizer until soil temperature reaches the order of 10°C (50°F) at 25 cm (10 in), when growth really begins to take off (Appendix A).

Scarification

According to the amount of grass growth and mowing over winter, there may be some need to clean out the base of the sward and lift any sprawling horizontal shoots. Use a scarifying wire brush or verti-cutting mower to clean the surface top without penetrating the soil before fertilizing to promote new vertical growth in the spring. Deep scarification would not be advisable in the spring as the dry conditions of summer will discourage the healing over of any score lines.

Weed and moss control

Spring is the best time to weed kill as some weed killers damage young grass and, in any case, weeds are most susceptible when new leaves are exposed and the growth is thin-walled and lush. The grass, when growing vigorously, will rapidly fill in. The same can be said for moss killing though moss should not be there if maintenance and management are correct. Moss has no true roots and cannot compete; it can only fill in where damage such as tear wear or scalping has been caused and no immediate steps have been taken to achieve the necessary repair.

If certain weeds continually reappear consideration should be given to the possibility that these may originate either in the topdressing, *Spergularia* (Sandspurrey) being typical of dune sand, or in worm activity re-cycling buried, viable seeds from the underlying soil.

Fertilizing

The spring fertilizer should mainly be nitrogen to promote green growth. On very sandy media, however, potassium which, like nitrogenous fertilizers, is highly soluble and very prone to leaching, should also be regularly applied during the growing season. A suitable nitrogen (N) to potassium (K) ratio would be 12:8. When expressed as nitrogen (N):potassium oxide (K_2O) this becomes a ratio of 12:9. Apply on three or four occasions between the end of March and mid-August, using a rate of 35 g/m^2 (1 oz/sq yd) on each occasion. Do not apply in dry weather.

Avoid fertilizers that include much phosphorus during the growing season if they cannot be incorporated by burial. The buried autumn application will persist to carry the sward through.

Sand topdressing, light scarification and/or verti-cutting

With adequate staff and the facility to put greens temporarily out of use, topdress with 1 kg/m^2 (2 lbs/sq yd) of *topsoil sand* on each occasion after fertilizing during the spring and summer. This will cut down the need for a large autumn application. A policy of little-and-often is to be preferred. As already indicated, it would be advisable to use these occasions to include the recommended over-seeding with agrostis.

Prior to application, 'prick-spike' and recondition the turf surface with a verti-cutting mower or a wire brush type of scarifier to remove thatch. This will also provide a better seed bed and help any topdressing to integrate with the existing soil. However, as in the spring, do not cut into the soil as any desiccation will cause the cut to open up and persist, upsetting the true roll of a ball.

Prior to mowing, always give consideration to grooming. That means not just verti-cutting but combing and brushing to lift thatch or sprawling grass up to mowing height. For best effect, and certainly when preparing for a tournament, these operations should be repeated in two directions, each time finished off by mowing.

Mowing

Mowing should never be so low as to scrape the surface and should never involve removal of more than ⅓rd of the grown height. Since growth may easily achieve 25 mm (1 in) per week at the peak of the growing season this means that a maintenance height of 6 mm (¼ in) can only be achieved, without weakening the grass, if cut each day, i.e. after 3 mm (⅛ in) of growth. This certainly applies during May, June and July. Removal of more than ⅓rd of the grown height cuts into reserves required for tillering or vigorous regrowth and most certainly affects the vigour of the vertical-growing grasses, in particular, fescue.

Cutting daily at 3 mm (⅛ in) should be considered only for special tournaments, and then, only if the mower is perfectly set and the surface sufficiently smooth to avoid any risk of high spots being scalped. Severe mowing, i.e. close mowing at infrequent intervals, will weaken the sward and encourage the invasion of moss. Far better to concentrate more time on grooming and increased frequency of mowing rather than lower the height of cut.

Where close mowing cannot be achieved without some spots being scalped and others being left too lush, steps should be taken steadily to improve the grading of the surface. High spots can be progressively lowered by extracting cores with a hollow-tine fork and *not* filling back with topdressing. Low spots can be raised by selectively topdressing or by turves being undercut and folded back to allow for extra sand to be inserted below.

Good equipment, skilfully used and properly maintained, is essential. Nothing is more disastrous to the sharpness of a mower than mineral matter sticking to the grass at cutting height. This risk is most severe after scarification and sand topdressing, especially if regular increments of fine sand are applied during the growing season, following each application of fertilizer. However, trouble can be avoided, both from the sand, and from the fertilizer scorching in dry weather, if these various topdressings are washed into the base of the sward by irrigation.

Irrigation

Facilities for irrigation are of value but should only be used to thoroughly soak at infrequent intervals. That is to say, it should only be used for the benefit of the grass to avoid desiccation, to wash in fertilizer or to settle in a topdressing of sand. It should be regarded as an aid to maintenance and should never be controlled by players seeking to influence the pace of the greens. Little-and-often irrigation onto a dry soil will encourage shallow rooting and make the sward particularly sensitive to drought, disease and limited nutrient supply. However, little-and-often can be justified if started before the soil has dried out in depth. This should keep the whole soil moist and, although such a moist regime will encourage annual meadow-grass and discourage fescue it will not promote surface rooting, nor risk 'dry patch' (section F.3) and desiccation.

A viable compromise between these two extremes is to delay irrigation until there is a marked fall in the clippings harvest when mowing. Such a growth check during the growing season indicates that the moisture deficit, though still well short of wilting point, when death would occur, has reached the stage when cell enlargement and, therefore, growth is affected. At this point, irrigate to re-wet the top 50–75 mm (2–3 in) of the soil by 5–6 applications of 2–3 mm ($\frac{1}{10}$ in), stopping only long enough between applications to prevent surface flooding leading to wasteful runoff. Supplement with a wetting agent where there has been a history of dry patch problems. Thereafter, until the drought is broken, apply a single application of 2–3 mm ($\frac{1}{20}$ in) daily to replenish at about the average, daily rate of evapo-transpiration loss in summertime. This approach will not discourage deep rooting or the maximum exploitation of the pace potential of a dry surface. What is vital is the skill to recognize the growth-check symptom and the ability then to react appropriately. With the advent of simple probe moisture meters this could now be more easily monitored.

10.5.3 Note for home-lawn owners

Too often the home-lawn owner gets carried away with the immaculate appearance of the sward on the local bowling green or golf green and jumps naively to the conclusion that this is all a consequence of choosing the correct seed mixture, fertilizing, lowering the height of cut and removing all clippings. It is not always appreciated how devastating is the effect of mowing at 6 mm (¼ in), just once a week, or, worse still, once a fortnight. This alone leads to weak growth of grass, loss of fescue and, in the absence of earthworms, infill by moss, annual meadow grass and Yorkshire fog plus, with earthworms, daisies, plantains, and a wide range of other broad-leaved weeds. Most week-end gardeners would do better to maintain a sharp mower, raise height of cut to 25–35 mm (1–1½ in), and allow clippings to fly when they are fine enough not to smother. Then, in addition, lime, fertilize and weed kill in moderation, welcoming the assistance that earthworms can give with drainage, incorporation of organic residues and efficient root exploitation of the soil in depth (section 11.4).

Chapter eleven

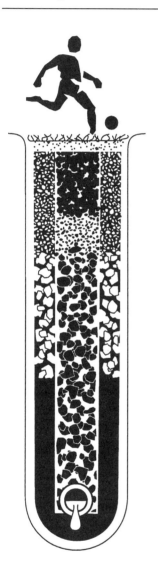
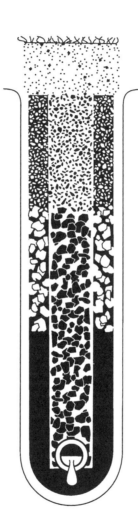
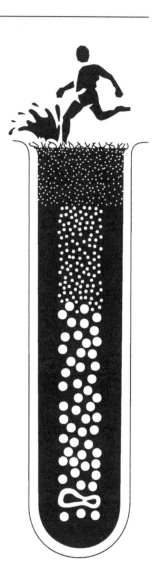

The slit approach, typically for vigorous winter games such as rugby and soccer

Winter use of natural turf for sports requires the surface to remain tractively efficient throughout the time of year when, in Britain, weather conditions are far from favourable. Because temperatures are low the grass growth is minimal, and because rainfall much exceeds evaporation the shear strength of the turf is threatened by physical damage to the grass and excessive wetness in the soil. To withstand the severe wear that vigorous play with studded footwear can cause, the sward must enter the playing season thick at the base and deeply rooted. Damage to the grass will tend to accumulate until repair by re-growth becomes possible the following spring. When conditions are not ideal therefore, the need for damage limitation may require discretion in use. Of the things we can do to help, efficient soil drainage should be regarded as the top priority.

11.1 Sand/gravel slits under coarse turf

11.1.1 Function

A slit system is merely the sports-field equivalent of the mole-assisted pipe system used in agriculture (Chapter 2, page 28). However, in sports turf, because we are working with a permanent sward not subject to periodic ploughing and re-seeding, the mole drainage approach can be made more efficient by concentrating and stabilizing the vertical slit with permeable fill – top half sand, bottom half gravel.

As the first task of a sand/gravel slit system is to intercept excess rainfall that would otherwise pond on the surface, the permeable fill must be brought right through to the surface. To maintain the infiltration routes clear, the top must be kept sandy, either by regular

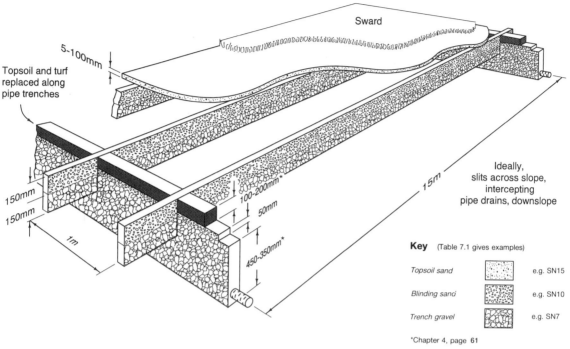

FIGURE 11.1 Diagram of a standard slit system. Note that 15 cm of *trench gravel* in the base of slits allows 15 m spacing between pipe underdrains (Chapter 7, page 114).

topdressing, never more than the existing sward can rapidly grow through, or by covering with a deep sand carpet on which the sward has to be established anew.

In a slit system the function of the pipe underdrains is to intercept and discharge the water brought to them by the slits. The pipes, therefore, can be allowed to run in parallel succession down slope. The slits are required to intercept water flowing over the surface or through the topsoil and, therefore, should run generally across slope. To limit the distance they have to convey water to a drain, they should run across the pipe system more or less at right angles, Figures 11.1 and 11.2.

11.1.2 Pipe depth and pipe trench backfill

Assuming no subsoil impediment to trenching, pipe depth need only be what is required to

provide adequate protection for the pipe from the trenching operations involved in the installation of slits.

The backfill for perforated plastic pipes need be no larger than can be accommodated within the *Stewart zone trench gravel* and should extend upwards from the pipe to link cleanly through to the *trench gravel* in the slits, i.e. 50–75 mm (2–3 in) above the proposed depth of the sand/gravel slits. The surface of the gravel in the pipe trench should then be screened by a 25 mm (1 in) covering of *blinding sand* and the remaining depth made good with topsoil and turf.

Should, for some reason, extra pipe runs be added after slits have been installed, it would be as well to raise the top of the *trench gravel* in the pipe trench to coincide with the top of the *trench gravel* in the slit. This will ensure that water discharging laterally through the slit

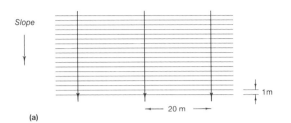

(a)

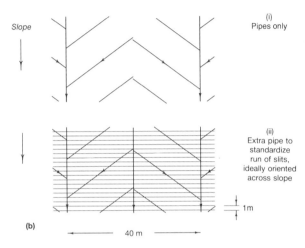

(i)
Pipes only

(ii)
Extra pipe to
standardize
run of slits,
ideally oriented
across slope

(b)

FIGURE 11.2 Layouts for slits and pipes: (a) ideal; (b) adapting to an existing, herringbone, pipe system.

will be in no way impeded as it enters the region over the pipe trench.

11.1.3 Slitting over existing pipe system

A herringbone pattern of pipe underdrainage is impossible to upgrade efficiently by super-imposing simple systems of mole drains or sand/gravel slits Either the slits have to change direction every time they cross a main or, when running all in one direction, they will vary in efficiency because of the varying lengths over which they accumulate water (Figure 3.1(a)). It is now generally accepted that supplementary provision for surface interception is essential on

loam and clay soils used at all intensively for winter games. In these circumstances therefore, a herringbone system of underdrainage is unhelpful when compared with a grid system in which the laterals run all in one direction to mains (Figure 11.2(a)). As Figure 11.2(b) indicates, upgrading a pitch with slits over a herringbone system of underdrains may well require the prior installation of yet more pipes.

11.1.4 Sand-capping the surface

Anyone installing slits should be forewarned of the need to take measures to counteract the inevitable tendency for soil to cap over the surface. Sand and gravel in slits will respond differently to repeated cycles of wetting and drying compared with the adjacent soil. The end result is that the level of the sand and gravel in the slits progressively sinks relative to the soil and, if the sand level is not maintained by topdressing, the soil will eventually seal over the surface (see the sequence in Figure 6.1). It is essential, therefore, that a slit-drained surface be protected from the start by an adequate, overall capping of sand. This may involve either a substantial topdressing repeated annually, or a deep carpet of 75–125 mm (3–5 in) depth on which a new sward will have to be established. Alternatively, provision will have to be made for some form of regular, repeat micro-slitting, as described in Chapter 2, page 43.

11.1.5 Upgrading the original soil surface before carpeting with sand

A sand-carpeted, slit-drained pitch will generally stand up well to intensive use, both in wet and dry conditions, but there have been instances where the quality of the sward has deteriorated, particularly in response to drought. This may arise where there is a lack of sufficient root penetration into the soil beneath the sand carpet.

Such a problem can originate in the sand having been laid directly over a made-up or degraded soil surface; for example, a soil without a satisfactory initial structure or an earthworm population capable of developing the structure that is so essential for a healthy rooting environment. As a result, the effective rooting medium is no more than the sand carpet itself, which may soon become exhausted of its initial organic and chemical supplements and will be very limited in its water reserve. Though the original soil surface in a sand carpet construction is to be buried out of sight, its quality should not be ignored. The long-term viability of the system depends on its biological vigour.

Therefore, before capping the surface with sand, consider what long-term advantages are to be gained from either of the following soil treatments carried out prior to slitting:

1. mechanical action to relieve soil compaction;
2. incorporation of lime and phosphate to counteract any acidity unfavourable to earthworms and encourage invading roots to proliferate by branching;
3. delay for a year before proceeding to slitting so as to superimpose a minimum of 100 mm (4 in) of fresh, good quality topsoil, after the installation of the pipe drains. This would also entail raising the level of the top boundary of the gravel in the pipe trenches by an extra 100 mm (4 in), and establishing a temporary sward to re-stabilize the surface before starting the slitting operation.

11.1.6 Grassing up

The working-up period after seeding a new construction can be difficult. The contractor may be given the responsibility for the establishment of the sward but will be unhappy about keeping men hanging about to ensure that all the necessary small operations are carried out at the right time for maximum benefit. The local authority maintenance team will already have a full schedule of routine work and may be disinclined to take on an additional commitment amounting to the medical equivalent of a period of intensive care.

In dry weather the establishment of a grass sward from seed on a sand surface is virtually impossible. The problem is to keep the seed in contact with moisture long enough to effect germination and then sustain the seedling until its roots have extended into a soil moisture reservoir. This is likely to be particularly difficult along a slit as there is nothing immediately beneath the surface but sand and gravel. The adjacent soil, though potentially a moisture reservoir, may intensify the desiccation threat initially by abstracting stored water from the sand.

To assist sward establishment the main aim should be to catch a period at the end of the growing season when the soil is moist but still warm (section G.2 and Figure G.1). Then, as a further precaution against surface desiccation, cover the seed with a mulch of grass clippings. Keep irrigation in reserve to sustain growth should the weather turn dry enough to threaten seedling establishment after germination has been achieved. No play should be contemplated until the whole surface has been stabilized by a well-rooted sward. Once rooted into the adjacent soil the grass along the slit will be remarkably persistent.

The sand-carpet-over-soil situation is likely to be less of a problem provided the seed is well incorporated to a depth of the order of 10 mm. Thus buried, the seed will be protected against all but the extremes of desiccation and, with only loose sand to displace, there is no risk of a cap impeding shoot emergence. Even if the sand carpet eventually dries out it will still act as a dry mulch to conserve water in the soil beneath. A major aim during the period of sward establishment should be to coax the roots through the moisture and nutrient reserves in the buried soil layer, then keeping

them there by avoiding the surface accumulation of organic debris and phosphate.

On any sand surface wait patiently for
complete grass cover before allowing use.

11.1.7 Special maintenance required to sustain the efficiency of sand-capped and sand-carpeted slit surfaces

General advice on maintenance is given in
section 11.4.

With a slit system of drainage brought
through to the playing surface there is an
inevitable need to topdress the surface with
sand annually. A substantial quantity of fine
sand will be required to make good the settlement along the line of the slits and maintain the
freely permeable link right through to the
surface.

For the sake of the quality of the soil between
slits, earthworm activity should be encouraged
by adding lime to maintain the pH above 6.

With inappropriate maintenance a sand-
carpeted, slit pitch, devoid of worms, will first
become green and mossy and then capped by
an organic, phosphate-rich thatch, encouraging
surface rooting and sensitivity to wear. Alternatively, with earthworms present to continually
incorporate and recycle organic debris, there is
then the problem of fine soil brought up in casts
gradually transforming the texture of the original sand surface. Although one or the other of
these adverse trends must be anticipated right
from the start, in either event the remedy is the
same. An annual sand topdressing will be
required either to dilute and bury organic and
fertilizer residues or dilute the fine particle
content of earthworm casts.

11.2 Possibilities for the use of mini-slits under fine turf

Mini-slits are generally 15–30 mm (⅜–1¼ in)
wide, 200–300 mm (8–12 in) deep, and spaced
200–300 mm (8–12 in) apart. They are so thin

they can be inserted by trenchless methods,
without excavation, and without undue
damage to the surface (Chapter 2, page 42).

The slit drainage approach to efficient
drainage was developed originally to meet the
needs of coarse turf used for vigorous winter
games (e.g. as illustrated in Figures 11.1 and
11.3). If miniaturized, however, it is possible to
conceive of this same general approach to
drainage being used under the fine turf of
bowling and golf greens, tennis courts and
croquet lawns, cricket outfields and hockey
pitches. To achieve this three potential
problems have to be overcome.

1. Different growing conditions are offered to
   grass rooting into the sand of a slit, or a
   pipe trench, compared with grass rooting
   through any general sand cap to the underlying topsoil.
2. Differential settlement of the surface is
   caused by the dissimilar swelling and shrinking of the sand in a slit compared with the
   adjacent soil.
3. For golf and crown bowling greens, there is
   the need to adapt the normal, rectilinear
   grid layout of pipes and slits to cope with
   surfaces that slope irregularly.

On the plus side, if the grass roots through the
surface capping of ameliorated sand to exploit
water stored in the underlying soil, this type of
construction is less vulnerable to drought than
a construction rafted over a drained gravel bed.
Thus, elaborate provision for irrigation is less
essential but, at the same time, a generally drier
soil-moisture regime can be maintained which
is more favourable to fescue and less favourable
to annual meadow-grass.

However, even if a drainage rate similar
to that of a standard slit system is achieved –
2 mm/h (2 in/day) – this is only a tenth of that
which might be expected when rapid infiltration is possible over the entire surface of an
all-sand topsoil, rafted over a drained gravel

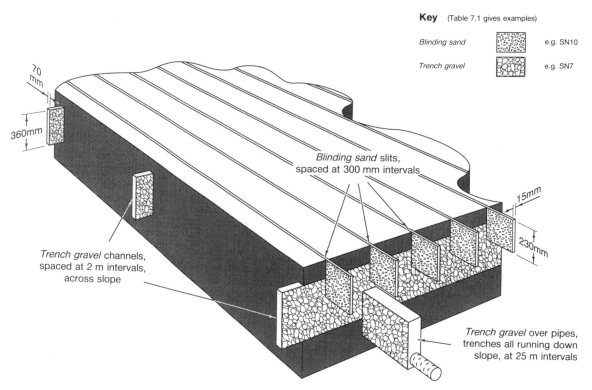

Key (Table 7.1 gives examples)

Blinding sand   e.g. SN10

Trench gravel   e.g. SN7

70 mm

360mm

Blinding sand slits,
spaced at 300 mm intervals

15mm

230mm

Trench gravel channels,
spaced at 2 m intervals,
across slope

Trench gravel over pipes,
trenches all running down
slope, at 25 m intervals

FIGURE 11.3 Drainage scheme for football pitch with pipes, channels and slits, installed by trenchless methods. Delay slitting until surface is cultivated, de-stoned, re-levelled and stabilized by grassing over. After slitting, topdress standard sized pitch with 25–50 tonne of *topsoil sand*. Repeat annually thereafter.

bed. Thus, to cope with periods of intense rain, thought will have to be given to assisting runoff by suitably sloping the surface.

Slits are normally aligned across slope to maximize their efficiency for the interception of water moving over and through the topsoil. By contrast, the pipe underdrains, which are there to intercept and clear water from the slits, should, ideally, run down slope. This leads to a simple, rectilinear layout when the surface slopes uniformly in one direction. However, to adapt such a system to the gentle but irregular sloping surface of a golf green, the slits will all have to tend to follow the contour lines and may not be evenly spaced. Similarly, the under-drainage will have to follow any well-defined troughs that slope steadily in the general direc-tion required, crossing the slits at right angles.

11.2.1 Mini-slit drainage on a plane surface

Because mini-slits are thin and filled with one material, typically *blinding sand*, their limited capacity requires their relief into a linked system of underdrains at relatively short inter-vals. If this is all to be done by trenchless methods, using the three-tier design illustrated in Figure 11.3, it is best accomplished in two stages. First, the pipe trenches and gravel channels should be installed on an exposed, sub-surface layer where any heave can be levelled out prior to the topsoil being super-imposed, and without undue concern for cap-ping. Then, after the carpet of topsoil has been superimposed and stabilized by grassing over, a direct link between the surface and the under-drains can be established by installation of the mini-slits. Alternatively, the gravel channels can be piped to extend their length of run so as to complete the scheme in just two tiers of artificial drainage.

Obviously, regular sand topdressing or repeat mini-slitting will have to be a feature of maintenance if the thin slit system is to remain linked directly through to the surface.

11.2.2 Possibilities for mini-slit and other forms of drainage on an irregularly sloping surface

On a smooth surface, runoff will clear all excess water from the steeper slopes but will add to the excess water accumulating on the longer, gentler slopes, and in the receiving hollows. The only practical alternatives available to cope with this situation are either to eliminate the hollows or introduce underdrainage beneath the hollows, linking this with the surface through topsoil organized to provide for the necessary infiltration.

The simplest and probably the cheapest approach is to mould the required surface from the existing topsoil, grading throughout so as to avoid internal hollows and shed all surface water to soakaways beyond the perimeter. Gradients, not less than 1:60 nor more than 1:20, will probably suffice to provide for continuous flow within an overall configuration acceptable for play.

If an unwanted, enclosed hollow develops on a made-up surface, as a result of differential settlement, then either the hollow should be filled in or provided with effective underdrainage.

To eliminate an enclosed hollow by infilling, fold back the turf and build up with more soil similar to the existing, grading as required to maintain surface flow across the new surface. A depression that is merely infilled with sand will leave the water-holding surface intact and the sand will do no more than mask the presence of the water held above the buried soil layer. Only when a uniformly textured, continuously shed-

ding surface has been established should topdressing with sand be contemplated.

If an underdrain is to be inserted through a fine-turf surface the job will have to be done very neatly. Using boards to work off, first remove cleanly cut turves along the line of the pipe trench and store carefully for subsequent replacement. Excavate through the exposed soil a narrow trench no more than 50–75 mm (2–3 in) wide, i.e. the minimum necessary to allow for the insertion of the pipe. The object being to intercept surface water and discharge it directly into the pipe, the trench need be no deeper than is required to provide for any necessary grading to the outfall and to keep the pipe clear of all spiking operations; 300–450 mm (12–18 in) would normally be adequate. Backfill over the pipe with *trench gravel* to 150 mm (6 in) from the new surface, then blind with 50 mm (2 in) of *blinding sand* and continue through to the new surface on which the turf is to be replaced, using *topsoil sand* ameliorated with 2% seaweed meal, and 2% horticultural lignite or equivalent. Topdress with a phosphate-rich fertilizer, saturate and then neatly replace the turf.

If the original soil is not particularly sandy, then replace the *topsoil sand* at the top of the pipe trench with some of the original, excavated topsoil. Thin, sand-filled mini- or micro-slits can then be inserted across the trench to effect surface interception and link below into the layer of *blinding sand* in the pipe trench. Slicing open thin slits with a spade may well be all that is necessary but may have to be repeated periodically.

As with all made-up soils, the backfill in the pipe trench should be consolidated into place to reduce the extent of any subsequent, long-term settlement. This process should be repeated as each layer is put into place. Any residual settlement will have to be taken out by careful luting along the line of the trenches whenever a topdressing of sand is applied subsequently.

The pipe trenches – often only one – should

run through the base of the receiving hollows, aligned with slope. Any extension of the system will normally require only gravel-filled channels or slits. The channels can be used to extend the underdrainage into subsidiary, receiving hollows, the backfill matched to that in the pipe trench with which it is linked.

Slits to improve surface interception on the gentler slopes where runoff is sluggish should be aligned across slope, traversing around the contour. Should there be any problem about defining a contour it might not be inappropriate to apply the simple technique traditionally used in India for laying out irrigation channels. This makes use of a man-sized A-frame with plumb bob suspended from the apex to swing free just below the level of the crossbar. The two feet of the frame will be at the same level when the plumb line intersects the crossbar at the mid point. Steady progress around a contour can then be achieved by rotating the frame in half circles, one leg, the trailing leg, lifted clear of the ground at each turn. Pegs should be inserted to define the line as you go.

Because a uniform, smooth surface is essential for golf and bowls, the pipe-trenched and sand-slit surface should be masked by a uniform carpet of sand. The depth of the sand carpet must allow for effective infiltration and lateral discharge to the underdrainage system. With underdrainage interception at 1–2-m (1–2-yard) intervals a 100-mm (4-in) depth of a *topsoil sand* carpet will generally be adequate except, perhaps, in the receiving hollows. Above the sand carpet, however, a turfed surface layer will develop which, if fine sand, loamy sand or organic matter dominated, could become persistently wet, especially if perched over a coarser, e.g. medium-textured, sand carpet. It is important, therefore, that the surface should be managed so as to maintain the whole turf layer similar to, or coarser than, the texture of the underlying sand carpet. Alternatively the sand carpet should be kept permanently linked through to the surface by hollow-tine core holes filled with sand of texture similar to, or coarser than, that of the sand carpet to which it is linked.

Clearance of water through the sand carpet will depend on the nature of the underlying soil and the combined effect of sand depth and slope on the ability of the sand to pull water down from the surface. There will be a tendency for the high spots to dry off excessively but this can be counteracted by differential maintenance, e.g. less intensively hollow tining the high spots, or core filling with a finer textured sand. In low-lying areas the sand depth, from the top of the sand carpet to the top of the gravel layer in the underdrainage trenches, should exceed the critical tension of the carpet sand (Figure 4.3(b)).

Do not ameliorate the sand carpet with either soil or peat as this will encourage water retention and risk souring the root zone by promoting anaerobic decay.

11.3 Upgrading an existing pitch for improved performance in winter

11.3.1 Initial state

Figure 11.4(a) illustrates two traditional constructions where surface drainage will almost inevitably break down under the strain of intensive winter use. Figure 11.4(b) illustrates how each may be improved. In one case a rubble foundation was intended to provide for all the necessary drainage; in the other, an agricultural pipe system. In effect, both have been provided with a potentially efficient underdrainage system but neither anticipates any problem in getting excess surface water through a topsoil destructured by treading. Both cases require provision to allow for adequate surface infiltration and the direct channelling of any excess into the underdrainage provided.

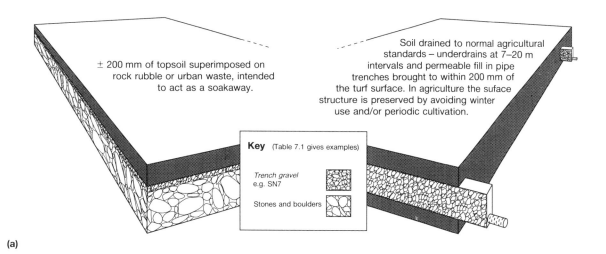

± 200 mm of topsoil superimposed on rock rubble or urban waste, intended to act as a soakaway.

Soil drained to normal agricultural standards – underdrains at 7–20 m intervals and permeable fill in pipe trenches brought to within 200 mm of the turf surface. In agriculture the suface structure is preserved by avoiding winter use and/or periodic cultivation.

Key (Table 7.1 gives examples)

Trench gravel e.g. SN7

Stones and boulders

(a)

Problem: the topsoil becomes compact, remaining saturated for long periods and vulnerable to the adverse affects of frost.

Problem: under intensive winter use for sport the soil structure collapses and surface water can no longer clear rapidly through the topsoil to underdrains.

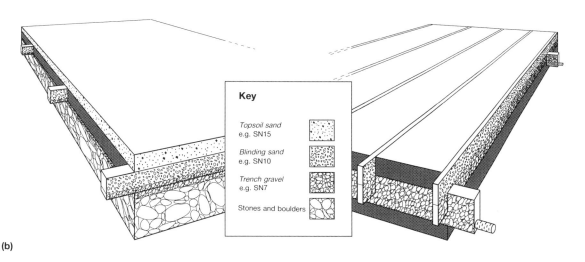

Key

Topsoil sand e.g. SN15

Blinding sand e.g. SN10

Trench gravel e.g. SN7

Stones and boulders

(b)

Remedy: install *blinding sand* slits with *trench gravel* base to bypass the compacted topsoil at 1 m intervals and link with the free-draining surface of the foundation soakaway. Increase soil depth to about 350 mm by superimposing the required amount of loamy sand soil, or *topsoil sand*, suitably enriched with compost. Re-grass surface surface and topdress annually with 25 tonne/ football pitch of *topsoil sand*.

Remedy: install sand/gravel slits at 1 m intervals, clearing excess water directly off the surface of the permeable fill in the pipe trenches. Restore sward and topdress the whole surface with *topsoil sand* (25–50 tonne/football pitch), and repeat thereafter annually.

FIGURE 11.4 Adaptations required to upgrade traditional constructions which have failed to drain adequately for winter use: (a) problems; (b) remedies.

Where a pipe system of underdrainage already exists it may well be intact but show little sign of use. Whether or not all or just parts of such a pipe system can be integrated into the upgrading plan will depend on:

- the condition of the original pipes;
- the extent to which the laterals are all aligned in one direction;
- the nature of the pipe-trench backfill and its proximity to the surface.

Pipe interval is seldom a problem – the discharge potential of the pipe system usually being more than adequate.

11.3.2 Example of an advisory report on two slit systems

Pitch A is a slit system with progressive accumulation of a sand-capped surface, whereas pitch B is a slit scheme immediately covered with a thick, ameliorated, sand carpet.

Having seen the soils on pitches A and B there is no doubt that both require a scheme of sand/gravel slits to efficiently infilter surface water through to an upgraded system of pipe underdrains. Under both pitches there is an intact pipe system of underdrains, but neither is organized to intercept through to the surface. From the dry, clean state of the chambers it seems unlikely that they have ever been called upon to carry very much water.

In A, because there is no stone restriction to deep trenching and the depth of the topsoil is satisfactory, a normal slit system can be introduced without difficulty, and sand topdressing restricted merely to that required annually to protect the slit surfaces from becoming capped by soil. In B, however, a relatively deep surface carpet of sand is required, not only to protect the slits from soil capping but, as we shall see, to deepen the topsoil.

Sands and gravels are defined according to the *Stewart zone* system (Chapter 7, page 114).

Preliminaries

1. The sward on both pitches is very weedy. An effort should be made to get on top of this problem as soon as possible by using an appropriate weedkiller. Consideration should then be given to controlling the growth of the existing swards by mowing. To avoid rank growth during the reconstruction operations, do not apply fertilizer.

2. At A the surface is very uneven and requires re-truing. This should be achieved by minimum disturbance, importing good topsoil of similar texture to the existing to fill in the depressions. Consolidate any introduced soil, supplementing further if necessary to achieve true level, then re-loosen the surface to seed.

3. At B there is a need to increase the depth of the topsoil. At present it is only of the order of 100–125 mm (4–5 in) and lies directly over a compact subsoil with tip rubble beginning at 400 mm (16 in). This extra depth of topsoil can be an ameliorated sand carpet introduced after the pipe drains and slits have been installed.

Pipe drainage

1. In general, on both pitches, pipe provision should aim to support an overall design rate of 50 mm (2 in) per day. Choice of pipe will depend on area served, gradient and function (Table 2.1).

2. The pipe laterals that intercept the slits should run in parallel succession at 15-m (17-yard) intervals, directly downhill, linking into the existing catchment drains that run along the down-slope margins. The links should be achieved by purpose-made junctions causing no interruption to flow.

3. The pipe laterals at A should be installed at a depth of 600 mm (24 in), below the depth of the existing herringbone system. All severed, old pipes to be positively linked into the new system from the uphill side.

Downhill the old pipes should be closed off by an appropriate cap.

4. At B place laterals at the shallow depth of 450 mm (18 in). This will avoid most of the major obstacles in the rubble substratum.

5. The new laterals should be backfilled with *trench gravel* to within 150 mm (6 in) of the existing surface and, thereafter, 50 mm (2 in) of *blinding sand*, followed by replacement of the original turf, bedded in topsoil.

6. Examine all links into chambers and correct any adverse consequences of scour and differential settlement in the pipe trench adjacent to the chamber.

Aim to complete 1–6 by the end of autumn. Assuming the re-turfed and seeded areas take successfully it may be possible for both pitches to be used with discretion over winter.

Slits and surface

1. Work to install slits in both pitches should begin as early as possible in the following spring.

2. The slits should be 50 mm (2 in) wide, 150 mm (12 in) deep, and should run in parallel succession at 1-m (1-yard) intervals, across slope, i.e. at right-angles to the lateral pipe system. Backfill should consist of a lower, 150 mm (6-in) layer of *trench gravel*, and an upper, 150-mm (6-in) layer of *blinding sand*, the sand layer being brought right throught to the surface.

3. At A, the slits should be over-topped to a height of 25 mm (1 in) with *topsoil sand*, ameliorated with 2% seaweed meal and 2% horticultural lignite (or an equivalent organic compost). Topdress overall with pre-seeding fertilizer and then overseed with a dwarf ryegrass/fescue-dominated seeds mixture, aiming to place the seed within the immediate surface of the sand. Make a second seeding pass along the line of each slit and then, rolling parallel to the slits, firm the sand around the buried seed.

4. At B, spread 100 kg/ha of urea and 300 kg/ha of ground rock phosphate (or similar). Spread 480 t (dry weight) of *topsoil sand* per hectare, plus 30 t of horticultural lignite and 30 t of seaweed meal (or equivalent organic compost). Then cover with another 1120 t/ha (dry weight) of *topsoil sand*.

Using a spring-tine harrow (or similar), set to skim over the top of the original, buried soil, work the organic material up towards the surface. Two slow passes at right angles should be adequate. The aim is to mix but not bring very much of the buried organic matter right through to the surface. Roll and re-level repeatedly, using machinery that will avoid rutting. Use a 3 m (9–12 ft wide) bar-grader to achieve the final, consolidated, true surface. Protect against windblow by watering if necessary.

Topdress with pre-seeding fertilizer and seed with a dwarf ryegrass/fescue-dominated seeds mixture. Insert seed by means that will work most of the seed some 10 mm (¼–½ in) under the surface. Roll to consolidate sand around the buried seed.

5. After seed germination, maintain both pitches as prescribed in the attached maintenance schedule (section 11.4).

6. Slitting and surface renewal may be achieved by the autumn, but ideally no play should be allowed on either pitch until the following year. Growing season conditions will be required to develop a vigorous, thick sward and, in the case of pitch A, to apply protective topdressings of *topsoil sand*. These sand topdressings may well have to be concentrated first in the vicinity of the slits so as to counteract any tendency for the surface in this area to slump. And note, even on pitch B, where a deep, sand carpet will have been introduced, there will still also be a need for annual topdressings of sand to counteract any tendency to develop an organic or fine-soil cap (section 6.3.1).

11.4 General guidance on coarse turf maintenance where, on balance, earthworm activity is considered to be potentially beneficial

Greater discretion in use and an improved programme of maintenance may alone achieve all the improvement that a beleaguered groundsman may require but, frequently, some inherent limitation of the site has to be overcome before even good maintenance can hope to be effective.

Before proceeding with any expensive construction or re-construction programme it is important to realize the nature of the maintenance that will be necessary if all the potential benefits from the construction work are to be realized. Nothing created in sports turf will remain for long as constructed unless maintained in a manner sensitive to the inevitable trends towards change that have to be continually controlled.

Much of the advice given under the heading of maintenance for fine turf (section 10.5) applies equally to a worm-worked sward. The features listed below simply draw attention to those which are of special significance for winter games pitches where stud wear is an inevitable hazard and, on balance, the effects of earthworm activity are considered to be beneficial.

11.4.1 Liming, fertilizing, weed-killing and over-seeding

1. Maintain soil pH above 5.5 by application of ground limestone. Where necessary, treat initially by means of a single application at the rate of 5 tonne/hectare (2 tons/acre). Spread evenly in calm, dry weather, at any time of the year. Check pH again after 2 years and thereafter every 4 years. Monitor pH only within the top 75 mm (3 in) of the soil.

2. In mid-April, or when soil temperature at 250 mm (10 in) has reached 10°C and there is ample evidence of renewed growth,

consider if the sward needs weed killing as well as fertilizing. Remedy as necessary and apply the first of three fairly light, spring and summer dressings of a fine-particle fertilizer, supplying mainly (or solely) nitrogen and potassium. Repeat mid-June and mid-August. Do not apply in drought but when rain is expected within 24–48 hours. Eliminate one dressing if drought persists.

Each second year, apply a standard high-phosphate, low-nitrogen autumn dressing (mid-September), on a thoroughly spiked or slit surface.

To boost growth along sand- and gravel-filled drain trenches, consider applying nitrogen and potassium as a liquid feed at low concentration along the trench runs, using a sprayer or watering can. Treat during the growing season whenever the yellowing symptoms of nitrogen deficiency show up.

3. Do not leave bare patches to seed themselves or nature may insert a broad-leaved weed, an unsuitable grass, or moss. Immediately heel back all displaced turf after play and consider the need for selective over-seeding both in spring and autumn. Though early autumn is usually the best time to seed, over-seeding may well be necessary in spring to treat damage caused by winter use. If a machine that places seed directly into the surface of the soil is not available, prepare the surface by raking or close, shallow spiking. On sandy surfaces, roll after seeding to improve seed contact with the soil.

11.4.2 Mowing, brushing and sand topdressing

1. During the growing season use a sharp mower to cut at 50 mm (2 in) for rugby or 30 mm (1¼ in) for soccer, whenever the general growth height reaches 75 mm (3 in) and 50 mm (2 in) respectively. When the

grass is growing well this will mean cutting once a week for rugby and once every 4–5 days for soccer. Remove clippings if earthworms are not active or if the grass is at risk of being smothered by clippings lying in swathes. To cut effectively at a height of 20–50 mm (1–2 in) a mower requires to be sharp. This means regular servicing, at the very least once a year in late autumn, after all topdressing and mowing has virtually ceased for the season.

2. Though worm activity can greatly benefit grass growth their casts will smear and give an unsightly appearance if the grass is cut too low. They can also be sites for weed invasion. For both these reasons it is desirable periodically to disperse the casts by brushing. A good rotary brush or a heavy drag brush can be effective for this purpose if the casts are fairly dry and crumbly at the time. Brushing is most likely to be required in spring and autumn when earthworm activity peaks. Brushing will also assist in grooming the sward, bringing sprawling shoots up to the mower for cutting.

3. Sand topdressing is essential to maintain the efficiency of modern sports-turf constructions where drainage depends on the maintenance of free-draining pathways, continuous from the surface right through to the pipe underdrains. In effect this means maintaining a sand surface overall, or at least along the surface of the installed drainage slits. Slits can be progressively down-graded by soil contamination resulting from foot traffic and earthworm activity. To counteract this, a uniform topdressing of the order of at least 40 tonne/hectare (16–17 tons/acre) of *topsoil sand* should be applied each summer during dry sunny weather. Spread the sand out in an evenly spaced arrangement of piles or wind-rows, until powder dry, then according as the priority is to true or merely topdress, lute or drag brush into the base of the sward.

11.5 A cautionary tale illustrating what can go wrong during and soon after construction

11.5.1 The initial concept

This is a story of unscientific design, inefficient workmanship, inadequate supervision and inappropriate maintenance. It concerns a scheme of drainage for a new 14-hectare (35-acre) sports ground, 700 m (765 yards) long, across slope, and 200 m (218 yards) wide, down slope. The final surface sloped uniformly at a gradient of 1:100 and was made up of material similar to subsoil.

Apart from two pitch areas set aside for hard porous and sand carpet constructions, the whole of the playing field was underdrained by pipes laid out in a herringbone pattern. Mains were all directed down slope, laterals coming off alternately right and left, orientated diagonally across slope. As Figure 3.1(a) indicates, if such a system does not suffice on its own the orientation of the laterals makes it difficult to up-grade efficiently without adding more pipes. This is not to make good any shortfall in number but to compensate for a layout that unnecessarily complicates the introduction of an efficient system of sand/gravel slits.

One of the two special areas was underdrained by mains and laterals laid out in a grid system, then sand/gravel slit and deeply sand carpeted. Initially, it was the only grass surface on which it was possible to achieve a sustained programme of winter use. The other special area was laid out as a hard porous construction like that discussed in Chapter 13.

11.5.2 Ensuing problems

All available funds having been spent on the initial construction, the groundsman was then left to carry on as best he could with two potentially useful pitches and the rest of the area rapidly falling out of use because the herringbone underdrainage was unable on its own to prevent winter use churning the surface to mud. However, when the groundsman began to investigate his problems, he started by looking at several persistent wet areas over drain runs. This revealed that he not only had problems of design but also inefficient installation. It was at this stage that outside advice was sought.

Field evidence and the lessons to be learnt

1. Many wet areas were associated with pipes crushed flat. In one instance this damage extended for a distance of 6 m (20 ft), presumably the result of heavy wheel pressure transmitted directly onto the pipes through the loose gravel backfill. Elsewhere, gaps were found at the junctions between laterals and mains, and wide gaps, up to 1 m in length, were found at junctions along mains. One pipe was found broken where it had been laid across a sharp piece of buried metal. Twelve such faults were found on one pitch alone.

   How did all this come about? Where was the clerk of works at the time of installation? What of the principle of inspection before cover? What should be our attitude now to weekend work, popular with contractors working away from home but unlikely to be capable of close supervision? How could such faults arise? Could some methods of installation involve an unsuspected measure of drag, when the pipe is covered immediately by backfill? Should we require a simple locking system at junctions?

2. On the sand-carpeted pitch the underdrainage consisted of a parallel succession of pipes running downhill at 15-m (16-yard) intervals and 500–600-mm (20–24-in) depth, plus gravel-filled trenches, running across slope at 2-m (2-yard) intervals and 350–400 mm (14–16 in) in depth. Here, seven instances were found of crushed or broken pipe where the gravel-filled trenches crossed the pipe system.

Could this evidence be indicating an effect of downward pressure from trencher tines transmitted through loose gravel? Or could it be an effect of one person's eccentric method of backfilling and consolidating gravel within narrow trenches?

The fully integrated methods now used for cutting trenches, laying pipes, placing and consolidating fill, all in just one or two passes of heavy machinery, may be quick and superficially tidy but who has checked to see the consequences below ground?

3. When a new contractor was called in to achieve a complete reconstruction, a new drainage system was superimposed with pipes running downslope 450 mm (18 in) deep, about the same depth as the suspect pipes in the original herringbone system. However, to avoid risk to the new pipes during subsequent slit trenching, the decision was made to first install gravel filled, slit trenches at fairly close intervals, across the slope, and then intercept these with the new pipe drains running downslope. Finally, close-spaced, sand mini-slits were injected downslope to direct surface flow to the gravel slits and thence to the new system of pipe underdrains.

   Great difficulty was experienced from the start because the trenchable topsoil that should have been installed to a placement depth of 30 mm (12 in) was found to be less than 150 mm (6 in) deep, and there it rested directly on a consolidated, stony subsoil of tipped rubble. The slit trenches were bound to be difficult to excavate to any depth and, since they were dug before the installation of the new pipe system, progress was further hampered during bad weather by the progressive accumulation of water within the working area.

   In this case the slits were installed in succession from the bottom to the top of the slope. Had this been done in reverse, i.e. top to bottom, the first slits installed might have helped to maintain the downslope area free of surface runoff, allowing progress to be maintained through a period of unsettled weather.

Subsequent installation of the new pipe system by trenchless methods was also very difficult because the soil was still wet and this increased the risk of further damage to the original herringbone pipe system. Timing should always make generous allowance for this type of work to be carried out only when the soil is adequately dry.

When upgrading an existing, suspect, drainage system by the introduction of new pipes, it is important not to superimpose the new pipes over the old without first checking that the old pipe system will still clear any water they intercept. Generally it is safer to trench-in the new pipes lower than the old, making positive links between the two systems wherever they cross, capping off the open end of the severed pipe on the downslope side of the trench. However, nothing of this can be achieved if the new pipes are installed by trenchless methods.

Considering the difficulties the contractor got into on the site in question, one wonders where the trained design team had got to. Was it yet another case of a foreman, far from base, abandoned to his own devices?

4. Once the mini-slit system had been installed at right-angles to the gravel filled slits, the sward recovered and, despite all the reconstruction difficulties, the surface performed well enough for two seasons. Then both slit systems were found to be capped over by soil to a depth of 20 m (¾ in).

As has already been said (section 6.2.1), it is of the utmost importance that anyone installing slits should be forewarned of the need to take measures to counteract the inevitable tendency to soil capping. Sand and gravel in slits will respond differently to repeated cycles of wetting and drying compared with the adjacent soil. The end result

is that the level of the sand and gravel in the slits progressively sinks relative to the soil and, if the sand level is not maintained by topdressing, the soil eventually seals over the surface. This inevitable trend should be anticipated, and provision made from the start for protection by either regular sand topdressing or regular, remedial micro-slitting.

5. For the first seven years the sand-carpeted pitch and the hard porous pitch had to carry virtually the full burden of use for which the whole field was originally intended. Despite the problem of washouts, originating in storm runoff accumulating in blocked drains, the sand-carpeted pitch stood up well to intensive use. However, the quality of the sward deteriorated, particularly in its response to drought. This seemed to be related to the lack of any root penetration into the soil beneath the sand carpet.

The sand had been laid directly over the formation layer of subsoil and stony rubble. This degraded material had neither a satisfactory initial structure nor an earthworm population capable of assisting soil development in depth. The effective rooting medium was no more than the sand-carpet itself and this was now exhausted of its initial organic and chemical supplements. The message is that although the original soil surface in a sand-carpet construction is to be buried out of sight, its quality cannot be ignored; the long-term viability of the sward depends on its biological vigour.

11.5.3 Addendum

It should not be assumed that the case history described above is an isolated example. Other sites, if investigated as assiduously, might well reveal similar shortcomings. The money having all been spent, the inclination then is for the architect, the clerk of works and the contractor to withdraw, leaving the groundsman to pick up the problems and the brickbats.

Design is clearly one thing; implementation quite another. Had the groundsman in this case been appointed and on site during the construction period, the story might well have been very different.

11.6 Some other errors encountered

Examples of other problems encountered are listed below.

1. The slit capacity was unduly stretched by not being oriented at right-angles to the pipe trenches; in two instances they were aligned parallel to the pipe drains and therefore lacking any outlet whatsoever!
2. The slits were spaced too wide apart in a misguided attempt at economy: for example, sand/gravel slits on a flat site spaced at intervals of 2 m (2 yards) or more.
3. Some slits had inadequate capacity because of inappropriate dimensions or inappropriate backfill.

4. The slits and pipe drains failed to link because the permeable fill in the two trench systems was inappropriately matched, or the two systems failed even to intersect.
5. The slits were inadvertently covered with soil at time of construction. This can arise if soil debris or heaved ridges of topsoil are present on either side of a trench when backfilling takes place. Mould boards at the rear of a backfilling hopper may then drag soil into the slit as well as sand overspill. A following roller presses the mixture into the slit and this may then be obscured by a further covering of sand. The same risk arises when heavy machinery slithers about on too wet a surface.
6. The slits became capped with soil because of failure to maintain a freely permeable cap by regular, sand topdressing.
7. The slit surface was carpeted over with an insufficiently sandy soil.
8. Precipitate use before full grass cover had been established along the line of pipe trenches and slits.

Chapter twelve

Cricket

12.1 Introduction

In cricket, even more than in golf, the reactions of the ball off the surface form an integral part of the game. If predictable, its qualities can be exploited by those with the necessary skills but, if unpredictable, it can thwart the intentions of the skilled and unskilled alike. Thus the character of the game can be determined by factors that affect the reactions of the playing surface: the weather, the soil and the skill of the groundsman.

The grass is scarcely visible above ground on a Test pitch prepared for play. It has to struggle to survive because most of what the groundsman has to do when preparing a pitch is quite contrary to what he would choose to do to maintain the soil in good heart and the sward vigorous.

The information presented in this chapter derives mainly from a research study carried out in the 1960s and reported to the First International Turfgrass Research Conference held in Harrogate in 1969 (Stewart and Adams, 1969), plus further field-work carried out in Australia and New Zealand in the 1980s. Though the main object of this research was to investigate how best to achieve good pitches for County and Test matches, the field evidence soon showed how variable the standard of performance can be from one County ground to another, and even from one pitch to another on the same square (Table 12.1). Later, as the study was extended overseas, it became evident how vastly different is the potential for pace at Test venues world-wide (see Table 12.5). Meantime, P.L.K. Drury, 1978, County Playing Fields Officer, Nottinghamshire, has shown how big a difference there is between the pace achieved on ordinary club and school grounds compared with that achieved at County level (Table 12.1 footnote).

In effect, the main differences between the highest and lowest standards reflects either differences in preparation time or the combined effects of climate and clay content of the soil. Thus, on County grounds, pitch preparation is likely to extend over a period of 10–14 days; this in addition to end of match, end of season and pre-season work. By contrast, most school and local club pitches are prepared in just one day or on the morning of the match. Overseas we see many potentially very fast pitches based on soils much richer in clay than could ever be regularly dried out in a normal British summer. No wonder our top players require time to adapt as they move from one country to another.

Consistency at a modest pace is really all that the lesser clubs and schools can aim to achieve with only a modest period of preparation. This eliminates the use of soils and soil conditions upon which the development of real pace depends. However, with the confidence that consistency allows, basic skills can be learnt that may flourish when tested at more demand-

TABLE 12.1 Range of average bounce values from 16 ft (4877 mm) for county pitches assessed after close of play on the final day

Clay[a] (%)	Average of 4[b] (in)	General[c] (in)	Pitch (date)	Clay[a] (%)	Average of 4[b] (in)	General[c] (in)	Pitch (date)
37	15	14	Edgbaston – Old Square (6.7.66)	19	13	11	Old Trafford (20.7.67)
32	18	17	Leicester (27.6.66)	42	19	15	Gloucester (10.7.67)
35	20	17	Swansea (27.5.66)	15	17	15	Cardiff – Sophia Gardens (1.8.67)
36	20	19	Lord's (26.8.66)	26	22	16	Hove (19.8.67)
29	21	19	Northampton (4.7.66)	30	21	19	Swansea (13.6.67)
29	23	22	Derby (23.8.66)	32	26	19	Worcester (18.7.67)
32	23	23	Oval (26.8.66)	21	26	21	Chelmsford (28.8.67)
29	26	23	Cardiff – Arms Park (22.7.66)	36	27	21	Edgbaston – New Square (25.7.67)
34	28	27	Trent Bridge (19.8.66)	29	24	22	Taunton (30.6.67)
42	31	30	Worcester (1.7.66)	27	24	22	Leicester (14.8.67)

[a] Percentage clay in mineral fraction of top 2 cm.
[b] Average of 4 highest bounces, 2 from each end.
[c] General average for pitch.
The extent of the difference between [b] and [c] is a measure of the general variability in bounce on the pitch.
Note: Concrete under equivalent conditions gives a value of 52 in. P.L.K. Dury has shown, for the Nottinghamshire area, that the average club or school pitch is unlikely to exceed 15 in, 11 in being typical. (Cricket Pitch Research, published in 1978 by Education Playing Field Service, Nottinghamshire.)

ing standards of pace. This same argument can be used in support of synthetic surfaces where resources are inadequate for the proper management of turf.

A game should involve skill, variety and fun; the element of fun normally arising from the intervention of chance changing the odds. The peculiarities of different soils and the vagaries of the climate are elements, therefore, that should not be entirely eliminated from the game of cricket, but scientific research aimed at understanding their influence on pitch performance can help to strike the balance that the game requires.

12.2 Pitch assessment

In the 1960s Imperial measurements were in common use; therefore, measurements in this chapter give these units priority.

12.2.1 Bounce test

The Test and Counties Cricket Board, which is now responsible for the selection of the English national team, is concerned that first-class cricket should be played under conditions conducive to the promotion of the skills necessary for success at international level. They

TABLE 12.2 Examples of variability in bounce on County pitches

Ground	Sampling date	Bounce (in) for ball dropped from 16 ft											
		New Road end											
Worcester	18.6.67	9	12	13	14	18	22	19	31	17	17	16	16
		Scoreboard end											
		25	17	20	20	24	23	24	20	22	22	11	10
		Pavilion end											
Edgbaston	25.7.67	17	23	28	26	16	28	13	21	18	28	16	17
		Constance Road end											
		21	22	22	14	22	18	15	26	24	23	13	17
		Pavilion end											
Oval*	26.8.66	25		25		24		25		25			
		Vauxhall End											
		20		21		20		18		19			

* Fewer samples taken at wider spacing on some pitches in the initial, 1966 survey.
The variability in bounce on the pitch at Worcester was caused by the pitch breaking up. The variability at Edgbaston was caused by turf cracks still present 32 months after the surface had been renovated by re-turfing. The pitch at the Oval showed a clear pattern of variation between ends which the players recognized.

believe that this requires the game to be played on fast, true pitches. Trueness is a matter of consistency, pace a matter of bounce. Consistency of bounce, therefore, is not a bad measure of pitch quality.

Method

The simple procedure which Stewart and Adams developed in the 1960s to measure bounce was to drop a once-used (60 overs), but sound, cricket ball vertically onto the surface of the pitch from a fixed height of 16 feet (just less than 5 metres). Under these conditions a sound, English ball will rebound off solid concrete to almost exactly one quarter of the dropping height. Sighting the top of the ball against a board marked off at inch intervals, the bounce off concrete is of the order of 52 inches (1321 mm).

The figures for pitches reported in this chapter were all taken after close of play on the final day of three- or five-day matches. They indicate the extent to which the important qualities of uniformity and solidity have survived the full match treatment. The aim, not always achieved, was to record 12 bounces within an area of 2–5 yards (1.8–4.6 m) in front of each wicket. Intact soil cores were then taken from the same areas for subsequent laboratory study.

Review of bounce evidence related to clay content of soil

Table 12.1 indicates the great range in pace to be found on County pitches. Some of this could be related to differences in moisture content, some to variations in soil strength as determined by clay content, but the worst cases of inconsistency had their origin in recent pitch reconstruction or imperfect preparation (Table 12.2).

Outwith the extremes of Old Trafford, which at the time was notoriously easy paced, and Gloucester, where the difficulty was to get the soil adequately dried out in depth, clay content was found to be remarkably uniform, most being within 5% either way of an average of 31%. Note, however, this is half the clay content that might be considered normal in Australia.

TABLE 12.3 Comparative values for pitch consolidation

Ground	Date sampled	Air dry bulk densities (gm/cm³)		Rolling efficiency – field density as % of density after remoulding
		From field condition	After remoulding	
Chelmsford	28.8.67	1.286	1.482	89
Worcester	1.7.66	1.473	1.655	89
Worcester	18.7.67	1.464	1.674	88
Taunton	30.6.67	1.514	1.720	88
Hove	29.8.67	1.358	1.573	86
Old Trafford	20.7.67	1.346	1.529	86
Cardiff – Arms Park	22.7.66	1.269	1.531	83
Cardiff – Sophia Gdns	1.8.67	1.195	1.473	83
Oval	26.8.66	1.296	1.560	83
Edgbaston – new	25.7.67	1.203	1.498	82
Leicester	14.8.67	1.233	1.507	82
Lord's	26.8.66	1.482	1.815	82
Trent Bridge	19.8.66	1.300	1.580	82
Derby	23.8.66	1.185	1.458	81
Leicester	27.6.66	1.306	1.625	79
Swansea	13.6.67	1.161	1.559	79
Edgbaston – old	6.7.66	1.269	1.638	78
Gloucester	10.7.67	1.219	1.656	76
Northampton	4.7.66	1.249	1.673	75

Values for rolling efficiency based on a comparison of the bulk density of carefully removed field cores, wetted and centrifuged to re-consolidate before air drying, with the same material air dried after remoulding moist.

12.2.2 Surface consolidation

Comparison of the bulk density of the soil cores in their field condition compared with the density of the same material remoulded and air dried in the laboratory (Table 12.3) indicated considerable variation in efficiency of consolidation during pitch preparation.

12.2.3 Visual evidence of management in soil cores

Visual evidence from soil cores, viewed in section, revealed considerable variation in soil management. This ranged from a neat succession of thin topdressing layers at the Oval, to much coarser, irregular layering at Lord's and Swansea, and in unlayered uniformity in the worm-worked soils at Worcester and Taunton.

12.2.4 Results of laboratory soil tests

A clear relationship was established in the laboratory between clay content and measurements of soil binding strength (see ASSB ratings, Appendix 1). In the field there was found to be general agreement between the bounce measurement and player opinion on pace. When those pitches were excluded which the density measurements suggested were least well prepared, i.e. those with rolling efficiency values less than 80% (Table 12.3), and values for dry binding strength were then compared with the average of the four best bounce values, the following strong relationship emerged:

bounce height (in)
= 0.1 × ASSB rating (lbs) + 9.0.

Alternatively, if values for clay content are used instead of the more immediately relevant

TABLE 12.4 Interrelationships between soil properties, bounce height and pace

Clay (%)	Dry strength		Bounce from 16 ft		Pace
	(lb)	(kg)	(in)	(mm)	
45	over 210	95	over 30	762	Very fast
34	160	73	25–30	635–762	Fast
22	110	50	20–25	508–635	Moderately fast
10	60	27	15–20	381–508	Easy paced
0	10	5	below 15	381	Slow

quality of binding strength, the relationship takes the form

bounce height (in) = 0.43 × clay % + 10.6.

However, this relationship between bounce and clay content applies only for clay contents between 20 and 40% and, on average, may be wrong, for one case in twenty.

12.2.5 Pitch and soil tests for cricket groundsmen

An important outcome of the research reported above is that it removed a lot of the mystique from the preparation of cricket pitches. It made it possible for a groundsman to objectively assess his achievement and to confirm or refute the subjective and often prejudiced opinions of the players, spectators and commentators. It made clear how the fundamental character of clay content in the soil could limit the pace potential that even a well-prepared pitch could achieve. It made it possible to distinguish a problem of an unsuitable soil from a failing in pitch preparation, and it provided simple criteria on which to base the selection of soil for topdressing and pitch construction.

Bounce height

Using the method described on page 183 the significance of the bounce height values obtained can be interpreted by reference to the standards listed in Table 12.4.

Low values, under 20 in (508 mm) or, worse still, under 15 in (381 mm) indicate a marked weakness in soil strength. This may be caused by any one of a combination of factors: a soil with an inadequate content of clay; unsatisfactory pitch preparation; or something unsatisfactory in the general management of the square. For example, on the pitches recorded in Table 12.1, the poor performance of the old part of the square at Edgbaston in 1966 could not be attributed to the clay content of the soil, whereas this clearly was the problem at Old Trafford in 1967. The bounce values alone could not have made this distinction.

A pitch, bouncing consistently between 25 and 30 in (635 and 762 mm) when a cricket ball is dropped vertically onto it from 16 ft (4877 mm), probably represents a good standard for Test and County play, but the normal club or school game is played on turf pitches that seldom bounce more than 15 in (381 mm).

Particularly high bounce values were recorded at Abbeydale Park, Sheffield in the mid 1970s. Values consistently around 35 in (889 mm) were recorded on the pitch used for the Yorkshire/West Indies match in 1976, and values two or three inches either side of an average of 37 in (940 mm) for the Yorkshire/Middlesex match in 1976. All this was achieved with a surface clay content of 35%. The injuries experienced by the Yorkshire players on both these occasions suggest that such pitches, even when consistent, are more lively than all but the most talented English batsmen can cope with, certainly when encountered unexpectedly, and the fast bowlers are West Indians.

Consistency of bounce

From field observations and the data recorded in Table 12.1 it would seem reasonable to postulate that a discrepancy of more than 2 in (50 mm) between the general average for 12 bounces at either end of a pitch (third column in Table 12.1), compared with the average of the two highest from either end (second column in Table 12.1), indicates some feature of management requiring attention, irrespective of any problem over clay content. Some examples now follow.

1. At Gloucester (1967) the immediate surface had cracked into a mosaic of very small hard blocks while an inch (25 mm) down, the strong clay soil was still moist enough to be plastic.
2. At Hove and Edgbaston (1967) both pitches were affected by abnormally low bounces along turf lines.
3. At Worcester (1967) the strong clay soil had not been adequately re-wetted and re-consolidated by rolling after previous use and so had cracked up dangerously by the end of the match, much to the benefit of the bowlers.

Soil strength

A simple ASSB or **motty test**, described in Appendix 1, will indicate any soil strength limitation inherent in the clay content of the soil. For well made 'motties' every 4½ lb (2 kg) of breaking strength is equivalent to 1% clay. However, with Australian soils in mind, it should be pointed out that this applies best for clay contents within the range 20–40% and where the clay is not chemically dispersed, e.g. by incautious de-salination.

Interrelationships between soil properties, bounce height and pace

Table 12.4 shows how values obtained in the survey of County pitches carried out in 1966 and 1967 allowed relationships to be made between clay content and dry strength of soil, and between bounce values for a cricket ball dropped vertically onto the surface from 16 ft (4877 mm) and player opinion of pace.

On a properly prepared, dry pitch, bounce height and true pace are likely to be related because both are beneficially affected by the extent to which the surface remains hard and unyielding on impact. Any give, or collapse, will reduce the rebound height and also check forward movement so that a player will complain of the ball not coming nicely onto the bat. The exaggerated forward movement of a ball skidding horizontally off a wet, or excessively lush, green surface is false pace. True pace, where the angle of departure is virtually the same as the angle of incidence, is what the player should be able to anticipate when making an attacking stroke to a guileless delivery. By contrast, false pace will deceive even the well-intentioned stroke. The potential to skid is not covered by the vertical bounce test and could not be predicted from the soil qualities of clay content or dry strength.

12.3 Critical factors in pitch preparation

12.3.1 Achieving the soil's maximum binding strength – theory

Using a soil sample from which gravel and stone have been removed, moisten just enough to allow any previous aggregation to be worked out by rubbing. Then, by rolling between cupped hands, form the whole mass into a firm, coherent plastic ball (motty) with a smooth, flawless surface. If the soil is too wet it will stick to everything; too dry it will not cohere enough to avoid breaking up when rolled; just right it will mould reliably without cracking, sticking to itself but leaving other surfaces clean. The last stage is known as 'sticky point'. It can be achieved in any soil that has sufficient fine particles for a continuous moisture matrix to provide the necessary flexible cohesion.

On further drying, the water matrix is broken and plasticity gives way to a kind of brittleness, like that of partially set cement. This stage coincides with the colour change from dark to light because the removal of water by evaporation causes drying of the surface first and entry of air into peripheral pore spaces.

Finally, as the soil is left to dry out completely in the air, the residual films of water between clay sheets get thinner, contraction ceases and soluble cementing agents, concentrated by the loss of moisture, solidify to form rigid bonds of varying degrees of permanence.

It is this sequence of events which a groundsman should keep in mind when setting about the task of preparing a cricket pitch for play.

12.3.2 Linking theory to practice

When preparing a pitch for play a groundsman should attend to the following points.

1. He should make his soil sufficiently moist to enable him to achieve integration by rolling into one, coherent, plastic mass. The more clay-rich the soil the more difficult this will be. Hence, a clay content of 40% should be considered the upper limit for cricket pitch soils in Britain. Above this percentage the soil would be difficult to dry out in our climate anyway.
2. Rolling should continue so long as the soil remains plastic, but never drier than sticky point. That is, he should roll only so long as the surface remains dark in colour, or so that the dark colour can be restored by

squeezing up moisture from below. If rolling is continued through to the brittle stage it will merely result in fine cracking, making the surface liable to break up during play. Re-wetting the surface from above may well trap air that will balloon on rolling to disrupt the soil horizontally. This may be the reason why the combination of spiking and rolling is a particularly effective way of achieving consolidation.
3. Final hardening of the pitch should be left to the drying of the atmosphere. Rolling of a thoroughly hard pitch may do no harm, but then neither does it do much good, except temporarily to tidy away loose soil and debris that shouldn't be there in the first place.

12.3.3 Surface consolidation

Problem of soil layering

Though an open soil is required for the deep rooting that benefits growth, a hard, compact, level surface is required for the game of cricket. This can be achieved only by a system of management that involves heavy rolling during pitch preparation. Topdressings of heavy loam, 2–3 mm ($\frac{1}{10}$ in) thick, should be applied annually to revive the sward, re-true the surface after scarification and spiking, incorporate fertilizer and seed, bury exposed roots and maintain the clay-rich character of the playing surface. This is the work which Man must take on to mimic the natural processes of opening the soil, burying organic residues and topdressing the surface, these being achieved by earthworms in a fertile pasture. Whereas the natural process of earthworm churning succeeds in maintaining a soil homogeneous, the field evidence points strongly to the man-made alternative ending up as a succession of horizontal layers.

Wheeled traffic across a bare soil will lead to the surface developing a platy structure. This happens even in a uniform soil, let alone one that begins already strongly layered because of the build-up of successive layers of topdressing. While the soil is still moist, rolling may temporarily achieve a measure of cohesion between the layers but the mass as a whole will only remain strongly coherent if nothing incompatible intervenes. This means that soil topdressings must be applied to a clean surface, and the applied soil must be similar in its swelling and shrinking characteristics to the soil already in place. If not, the layers are liable to separate on drying with adverse consequences for pace. Compatibility can be assessed by a modification of the ASSB test described in Appendix A1.3.

Heterogeneous layers will react differentially in response to the uptake of water and the disruptive action of frost. Therefore, reconsolidation of the soil in depth must be given due priority in early spring, making use of the spike and roll combination to aid integration and release trapped air.

Role of grass

To many, cricket is a game played on grass but, at County standard and above, a pitch when ready for play is 90% bare soil. However, grass on a square does have a role to play apart from just blending with the outfield when out of use. If the grass is well rooted in depth it can not only help directly with surface integration, it can help indirectly by actively extending the drying process deeper into the soil. The builders of clay-walled houses used to include straw in the mix to ensure steady drying in depth and prevent the surface flaking off in layers, so the roots and stem bases of the sward will do likewise on a pitch. The premature drying of a surface skin is something that should be avoided.

Earthworms – are they welcome on a cricket square?

Despite the problem of surface casting, which some groundsmen seem to find insuperable, there would seem to be much to be said for learning to work with earthworms, even on a cricket square. However, this is only true if the cast material that the worms bring to the surface is of an adequate clay content to act as a topdressing for the promotion of pace. That means the clay content of the whole soil is important and not just the playing surface. It is probably this limitation that accounts for the different prejudices of groundsmen who have had experience of earthworm activity on their squares.

At the start of the research survey carried out in the 1960s, a gathering of ex-England captains agreed that three County grounds stood out as having been renowned for the satisfactory pace of their pitches over the years: Worcester, Portsmouth and Taunton. On completion of the survey, and despite a general prejudice against the presence of earthworms on cricket squares, it was found that at three grounds earthworms had been retained:- Worcester, Portsmouth and Taunton.

If a groundsman inherits a square on which earthworms are active, and the soil they bring up in their casts is sufficiently clay-rich to act as a suitable topdressing for the promotion of pace, he would do well to try and learn to live with them. Their burrowing and soil mixing activities will benefit drainage, avoid layering and the development of thatch, and encourage deep rooting. Casts can be a problem when mowing or rolling but this problem gets less as the surface dries out during pitch preparation, and any casts that do appear can be removed by brushing.

With modern chemicals, earthworms can readily be exterminated, thereby eliminating the problem of surface casts, but the groundsman must then take on all the jobs that the

TABLE 12.5 Percentage clay values characteristic of soils used for test matches worldwide

Ground	1932[a]	1964[b]	1968	1970	1974	1975[c]	1980	1982[c]	1984	1986	Local average	General average
England												
Edgbaston			38				34		34		35	
Headingley			34				38		39		37	
Lord's			38	36			28		31		33	33
Old Trafford			20				37		35		31	
Oval			35	30			30		26		30	
Trent Bridge			32				29				30	
Australia												
Adelaide	56	52				53					54	
Brisbane	71	73				72		85			75	
Melbourne	68	48				51					56	66
Perth						74		85			79	
Sydney	73	52				54					65	
New Zealand												
Auckland				46								
Wellington				35								
Jamaica												
Sabina Park			49									
UAE												
Sharjah										59		
(Lahore Loam)												
South Africa												
Cape Loam					68							
Natal Loam					56							

[a] Piper, C.S. (1932) included in data from Greenland and Quirk (1966).
[b] Greenland, D.J. and Quirk, J.P. (1966) Waite Research Institute, University of Adelaide. Personal communication, received 3 May 1966.
[c] McIntyre, D.S. (1983) Australian cricket pitch soils and profiles, in The National Seminar on Turf Management, ACT Region, Royal Australian Institute of Parks and Recreation, Canberra. Data re-calculated for mineral skeleton only.

earthworm would otherwise do. Eventually he may be faced with a surface so excessively layered that complete reconstruction becomes necessary.

12.4 Overseas comparisons

12.4.1 Clay content

As shown by the data in Table 12.5, the soils encountered by our Test players overseas may be very different from those to which they have become accustomed in Britain. Best documented is the information from Australia. This indicates a preference for soils with a clay content exceeding 50% and a type of clay which, by comparison with that used in Britain, is markedly swelling in character. Their soils expand and contract a great deal in response to wetting and drying and, by this means, readily fracture.

The use of self-mulching, high-clay soils on cricket squares only begins to make sense when it is realized that first, cricket squares in Australia often form part of pitches used for various types of football during the winter, and secondly there can be a problem of salt accumulation at the surface which has to be leached away through the soil periodically.

Strange though it may seem to use the hallowed turf of the square for vigorous games in the winter, there is some reason to believe that it is the winter game rather than the summer game that suffers most from this pattern of use. The change in the feel underfoot is somewhat disconcerting to a player striding out at full pace. However, studded footwear probably achieves a useful amount of churning to homogenize the topsoil, and any cracking will assist drainage and the removal of salts.

12.4.2 Grass

The preferred grass used in Australia, and other countries with a warm climate, is *Cynodon dactylon*. This grass spreads very rapidly by surface runners and underground rhizomes. Its common name in Australia is 'couch', one of the names we use in Britain for the rapidly spreading, troublesome weed grass, *Agropyron repens*. Because *Cynodon* dies back in the winter it benefits from the fine cracking of a strong clay soil to regenerate from below when the increase in temperature allows.

It may also be this contrast in origin of the renewal shoots that accounts for a difference in expression of our thatch problems. A strong clay pitch in South Africa is said to be at its best only for the first two years after the surface has been renewed. Thereafter it becomes more and more difficult to re-integrate by rolling. From the visual examination of intact, core samples it would appear that this problem results from the progressive build-up of grass fibre in an array of vertical cracks leading through to the surface from below. Contrast this with the horizontal orientation of our

thatch problem in Britain where organic residues inhibit the integration of annual increments of topdressing. Since there is no mention of any similar problem of vertical integration in Australia, could it be that this is another favourable consequence of the churning achieved by winter use and the annual need for some measure of surface renewal?

12.3.3 Tips from down-under on surface consolidation

When making motties, for the soil strength test, it is useful to check periodically if the soil ball being moulded is still moist enough to stick to absorbent paper pressed against it. Continued rolling beyond this critical limit of stickiness will risk the whole surface breaking up into a mosaic of fine cracks. This is a useful way of demonstrating to groundsmen why, valuable as rolling is for integrating a moist soil in depth, it should not be continued through to the brittle stage.

This same message comes through from two practical procedures used in pitch preparation in the southern hemisphere. In South Africa there is a tradition of rolling over a covering of hessian, stopping rolling when the hessian no longer sticks to the soil, then leaving the surface to bake hard in the sun. In Australia the advice is to scatter fresh grass clippings on the moist soil then roll, squeezing up water from depth, stopping when the clippings fail to adhere to the soil. These practical procedures seem to be aimed firstly at keeping the soil plastic until uniformly consolidated in depth, and secondly at using the evidence of loss of surface stickiness to indicate the point on the drying cycle when rolling should cease and any further consolidation left to the desiccating effect of the atmosphere. This could be useful advice for all groundsmen who are faced with the task of consolidating a strong soil in depth without the surface drying out prematurely. (Refer back to the problem pitch at Gloucester – Table 12.1 and pages 183 and 186.)

12.5 Creating a cricket field

In practice, there are two main approaches to the construction of a cricket field – one puts the emphasis on site selection and the other is man-made and expensive.

12.5.1 A natural cricket field

The simplest approach is to chose a level or gently sloping site that already has in place an earthworm-worked, clay loam or silty clay loam soil, 25–40% clay. Any problem of encroaching ground water should be controlled by peripheral ditches or catchment drains, placed beyond the boundary of the outfield. The surface, from the centre of the square to the periphery of the outfield, should be trued by minimal soil disturbance, aiming to assist the run-off of surface, storm water all the way to interception drainage beyond the boundary.

With summer use only, this could well suffice so long as management is sensitive, not only to the needs of the players, but also to the welfare of the earthworm population that is essential for the conditioning of the soil. Without some effort to avoid acidity and to feed the earthworms by return of clippings, numbers will fall and the natural drainage of the soil will suffer in consequence. Allowed to go too far, this may then require the assistance of a full, sand-capped, slit system of drainage in the outfield, and a catchment drain around the square.

12.5.2 A purpose-made cricket square

Problems arising from the nature of the game

A clay loam, cricket square soil is required to remain level, grassed and consolidated throughout the summer but, as such, it is unlikely to contribute much to its own drainage. Priority has to be given to organizing interception of encroaching ground water and surface runoff without interfering with play. Typically this is what a 'French' drain is meant to do but the problem is to fit such a drain around the periphery of the square without unsightly consequences for the growth of the grass, or undue interference with play. Dividing the square into well defined, pitch-wide strips, bordered by sand/gravel slits might appear to be another similar option. The problem with this would be to maintain the slit surface freely permeable and level with the rest of the square without extending the area of sand contamination onto the playing surface of the pitches.

Unlike the situation with winter games pitches, where topdressing with sand is recommended, sand, or even a sandy loam, should be kept off the clay-loam surface of a good quality cricket square. A light dusting of sand onto the surface of a prepared pitch could be used to enhance response to spin but would not be considered sporting, especially if applied surreptitiously to influence the course of a game. But apart from these sporting considerations, it could have long-term, adverse effects on the performance of the playing surface. It will not become properly integrated into the existing surface soil, and any subsequent clay-loam topdressing will be difficult to integrate through it with the layer below. As a result, the weak binding link at the junction will lead to horizontal cracking as the soil dries out after rolling. This will deaden the bounce and eventually cause the surface to disintegrate.

Soil consolidation, like drainage, requires displacement of air and water. Both these potentially mobile components of soil can to some extent be brought up to the surface by spiking and rolling but it is also possible to impel them down through the soil if there is an underlying, drained gravel bed not too far below. Thus, though much attention is concentrated on treating the surfaces of cricket squares to improve pitch performance, there is also scope for rational interference below ground with the same ultimate objective in mind.

Construction

The need for soil compaction being inevitable, the soil on the square should be kept as shallow as possible, and rafted over a drainage bed of gravel. In design it can be very similar to the bowling green described in Chapter 10, but with the topsoil, above the coarse sand blinding layer, consisting of 100 mm (4 in) of a fertile, loamy sand soil, with 100 mm (4 in) of a fertile clay loam, or silty clay loam soil to form the actual playing surface. Allowance should be made at time of placement for long-term settlement, of the order of one sixth, after the initial firming down of each soil layer. This shallow soil construction is typical of what is at present used in Britain and Australia though there is, as yet, very little experimental evidence to support it in detail.

To assist the movement of wheeled traffic traversing the site during construction, and to add to the stability of the shallow soil profile, it would be advisable to choose an angular, fine version of a *trench gravel* for the gravel bed, and an angular, *blinding sand* to separate the gravel from the loamy sand soil above. Where ease of rolling out and trueness are even more important than fast pace, for example at school and club level, the extra silt in a silty clay loam could be beneficial for the actual playing surface.

Essential aids to soil-moisture control

Covers

In the process of pitch preparation it is essential that the soil surface is allowed to dry out progressively after having been fully integrated by rolling out when moist. Any re-wetting will cause swelling and some risk of disruption which may then require re-integration by going right back to the initial stage of rolling out moist. Since the process of drying out may take anything from three to five days the protection of covers is essential if the process is to be completed by a specific date. There may then be other uses for covers during the period of play but, whatever the prevailing rules of the game allow in this respect, the vital role of covers in pitch preparation will remain. As a consequence, provision must be made for intercepted rainfall to be discharged from hosing attached to the gutters directly into the drainage system at either end of the square.

Irrigation

The deep rooting of grass in a worm-worked soil is the best natural insurance against the risks inherent in drought but earthworms, more often than not, are by no means abundant on our major grounds. The alternative of effective irrigation is still something of a luxury in Britain as, so often during a drought, water use is restricted.

It is essential, however, that a water source should be installed, accessible from the surface, and near enough to the square to assist with the irrigation required for preparation and end renovation.

With a shallow soil in place over a drained gravel bed, sub-irrigation would seem to be an option that could help in pitch preparation and maintenance. The construction would have to allow for each pitch area to be serviced separately. However, at this stage any move in the direction of sub-irrigation would have to be considered experimental, as capillary flow through a compact clay loam will be very much slower than through sand.

12.5.3 A purpose-made outfield

A cricket outfield covers of the order of 1½ hectares (3–4 acres), a very large area of grass to maintain merely for cricket use in the summer. Alternative use varies from the rigours of a full winter programme of football to occasional use for the more compatible game of hockey, or reversion to public use as might be the case on a village green. Over such a wide range of use no one prescription for construction and management could be expected to apply, but there are certain general requirements that should be given precedence if opportunity allows. These are:

- efficient drainage
- evenness of surface
- uniformity of grass cover.

Efficient drainage is essential, even for a summer game, as play cannot take place on a surface that remains ponded after rain. It is not unknown for resumption of play in a Test match to be delayed because of water lying in the outfield.

Earthworms are invaluable for their assistance with drainage and the recycling of organic residues but regular brushing and weedkilling will be essential to maintain an even, uniformly grassed surface suitable for close mowing and acceptable to fielders relying on the true roll of the ball.

Elimination of earthworms or intensive winter use means that, except on steeply sloping land or sand, drainage assistance will be essential. The form this takes will almost certainly involve surface interception by slits linked to pipes. If the system chosen makes use of 50 mm (2 in) wide, sand/gravel slits, the combination of an even surface for cricket and intensive use for vigorous play in winter favours covering the slit surface with a deep carpet of ameliorated fine sand (section 11.2.2, pitch B). If surface interception is ultimately placed in the hands of a mini- or micro-slit system, then surface trueness will be less at risk from slit settlement but regular attention will still have to be paid to sand topdressing and/or repeat slitting to maintain the thin slits functional (Chapter 2, pages 42 and 43).

Chapter thirteen

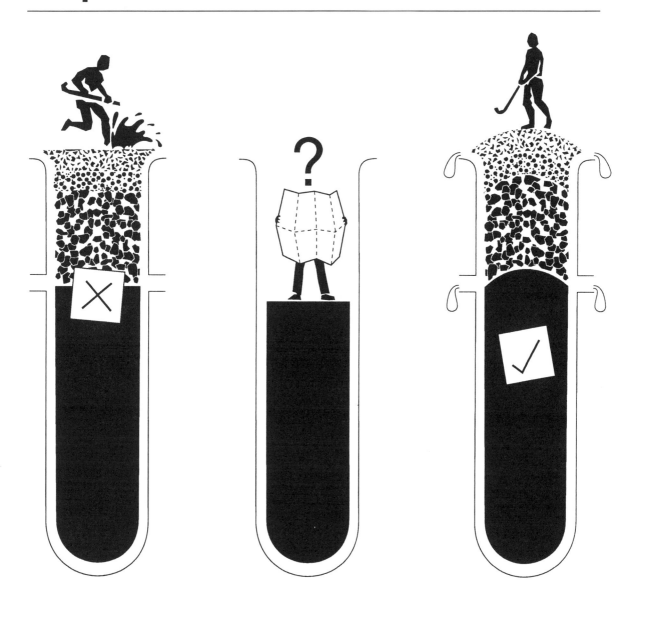

Water-bound hard porous pitches

13.1 Function

The hard porous pitch is a non-grass surface rafted on a drained, gravel base. The surface functions very like the smooth, water-bound sand that forms continuously renewable surfaces for play on our beaches, between tide levels.

This type of pitch does not provide the best surface for sport but it is an option that should be considered when grass cannot cope and a synthetic alternative threatens to be far too expensive. It can be a useful workhorse provided it is sensibly constructed and adequately maintained.

Unlike the expensive, wholly synthetic pitches, hard porous pitches are formed entirely from particulate mineral matter and draw on the same scientific skills for design as have already been discussed in relation to soil-based sports turf. However, in this case, we have no biological component to worry about and can give priority to factors such as drainage, surface trueness and ease of management, albeit at some sacrifice to tractive efficiency and comfort underfoot. It would be a pity if this simple and relatively cheap, non-grass playing surface were to lose out entirely to the sales pressure behind the much more expensive synthetic carpet approach because of poor choice of materials and inefficiencies in design, construction and maintenance.

13.2 General features of design

13.2.1 General layout appropriate to hard porous areas

Dissatisfaction with the performance of hard porous pitches has often been associated with persistent ponding in dished areas holding up play long after rainfall has ceased. This reflects the limited infiltration rate of the surfacing material and a surface configuration inadequately sloped to clear surplus water all the way to the periphery. Excavation through to the gravel layer beneath ponded areas will show that it is **access** to the gravel layer, not **flow through** the gravel layer that is the cause.

The design of a hard porous pitch can take two forms: a uniform slope all the way across, or a central crown with even falls to a level perimeter. Choice is governed mainly by the size and shape required, and cost. An exception is where the area is encircled by a running track, when only the crowned type of construction is suitable. A hard porous surface for the central area of a track may enable increased use for games throughout the year but has the disadvantage that the hammer, discus and javelin cannot be thrown within the arena and a special grass area must be provided outside the track for these events.

13.2.2 General form of the surface

The factor most likely to determine which form the design should take is the distance surface water will have to travel to reach the perimeter and the steepness of the slope over which it will have to flow. Heavy rain on a long and/or steep slope is likely to result in severe scouring of the surface towards the bottom of the slope and a risk of fine surface material being deposited in the drains and on adjacent land. To minimize this risk it is inadvisable to accept general gradients steeper than 1:80, especially where such slopes exceed a distance of 45 m (50 yards). On the other hand, too gradual a general slope, i.e. less than 1:120, is liable to result in excessive ponding in localized depressions.

Where the area to be surfaced is wider than would be permitted by the above limits, the crown method of design should be adopted. This has the effect of limiting the length of slope to half the width of the hard porous area, thereby greatly reducing the risk of scouring.

13.2.3 Materials used to construct the playing surface

Without the assistance of root-binding and sward cover, surface stability on hard porous surfaces can only be achieved by choosing materials of mixed particle-size composition and angular shape. The pore system must transmit water at more than 2–3 mm/h ($\frac{1}{10}$ in) but must not empty by gravity, drying out instead by the relatively slow process of evaporation upwards, e.g. a layer of fine-to-coarse sand, less than 150 mm (6 in) deep, placed over a bed of fine gravel. (Refer back to section 4.2 for a full discussion of the significance of critical tension and its role in the retention of water.) Water-binding is an essential feature of the surface layer, contributing to tractive efficiency and resistance to wind erosion.

The most readily available materials used for the surface are by-products from stone quarries involved in rock crushing. These are mechanically crushed rocks with particle-size composition as summarized in Table 13.1 and Figure 13.1. A typical example, SN9, is included in

Table 7.1. Because the particles are sharply angular and vary in size they will interpack to form a relatively dense, rigid surface, retentive of water when placed in a thin layer over gravel. Drainage is controlled by the rock dust component of silt- and clay-sized particles present. When fine particle segregation reduces the infiltration rate of the surface to something less than 2–3 mm ($\frac{1}{10}$ in)/h, even short bursts of intense rainfall may give rise to surface flow.

Based on a survey of 15 samples, representative of nine different, marketed products available in the 1970s (Table 13.1), hard porous materials are likely to contain of the order of 30–40% fine gravel, 15–20% medium-plus-fine sand, and 10–15% silt-plus-clay, with a fairly even spread between. However, this composition probably owes more to the ready availability of these by-product materials than to scientific investigation. Further experimentation could usefully explore the extent to which the silt-plus-clay component could be reduced and the gravel component eliminated.

Despite the preponderance of coarse particles in hard porous, surfacing materials, it is the finer material packed into the pores between the larger particles that ultimately controls the rate at which water will pass through. Though the hydraulic conductivity of these materials, measured in the laboratory or predicted from particle-size composition D_{10}, is likely to indicate values of the order of 25 mm/hour (1 in), irrigation water applied to established surfaces at rates one-tenth of this have been observed to pond. This discrepancy is to be related to the practical problem of air entrapment. It further emphasizes the importance of adequately grading the surface so that any temporary excess of rainfall over infiltration can clear all the way to a catchment drain at the periphery.

Wind and water movement inevitably result in the finest particles being either blown away or washed downslope. With soft rock materials, such as 1–3, 9–11 and 15 in Table 13.1, fine-particle replenishment will result from

TABLE 13.1 Crushed rock materials used in the 1970s for hard porous, water-bound, reacreation surfaces

Attribute	Measurement value														
Percentage by weight for graded particle diameters (mm)	Material number[c]														
	1	2	3	4	5	6	7	8	9	10	11	12	13	14	15
Stones over 8.000															
Coarse gravel 4.000–8.000	7	5	1	2	5	1	8	4	10	7	6	3	2	7	6
Fine gravel 2.000–4.000	36	33	20	31	24	17	36	42	53	49	21	21	34	22	23
Very coarse sand 1.000–2.000	12	10	20	8	9	38	8	15	12	15	13	20	20	30	21
Coarse sand 0.500–1.000	11	13	14	15	14	12	14	11	8	7	15	17	16	11	17
Medium sand 0.250–0.500	7	8	8	13	14	8	8	7	2	4	16	12	10	8	11
Fine sand 0.125–0.250	5	6	5	9	12	7	7	5	1	3	13	7	5	7	6
Very fine sand 0.060–0.125	5	6	7	5	6	5	6	5	2	1	8	5	3	2	4
Coarse silt 0.020–0.060	8	12	13	4	4	2	6	5	5	6	5	5	3	4	5
Fine silt 0.002–0.020	5	6	6	6	7	6	4	3	5	6	3	6	4	5	4
Clay less than 0.002	3	2	5	6	5	6	3	3	1	2	2	3	3	5	2
Dispersion coefficent – percentage of total clay dispersible in water	14	13	53	68	71	96	59	63	36	25	82	63	94	57	53
Hardness class[a]	2	1	1	6	4	5	3	4	1	2	2	5	3	4	2
pH using glass electrode – water:soil ratio = 5:2	7.8	7.7	7.8	7.2	7.3	–	7.2	–	8.0	7.8	7.1	7.6		7.2	7.1
Lime status[b]	HC	HC	C	SC	SC	SC	SC	NC	HC	HC	NC	HC	SC	SC	HC

When homogeneously mixed all these materials could be characterized by their 10% summation value (D_K 10%). This suggests that, on average, their hydraulic conductivity when newly laid should be approximately 25 mm (1 in)/hour. In time, however, being loose materials, particle segregation will tend to concentrate the coarser particles onto the surface, leaving the fine particles to form a much less permeable layer below.
[a] Hardness class: 1, very soft; 2, soft; 3, fairly hard; 4, hard; 5, very hard; 6, extremely hard.
[b] Lime status: NC, non-calcareous; SC, slightly calcareous; C, calcareous; HC, highly calcareous.
[c] Materials (trade names): 1, Redgra 1; 2, Redgra 2; 3, Redgra 3; 4, Dripla 1; 5, Dripla 2; 6, Dripla 3; 7, Oliset 1; 8, Oliset 2; 9, Nortex 1; 10, Nortex 2; 11, PPS Redland; 12, Fyset; 13, Bolbriggan; 14, Coatsgate; 15, Red Blaes – used extensively in Scotland.

wear so long as coarse-particle replenishment is maintained by topdressing. With a surfacing material from a hard rock source it could be that the dust component itself may require replenishment from time to time, but before moving in this direction, it would be as well to seek clear evidence of need from an analytical survey.

As these hard porous materials can be expensive there is no point in building up a layer thicker than is necessary to avoid stud penetration through to the gravel layer beneath. Experience points to a minimum, consolidated depth of 35–40 mm (1⅜–1½ in).

13.2.4 The sub-structure

Without trying to provide for extreme conditions, it would be reasonable to design hard porous pitches in Britain to cope with a maximum, steady discharge of the order of 6 mm (¼ in) per hour through the gravel drainage bed. In most circumstances this will be more than adequate.

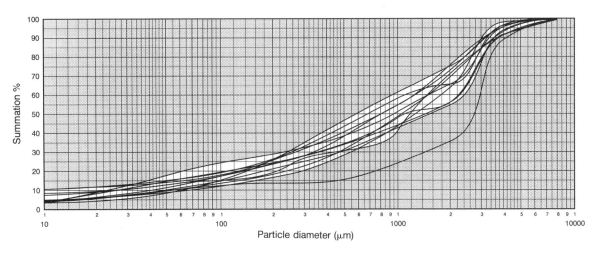

FIGURE 13.1 Summation graph showing the particle-size composition of the hard porous materials listed in Table 13.1. The unshaded area defines the particle-size zone typical of materials that have been used traditionally for surfacing hard porous pitches. Because of the very wide range of particle sizes present in crushed rock materials there is a great deal of scope for reconsolidation by interpacking. To determine D_K from Figure 13.1 and hence, by reference to Figure 7.7, predict the order of hydraulic conductivity to be expected from these materials when settled on site, use the particle-size value which corresponds with the 10% value on the summation scale. This prediction procedure indicates that hydraulic conductivities between 5 and 30 mm/h will be typical. Thus, as experience confirms, surface flow may well lead to localized ponding during bursts of intense rainfall unless the surface is graded to ensure that all excess will clear to the periphery.

The gravel drainage bed itself is usually over-generously designed and can offer a considerable amount of spare, temporary storage capacity. The actual capacity will depend on the depth of the gravel bed and the slope of the base, but could well extend to an amount in excess of 150 000 litres (33 000 gallons). Where a pitch is located at the foot of a slope and is liable to flooding, a catchment drain will be required to intercept extraneous water arriving as runoff from the hill above. However, the drain may not be adequate to cope with exceptional storm conditions and it might then be helpful if the storage capacity beneath the pitch could be utilized as a flood-control reservoir. This could be achieved by linking the gravel bed through to the gravel fill above the pipe in the catchment-drain trench, making it possible, under exceptional circumstances, to allow excess water to overflow from the catchment drain

trench into the available space for temporary storage in the gravel bed beneath the pitch.

If the crushed rock forming the playing surface is to be encouraged to remain water-bound and minimally disrupted by frost, there must be no capillary continuity between it and the underlying soil. This is something which the gravel bed must achieve in addition to drainage, and explains why solid gravel is to be preferred to cinder.

13.3 Two standard designs for low cost, quick-draining, water-bound, hard porous pitches

13.3.1 Theory

An area of a size suitable for a single pitch can be designed to grade uniformly, all in one direction, or either way off a central, goal-to-goal crown. The first option might be more appropriate for a site which already slopes in one direction; the second would be a good option for a flat site, for example, a pitch within a running track. With clearance one way there is a risk that surface flow will so accumulate downslope that, during heavy rain, surface erosion becomes a real possibility. With a crown, the change in slope across the midline tends to visually exaggerate the steepness of the slopes that fall away either side, unless the grade change at the crown is very gradual. Figure 13.2 illustrates the two options by means of transverse sections across the width of the pitch.

The gradients chosen for the surface must be a compromise, arbitrarily chosen to enhance surface flow and avoid ponding while, at the same time, minimizing the risk of erosion and not noticeably interfering with play. The gradient of 1:90 chosen for the surface sloping all in one direction is probably the maximum that should be risked for the 60 m (66 yard) run across the width of a pitch. A lesser gradient might seem a safer option but this will increase the risk of localized ponding in areas left slightly dished after construction or becoming dished subsequently as a result of differential settlement. The greatest risk of erosion damage arises when areas ponded upslope eventually overflow, causing gullying to start at the point of release. A steeper slope will keep water on the move but, on a long slope, the risk of sheet erosion will increase as runoff accumulates and the speed of flow accelerates. Thus, though a slope that will help discharge surface water to the periphery is desirable, the length in any one direction should be kept to a minimum. This means orienting the slope across the width of the pitch, ideally splitting it to run either way off a goal-to-goal crown.

Creating a surface that will initially shed excess water very effectively is not enough: it must remain effective. This requires that all

layers are properly consolidated at time of construction and any adverse effects of long-term settlement are taken out by appropriate topdressing with additional surface material.

At either side of the pitch there may have to be drains organized to intercept water encroaching from outside the playing area, and the same system can be used to clear surface and ground water directed to it off the pitch. An additional pipe, running lengthwise down the pitch, may be used to allow a marked reduction in the depth of gravel required to form the drainage bed beneath a pitch sloping all one way. Under a crowned pitch, the depth of *trench gravel* required to clear the drainage water all the way to either peripheral drain is only of the order of 100 mm (4 in). This is not much more than would be required to form a satisfactory capillary break between the underlying soil and the layer of crushed rock forming the water-bound surface. Thus, for a crowned pitch, the only pipes required are the catchment drains at the periphery.

Traps and inspection chambers should be installed at either end of each pipe run to assist with the interception and clearance of silt. The looseness of the crushed rock surface and the sorting effect of treading disturbance and frost heave will allow the fine, water-holding particles to escape into the drainage system. As this risk is greatest during construction and the initial, settling down period, inspection prior to handover would be a wise precaution.

The two pitches illustrated in Figure 13.2 aim to offer the best, low-cost alternatives for workaday pitches, designed to carry all the hard wear from which the grass pitches in a playing field need to be protected. The general form of the surface is established by the form into which the exposed, subsoil surface is graded, then above this, layers of *trench gravel*, *blinding sand* and crushed rock, hard porous material can be laid, each of uniform thickness. The *trench gravel* for the crowned pitch should be 105 mm (4¼ in) deep, and for the pitch

Water-bound hard porous pitches

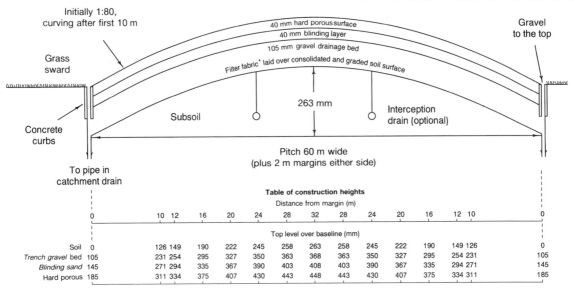

Table of construction heights														
Distance from margin (m)														
0	10	12	16	20	24	28	32	28	24	20	16	12	10	0
Top level over baseline (mm)														
Soil 0	126	149	190	222	245	258	263	258	245	222	190	149	126	0
Trench gravel bed 105	231	254	295	327	350	363	368	363	350	327	295	254	231	105
Blinding sand 145	271	294	335	367	390	403	408	403	390	367	335	294	271	145
Hard porous 185	311	334	375	407	430	443	448	443	430	407	375	334	311	185

(a)

*If filter fabric replaced by 30 mm of *blinding sand*, deepen construction by 30 mm to accomodate.

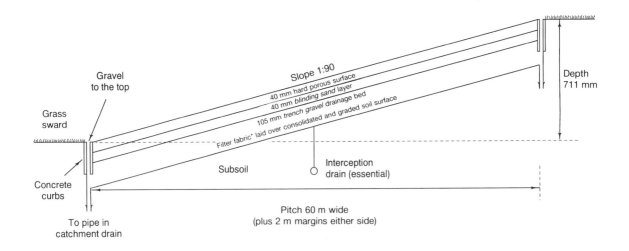

(b)

*If filter fabric replaced by 30 mm of *blinding sand*, deepen construction by 30 mm to accomodate.

FIGURE 13.2 Transverse sections of hard porous pitches: (a) sloping either way off a central, goal to goal crown; (b) sloping uniformly across the pitch.

sloping all one way, 210 mm (8½ in) deep or, with an additional central pipe, 105 mm (4¼ in) deep. The layers of *blinding sand* and the hard porous surface should both be about 40 mm (1½ in) deep, irrespective of other details of the construction.

Two catchment drains are shown running longitudinally down either side of each pitch.

Only on the pitch with 105 mm (4¼ in) deep drainage bed, sloping all one way, is it necessary to introduce one additional drain to run longitudinally down the centre. The grading and linkage of the drain pipes will depend on the location of the final outfall and all the other factors normally involved in the design of pipe, underdrainage systems (section 2.1).

13.3.2 Calculation

Pitch sloping all one way

To calculate H, the depth of the gravel bed, follow procedures described in Appendix E2.2 (also refer to Figure 13.2(b)). The following are known:

V – the overall design rate   6 mm/h

S – the width of the pitch including surrounds (drain to drain)   64 000 mm

$\dfrac{G}{S}$ – the slope   1/90

K – the hydraulic conductivity of the trench gravel used to form the bed   100 000 mm/h.

Step 1: determine α using equation (E.31):

$$\alpha = \frac{1}{2} \times \frac{G}{S} \times \sqrt{\frac{K}{V}}$$

$$= \frac{1}{2} \times \frac{1}{90} \sqrt{\left(\frac{100\,000}{6}\right)}$$

$$= 0.717.$$

Step 2: determine β using relationship to α as described in the graph, Figure 13.3(a): when $\alpha = 0.717$, $\beta = 0.435$.

Step 3: from equation (E.32)

$$\beta = \frac{H}{S} \sqrt{\frac{K}{V}}$$

giving

$$H = \beta S \sqrt{\frac{V}{K}}$$

$$= 0.435 \times 64\,000 \sqrt{\frac{6}{100\,000}}$$

$$= 216 \text{ mm } (8\frac{1}{2} \text{ in}).$$

Knowing H, the depth of the gravel bed, and G, the difference in height either side of the pitch, we can if necessary calculate any one of S, K or V, knowing the other two. This can be done using equations (E.31) and (E.32), provided we can obtain values for α and β.

Step 1: from equations (E.31) and (E.32) we can relate α to β as follows

$$\frac{\beta}{\alpha} = \frac{\dfrac{H}{S}\sqrt{\dfrac{K}{V}}}{\dfrac{1}{2}\dfrac{G}{S}\sqrt{\dfrac{K}{V}}} = \frac{2H}{G},$$

and

$$\beta = 2\frac{H}{G} \times \alpha.$$

This is a straight-line relationship, passing through the origin.

Step 2: plot the straight-line relationship between α and β on the graph (Figure 13.3(a)) which describes the physical relationships involved in the actual construction. This can be done by making use of the fact that when $\alpha = 0$, $\beta = 0$ and when $\alpha = 1$, $\beta = 2H/G$, i.e.

$$\beta = 2 \times \frac{216}{711} = 0.608.$$

The intersection between this line and the curve on the graph gives values $\alpha = 0.717$, $\beta = 0.435$.

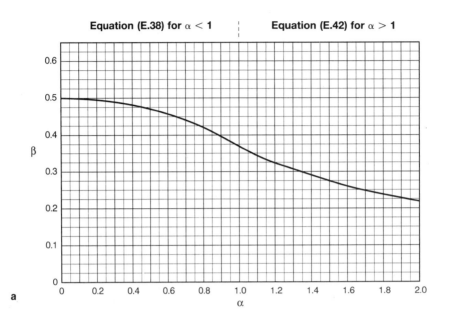

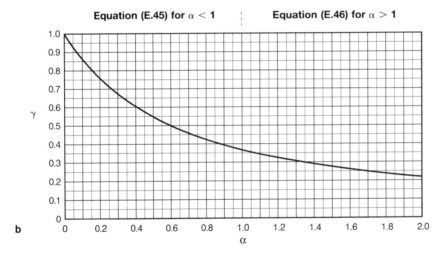

FIGURE 13.3 (a) Relationship between α and β for pitches with drainage bed sloping all one way, using equations (E.38) and (E.42). (b) Relationship between α and γ for crowned pitches with drainage bed sloping down to either side off a central crown, using equations (E.45) and (E.46).

Step 3: Using these values for α and β, equations (E.31) and (E.32) can then be used to obtain values for either S, K or V.

Instead of using 210 mm of gravel it may well be cheaper, and just as efficient to introduce an additional pipe drain to run lengthwise down the centre of the pitch, reducing S to 32 000 mm and gravel depth H to 105 mm (4¼ in).

Pitch clearing excess water to either side off a goal-to-goal crown

In the following calculations it is assumed that no gradient should exceed 1:80 and it would be practically more desirable to have a uniform, fixed depth for the gravel drainage bed.

To fix precise values to key features of the construction, follow calculation procedures described in Appendix E.2.3 and the definitions listed below; also refer to Figure 13.2 (a).

V – the overall design rate (6 mm/h)

G/S– the 1:80 gradient for the straight portion at either edge of the cross-sectional profile of the pitch

H – the depth of the gravel drainage bed (mm)

K – the hydraulic conductivity of the *trench gravel* used to form the drainage bed (100 000 mm/h)

x_1 – the total distance from the centre of the pitch to a peripheral drain, measured horizontally (mm)

x – any distance from a drain measured horizontally across the pitch (mm)

x_0 – the point along the horizontal above which the curving portion of the profile begins (mm)

g – the height above the horizontal base line (mm).

Step 1: determine α using equation (E.31):

$$\alpha = \frac{1}{2} \frac{G}{S} \sqrt{\frac{K}{V}}$$

$$\alpha = \frac{1}{2} \times \frac{1}{80} \sqrt{\frac{100\,000}{6}}$$

$$= 0.807.$$

Step 2: determine γ using relationship to α as described in the graph, Figure 13.3(b): when $\alpha = 0.807$, $\gamma = 0.422$.

Step 3: using equation (E.51)

$$\gamma = \frac{H}{x_1} \sqrt{\frac{K}{V}}$$

giving

$$H = \gamma x_1 \sqrt{\frac{V}{K}}$$

$$= 0.422 \times 32\,000 \sqrt{\frac{6}{100\,000}}$$

$$= 105 \text{ mm (4¼ in).}$$

Step 4: using Equation (E.47), determine x_0, the distance from a drain at the edge of the pitch that defines the point on the surface where the uniform, 1:80 gradient begins to fall off to a steadily curving profile over the crown.

$$x_0 = x_1 - \left(\frac{K}{V} \frac{G}{S} H\right)$$

$$= 32\,000 - \left(\frac{100\,000}{6} \times \frac{1}{80} \times 105\right)$$

$$= 10\,100 \text{ mm (11 yards).}$$

Step 5: using equation (E.50), determine the height (mm) of the top of the soil formation surface above a series of base line values for x. Choose values for x that will facilitate construction of the profile required. Height g at point x (valid only for curved portion of profile):

$$g(x) = \frac{G}{S} \left(x_1 - \frac{1}{2} \frac{K}{V} \frac{G}{S} H\right)$$
$$- \frac{1}{2} \frac{V}{KH} (x_1 - x)^2.$$

For $x = 10\,100$ mm (i.e. x_0)

$$g = \frac{1}{80} \left(32\,000 - \frac{1}{2} \times \frac{100\,000}{6} \times \frac{1}{80} \times 105\right)$$

$$- \frac{1}{2} \times \frac{6}{100\,000 \times 105} (32\,000 - 10\,100)^2$$

$$= 126 \text{ mm (i.e. for distance of 10 100 mm at gradient of 1:80, rise = 126 mm).}$$

Similarly, after simplifying the calculation to

$$g = 263 - 0.286 \times \left(32 - \frac{x}{1000}\right)^2,$$

for $x = 12\,000$ mm $g = 149$ mm
  $x = 16\,000$ mm $g = 190$ mm
  $x = 20\,000$ mm $g = 222$ mm
  $x = 24\,000$ mm $g = 245$ mm
  $x = 28\,000$ mm $g = 258$ mm
  $x = 32\,000$ mm $g = 263$ mm,

and again in reverse order for the far side of the crown.

This profile is then repeated 105 mm, 145 mm and 185 mm higher, for the top of the gravel bed, the top of the layer of *blinding sand* and the top of the crushed rock, surfacing material respectively (Figure 13.2(a)).

A crowned profile of this form could well be considered for use elsewhere than for hard porous pitches, e.g. beneath a suitably resilient surface, such as an outside arena for horse riding.

13.3.3 Outline specification

1. The formation layer should be excavated and shaped to create a stable, consolidated surface of subsoil conforming exactly with one or other of the profiles illustrated in Figure 13.2. After initial site preparation the consolidated soil surface, covered with either filter fabric or 25 mm (1 in) of *blinding sand*, should be at a depth below the general level of the adjacent, undisturbed soil equal to the combined depth of the *trench gravel*, *blinding sand* and crushed rock layers used to create the drainage bed and playing surface. It is vital that the soil is disturbed as little as possible below excavation depth and is properly re-consolidated every 150 mm (6 in) where used as fill. Differential settlement after the whole construction is in place is a major hazard and care is required to minimize this risk.

2. Install perimeter drains along each side so as to intercept water reaching the area from surrounding land and to take water flowing out of the gravel foundation. The drains should run just inside a concrete edging, the trench at least 200 mm (8 in) wide. Pipes should be between 100 and 150 mm (4 and 6 in) in diameter according to the size of the area and the amount of water likely to be intercepted from surrounding land. See back to section 13.2.4 for a modification where precautions need to be taken against a risk of site flooding.

   Ideally, the pipes should be laid to a fall of not less than 1:100, with depth to invert not less than 300 mm (12 in) below the level of the formation surface. Permeable backfill should be *trench gravel*, finishing at least 50 mm (2 in) proud of the formation surface so as to protect the freely porous backfill from becoming contaminated by soil as the work proceeds. They should link with other pipes via chambers with silt traps, and have access points along their length to aid inspection and jet clearance of silt.

   If additional, longitudinal drains are used within the pitch area they should be similar to those at the periphery.

3. Round-topped precast concrete edging, 150 × 50 mm (6 × 2 in), should be laid round four sides, bedded and haunched in concrete so that the top lies flush with the final surface level.

4. After applying total weedkiller to the formation surface and margins, the formation soil surface should be blinded with 25 mm (1 in) of *blinding sand*, or synthetic fabric filter, anchored by tucking the edge down the inner wall of the peripheral drain trenches.

5. Lay and spread a foundation, drainage layer of *trench gravel* to the depth indicated as appropriate in Figure 13.2. If a somewhat angular gravel is used this will assist trafficking during construction. Take pains to consolidate and true the surface to the required configuration.

6. Evenly blind the gravel drainage bed with 40 mm (1½ in) of *blinding sand*; true and consolidate.

7. Lay and spread approved, crushed-rock surfacing material to an even, consolidated depth of 40 mm (1½ in) so as to finish flush with the top of the edging.
8. Initially the surface will be loose and inclined to be churned up by use unless gently firmed down, for example, by the continuous patter of feet when moist. Top-dress with crushed rock to true off to the required profile overall.
9. The build-up over the level pitch margins and peripheral drains should conform with that of the pitch in general. As experience indicates where surface runoff accumulates, make local provision to clear ponded water directly into the gravel bed through a layer of fabric filter, buried at shallow depth beneath a cosmetic covering of the gravel fraction sieved out of the crushed-rock surfacing material.

13.4 Maintenance

13.4.1 Special problems likely to be revealed soon after construction

The main task of maintenance on water-bound, hard porous pitches is to keep the surface uniform in composition, consolidated and true, despite the tendency for a particulate, multi-particle-sized material to segregate when churned up by energetic play. This problem will be worst immediately after construction but should decrease as more effective particle packing allows the surface to stabilize.

Differential settlement, which is also likely to be most pronounced in the initial years following construction, may be sufficient to cause local, dished areas, liable to accumulate surface runoff. These should be eliminated by topdressing with more surface material before a deposit of eroded fine particles builds up to adversely affect infiltration. A reserve of 4–6 tonne of

surfacing material will be required annually for re-truing and the replacement of losses brought about by comminution and surface erosion.

Persistent problems of surface ponding should not occur if the surface is smooth and suitably graded so as to clear all surface water to the periphery. However, if designed too flat, problems of persistent surface ponding may require attention. This can be approached in two ways. A disc, slicing device can be used to slit through the surface material and reach the clean gravel below. If the slit is oriented across slope and filled with coarse particles, either brushed off the surface or separated by sieving from the bulk reserve, it will function to intercept surface flow. However, any beneficial effect is unlikely to persist for more than a few months as surface wear will soon ensure fine-particle invasion of the coarse backfill. Alternatively, install, a small, 150 mm (6 in) diameter, readily accessible outfall in the base of each major depression so that it can be opened up to clear ponded water quickly when necessary. These covered outlets should take the form of wide-necked funnels, each anchored with its neck in the underlying gravel bed and bowl opening just below the surface. The inlet should be protected against silting by covering with a renewable, fabric filter, shielded against physical damage by covering with a removable, wooden cap, lying flush with the surface.

13.4.2 Surface renovation and surface protection

Routine maintenance involves luting, drag matting, brushing and rolling. Scarification will also be required, but only when the top needs opening up to help integrate a surface topdressing. Since agitation will inevitably lead to segregation of coarse particles onto the surface, rolling should be carried out when the whole top is moist. This will make it easier for the coarse particles to be pressed back into the finer material below. If not, they will remain as a loose covering, unfavourable to efficient traction. The late F. W. Smith, the first Grounds Superintendent at the University of Lancaster, and great advocate of hard porous surfaces, used to strongly advise rolling in the rain.

Provision for irrigation should be considered essential as the shallow, surface layer will readily dry out in hot weather, and then be vulnerable to windblow.

Hard porous materials are often wrongly described as 'all weather'. In fact there are two weather-induced conditions when use should not be contemplated. Do not risk loosening the surface if irrigation cannot be used during hot weather to prevent the fine particles required for water-binding being selectively removed by wind erosion. On no account use a hard porous surface after frost until it has thawed out and been thoroughly re-consolidated by rolling. The expansion that follows the freezing of retained moisture may lead to considerable surface heave.

Salt will help to keep this type of surface 'greasily' moist through a dry spell and less inclined to freeze up in winter, but it will readily wash out and then encourage the leaching away of any clay component.

13.4.3 Manpower

Though much more suitable for programmed use than the normal, soil-based, grass surface, to sustain performance, provision must be made for frequent surface renovation. In practice, therefore, this type of non-grass facility should not be looked upon as allowing any very significant saving in maintenance manpower.

13.5 Further developments in the hard porous approach

13.5.1 Surfaces for schooling horses

If the *blinding sand* layer of a hard porous construction is overlaid with 100 mm (4 in) depth of *topsoil sand*, or any other medium approved for the purpose, it might well serve for the schooling of horses. In these circumstances the sand, or special alternative layer, should be placed over a layer of fabric filter to facilitate surface renewal without risk to the integrity of the drainage bed. Provision for irrigation will be necessary to keep the surface firmly water-bound.

13.5.2 Nottinghamshire envelope system

Peter L. K. Dury, working in the Nottinghamshire playing-field service, has developed the idea of enveloping hard porous and dune-sand-like materials within free-draining and tractively efficient, filter fabrics (geotextiles). The early promise of this approach has now led on to diversification into a wide range of amenity applications from safe surfaces for child play to cricket pitches, tennis courts and full-scale pitches for hockey and soccer. All of these have infill and surface fabrics matched to the special requirements of the user. Here then is a halfway house between the very expensive, wholly synthetic surfaces, claimed to be all-weather, and the much less sophisticated but relatively cheap workhorse, the original hard porous pitch. They all aim to provide surfaces better suited than grass for intensive, programmed use.

Chapter fourteen

PATENT
PENDING

DIY construction, package deals, patents, trade names and trade-sponsored literature

14.1 DIY approach to construction

14.1.1 Introduction

A well-managed complex of facilities that included, for example, a bowling green, a children's play area, an orderly arrangement of allotments and a multi-purpose playing field, all laid out around a club house, car park and maintenance yard, could do much to meet the social needs of a community. In many circumstances the provision of just one of these facilities would be a welcome move in the right direction.

It has been a primary aim of this book to give practical support to the ideals and objectives of the National Playing Fields Association. This is a charity whose purpose is to help those who wish to use outdoor facilities for recreation. It provides grants and advice either to assist in the improvement of existing facilities or to help create something entirely new. Being a charity with very limited resources it must be particu-

larly concerned to achieve maximum benefit for minimum cost. One way of achieving this is to encourage community involvement in a DIY approach which may have the added bonus of community concern for aftercare.

14.1.2 Advisory services

In previous chapters general guidance has been given to illustrate how theoretical principles work out when applied to typical, practical examples. This guidance should be adequate to enable organizations intent on adopting a DIY approach to achieve this with the technical support of the NPFA or an independent consultant.

Role of the adviser in a DIY project

1. To assist with site selection;
2. to provide the technical vetting that can eliminate mistakes in design and choice of materials;

3. to inspect and provide guidance at critical periods during construction.

Role of the community in a DIY project

1. Planning permission must be obtained, and checks made with the local authority on arrangements for discharge of drainage water and obligations with regard to public utilities.
2. The adviser will require support in designing the various facilities, preparing layout and construction drawings, specifying the materials and staging the work.
3. The site will require marking out and checking against the specification.
4. As the construction work proceeds, it will be necessary to call on the adviser to inspect and instruct as each pre-determined stage in the construction is reached and before the next stage begins.
5. Working with the adviser a detailed programme of maintenance must be agreed, care having been taken at the planning stage to point out the general nature of the maintenance that will be required according to the scheme of construction adopted.

Payment

Independent advice can be a much undervalued commodity. We are happy to pay for goods but we expect advice to be given free on the packet. The value of advice is often not immediately obvious and, if given verbally, tends to be regarded as a goodwill offering. However, knowledge is a commodity well worth paying for and should not be confused with sales talk.

An independent consultant will either work to a scale of fees based on time and expenses, or charge a fixed percentage of the contract price. The NPFA expect the client to cover all the expenses involved in advisory visits but may use charity money to cover the cost of the adviser's time.

14.1.3 Organizing community effort

Tasks

Working together can strengthen a community so that much is to be said, in a DIY project, for spreading around the variety of tasks involved. These include:

- fund raising;
- financial control;
- design, preparation of drawings, specification of work and marking out;
- timely ordering and provision of approved materials, equipment and mechanical aids;
- timely provision of skilled manpower and willing labour;
- site management to organize each stage of the work, to check on the standard of workmanship and to maintain a tidy, well-organized site;
- organization of maintenance, from seeding onwards.

Each stage of the work should be finished off securely so that no harm will come to the progress of the work should a long interruption intervene. Holes, trenches and depressions should not be left to fill up with water because no provision has been made to protect them against surface-water flooding, or to clear accumulating water to a safe outfall. When working in the open the aim should be never to start what cannot be cleared up and made safe before leaving.

Personnel

Recreational activities can attract a wide range of personalities. When allocating tasks for a DIY project it would be as well to remember how a psychologist is said to have classified personality according to activity and intelligence:

- the active and intelligent – they are liable to develop neuroses and burn out early;
- the inactive and unintelligent – they do not

achieve very much but neither do they do much harm;

- the active but unintelligent – they are likely to be a menace;
- the inactive but intelligent – these are the most useful because they will think twice before committing themselves to action.

Beware the macho man, revved up with horsepower and impatient to get started. Be on site early to think ahead for him. Give simple, clear instructions for just one phase of the work at a time and keep your own, more reliable manpower to clear up afterwards. Be on site to observe the large boulder that might otherwise end up just below the surface, or the topsoil that was about to be buried when it should have been preserved for better use elsewhere. Reject no genuine offer of help but supervise diligently until experience justifies confidence.

14.2 Package deals

It is possible, at extra cost, to obtain package deals from consultants and contractors which may include:

1. details of model schemes requiring only local modification to fit the peculiarities of a particular site;
2. plans, specifications and details of quantities to achieve a specified purpose on a particular site;
3. a total package deal, covering both design and construction, plus immediate aftercare through to the point of handover for play.

The NPFA endeavours to keep abreast of this information and should be contacted by those wishing to purchase information sheets listing appropriate consultants and contractors.

Beware the tendency for package deals to escalate. From the contractor's point of view the bigger the package that he can conveniently handle the better the financial prospects of the deal. And the more ancillary aids he can build

in, the less risk of failure. This will protect the contractor against litigation, and suits the big-spending professionals who demand play at any cost. It may well be cheaper to include irrigation and undersoil heating in one package along with drainage, but in most circumstances drainage along will suffice. Improved drainage, to the extent that it will keep the soil drier, will bring with it less risk of damage from frost heave, and because of improved soil aeration, will encourage deeper rooting and therefore lessen the risk of sward damage from desiccation.

Many things are useful but that does not mean they are essential. Prudent spending requires that priorities are critically assessed, particularly when spending other people's money.

14.3 Patents

14.3.1 Extent of cover

Periodically, one is liable to come across mention of the fact that a particular construction is protected by a patent. Sometimes the way this information is presented can mislead the reader into thinking that the patent covers every feature of the construction. This may raise doubt as to the freedom with which others may develop their own design or implement even traditional techniques to achieve their purpose.

The following advice on patent law has been checked by the NPFA and may be used as general guidance.

1. Nothing which is common knowledge can be patented. This covers traditional procedures and information freely available in the standard literature.
2. To secure a patent the inventor has to draw attention to the features of his invention

that are novel and it is these only that the granting of a patent protects.

3. The impression of quality and reliability that might be given by association with the backing of the law is not always justified in practice because, for an invention to be patented, it does not necessarily have to work.

4. The DIY enthusiasts have little to fear in the patent world so long as no one involved in the special nature of the construction is using the invention for financial gain.

14.3.2 Examples

1. One sub-irrigation system of construction involves tanking an excavation with polythene, laying pipes and building a soil of a closely specified sand. The construction is said to be covered by a patent. Does this mean that any system of sub-irrigation or any sand construction is covered? In fact, sub-irrigation and constructing with sand are old ideas. In this case, all the patent actually protects is the ingenious way devised to ensure that laterals off the main fill up in an orderly succession, but this patented technique is not the only way of achieving the benefits of sub-irrigation.

2. A construction involving a thick, surface carpet of sand, used to be widely advertised, like the last, under a trade name. It drew attention to the fact that it was covered by a patent, but this lapsed in 1990. In this case sand is spread as a thick carpet over a soil drained by an integrated system of gravel channels and pipes, the sward being established directly on top of the sand carpet. Such a design sounds as if it might cover any sand-over-soil construction, but the novel feature of the invention referred to the belief, heretofore, that it was not practicable for grass seed to germinate in 'uncontaminated sand'. The patent, therefore, only

referred to a construction in which the sward was established from seed sown directly onto a surface layer of **uncontaminated sand**, at least 3–4 in in depth. Since it was unlikely that many people would want to use sand for this purpose without including some soil, peat or other amendment, the patent had very little practical significance.

3. A lapsed patent for which application was first made in Austria in January 1965, appeared to cover all slit systems of surface drainage, but it repeatedly stressed the advantage in the invention of first strongly compacting the soil surface before slitting and seeding. The application of this patent, therefore, was again very narrowly defined, especially so when in the preamble it made clear that the strong compaction referred to was such as could be achieved by a road roller! No wonder the invention also referred to a special method of seeding involving a surface covering of straw, coated with asphalt.

It is obviously a very difficult thing to acquire the sort of all-embracing patent that advertisements seem sometimes to wish to imply. If in doubt, obtain a copy of the patent from The Patent Office, London WC2A 1AY.

14.4 Trade names

When a novel approach reaches the stage of commercial exploitation, minor variations which at best differ only marginally in principle, are hijacked by the marketing men for special promotion. This can then lead to exaggerated claims for significance based on pseudo-scientific terminology and the bogus distinction implied by a trade name. Fertilizers, weedkillers, hard porous surfacing materials, sand constructions and slit systems of drainage, the less they differ in principle the more it seems that the distinction of a trade name is required to secure a substantial share of the market.

14.5 Trade-sponsored literature

It would be naive to expect literature supported by advertising to be free of commercial pressures. Even technical articles are liable to be merely extensions of advertising. This is not the type of literature to which scientists normally refer, but in a free market economy we must all learn to recognize partial information that is 'economical with the truth', and evaluate it accordingly.

The enthusiasm of the salesman should not be allowed to carry more weight than experience justifies. Though there must be some virtue in a well-tried recipe, for the salesman it is essential to project the idea of novelty. Each year the market needs reviving and last year's novelty has to be projected as superseded or set aside as obsolete. Too often we have seen a minor innovation immediately proclaimed as a significant breakthrough, but trades literature does not give equal prominence to its subsequent demise. No sales representative is going to help you to discover the weak features of his product; you must seek independent advice and then think things out for yourself, or find out by experience, too late. Listening, viewing and reading critically are skills which require effort to acquire, but acquire them you must if you are to survive in a free market system.

Part Three

Appendices

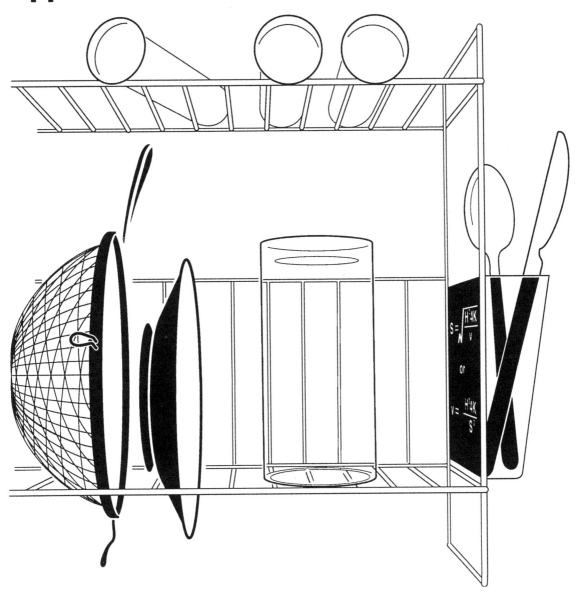

Simple tests for the determination of soil texture and topsoil quality

A.1 Soil texture assessed by handling properties

1. Moisten 10–20 g (i.e. a dessert-spoonful) of soil and knead into a firm dough – sand will feel gritty, silt will feel soft and silky, clay will be stiff and tenaciously sticky.
2. By trying to form shapes in the sequence 1–5 in Table A.1 the shape achieved furthest down the list will indicate the soil texture class.

A.2 Clay content assessed by the Adams and Stewart soil-binding test (ASSB or 'motty test')

A.2.1 Procedures

Because of the risk of errors in preparation it is advisable always to include a standard soil with each batch of determinations.

1. Place on a saucer a golf-ball-size sample of soil roughly 50 g (2 oz) for a mineral soil. Then add 15–20 ml of water, the lesser quantity for sands.
2. Rub down by firm thumb pressure, smearing on the surface of the saucer to break down all aggregation.

3. (a) Make into a ball and thump down on to absorbent paper to test for, and eliminate, excess moisture. Samples that are too wet will smear and stick to the paper; too dry samples will shatter and crack.
   (b) If too wet to thump drier, leave to stand for a while in contact with absorbent paper.
   If too dry, add 1 ml water, knead to incorporate and try (a) again, adding further 1-ml increments of water if necessary.
4. Place clod on dish in one drop of water, and cover with a small glass or cup. Leave to stand for several hours, e.g. overnight. This will allow time for the water to become uniformly dispersed.
5. Check on the moisture state of the clod after equilibration, then:
   (a) if too dry the surface will be dull and a further drop of water may require to be added;
   (b) if too wet there may be a pool of water in the dish and the clod will glisten. Pour off any free water and leave the

TABLE A.1 Handling properties and soil texture class

Shape	Texture
1. Cone only	Sand
2. Cone and ball only	Loamy sand
3. Cone, ball and worm formed, worm cracks when bent; ball inclined to be soft-centred	Silty loam
4. Cone, ball and worm formed, but worm cracks when bent; ball not noticably soft-centred	Remainder of loams
5. Cone, ball and worm formed, but worm not cracked when bent into a ring around finger. Ball typically stiff to work and difficult to round off into a perfect sphere when just moist enough to mould without cracking. The surface will readily take on a polish.	Clay

wet clod to dry for a while on absorbent paper;

(c) if ideal, the soil ball will be glistening wet but there will be no free water in the dish.

6. When the clod is satisfactorily wet, re-work in the hand and then roll into a cylinder 25 mm (1 in) in diameter. Avoid incorporating folds and cut off any involuted ends. Cut the cylinder into three or four, 20 mm (¾ in) lengths, discarding any residue. Ensure that all sections used are of equal size.

7. Mould cylinder sections into round balls, avoiding folds. Add one drop of water and thoroughly re-work if there is a tendency to crack. Round off by progressively rolling more firmly between the palms of both hands for at least 45 seconds.

With strongly coherent soils such as loams and clays, maximize consolidation by repeatedly throwing the ball down on to a smooth, solid surface covered with clean absorbent paper. Roll to restore shape after each throw. Continue until the reduced earthy staining of the paper on impact indicates that all excess water has been squeezed out, then round off for the last time, aiming to form a perfect sphere with a smooth, polished surface.

With silts and sands there may well be insufficient cohesion to enable a moist ball to hold together on impact. Therefore, consolidation and removal of excess water will have to be achieved at the ball-forming stage by very careful squeezing and blotting during the rounding-off process. If the ball is left to stand periodically on absorbent paper, this can help, but great care will be required when handling during the rounding-off process as any motty, with little or no clay, will become brittle as it dries out.

In every case, aim to form a perfectly smooth, well-consolidated sphere, with no cracks.

8. Leave the moulded soil balls uncovered overnight to begin drying. If they have been rolled too wet they will be moist and flattened at the base next morning and may stick to the dish. They should be left to dry out completely over a period of 5 days at normal room temperature.

9. On the sixth day, crack the dry motty between two, smooth, hard surfaces laid one over the other on the platform of a bathroom scales. Apply foot pressure from above and record weight required to shatter the dry motty. Zero the scales, plus any base plate used, before applying pressure

TABLE A.2 Classification of clay content and breaking strength (ASSB) values

ASSB value		Equivalent clay content for well-made motties	Strength category
113 kg	(250 lb) and over	over 55%	Exceptionally strong
91–113 kg	(200–250 lb)	44–55%	Very strong
68–91 kg	(150–200 lb)	33–44%	Strong
45–68 kg	(100–150 lb)	22–33%	Moderately strong
23–45 kg	(50–100 lb)	11–22%	Weak
9–23 kg	(20–50 lb)	4–11%	Very weak
under 9 kg	(20 lb)	below 4%	Non-binding

from above. If the motty is well made the shatter point will be well defined and sudden.

10. Because of the risk of errors in preparation affecting individual motties, eliminate the lowest breaking value in every three determinations before averaging the remaining values to give the rating for the sample.

A.2.2 Interpretation of breaking strength values

Table A.2 classifies ASSB breaking strengths for well-made, properly air-dried motties of normal topsoil. Every 2 kg (4½ lb) of breaking strength corresponds to approximately 1% of clay but, for those inexperienced in motty making, assume 1.6–1.8 kg (3½–4 lb) of breaking strength corresponds to 1% of clay.

If you regard efficient motty making as a skill worth acquiring, then practice with materials of known clay content.

Clay type and degree of dispersion can affect the ASSB value. Small, potentially very active clays, and marked dispersion typical of structurally degraded and salt-affected soil, both increase the binding strength of a given quantity of clay. However, these effects will also be expressed in the field so that, if regarded as a measure of the degree to which a soil will display the characteristics typical of its clay content, clay type and state of dispersion, then ASSB rankings will not mislead.

A.3 Modification of the motty test to assess topdressing compatibility with the topsoil already in place

As reported in *Parks and Sports Grounds*, May, 1987, Dr W. A. Adams has now introduced a modification to the motty test which is of particular value for checking on the compatibility of different clay soil top-dressings used to promote pace on cricket pitches. The modification involves joining two half-motties together along the flattened face of each hemisphere. To help achieve a firm join, avoid trapping air along the junction by ponding water over the upturned face of one hemisphere, then, after wetting the face of the other hemisphere, bring the two together by inverting the second hemisphere over the ponded surface of the first. Place the composite motty on absorbent paper for a while to dry off excess water, and when no longer too tacky to handle, remould and consolidate into a ball, dry and determine breaking strength, as recommended for loams and clays in paragraphs 7–9 of section A 2.1.

If there is excessive differential shrinkage between the two halves on drying then the motty will readily separate along the boundary. Compatible soils will hold together until the whole motty shatters at random. This difference cannot be confidently predicted from differences in clay content alone, other factors such as clay type and state of dispersion also being involved.

Needless to say, only materials that cohere well in such a test with the existing surface soil should be used for topdressing. This also suggests that when trying to effect change by upgrading the binding strength of the soil used for topdressing, progress may have to be gradual.

A.4 Sand content assessed by decantation of the silt and clay

When all the mineral particles in a soil have been freed to act as individuals they settle out in water at very different rates according to size. From a totally dispersed sample, 180 mm (7 in) deep, left to sediment out in still water, all the sand will have settled to the bottom in one minute. A decantation of the supernatant will then contain only silt and clay. Repeated dispersions, followed by decantation, will eventually remove all the silt and clay, leaving only the sand.

For practical reasons it is probably best to carry out this determination starting with a cup-sized sample of soil left to dry for a week at room temperature and passed through a 2 mm sieve. From this weigh out 110 g (4 oz will do) for typical topsoil (5–10% organic matter), or 103 g for subsoil, and then puddle, using no more than a cupful of water. Work in a 9-litre (2-gallon) bucket, and rub the soil against the wall of the bucket with a pliable spatula. To assist with clay dispersion, add to the water a pinch of table salt and a pinch, or a few drops of a non-frothing detergent (e.g. Calgon). The aim should be to free the individual soil particles by rubbing down any granular aggregations between the fingers. Once the soil has been converted to a smooth paste, make up with water to a height of 200 mm (8 in) from the base and stir vigorously to try and form a uniform suspension of the soil in the water. Quickly counter any residual swirling motion in the water and note the time when sedimentation is allowed to begin.

Exactly one minute later carefully tip out most of the supernatant liquid, in a continuous, steady stream, leaving only the equivalent of 20–30 mm (1 in) of water to remain in the bucket. Refill with water to the 200 mm (8 in) height and repeat for a total of four decantations. By the fourth decantation the supernatant liquid will scarcely be cloudy and it will be possible to pour off virtually all the free water, including any sludge or organic debris half suspended in the last dregs of the water. The total sand fraction should be dried, e.g. at 100°C in an oven or near a room heater, until it flows easily without sticking, then weigh. The weight in grammes will represent the percentage sand in the mineral skeleton of the original sample. A value in excess of 70 g (2½ oz) will indicate a soil with the workability and free-draining characteristics of a sand, i.e. a soil particularly prone to be hungry and thirsty unless maintained well-supplemented with organic matter. A value falling short of 70 g (i.e. less than 70% sand) will indicate a loam or a clay, requiring further investigation by means of its reaction to the 'worm' test, as described in section A.1, or by the breaking strength of its motty being higher or lower than 80 kg (180 lb). However, from the evidence of sand content alone, the probability zone on the triangle of texture (Figure A.1) indicates that the soil is very unlikely to be a clay unless the sand value is less than 40 g (40%).

A.5 Designation of soil texture classes

A.5.1 Considering the mineral, fine earth only

From systematic sampling of soil data, it would appear that 90% of the soils in England and

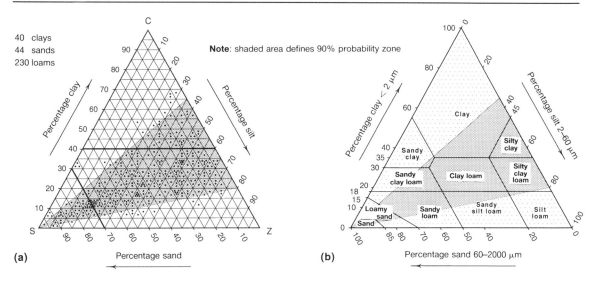

(a)

40 clays
44 sands
230 loams

Note: shaded area defines 90% probability zone

(b)

Systematic sampling of soil survey data for England and Wales suggests that 1/8th of our mineral topsoils are likely to be sands and another 1/8th clays, but 3/4 are likely to be some form of loam (Stewart *et al.*1980).

FIGURE A.1 Triangles of texture defining 90% probability zone for topsoils in England and Wales. (a) Plot of systematically sampled data for topsoils in England and Wales. (b) 90% probability zone superimposed on triangle of texture defining commonly used BS particle-size classes.

Wales lie within the probability zone defined in Figures A.1 and A.2 and most of these lie close to the line X–Y (Figure A.2).

For practical purposes, when dealing with normal soils which are neither markedly organic nor excessively stony, there is much to be said for limiting the objective to the recognition of just the three texture categories shown in Figure A.2. These can fairly readily be recognized by their handling properties but, as corroborative evidence, the ASSB value or the sand content will provide quantitative data indicating lines for clay or sand content along which the sample must lie. Plotting both for sand and clay will give an intersection defining the texture exactly. However, if only one of these – sand or clay – is known, a projection into the 90% probability area will give useful general guidance which the handling properties will refine sufficiently to enable a choice to be

made between the three simple categories on offer.

Alternatively, as the data for England and Wales indicate that most soils contain silt and clay in a ratio close to 6:4, an estimate of any one fraction, sand, silt or clay, will also allow an estimate to be made of all three. For example, if clay content is 20%, silt is likely to be of the order of $20 \times \frac{6}{4} = 30\%$ and sand $100 - (20 + 30) = 50\%$.

A.5.2 Taking account of stones and organic matter

Stones contribute very little other than weight to a soil. They are essentially inert filler, occupying space without contributing to water or nutrient supply. They dilute the influence of the active soil.

Organic matter is itself a significant source of

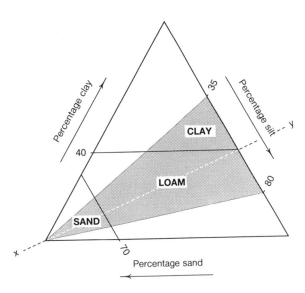

FIGURE A.2 Triangle of texture showing particle-size classes reduced to just three major categories: sand, clay and loam.

a wide range of nutrients beneficial to plants and soil organisms, and it may supplement the available water reserve. However, organic matter is light in weight and, when dominant, as in peat, may adversely affect anchorage.

Both components should be commented upon in a full texture description as they can significantly modify predictions based solely on the particle-size composition of the mineral, fine earth.

Classifications of stone and organic matter contents are subjective, like the particle-size classes used to define the texture of the mineral, fine earth. They tend to be ignored, and no one system of classification seems yet to have found general acceptance, but for precise specification it is essential that categories are defined.

Stones

Table A.3 defines categories based on size and quantity. These are used by soil scientists for general descriptive purposes. Note, this system dispenses with the idea of distinguishing the finer fractions described in Tables 7.1 and 13.1 as fine and coarse gravel particles (2–4 mm and 4–8 mm in nominal diameter). Based on these categories, a loam with 50% stones by weight (35% by volume) would be more correctly described as a very stony loam and, if some of the stones were boulders, these would have to be specifically mentioned also.

To assess stone content accurately requires very large samples, and correspondingly robust equipment, but it can be assessed adequately enough in the field by eye using the volume categories as guidance.

On sports fields, boulders are never welcome within drain trenching depth, and if less than 2–3 m apart, they will severely impede tillage and subsoiling. Stones over 6–8 cm will interfere with efficient slit trenching and spiking. Ideally a topsoil for sports turf should not contain stones much larger than 2 cm, especially if sharply angular and liable to cause injury.

A topsoil classified in Table A.3 as more than slightly stony should be considered undesirable, especially if it is to be imported. By the time it has been spread, harrowed, levelled and seeded, the mechanical agitation will have brought the stones to the surface, concentrating them where they are least welcome. Any process involving soil agitation, such as cultivation or frost heaving, will cause stones to rise because the fine soil will more easily slump back into place. The only natural processes that will tend to bury stones are the surface casting of earthworms, and in the absence of earthworms, the accumulation of a surface, organic mat. Under sports turf the former will at best take years to build up; the latter is undesirable. Better to avoid the problem by choosing a soil that is no more than slightly stony in the first place.

Organic matter

Table A.4 indicates categories of organic matter content that should be used to qualify a texture classification. For example, a natural loam soil

TABLE A.3 Ranking of stone and boulder categories – sizes and quantities

Longest diameter (mm)	Size category	Percentage by weight	By volume (approx %)	Classification
over 600	boulder	under 1		stoneless
600–200	V.L. stone	1–5	under 3	V.S. stony
200–60	L. stone	6–15	3–8	S. stony
60–20	M. stone	16–35	9–21	M. stony
20–6	S. stone	36–70	22–53	V. stony
6–2	V.S. stone	71–80	54–66	Ex. stony
under 2	Fine earth	over 80	over 66	Insufficient fine earth to fill cavities between stones

TABLE A.4 Rough guide to the significance of organic matter content in British soils

Percentage by weight (oven dry)	Percentage by volume (oven dry)	Practical significance
under 3	under 16	Mineral soil with organic matter in short supply; typical of subsoils and degraded topsoils
3–10	16–38	Mineral soil, adequately organic enriched; typical of worm-worked topsoil
10–25	38–65	Humose – organic matter content beginning to dominate soil properties; organic decay probably restricted seasonally by low temperature and/or excessive wetness
25–35	65–75	Peaty – soil essentially organic because site and/or climate has caused organic decay to be impeded by persistent waterlogging
over 35	over 75	Peat – an accumulation of organic residues where decay has been arrested by site and climate combining to cause permanent waterlogging

containing 12% organic matter by dry weight (about 43% by volume) should be described as humose; a loam containing 6% organic matter by dry weight (about 25% by volume), loam with normal topsoil organic matter content. (Figure A.3 gives weight/volume conversions.)

The organic matter categories defined in Table A.4 have practical significance. Below 3% organic matter by dry weight (about 16% by volume) there begins to be insufficient organic matter to benefit structure. Organic matter contents of around 6–8% by dry weight (25–31% by volume) are typical of natural topsoils in Britain sustained in good heart by earthworms. Organic matter contents in excess of 10–12% by dry weight (37–43% by volume) indicate soils in which there has been at least some seasonal restriction in organic matter decay, probably low temperature and/or excess moisture, slowing down biological activity. At

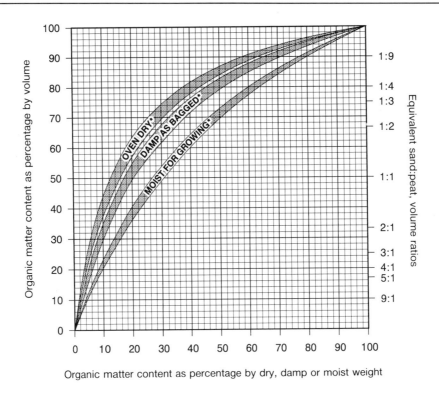

Oven dry: moisture content of organic component 0% of dry weight.

Damp: Moisture content of organic component 66% of dry weight/40% of damp weight.

Moist: Moisture content of organic component 234% of dry weight/70% of moist weight.

FIGURE A.3 Rough guide to relationship between percentage organic matter by weight and percentage organic matter by volume. In each zone the upper margin relates to sand/peat mixtures; the lower margin to mixtures in which the mineral component is loam in particle-size composition. A strongly granulated soil would lie outwith the lower margin.

over about 25% organic matter by dry weight (65% by volume) the material is peat in origin, a product of prolonged waterlogging arresting organic decay.

However, as organic matter contents can be enhanced artificially, organic matter content alone should not be used as definitive evidence of topsoil quality. For loams and clays in particular, there needs also to be satisfactory evidence on water-stable structure.

A.6 Practical significance of the three primary soil texture classes: sands, clays and loams

A.6.1 Strong clay soils

Winter games

Soils with a binding strength of over 82 kg (180 lb), equivalent to clay content of 40% are likely to be strong cracking clays, i.e. given the opportunity to dry out thoroughly, as in a long dry summer, they will form a system of deep cracks. If these are filled from the surface with fine, dry sand they will continue to assist with surface drainage throughout the succeeding winter.

To ensure a good packing of sand within the cracks, the sand-filling operation should be carried out with a uniform fine sand, when both sand and surface are dry, and the cracks wide open. Six millimetres (¼ in) of sand, equivalent to 100 tonnes/hectare (40 tons/acre), spread over the surface and brushed into the cracks, would not be an over estimate of the amount of sand required in the initial application. Topping up will be necessary in succeeding years when conditions are dry enough to re-open the cracks again.

Because of the tendency for strong clay soils to structure themselves by cracking, and then to maintain this form by virtue of their binding strength, they are the soils most likely to respond favourably to mole ploughing (Chapter 2, page 35). For this reason, true clay soils are a much better proposition for drainage then the silty soils with which they are so frequently confused. It is inadvisable therefore, to assume a texture based solely on superficial evidence without checking by means of a motty test. The difference in binding strength between silt and clay is so obvious that it leaves no margin for doubt.

Cricket tables

Pace is an essential feature of the performance of a cricket pitch and for this the clay content of the soil is critical (Table 12.4, page 185). Appropriate ASSB values are as follows:

1. school and club standard, where durable pace is secondary to trueness and ease of preparation, 36–64 kg (80–140 lb);
2. first class County standard, where skilled time-consuming preparation is essential, 64–82 kg (140–180 lb);
3. breaking strength at which pitch pre-

paration is likely to be difficult, and an inadequately prepared pitch dangerous, 82 kg (180 lb) and over.

A.6.2 Weak, very sandy soils

Soils with a binding strength of under 18 kg (40 lb), equivalent to a clay content of 9%, are likely to be sands, loamy sands or low clay versions of silt loams. To further distinguish between these three alternatives, use handling properties or visual examination (section A.1).

If revealed to be a loamy sand, such a soil can be expected to retain a useful amount of rapid drainage, even when compact, providing the infiltered water can be adequately discharged below ground.

If revealed to be a sandy silt loam or a silt loam, (i.e. less than 70% sand and less than 10% clay) such a soil should be avoided where, as under sports turf, it cannot be repeatedly cultivated. It will be inclined to slump and retain moisture. Water may not lie for long on the surface but the problem will be to clear water from the uniform, fine pore system of the soil itself.

Even amongst soils more than 70% sand, problems of drainage can arise.

1. If the sand component is not of a uniform, particle-size composition, e.g. if it does not have of the order of 80% in the medium-to-fine (0.125–0.500 mm) particle-size range. Too wide a range of particle sizes allows for a substantial amount of interpacking within the sand itself, reducing the amount of silt and clay required to block the remaining pore space. Contrast the cement required to make up a cement mortar with that required for an equal volume of concrete. Where there is a wide range of particle sizes present in a sand, e.g. no two adjacent categories together exceeding 80%, then it may not be until the total sand content exceeds 90% that there will be insufficient silt and clay to

fill the available pore space when the soil is compact.

2. If the silt and clay present is allowed to segregate into layers. This is particularly liable to happen if the clay is freely dispersible in water, i.e. not associated with organic matter in water-stable clusters. Such a dispersed state is typical of soil that has been stockpiled (refer to section A.7).

A.6.3 Loamy soils

The sands and strong clays together constitute only one quarter of the soils of England and Wales. The loams, that is soils with no more than 70% sand or 40% clay, are by far our commonest soils. For them particle aggregation is essential to provide the proper balance of water retentive (small) and free-draining (large) pores required to ensure an acceptable air/water balance. As already discussed in section 1.4, with a fairly balanced mixture of particle sizes we do not automatically get the nice mixture of large and small pores that one might expect because the different particle-size grades tend to interpack, leaving the finer grades in control of the pore space. Therefore, to provide a free-draining, macro-pore system in a loam-textured soil some form of aggregation into water-stable granules is absolutely essential.

Soil granulation in the loams is primarily a by-product of the processing of soil by earthworms, as they burrow and process fresh organic residues into the mineral soil. Typically it occurs under grass but only when earthworms are present.

In sports turf the twin problems of soil compaction and thatch appear when earthworms are absent. Associated features are: surface rooting, sensitivity to drought, and problems with those pests and diseases that are encouraged by an organic-rich surface and the absence of earthworm browsing.

However, water-stable, soil granulation, though fairly stable to the patter of raindrops,

cannot survive the sort of foot traffic that a football pitch receives in the winter. When present in such circumstances earthworms will continually re-open their burrows and thereby contribute to drainage, but the loss of soil granulation between the worm burrows ensures that the bulk of the soil is compact and water holding. When earthworm activity is absent, as on many made-up sites, or discouraged by the acidity promoted by sulphate-rich fertilizers, or failure to lime, a loam can rapidly become surface waterlogged, even when perched over a free-draining gravel bed that is no more than 150 mm (6 in) under the surface.

Where a loam soil is to be subject to intensive winter use, beyond the capacity of an active earthworm population to continually rehabilitate, spiking and surface sanding can at best provide only temporary relief. In fact, spiking, if overdone, can lead to new problems of sub-surface compaction. The only long-term solution for sports use is to install an intensive system of surface-opening, vertical slits, stabilized by appropriate permeable fill, and linked for discharge below into a pipe, or soakaway system.

A.7 Assessment of topsoil condition in loamy soils

A loam in good condition is likely to be associated with visual evidence of the presence of earthworms, including their casts and burrows. There will be no evidence of a surface, organic mat. Instead, the organic matter content (5–10%) and the roots will be evenly distributed throughout a surface layer of soil, typically 225 mm (9 in) – 300 mm (12 in) deep, well aggregated and water stable. The pH will probably lie between 5.5 and 7.5, limits ideal both for earthworms and grass.

As the water-stable aggregation is both **the consequence** of all the conditions being right to encourage earthworm activity, and **the cause** of the fertility which benefits grass growth, a test to assess the degree to which a loam soil is water-stably aggregated can be used as a general criterion of quality.

To carry out the simplest form of this test, air dry the soil, then sieve off any loose particles that will pass a domestic, culinary or flour sieve. Place a dessert spoonful of the material retained on the sieve into a glass containing approximately 100 mm (4 in) depth of cold water. Leave to soak for five minutes and then swirl ten times. If the solution rapidly clears and the granules of the soil remain more-or-less coherent, the structure is water stable and the soil could be expected to be of a kind that a farmer would describe as topsoil in 'good heart'. Check if the soil units that appear to be stable are indeed single, solid particles, or aggregates of particles that will crush down further to smaller components merely under finger pressure.

This test is not appropriate for sands, loamy sands and loams which have insufficient clay (less than 10%) to hold a structure. They will probably break down completely at the dry sieving stage anyway. However, of these, the sands and loamy sands have more than 70% sand and can be readily amended for use as free-draining topsoils, merely by the addition of an organic compost. Loams with less than 10% clay are uncommon and are potentially quite difficult to manage, even for agriculture, unless the cropping system and the climate allow for periodic, mechanical disturbance to relieve compaction.

To improve the quality of the water-stability test there are several modifications that should be considered:

1. The whole sample can be used – set aside until just brittle-dry, then ease clods apart, teasing out roots so as to create a tilth that will all pass a 10-mm (¼–⅜-in) riddle. Avoid working the soil when it is inclined to smear or dust.

2. Sub-samples of the total soil sample prepared as above should be compared with:
   (a) samples of similar texture but of known subsoil origin;
   (b) a selection of earthworm casts from the surface of a soil of similar texture, under grass, and/or topsoil from undisturbed land around the edge of the field.
   The aim should be to provide a scale of comparison ranging from the worst to the best that could reasonably be expected for the texture of the soil under examination.

3. Allow about one hour for the soil to soak, then swirl and allow five minutes for the material to settle. Note the relative cloudiness of the supernatant liquid. Looking up through the base of the glass beaker, against the light, decant off the supernatant if particularly cloudy, and then observe the extent to which the aggregation has remained water stable. The less cloudy the supernatant and the greater the amount of water-stable aggregation the better is the condition of the soil.

4. A loam or clay in good heart will settle out in water to leave a clear, or translucent, supernatant solution with light showing through the gaps between granules. This is best seen when the solution is gently agitated and viewed from below, against the light. A loam, or clay in poor condition will leave a cloudy effect in the supernatant solution, varying a little in proportion to the silt and clay content of the soil; any aggregation will collapse to form an opaque sludge at the base of the beaker. A chalk or limestone soil, because of its high lime content, may cause the supernatant solution to clear by flocculating any suspended clay. However, the true state of affairs will be evident in the curdiness of the flocculated deposit compared with the discrete, granular character of water-stable aggregates.

Simple tests for *Stewart zone* materials

For all materials it is assumed here that particle shape and mineral composition is satisfactory.

B.1 *Stewart zone topsoil sand* (uniform fine sand)

Often, small local suppliers are unable to provide numerical data to assist with the selection of appropriate sands. However, they are usually aware of the general nature of their materials and describe them either in terms of their use, or their source. Sands, described variously as dune, building, plaster, masonry, foundry or filter sands are all candidates for consideration as *topsoil sands*. First eliminate the coarse, concreting and horticultural sharp sands by carrying out the sieve tests in section B.2 below. Use can then be made of a simple, infiltration test to weed out those that are too fine and dusty to do the job efficiently.

To carry out the hydraulic conductivity test use a cylindrical container, ideally 100–150 mm (4–6 in) tall, such as an old tin or plastic flower pot with the base removed and replaced by a muslin-covered fine mesh filter. The muslin should not be so coarse as to allow more than dust through from the fine sand, and should not be so fine as to prevent water passing through in a matter of seconds rather than minutes.

With the filter in place, fill the container half full of the fine sand under test, leaving 75 mm (3 in) empty above. Stand in a bowl so that the base of the container will allow water access from below. Fill the outer bowl with water to above the level of the sand in the inner container, maintaining this level until the surface of the sand within the container becomes wet. Tap the container to eliminate air bubbles and settle the sand, then top up with more sand if necessary to compensate for any fall below halfway. Fill both the outer bowl and inner container with water until flush with the rim of the inner, sand-filled container.

Starting with the sand container brimming with water, lift it out of the bowl, resting it on a makeshift stand that will allow free drainage. Note the time taken for the water level in the sand container to fall from the rim of the container to the surface of the sand. The sand taking the least time to clear the 75 mm (3 in) column of water, from the rim to the surface of the sand, will be the best. Times taken may vary from a few minutes to a few hours, but a suitable material would take something of the order of 5–10 minutes.

B.2 *Stewart zone blinding sand*

The hydraulic conductivity test is not alone sufficient for selecting *Stewart zone blinding sands* from amongst fine sands, concreting sands or sharp sands. Its hydraulic conductivity, measured in the manner described in section B.1, is similar to or only a little faster than that of a *Stewart zone topsoil sand*, i.e. typically 1–5 minutes. However, it will have to be distinguished further by having 20–50% of coarse particles larger than 1 mm (i.e. failing to pass a domestic flour sieve).

B.3 *Stewart zone trench gravel*

A typical *Stewart zone trench gravel* will have 90% of particles between 2 mm (¹⁄₁₂ in) and 12 mm (½ in) in effective diameter, with the great majority close to 6 mm (¼ in). This can be checked by using appropriate sieves or, more simply, by direct measurement of individual particles, using a ruler.

Soil and sand amelioration

C.1 Soil amelioration with sand

The long-term benefits from adding sand to soil as a means of improving drainage are generally much overrated. Theoretically, silt and clay need not be present as more than 40% of the whole to fill all the pore space in the sand and thereby control drainage. However, even if the silt and clay content is reduced to just 10–15% of the whole it may still have a dramatic adverse effect on water flow, despite not filling all the pore space. Silt and clay particles are so much smaller than sand particles that they may filter down and concentrate in layers, e.g. above a filter fabric barrier. Alternatively, as one marble in the right place can control drainage through the neck of a funnel, so silt and clay can do likewise by blocking the narrow necks in a closely packed arrangement of sand particles.

To ameliorate a loam or clay-textured soil for use under sports turf, the minimum aim should be to retain an excess of free-draining pore space (macro-pore space) over that which could be filled by the available silt and clay. In practice this means that we should bring the medium-to-fine sand content in the mix to a minimum of 75% (e.g. SN18 in Table 7.1). To achieve this with the minimum amount of sand, the sand itself must have a medium-to-fine sand content of the order of 90% or over.

As a general rule, adding sand is most effective in improving drainage when it is kept apart from the original soil, in core holes or vertical slits. When ameliorating a soil with sand, therefore, it would seem to be inappropriate to struggle too hard to achieve an intimately blended mixture when a more heterogeneous, randomly streaky mixture could be more effective. In the same way, every effort should be made to preserve any natural granulation in the original soil rather than cause this to collapse through a mixing process akin to grinding.

Because so much sand is normally required to effectively ameliorate a problem soil, some thought should be given to the object of the exercise as a whole. This is especially so when, as is generally the case, soil ameliration alone may achieve little unless provision is also made for the effective release of excess water to drainage from the base of the ameliorated layer. As suggested in the example that follows, it may well be more effective to improve the drainage and nutrient status of the existing soil, then simply cover the surface with sand as in a sand-over-soil construction (section 11.3.2).

C.1.1 Calculation

To bring a given depth of existing soil up to a minimum content of 75% medium-plus-fine sand, use the following procedure.

1. Determine the medium-plus-fine sand content of the mineral skeleton of the original

soil, i.e. the percentage by weight of particles of 0.125–0.500 mm in diameter.

2. Use as the amending sand a material with at least 80–90% of its mineral particles in the medium-plus-fine sand range; the higher this percentage the better. Where possible, choose a sand more biased towards either the medium or fine end of this range so as to match the sand particle size most abundant in the soil. The higher the content of this narrow range of particle sizes in both the soil and the sand the less ameliorating sand will be required.

3. Calculate the effect on the mix of adding progressively more increments of the chosen sand until the desired percentage for the mix is reached.

C.1.2 Examples

The calculation assumes:

(a) the dry bulk density of the original soil is 1.26 gm/cm^3, which approximates to 126 t/ha/cm depth of mineral soil (126 tons/acre/inch);

(b) the soil contains 20% medium-plus-fine sand originally;

(c) the amending sand is 90% medium-plus-fine sand and bulk density 1.60 gm/cm^2, approximately 160 t/ha/cm (160 tons/acre/inch).

The trial-and-error calculation can then proceed as follows.

1. 1 cm of mineral soil plus 1 cm of sand, measured in

tonne/hectare $= 126 + 160 = 286$ t

Medium-plus-fine sand content
(tonne) $= 25 + 144 = 169$ t

medium-plus-fine sand content
as % $= 169/286 \times 100$

$= 59\%$ – unsatisfactory

2. 1 cm of mineral soil plus 2 cm of sand, measured in

tonne/hectare $= 126 + 320 = 446$ t

Medium-plus-fine sand content
(tonne) $= 25 + 288 = 313$ t

Medium-plus-fine sand content
as % $= 313/446 \times 100$

$= 70\%$ – better

3. 1 cm of mineral soil plus 3 cm of sand, measured in

tonne/hectare $= 126 + 480 = 606$ t

medium-plus-fine sand content
(tonne) $= 25 + 432 = 457$ t

medium-plus-fine sand content
as % $= 457/606 \times 100$

$= 75.4\%$ – satisfactory

From these calculations it can be seen that at least 3 cm of sand must be mixed into the soil for every 1 cm of the original soil requiring amelioration to over 75% medium-plus-fine sand. Alternatively, to ameliorate a bulk supply of the given soil, every 100 tonne dry weight of the soil will require 381 tonne dry weight of the given sand.

Volume mixes of 1:3 or 1:4 dry weight mixes are typical proportions for soil amelioration with uniform, fine sands, i.e. *Stewart zone topsoil sands* (Table 7.1 SN5, 6). This shows that it requires a large amount of sand to achieve the desired effect, so much in fact, that sand slitting or sand carpeting are often more attractive alternatives.

C.2 Sand amelioration with soil and/or peat

Where soil is used this must be done with a good, water-stable, granular topsoil, every care being taken during handling to preserve the granular aggregation. The aim should be to achieve a 'spotted dog' effect, preserving the granules of topsoil intact within a uniform background of sand. In the final mix the overall content of medium-plus-fine sand should exceed 75%.

Where in time earthworms can be expected to work up mineral soil from below, it may be better to begin just with a sand/peat mixture on top. In this case aim at a 3:1 by volume sand to shredded-peat mix (Table 7.1 SN16). This is equivalent to 5% organic matter by weight when dry, or about 7% by weight of peat packed slightly damp, 40% of the moist weight being water, see Figure A.3.

C.3 Sand amelioration with lignite and/or seaweed meal

Lignite is 'brown coal', a natural, mined product, intermediate in character between peat and coal. Its organic matter content is close to 50%. Unlike coal it is still potentially biologically active in soil but, being more slowly reactive than peat, is much more durable. When prepared for horticulture it is a lightweight, dusty version of the crushed rock materials used to surface hard porous pitches. Though lighter than sand, lignite is heavier than peat, and forms a more stable mix with sand. However, lignite is relatively expensive compared with peat and, therefore, is not likely to be used at concentrations much above 2% by weight. It should be placed strategically within the soil where root branching is to be encouraged.

Milled seaweed is a relatively non-fibrous, organic source that will decompose rapidly to release both structure-stabilizing gums and a wide range of nutrients. Though cheap for those willing and well-placed to collect it off a beach, it is fairly expensive to purchase in a prepared form from commercial sources. Like lignite, therefore, it should be used strategically, at around 2% concentration by weight, but in this case, near the surface to relieve the initial rawness of a sandy topsoil until any organic deficit is made good by the accumulation of root debris. Being relatively non-fibrous it will not leave a resistant residue to contribute to organic matter accumulation in the topsoil.

For equal dry weights, the relative bulk volumes of dune sand, crushed lignite and milled seaweed are of the order 2:3:4.

C.4 Mixing precautions when ameliorating sand with shredded peat, milled seaweed or crushed lignite

The problem, whether mixing is achieved off-site or on-site, is that the lighter, organic materials will tend to re-segregate if agitated, especially when dry. A slightly moist mix is more stable but may be more difficult to spread.

To mix *in situ*, place the organic components in a layer within cultivation depth by a spring-tine harrow (or some similar implement), then work carefully upwards through a covering layer of sand. Avoid excessive cultivation or most of the organic matter will end up on the surface where it should not be.

Gradients

D.1 Numerical definitions

In the past, gradients have usually been expressed in terms of a one unit rise over a given distance measured in the same units. With the coming of metrication, however, slopes are increasingly being expressed as percentages or degrees. Table D.1 lists numerical equivalents.

TABLE D.1 Interrelationships between different methods of defining slope

Slopes	Percentages	Degrees	(approx)
1 in 5	20.00	11.31	(11)
1 in 10	10.00	5.71	(6)
1 in 20	5.00	2.81	(3)
1 in 30	3.33	1.91	(2)
1 in 40	2.50	1.43	(1½)
1 in 50	2.00	1.14	
1 in 60	1.66	0.95	(1)
1 in 70	1.42	0.82	
1 in 80	1.25	0.72	(¾)
1 in 90	1.11	0.64	
1 in 100	1.00	0.57	(½)
1 in 110	0.91	0.52	(½)
1 in 120	0.83	0.48	(½)
1 in 150	0.66	0.38	
1 in 200	0.50	0.29	(¼)
1 in 250	0.40	0.23	(¼)
1 in 300	0.33	0.19	
1 in 400	0.25	0.14	

Drainage calculations

Contributed by
E. D. Stewart, MA, PhD.

E.1 Theory

E.1.1 General mathematical model

The flow of water in the watertable of a homogeneous isotropic soil is governed by Darcy's law:

$$\mathbf{v} = -K\nabla h \qquad \text{(E.1)}$$

where $\mathbf{v}$ is the effective velocity of water flow, K is the constant hydraulic conductivity, h is the hydraulic head.

The hydraulic head at any given point is

$$h = z + p \qquad \text{(E.2)}$$

where z is the gravitational head, i.e. the vertical height above the origin of coordinates, and p is the pressure head.

In this appendix only steady flows will be considered, i.e. flows where the watertable is in equilibrium, with rainfall balancing drainage. For steady flows, conservation of water implies that inside the watertable

$$\nabla.\mathbf{v} = 0 \qquad \text{(E.3)}$$

and so, from equation (E.1)

$$\nabla^2 h = 0. \qquad \text{(E.4)}$$

The boundary conditions for this equation are:

1. for an impermeable boundary

$$\mathbf{v}.\mathbf{n} = 0$$

where $\mathbf{n}$ is the unit outward-pointing vector perpendicular to the boundary of the watertable;

2. for an outflow face (Figure E.1)

$$p = 0;$$

3. for a free surface with rainfall V

$$p = 0$$

and

$$\mathbf{n}.\mathbf{v} = \mathbf{n}.(-V\hat{\mathbf{z}})$$

where $\hat{\mathbf{z}}$ is the unit vertically upward-pointing vector and so $-V\hat{\mathbf{z}}$ is the effective velocity of rainfall flow.

Using equations (E.1) and (E.2) these become, in terms of h:

1. $\mathbf{n}.\nabla h = 0$ (E.5)

2. $h = z$ (E.6)

3. $h = z$ and $\mathbf{n}.\nabla h = \dfrac{V}{K}\,\mathbf{n}.\hat{\mathbf{z}}.$ (E.7)

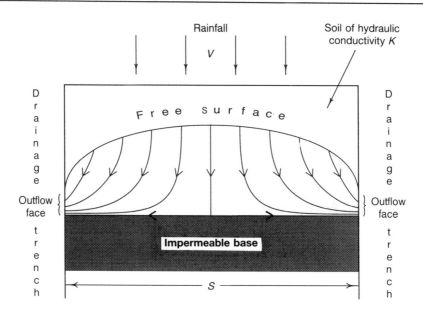

FIGURE E.1   Flow diagram.

E.1.2 Applying the general mathematical model to the case of two-dimensional flow on a horizontal, impermeable base, bounded by two drainage trenches, with rainfall V

From Figure E.1, the flow is clearly symmetrical so consider the right-hand side only (Figure E.2). This is a difficult problem to solve exactly

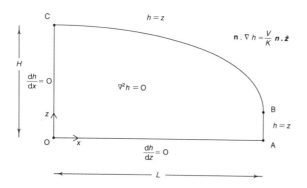

FIGURE E.2 Boundary conditions for differential equation.

but by using the following trick a bound can be obtained for H.

In the interior of the region OABC, $\nabla^2 h = 0$ and $\nabla^2 x = 0$ is an identity. Therefore

$$0 = \iint_{OABC} (h\nabla^2 x - x\nabla^2 h)dxdz$$

$$= \iint_{OABC} \nabla.(h\nabla x - x\nabla h)dxdz.$$

Now using the divergence theorem this is equal to an integral over the boundary of the region OABC:

$$0 = \iint_{OABC} \nabla.(h\nabla x - x\nabla h)dxdz$$

$$= \oint_{OABC} (h\mathbf{n}.\nabla x - x\mathbf{n}.\nabla h)ds$$

$$= \oint_{OABC} (h\mathbf{n}.\hat{\mathbf{x}} - x\mathbf{n}.\nabla h)ds$$

where $\hat{\mathbf{x}}$ is the unit vector $(1,0)$.

Now using the boundary conditions (Figure E.2)

$$0 = \oint_{OABC} (h\mathbf{n}.\hat{\mathbf{x}} - x\mathbf{n}.\nabla h)\mathrm{d}s$$

$$= \int_A^B z\mathrm{d}z + \int_B^C z\mathbf{n}.\hat{\mathbf{x}}\mathrm{d}s - \int_O^C h\mathrm{d}z$$

$$- L\int_A^B \frac{\partial h}{\partial x}\mathrm{d}z - \frac{V}{K}\int_B^C x\mathbf{n}.\hat{\mathbf{z}}\mathrm{d}s. \qquad (E.8)$$

But

$$\mathbf{n}\mathrm{d}s = (\mathrm{d}z, -\mathrm{d}x).$$

Therefore,

$$\mathbf{n}.\hat{\mathbf{x}}\mathrm{d}s = \mathrm{d}z \text{ and } \mathbf{n}.\hat{\mathbf{z}}\mathrm{d}s = -\mathrm{d}x$$

and since the watertable is in equilibrium with rainfall balancing drainage

$$VL = \int_A^B v_x\mathrm{d}z,$$

where $\mathbf{v} = (v_x, v_z)$ and so, from (E.1),

$$\int_A^B \frac{\partial h}{\partial x}\mathrm{d}z = -\frac{V}{K}L.$$

Thus, from (E.8)

$$0 = \int_A^B z\mathrm{d}z + \int_B^C z\mathrm{d}z - [hz]_O^C + \int_O^C z\frac{\partial h}{\partial z}\mathrm{d}z$$

$$+ \frac{V}{K}L^2 + \frac{V}{K}\int_B^C x\mathrm{d}x$$

$$= \tfrac{1}{2}H^2 - H^2 - \frac{1}{K}\int_O^C zv_z\mathrm{d}z + \frac{V}{K}L^2 - \tfrac{1}{2}\frac{V}{K}L^2.$$

Therefore,

$$\frac{V}{K}L^2 = H^2 + \frac{2}{K}\int_O^C zv_z\mathrm{d}z. \qquad (E.9)$$

But on OC, $v_z \leq 0$ and at O, $v_z = 0$ and at C, $v_z = -V$. Also, on OC, $\partial v_x/\partial x \geq 0$ and so, from equation (E.3) $\partial v_z/\partial z \leq 0$. Thus

$$0 > \int_O^C zv_z\mathrm{d}z$$

$$= [\tfrac{1}{2}z^2v_z]_O^C - \int_O^C \tfrac{1}{2}z^2\frac{\partial v_z}{\partial z}\mathrm{d}z > -\tfrac{1}{2}VH^2$$

and so, from equation (E.9)

$$\left(1 - \frac{V}{K}\right)H^2 < \frac{V}{K}L^2 < H^2 \qquad (E.10)$$

and so

$$\sqrt{\left(\frac{V}{K}\right)}L < H < \frac{\sqrt{\left(\frac{V}{K}\right)}L}{\sqrt{\left(1 - \frac{V}{K}\right)}} \qquad (E.11)$$

or equivalently

$$\frac{H^2}{L^2+H^2} < \frac{V}{K} < \frac{H^2}{L^2}. \qquad (E.12)$$

Now if $K >> V$ or $L^2 >> H^2$ (which are true for most practical cases) then a definite formula can be given:

$$H = \sqrt{\left(\frac{V}{K}\right)}L \qquad (E.13)$$

E.1.3 Approximate method that will be used for practical calculations

For this method it is assumed that

$$v_z^2 << v_x^2 + v_y^2 \qquad (E.14)$$

i.e. the flow is approximately horizontal.

Now from equation (E.1) condition (E.14) is equivalent to

$$h \simeq h(x,y).$$

But from (E.7), $h = z$ is one of the boundary conditions for the free surface of the watertable, therefore $h(x,y)$ now gives the height of the free surface of the watertable.

Also, since the flow is steady with rainfall V, conservation of water now gives

$$\nabla.(u\mathbf{v}) = V,$$

where u is the depth of the watertable and $\mathbf{v} = (v_x, v_y)$ and so from (E.1)

$$\nabla.(u\nabla h) = -\frac{V}{K}. \qquad (E.15)$$

The only sensible boundary condition is to set u

= 0 where the soil meets a drainage trench. For two-dimensional flow this reduces to

$$\frac{d}{dx}\left(u\frac{dh}{dx}\right) = -\frac{V}{K}.$$

Therefore,

$$Ku\frac{dh}{dx} = V(x_1 - x) \qquad \text{(E.16)}$$

with $u = 0$ at a drainage trench boundary and where $x = x_1$ is the point where there is no flow of water. Now for the case discussed in section E.1.2, $u = h$ and $x_1 = 0$. Therefore,

$$Kh\frac{dh}{dx} = -Vx$$

so that

$$\tfrac{1}{2}K(h^2 - H^2) = -\tfrac{1}{2}Vx^2,$$

where $h = H$ at $x = 0$ has been used. Therefore

$$h^2 + \frac{V}{K}x^2 = H^2$$

which is the equation of an ellipse.

Now setting $u = 0$ at $x = L$, i.e. $h = 0$ at $x = L$

$$H^2 = \frac{V}{K}L^2 \qquad \text{(E.17)}$$

which agrees with the result obtained in section E.1.2 in the limit $L^2 \gg H^2$, i.e. for an approximately horizontal flow.

E.2 Practical calculations

E.2.1 Three-dimensional flow on a horizontal rectangular impermeable base bounded by drainage trenches with rainfall V

The watertable (Figure E.3) is determined from equation (E.15)

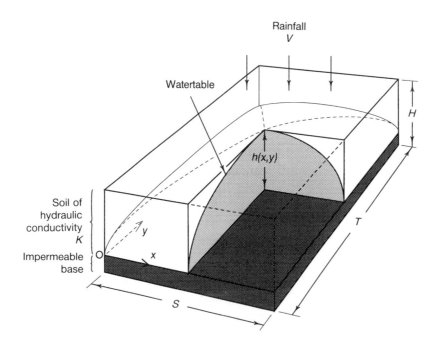

FIGURE E.3 Three-dimensional flow.

$$\nabla.(u\nabla h) = \frac{-V}{K} \qquad (E.18)$$

with $u = 0$ on the boundary. The impermeable base is horizontal, therefore $u = h$. Let

$$f = \tfrac{1}{2}h^2 \text{ and } \rho = \frac{V}{K} \qquad (E.19)$$

Then equation (E.18) gives

$$\nabla^2 f = -\rho \text{ with } f = 0 \text{ on the boundary.} \qquad (E.20)$$

Expanding in Fourier series,

$$f(x,y) = \sum_{n=0}^{\infty} f_n(y)\sin\left[\frac{(2n+1)\pi x}{S}\right] \qquad (E.21)$$

$$\rho = \sum_{n=0}^{\infty} \rho_n\sin\left[\frac{(2n+1)\pi x}{S}\right]. \qquad (E.22)$$

Now

$$\frac{2\rho S}{(2n+1)\pi x} = \int_0^S \rho\sin\left[\frac{(2n+1)\pi}{S}\right]dx$$

$$= \sum_{m=0}^{\infty} \rho_m\int_0^S \sin\left[\frac{(2m+1)\pi x}{S}\right]$$

$$\times \sin\left[\frac{(2n+1)\pi x}{S}\right]dx$$

$$= \tfrac{1}{2}S\rho_n$$

therefore

$$\rho_n = \frac{4\rho}{(2n+1)\pi}.$$

Now equations (E.20) − (E.22) give

$$\frac{d^2 f_n}{dy^2} - \left[\frac{(2n+1)\pi}{S}\right]^2 f_n = -\frac{4\rho}{(2n+1)\pi}$$

which has the general solution

$$f_n(y) = A_n \sinh\left[\frac{(2n+1)\pi y}{S}\right]$$

$$+ B_n \cosh\left[\frac{(2n+1)\pi y}{S}\right] + \frac{4\rho S^2}{(2n+1)^3\pi^3}.$$

The boundary condition (E.20) now gives

$$f_n(0) = f_n(T) = 0$$

Therefore

$$B_n = \frac{-4\rho S^2}{(2n+1)^3\pi^3}$$

and

$$A_n = \frac{4\rho S^2}{(2n+1)^3\pi^3}\left\{\frac{\cosh[(2n+1)\pi T/S]-1}{\sinh[(2n+1)\pi T/S]}\right\}$$

$$= \frac{4\rho S^2}{(2n+1)^3\pi^3}\left\{\frac{\sinh[(2n+1)\pi T/2S]}{\cosh[(2n+1)\pi T/2S]}\right\}.$$

At peak capacity $h(\tfrac{1}{2}S, \tfrac{1}{2}T) = H$, therefore

$$\tfrac{1}{2}H^2 = f(\tfrac{1}{2}S,\tfrac{1}{2}T) = \sum_{n=0}^{\infty} f_n(\tfrac{1}{2}T)(-1)^n.$$

Now

$$f_n(\tfrac{1}{2}T) = \frac{4\rho S^2}{(2n+1)^3\pi^3}\left\{1 - \frac{1}{\cosh[(2n+1)\pi T/2S]}\right\}$$

and

$$\sum_{n=0}^{\infty} \frac{(-1)^n}{(2n+1)^3} = \frac{\pi^3}{32}.$$

Therefore,

$$H^2 = \frac{1}{4}\frac{V}{K}S^2\left\{1 - \frac{32}{\pi^3}\sum_{n=0}^{\infty} \frac{(-1)^n}{(2n+1)^3}\right.$$

$$\left.\times \frac{1}{\cosh[(2n+1)\pi T/2S]}\right\} \qquad (E.23)$$

Note that as $T \rightarrow \infty$ the problem reduces to the two-dimensional problem and we recover the two-dimensional result (E.17), noting that $S = 2L$:

$$H^2 = \frac{1}{4}\frac{V}{K}S^2.$$

For $T \geq S$ the series (E.23) converges very quickly and can be very well approximated by

$$H^2 = \frac{1}{4}\frac{V}{K}S^2\left[1 - \frac{32}{\pi^3 \cosh\left(\frac{\pi}{2}\frac{T}{S}\right)}\right] \quad \text{(E.24)}$$

Of particular interest is the case of a square, $T = S$, when we get the formula

$$S^2 = 6.79\frac{K}{V}H^2. \quad \text{(E.25)}$$

E.2.2 Two-dimensional flow on an impermeable base with constant slope G/S bounded by drainage trenches with rainfall V

The situation is represented by Figure E.4. The watertable is determined from equation (E.16)

$$Ku\frac{dh}{dx} = V(x_1 - x) \quad \text{(E.26)}$$

with $u = 0$ on the boundary.

The left-hand side of this equation gives the flow of water in the negative x direction at any given point as given by Darcy's law, while the right-hand side gives the flow of water needed to maintain equilibrium. The impermeable base has constant slope G/S and so

$$h = u + \frac{G}{S}x. \quad \text{(E.27)}$$

$x = x_1$ is the point where there is no flow of water. Let $x = x_0$ be the point where the watertable touches the surface of the soil, i.e.

$$u = H \text{ and } \frac{du}{dx} = 0 \text{ at } x = x_0. \quad \text{(E.28)}$$

Now from equations (E.26) and (E.27)

$$KH\frac{G}{S} = V(x_1 - x_0),$$

therefore

$$x_0 = x_1 - \frac{K}{V}\frac{HG}{S}. \quad \text{(E.29)}$$

Also, from equations (E.26) and (E.27)

$$Ku\left(\frac{du}{dx} + \frac{G}{S}\right) = V(x_1 - x).$$

Let

$$t = 1 - \frac{x}{x_1}, \quad w = \sqrt{\left(\frac{K}{V}\right)\frac{u}{x_1}} \quad \text{(E.30)}$$

and

$$\alpha = \frac{1}{2}\frac{G}{S}\sqrt{\frac{K}{V}} \quad \text{(E.31)}$$

$$\beta = \frac{H}{S}\sqrt{\frac{K}{V}} \quad \text{(E.32)}$$

Therefore,

$$\frac{dw}{dt} = 2\alpha - \frac{t}{w}.$$

Let

$$s = \frac{t}{w}, \quad r = \ln w, \quad \text{(E.33)}$$

therefore

$$\frac{dt}{dw} = \frac{ds}{dr} + s$$

and

$$\frac{dr}{ds} = \frac{2\alpha - s}{s^2 - 2\alpha s + 1}$$

$$= -\frac{1}{2}\left(\frac{2s - 2\alpha}{s^2 - 2\alpha s + 1}\right) + \frac{\alpha}{(s-\alpha)^2 + 1 - \alpha^2}. \quad \text{(E.34)}$$

There are two cases:

1. Case for $\alpha < 1$:
   using the substitution $s - \alpha = \sqrt{(1 - \alpha^2)}\cot\theta$, equation (E.34) gives

$$r = -\frac{1}{2}\ln(s^2 - 2\alpha s + 1)$$

$$- \frac{\alpha}{\sqrt{(1-\alpha^2)}}\tan^{-1}\left[\frac{\sqrt{(1-\alpha^2)}}{s-\alpha}\right] + \text{constant}$$

Therefore, from equation (E.33)

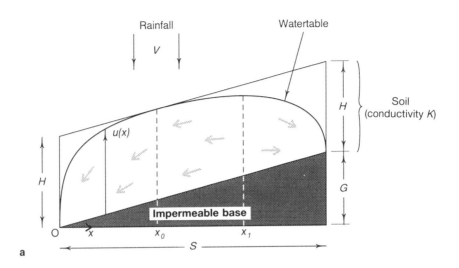

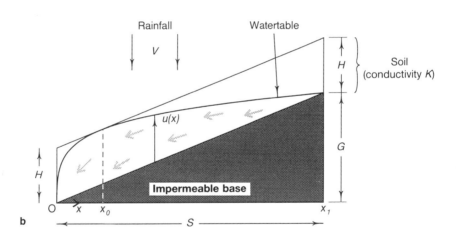

FIGURE E.4 (a) Two-dimensional flow on a constant slope with $\alpha < 1$. (b) Two-dimensional flow on a constant slope, with $\alpha > 1$.

$$\tfrac{1}{2} \ln(t^2 - 2\alpha tw + w^2) = -\frac{\alpha}{\sqrt{(1-\alpha^2)}} \tan^{-1}$$

$$\times \left[\frac{\sqrt{(1-\alpha^2)}w}{t-\alpha w} \right] + \text{constant}. \qquad (E.35)$$

Now the boundary condition (E.26) gives u

$= 0$ when $x = 0$. Therefore, from equation (E.30), $w = 0$ when $t = 1$, and constant $= 0$.

Also, from equations (E.28)–(E.32)

$$w = \beta \frac{S}{x_1}$$

when

$$t = 2\alpha\beta\frac{S}{x_1}.$$

Therefore, from equation (E.35) with constant = 0,

$$\ln\left(\beta\frac{S}{x_1}\right) = -\frac{\alpha}{\sqrt{(1-\alpha^2)}} \tan^{-1}\left[\frac{\sqrt{(1-\alpha^2)}}{\alpha}\right].$$

Therefore

$$\beta = \frac{x_1}{S} \exp\left\{-\frac{\alpha}{\sqrt{(1-\alpha^2)}} \tan^{-1}\left[\frac{\sqrt{(1-\alpha^2)}}{\alpha}\right]\right\}.$$

(E.36)

Also the boundary condition E.26 gives $u = 0$ when $x = S$. Therefore from equation (E. 30)

$$w = 0 \text{ when } t = 1 - \frac{S}{x_1},$$

and from equation (E.35) with constant = 0

$$\ln\left(\frac{S}{x_1} - 1\right) = -\pi\frac{\alpha}{\sqrt{(1-\alpha^2)}},$$

where $\tan^{-1}(0^-) = \pi$ must be taken for a consistent definition of $\tan^{-1}$. Therefore

$$\frac{x_1}{S} = \frac{1}{1+\exp\left[-\pi\frac{\alpha}{\sqrt{(1-\alpha^2)}}\right]} \quad \text{(E.37)}$$

and from equation (E.36)

$$\beta = \frac{\exp\left\{-\frac{\alpha}{\sqrt{(1-\alpha^2)}} \tan^{-1}\left[\frac{\sqrt{(1-\alpha^2)}}{\alpha}\right]\right\}}{1 + \exp\left[-\pi\frac{\alpha}{\sqrt{(1-\alpha^2)}}\right]} \quad \text{(E.38)}$$

Now equations (E.29), (E.31) and (E.32) give

$$x_0 = x_1 - 2\alpha\beta S.$$

Therefore,

$$\frac{x_0}{S} = \frac{1 - 2\alpha \exp\left\{-\frac{\alpha}{\sqrt{(1-\alpha^2)}} \tan^{-1}\left[\frac{\sqrt{(1-\alpha^2)}}{\alpha}\right]\right\}}{1 + \exp\left[-\pi\frac{\alpha}{\sqrt{(1-\alpha^2)}}\right]} \quad \text{(E.39)}$$

2. Case for $\alpha > 1$:
from equation (E.34)

$$\frac{dr}{ds} = -\frac{1}{2}\left(\frac{2s-2\alpha}{s^2-2\alpha s+1}\right)$$

$$+ \frac{1}{2}\frac{\alpha}{\sqrt{(\alpha^2-1)}}\left(\frac{1}{s-\alpha-\sqrt{(\alpha^2-1)}}\right.$$

$$\left.-\frac{1}{s-\alpha+\sqrt{(\alpha^2-1)}}\right).$$

Therefore,

$$r = -\frac{1}{2}\ln|s^2-2\alpha s+ 1|$$

$$+ \frac{1}{2}\frac{\alpha}{\sqrt{(\alpha^2-1)}} \ln|s-\alpha-\sqrt{(\alpha^2-1)}|$$

$$-\frac{1}{2}\frac{\alpha}{\sqrt{(\alpha^2-1)}} \ln|s-\alpha+ \sqrt{(\alpha^2-1)}|$$

$$+ \text{ constant.}$$

Therefore, from equation (E.33),

$$[\alpha-\sqrt{(\alpha^2-1)}] \ln|t-[\alpha+\sqrt{(\alpha^2-1)}]w|$$
$$=[\alpha+\sqrt{(\alpha^2-1)}] \ln|t-[\alpha-\sqrt{(\alpha^2-1)}]w|$$
$$+ \text{ constant.}$$

Now the boundary condition (E.26) gives $u = 0$ when $x = 0$. Therefore, from equation (E.30), $w = 0$ when $t = 1$.

Therefore

$$\{t-[\alpha+\sqrt{(\alpha^2-1)}]w\}^{\alpha-\sqrt{(\alpha^2-1)}}$$
$$= \{t-[\alpha-\sqrt{(\alpha^2-1)}]w\}^{\alpha+\sqrt{(\alpha^2-1)}} \quad \text{(E.40)}$$

Now $u = 0$ when $x = 0$ or $x = S$ and when $u = 0$, i.e. $w = 0$, equation (E.40) gives $t = 0$ or $t = 1$. Therefore, from equation (E.30),

$$x_1 = S. \quad \text{(E.41)}$$

Now from equations (E.28)–(E.32) $w = \beta$ when $t = 2\alpha\beta$.

Therefore, from equation (E.40)

$$\beta^{2\sqrt{(\alpha^2-1)}} = \frac{[\alpha-\sqrt{(\alpha^2-1)}]^{\alpha-\sqrt{(\alpha^2-1)}}}{[\alpha+\sqrt{(\alpha^2-1)}]^{\alpha+\sqrt{(\alpha^2-1)}}}$$

$$= \left[\frac{\alpha-\sqrt{(\alpha^2-1)}}{\alpha+\sqrt{(\alpha^2-1)}}\right]^\alpha,$$

giving

$$\beta = \left[\dfrac{\dfrac{\alpha}{\sqrt{(\alpha^2-1)}}-1}{\dfrac{\alpha}{\sqrt{(\alpha^2-1)}}+1} \right]^{\frac{1}{2}\frac{\alpha}{\sqrt{(\alpha^2-1)}}}.$$

(E.42)

Now equations (E.29), (E.31), (E.32) and (E.41) give

$$x_0 = (1-2\alpha\beta)S.$$

Therefore,

$$\frac{x_0}{S} = 1 - 2\alpha \left(\dfrac{\dfrac{\alpha}{\sqrt{(\alpha^2-1)}}-1}{\dfrac{\alpha}{\sqrt{(\alpha^2-1)}}+1} \right)^{\frac{1}{2}\frac{\alpha}{\sqrt{(\alpha^2-1)}}}.$$

(E.43)

In summary, to calculate H or G use

$$\alpha = \frac{1}{2}\frac{G}{S}\sqrt{\left(\frac{K}{V}\right)} \quad \text{and} \quad \beta = \frac{H}{S}\sqrt{\left(\frac{K}{V}\right)}$$

and the graph of Figure 13.3(a).

To calculate S, K or V draw the straight line

$$\beta = 2\frac{H}{G}\alpha$$

on the graph and the point of intersection will give α and β, and hence from

$$\alpha = \frac{1}{2}\frac{G}{S}\sqrt{\left(\frac{K}{V}\right)} \quad \text{and} \quad \beta = \frac{H}{S}\sqrt{\left(\frac{K}{V}\right)}$$

will give S, K or V. The graph is given by equations (E.38) for $\alpha < 1$ and (E.42) for $\alpha > 1$.

E.2.3 Two-dimensional flow on an impermeable base with optimum crowned profile bounded by drainage trenches with rainfall V

The situation is represented by Figure E.5. The profile is determined from equation (E.3)

$$Ku\frac{dh}{dx} = V(x_1 - x).$$

(E.44)

For $x < x_0$ the situation is the same as in section E.2.2. From equations (E.31)–(E.32)

$$\alpha = \frac{1}{2}\frac{G}{S}\sqrt{\left(\frac{K}{V}\right)}.$$

Now for $\alpha < 1$, equations (E.31), (E.32) and (E.36) give

$$H = \sqrt{\left(\frac{V}{K}\right)}x_1 \exp\left\{-\frac{\alpha}{\sqrt{(1-\alpha^2)}}\tan^{-1}\left[\frac{\sqrt{(1-\alpha^2)}}{\alpha}\right]\right\}$$

(E.45)

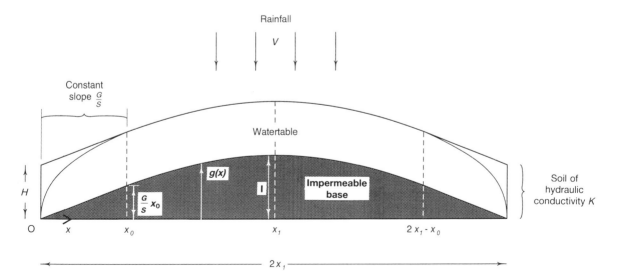

FIGURE E.5 Two-dimensional flow on a crowned profile.

and for $\alpha < 1$, equations (E.31), (E.32), (E.41) and (E.42) give

$$H = \sqrt{\left(\frac{V}{K}\right)} x_1 \left(\frac{\frac{\alpha}{\sqrt{(\alpha^2-1)}} - 1}{\frac{\alpha}{\sqrt{(\alpha^2-1)}} + 1} \right)^{\frac{1}{2} \frac{\alpha}{\sqrt{(\alpha^2-1)}}} \tag{E.46}$$

Now equation (E.29) gives

$$x_0 = x_1 - \frac{K}{V}\frac{G}{S}H. \tag{E.47}$$

For $x_0 < x < 2x_1 - x_0$, $u = H$ and $h = g + H$ and so, from equation (E.44)

$$\frac{dg}{dx} = \frac{V}{KH}(x_1 - x).$$

Therefore

$$g = I - \frac{1}{2}\frac{V}{KH}(x_1 - x)^2. \tag{E.48}$$

Now, when $x = x_0$, $g = (G/S)x_0$. Therefore, from equations (E.47) and (E.48)

$$\begin{aligned} I &= \frac{G}{S}x_1 - \frac{K}{V}\left(\frac{G}{S}\right)^2 H + \frac{1}{2}\frac{K}{V}\left(\frac{G}{S}\right)^2 H \\ &= \frac{G}{S}\left(x_1 - \frac{1}{2}\frac{KG}{VS}H\right). \end{aligned} \tag{E.49}$$

Therefore

$$g(x) = \frac{G}{S}\left(x_1 - \frac{1}{2}\frac{KG}{VS}H\right) - \frac{1}{2}\frac{V}{KH}(x_1 - x)^2, \tag{E.50}$$

where H is given by equations (E.45) and (E.46).

In summary, to calculate H, x_1 or G/S use equation (E.31)

$$\alpha = \frac{1}{2}\frac{G}{S}\sqrt{\left(\frac{K}{V}\right)}$$

and

$$\gamma = \frac{H}{x_1}\sqrt{\left(\frac{K}{V}\right)} \tag{E.51}$$

together with the graph of Figure 13.3 (b).

To calculate K or V draw the straight line

$$\gamma = 2\frac{H}{x_1}\frac{S}{G}\alpha$$

on the graph and the point of intersection will give α and γ, and hence from

$$\alpha = \frac{1}{2}\frac{G}{S}\sqrt{\left(\frac{K}{V}\right)} \quad \text{and} \quad \gamma = \frac{H}{x_1}\sqrt{\left(\frac{K}{V}\right)}$$

will give K or V.

The graph is given by equations (E.45) for $\alpha < 1$ and (E.46) for $\alpha > 1$.

The profile is given by

$$g(x) = \frac{G}{S}x, \qquad \text{for } 0 \leqslant x \leqslant x_0,$$

$$g(x) = \frac{G}{S}\left(x_1 - \frac{1}{2}\frac{K}{V}\frac{G}{S}H\right)$$

$$- \frac{1}{2}\frac{V}{KH}(x_1 - x)^2, \text{ for } x_0 \leqslant x \leqslant 2x_1 - x_0,$$

$$g(x) = \frac{G}{S}(2x_1 - x), \quad \text{for } 2x_1 - x_0 \leqslant x \leqslant 2x_1$$

and

$$x_0 = x_1 - \frac{K}{V}\frac{G}{S}H.$$

Grooming, verti-cutting, hollow-tine coring, and verti-draining as aids in fine-turf management for golf and bowls

These are procedures aimed at counteracting inevitable trends towards mat development and soil compaction which are inherent in a soil deprived of earthworm activity. They should be looked upon, not as alternatives, but as a combination of treatments which together can be used by the greenkeeper to maintain the surface fit for play.

F.1 Terminology

This subject is confused by the fact that, where earthworms are absent from the soil, very similar organic-rich surface conditions can arise in forest, pasture or sports turf, but their common origin has not been generally recognized. This is a pity, because all concerned could benefit their understanding by actively seeking out the additional knowledge on this subject that exists outwith their specialisms (Tables 6.1 and 6.2).

Foresters, agriculturalists and greenkeepers have developed their own terminology in isolation. Thus the forester's 'mor' is the equivalent of the agriculturalist's 'mat' and the greenkeeper's 'thatch'. The English words mat and thatch, however, have familiar meanings in other contexts and it would be helpful to our understanding if we now used these meanings to rationalize our terminology. Thatch implies something fairly loose, laid on top; mat (or matted), something held tightly together by the intertwining of threads. Thus, under grass, it would be appropriate to use 'thatch' to describe the fresh and decaying, fibrous debris that sprawls across or is deposited upon the surface from shoots and clippings. In the presence of burrowing earthworms this will be rapidly incorporated out of sight, into the underlying mineral soil. But in the absence of earthworms, it will remain to accumulate in a discrete, wholly organic layer, unless diluted with mineral topdressing. In the cool, moist climate of Britain, such a surface organic layer will not entirely disappear by decay in the course of a year. Annual increments will build up and in time become invaded by fungal hyphae and grass roots, so becoming stabilized like a mat. As the grass root system tends to die back and shorten in response to frequent close mowing, the matted condition can get progressively tighter and the competition for the water and nutrients within it, intense. This is the condition that can lead to a spongy, water-holding and slow-playing surface.

For the benefit of play, therefore, the greenkeeper should do everything he can to remove organic debris that would otherwise accumulate as thatch, doing this while it can be fairly easily worked out from between the grass shoots. But to re-invigorate the root system and extract organic matter from within the mat is by no means easy if the integrity of the sward is not to suffer. Thus it would be as well not to confuse the two terms, 'thatch' and 'mat'. Use 'thatch' when referring to the surface accumulation of loose, organic debris that can be removed continuously without harm to the aerial shoots of the grass. Use 'mat' for the root-bound sod that holds the surface together; it may lose its cohesion if sliced, or may rip out if snagged by a spike. If only one of these words has to be used for the combination of the two, then mat is probably to be preferred.

F.2 Mat development

Mat development is a natural and inevitable feature of any vegetated surface where earthworm activity is unavailable to incorporate organic debris, not otherwise removed off site. Microbial decomposition will achieve a certain reduction but, as with composting, much will remain to accumulate on the surface if not otherwise removed. Where earthworms are virtually absent, usually because of lack of appropriate food, acidity or other chemical irritants, a surface mat will develop in which a balance is eventually struck between the overall loss by microbial decomposition and input by litter deposition. In a cool temperate climate, this balance may only be struck, under natural conditions, when the mat is 100–150 mm (4–6 in) deep.

As such a mat accumulates, the development of new roots, and the disposal of the whole rooting system, becomes more and more confined to the older layers of composted material that lie beneath the latest increment of litter. Being ultimately dependent on such a rooting medium, the natural vegetation must be highly specialized in its feeding arrangements, and well adapted to cope with the twin stresses of periodic waterlogging and periodic drought (Table 6.1).

On worm-deficient sports turf the potential for mat development is much reduced because of the removal of clippings, but even here it can become over 50 mm (2 in) deep if other measures of control are not implemented. It is formed from clippings which escape the box, die-back from leaf bases, surface roots and moss, plus organic residues from inappropriate topdressings. At worst a mat becomes just a root-bound sod.

Whether earthworms are absent or not will determine whether organic matter deposited on the surface remains to form a mat or is intimately mixed with mineral soil and incorporated beneath the surface. In either case, decomposition will continue at a relatively fast rate, unlike in peat development where the persistence of anaerobic conditions, brought on by permanent waterlogging, effectively arrests decay.

F.3 Why bother anyway?

As organic matter decomposes at the surface, a greasy residue may impede drainage and foster persistent wetness by holding on to water. Surface rooting will be encouraged and consequences of poor aeration, such as denitrification and toxin production, will adversely affect plant growth. At the other end of the moisture range, during drought the shallow rooting will severely limit the exploitation of residual water reserves at depth. In the organic mat, fungi and insects, including some that parasitize living plants, will thrive alongside the other, more benign organisms, involved in processes of decay. In the case of *Fusarium*, a major grass disease, the fungus can survive for much of the time, living as a saprophyte on dead organic matter, and then invading living tissue as a parasite, when the atmosphere is humid and the sward is moist.

But not only is a surface mat a problem for the well-being of the grass; it is also, for players, a major cause of slowness of pace, except when threatening desiccation. Should it be allowed to desiccate, then it will behave as if waxy, failing to re-absorb water and threatening sward survival.

Mat development is the main natural problem which the greenkeeper has to strive continuously to control.

F.4 Measures to control thatch, additional to boxing off clippings

1. Brushing, combing or the use of grooming reels, are all aimed at lifting sprawling growth to cutting height so as to provide the tight, vertical growth required for a true playing surface. This is particularly important for agrostis (browntop bent) which can provide an excellent playing surface but has a marked tendency to sprawl. Incidentally, these procedures, aimed primarily at improving the quality of the surface for play, will also make a contribution to the removal of debris sheltering within the stem bases. When first used on a neglected sward they will expose bare patches smothered by sprawl and will noticeably roughen the surface. As routine procedures they are probably best carried out just once a week during the growing season.

2. Verti-cutting is a more vigorous form of grooming. The machine is a mower whose blades have to be kept sharp enough to cut through sprawling growth and remove the freed clippings. It must be treated with respect as a vertical mower and not blunted by the blades being lowered to scratch the surface of the soil. It contributes to thatch control by removing clippings that might otherwise escape a horizontal mower, and like grooming, helps to maintain the tight vertical growth required for a true playing surface. As a routine procedure it is probably best used once a month during the growing season, and always immediately prior to topdressing.

3. Topdressing with uniform, fine sandy material is intended, like grooming and verti-cutting, not only to help true the surface for play, but also to further reduce any tendency to mat accumulation by diluting the decomposing surface debris that escapes the action of the mowing and grooming procedures. As sand sticking to leaves would blunt both the horizontal and vertical mowers, it should be applied dry so that it can be worked into the base of the sward, and then watered to ensure that it settles firmly into the soil surface, out of the way of cutting blades. It is best added frequently, in monthly increments after verti-cutting, when it will have a good chance of uniformly diluting any residue of organic matter. The alternative of a relatively large, once-a-year autumn treatment, tends to encourage the layering that

interferes with uniform moisture and root distribution.

Topdressing, without prior removal of organic debris, risks burying trouble out of sight, for once below the surface, it will accumulate water and develop a sour smell as it continues to decompose anaerobically. In the past, most bought-in turf contained a rooting base of loam or peat, and most topdressings were similarly afflicted. The legacy for the greenkeeper has been the need to develop means to remove or bypass these materials so as to improve vertical drainage and prevent layers of anaerobicity developing as they sink out of reach from the surface, under successive layers of topdressing.

Providing the surface starts without a mat or soil-cap problem, the combination of horizontal and vertical mowing, plus boxing-off of clippings, grooming and sand topdressing should go a long way to controlling mat development without recourse to the remedial treatments discussed next.

F.5 Remedial treatments

These become necessary where continuous attention to thatch control has not been adequately implemented, or where former construction and maintenance faults are responsible for drainage problems built into the soil itself. Such problems may exist at the surface (mats and caps), or within the immediate topsoil (introduced layers of inappropriate material), and also at greater depth where the indigenous soil has become unduly compacted.

Initial poor construction, or subsequent differential settlement, may result in enclosed hollows where surface or subsoil drainage water may cause trouble by accumulating. This will further add to the problems associated with mat but will need more than standard maintenance techniques to remedy.

Soil examination in depth will be necessary before a logical decision can be made on the remedial action required.

F.5.1 Scarification

Where organic debris has not been adequately removed during the growing season, scarification will be required to remove it before the onset of winter restricts sward recovery. The tines of the scarifier are designed to cope with soil abrasion but this does not mean that they should be set to penetrate so deeply that the roots of the living grass are put at risk. Better to proceed cautiously, by means of several passes in different directions, but even then the treated sward may require extensive over-seeding.

To be consistently successful as part of an annual programme of maintenance, the work should begin early in September. This does not fit well with the requirements of year-round golf, nor with bowlers reluctant for the season to end.

F.5.2 Hollow-tine coring with sand infill

This is required when mat development has reached the stage of being root bound, or when an inappropriate layer of loam or peat enrichment has been introduced during turfing, or in subsequent topdressing. The aim must be to remove a substantial amount of the offending material and bypass the remainder with the sand infill; doing all this with minimum loss of use. Note that 12 mm 1½ in) diameter cores every 75 mm (3 in) or 15 mm (⅝ in) diameter cores every 50 mm (2 in) will remove only 5–8% of the offending layer in one pass, but the sward will require time and good growing conditions to recover.

To be successful, the coring must take place when the surface is just moist enough to allow for easy penetration and efficient core extration. Then, after core collection and removal, to achieve a satisfactory infilling of the core holes with tightly packed sand, the topdressing must be a dry, free-pouring sand, brushed into the core holes over a closely mown, clean, dry surface. Finally, to settle the sand firmly into the core holes, irrigate. When the surface is dry again, over-seed and apply a further topdressing of sand, then mat to level off the core holes and re-true the surface. All this points to treatment well before the end of the growing season, and greens put temporarily out of use to accommodate.

If the infill within the core holes is texturally similar to or coarser than the underlying material to which it is to form a drainage link, it will tend to empty as the final stage of drainage is reached, leaving the surface dry. However, if at least one particle-size category finer, the infill will tend to remain persistently saturated after rain. This may usefully enhance drought resistance on high spots, but more generally will be seen to discourage a thoroughly soaked surface from rapidly drying out (section 4.2.1).

Because of the importance of timing for successful coring and sand infilling this is not an operation that should be delegated to a contractor, or made dependent on hiring the necessary equipment. It requires the timeliness of astute greenkeeping, backed up by ready access to the necessary equipment and materials.

Note, even at St. Andrews, where there is an established programme of weekly grooming plus monthly verti-cutting and topdressing throughout the growing season, still six greens each year are given the hollow-tining treatment to guarantee effective mat control. If the management for mat control throughout the growing season is inadequate, then all greens may require the hollow-tining treatment annually. American literature suggests that hollow-tine coring may be carried out more than once a year, typically in spring and autumn. At this frequency there must be appropriate equipment on hand to take full advantage of ideal weather conditions, there must be adequate staff, and there must be alternative greens, or acceptable alternative arrangements, to allow play to continue.

F.5.3 Verti-draining

Where there is soil compaction impeding drainage at a depth beyond normal solid- or hollow-tine reach, it may be necessary to use the greater depth of action made possible by a verti-drainer. With this, the combined effect of penetration, lateral displacement and heave will tend to crack open the compaction and raise the surface uniformly so as to accommodate the extra pore space. If the problem is simply confined to an impeding layer which the verti-draining tines can bridge through to a free-draining material below, then this may be all that is necessary, at least to achieve a significant, temporary benefit. However, if the subsoil beyond the depth of tine penetration is not free draining, then it may be necessary to follow up with some form of continuous slitting to provide for the positive clearance of excess water sideways to underdrains.

Disruption of an unstable soil will alone achieve only a temporary effect. The rate of re-settlement will depend on the binding strength provided by the clay content. Only in a strong, clay soil could the beneficial effect of mechanical disruption be expected to last for more than one or two years. However, verti-draining equipment has now been adapted for deep hollow tining. Thus, positive steps can be taken to progressively remove an unfavourable material from depths down to 300–400 mm (12–16 in) and replace with sand. But, as with the normal, more shallow hollow-tining treatment, the condition of the infilling sand and the surface must be right, if the necessary substitution is to be wholly effective.

F.6 General hints on diagnosis and treatment

Be guided at first by the general performance of the greens in play, and the organic content of the top 50 mm (2 in) of the soil. If generally black in colour, sour in smell, and not very sandy in appearance when examined closely through a times 10 lens, then suspect an inadequate mat-control regime. Scarification and/or hollow-tine coring may well have to be introduced as an annual treatment until the surface of the soil has been re-conditioned. If it proves impossible, therefore, to get an appropriate grooming, verti-cutting and sand top-dressing programme implemented throughout the growing season, make do with what proves possible and continue to make good with remedial scarification and hollow-tining treatments each autumn. The players and the greens staff must accept one or other of these alternatives if they are ever to achieve the putting surfaces required.

If only particular greens are affected, examine the configuration of the surface to see if localized wetness could be resulting from surface water being shed into enclosed hollows. If so, consider how these hollows can be taken out. Slit draining through the hollow is an option, but the efficiency of the drainage through the surface to the drain will have to be frequently renewed by spiking and/or sand-filling hollow-tine core holes.

Where surface configuration does not appear to account for a particular problem of persist-

ent wetness, then examine the soil in depth, looking for a well-defined layer, suspended within the soil profile, that could be impeding vertical drainage. If present, decide if it could be treated satisfactorily by core extraction and sand in-filling. Aim to remove cores of the problem layer so as to link through to a free-draining material below, and then secure the bypass route by sand in-filling. The machine required will depend on depth.

Any general problem of soil compaction that continues in depth will originate in an inappropriate soil texture. To treat, this will require either deep disruption by verti-draining tines, sand-filling and provision for lateral discharge, or complete reconstruction with appropriate materials.

The ideal for any green is a good initial construction with appropriate materials, and a true, shedding surface, maintained throughout the growing season by routinely grooming, verti-cutting and sand topdressing. Scarification and hollow-tine coring then can be held in reserve for remedial treatment in those seasons when the normal maintenance programme has not been fulfilled, or when surface disruption is welcome because there is to be a major effort at overseeding.

Recording soil temperature

G.1 Procedure

Chose a maintained grass site that is level, freely drained, unshaded and with the soil unobstructed by stones or severe induration to a depth of 300 mm (12 in). Purchase from an ironmonger or garden centre a 300 mm (12 in) long, metal-sheathed soil thermometer and make up, or purchase, a 12 mm (½ in) wide, 300 mm (12 in) long, strong metal probe fitted

with a handle – an old fashioned, long chisel is ideal. The probe is required to create the hole into which the thermometer is to be neatly inserted to 250 mm (10 in) depth without risk of damage, the idea being to enable close contact to be maintained between the metal sheath and the soil.

Measure soil temperature at 250 mm (10 in) depth weekly (or twice monthly), between midday and late afternoon, leaving the thermo-

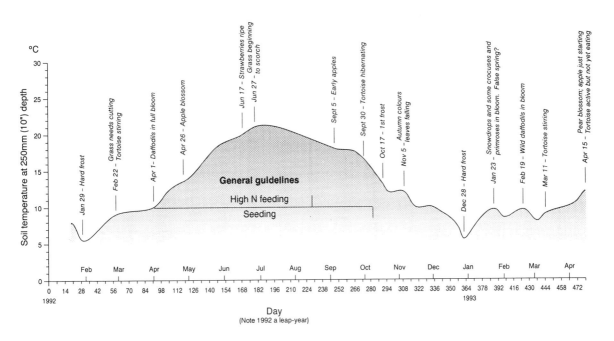

FIGURE G.1 Graph of 1992 soil temperature records as listed in Table A7.1.

TABLE G.1 1992–93 soil temperature records at 250 mm (10 in) depth beneath garden lawn near Aberystywth. Grass maintained during growing season by weekly mowing at not less than 25 mm (1 in); clippings mostly returned. Soil a freely drained, clay loam with earthworms present, therefore no surface mat.

Date		Temperature (°C)	Observations
January	19	8	Mild.
	29	5.5	Cold and frosty but also sunny.
February	27	9	Changeable; grass now needs first cut; some buds bursting; snowdrops and crocuses flowering; daffodils in bud; rhubarb shoots emerging; tortoise stirring.
April	1	10	Colder; some snow; grass needs second cut; crocuses, primroses and daffodils in flower; tortoise dormant again; birds nesting.
	12	12	Changeable; grass seeded end of March now germinating; buds of larger trees now bursting; tortoise lethargically active.
	26	13.5	Sunny but cool wind; fern shoots unwinding; apple blossom starting; tortoise still somewhat lethargic.
May	28	18.5	Dry and very hot; soft fruit forming up; tortoise lively and eating well.
June	17	20	Continuing hot and dry; strawberries ripe.
	27	21	Still continuing hot and now very dry; soil hard and no longer sticking to chisel; no growth, grass beginning to show signs of scorch.
August	4	20	Changeable; grass growing again; last of bilberries now being picked.
September	5	18	Changeable, wet and windy; grass growing well; starting to pick early apples and sweet corn; killing caterpillars on broccoli by hand.
	22	17.5	Wet weather continuing.
October	8	15	Colder and drier; grass growing well; pears ripening; caterpillars still very active on broccoli; earwigs and slugs on brussel sprouts but under control; tortoise dug in and hibernating since September 30.
	17	13	First frosty morning; weather mixed – cold, sunny and occasional showers. Autumn colours starting on aspen, fig and bilberries.
	21	12	Continuing wet/cold/sunny; pear leaves yellowing; grass seed sown October 14 now germinating.
November	5	12	Mild; full autumn colours; leaves starting to fall.
	15	10	Wet and windy; most trees now bare.
	29	10	Mild with some wind and rain; snowdrop and daffodil shoots emerging.
December	10	9	Frosty morning but previously mild, wet and windy, grass-seeded patches still only sparsely covered with seedlings.
	23	7	Cold and frosty but sunny; main lawn still growing slowly and should be trimmed to tidy.
	28	5.5	Continuing frosty and sunny; soil surface hard frozen.
January	1	6	Sunny and mild following a week of hard frost.
	23	9.5	Very mild, wet and windy; snowdrops all in flower plus occasional crocus and primrose; daffodils in bud; late-seeded grass still thin.
	28	9	Still mild and moist; main lawn requires mowing but too wet; bluebell shoots now emerging; tortoise still hibernating under her sheltered pile of pine needles – will she respond to this false spring as she did last year?
February	1	8.5	Mild, dull and damp.
	19	9.5	Continuing mild; fruit buds bursting grass growing well.
March	3	7.5	5 cold days; light snow and frost.
	11	9	Mild and sunny; tortoise stirring.
	24	10	Daffodils in full bloom and plum blossom fully out; grass due for third cut.
April	15	12	Apple blossom starting. Spring on its way. Tortoise active.

meter in place to equilibrate for a period of about 5 min. Record in a diary, along with notes about weather conditions, vegetation and other related observations, and enter as an additional plot on a continuously recorded, one-year graph. (Refer to Figure G.1 and associated observation records in Table G.1.)

Interest will develop as data accumulates to enable comparisons to be made, one year with another, and ideas about local norms and seasonal trends developed. This local knowledge will help to interpret variations in sward performance from one site to another and one year to the next, and will assist in the timing of management procedures such as fertilizing and seeding where the response is likely to be temperature dependent.

G.2 Aids to interpretation

1. The site to which the data in Figure G.1 refers is an unshaded garden lawn at 15 m (50 ft) above sea level, on the north side of a broad, east-west valley, 1½ km (1 mile) inland from the coast of mid-Wales, just north of Aberystwyth.

2. The soil temperature at 250 mm (10 in) tends to vary between a winter low of about 5°C and a summer high of about 20°C, with values of 9°C and above likely to promote growth, all other conditions being favourable. On this basis, the 1992 growing season began mid-March and continued until late November.

3. The soil temperature tends to rise at an average rate of 0.75°C per week through spring and into summer, falling again at a similar, or slightly slower rate, through autumn into winter. At these transition periods, however, a spell of low air temperatures will affect the surface of the soil and limit germination from seed and seedling growth.

4. Think of soil temperature, at or below 250 mm (10 in) depth, as reflecting the heat store available to warm the soil from below. However, once the soil surface becomes frozen the effect will reduce the influence of this heat store at least temporarily, but because it is maintained geothermally from below, the 250 mm (10 in) depth value will readily recover to its more normal winter range of 6–8°C, just enough to maintain a very slow rate of grass growth.

5. There is no point in applying highly soluble, readily leached fertilzers before soil temperature is adequate to enhance growth. Therefore, delay application of seed and nitrogen-rich fertilizer, until the spring surge of soil temperatures exceeds 9–10°C. In the autumn the fall in soil temperatures will lag behind the fall in air temperatures and this will affect the performance of seeds and seedlings at the surface. It is advisable, therefore, to avoid seeding in the autumn beyond the point at which soil temperature at 250 mm (10 in) falls below 14 or 15°C.

References

Al-Bakri, K.H. (1984) *Biological Influences on the Development of Soil Structure*. Ph.D. Thesis, University College of Wales, Aberystwyth.

Casagrande, A. and Fadum, R.E. (1940) *Notes on Soil Testing for Engineering Purposes*, Harvard Univ. Grad. School of Engineering, Publ. 268, quoted, p55, in *Soil Mechanics in Engineering Practice* by Karl Terzaghi and Ralph B. Beck, 2nd edn, Wiley, New York, 1967.

Drew, M.C. (1975) Comparison of the effects of a localised supply of phosphate, nitrate, ammonium and potassium on the growth of the seminal root system, and the shoot, in barley. *New Phytologist* 75, 479–490.

Houghoudt, S.B. (1940) Versl. Landbouwk, Ond., 46, pp. 515–707, reviewed in English by Luthin, J.N., *Drainage Engineering*, Wiley, 1966, pp. 149–158.

Kamenskii, G.N. (1938) Dvizhenie gruntovykh vod v mezhdurechnom massive. (The movement of ground water in interfluvial tracks) quoted in Aravin, V.I. and Numerov, S.N. (1953) *Theory of Fluid Flow in Undeformable Porous Media*. Translated from Russian, Israel Program for Scientific Translations, Jerusalem, 1965, p. 85.

MAFF (1976) *The Agricultural Climate of England and Wales*, HMSO, London

MAFF (1982) *The Design of Field Drainage Pipe Systems*, HMSO, London.

Salih, R.O. (1978) *The Assessment of Soil Structure and the Influence of Soil Treatment on This Property*. Ph.D. Thesis, University College of Wales, Aberystwyth.

Stewart, V.I. (1971) *Drainage Problems on Playing Fields*, National Playing Fields Association, London.

Stewart, V.I. (1985) Functions of the soil. Introductory paper for European Environmental Bureau Conference on Soil Protection in the European Community, Brussels, 1984, pp. 47–58. Reproduced in *The Royal New Zealand Institute of Horticulture Annual Journal*, (13) 1985, 45–48.

Stewart, V.I. and Adams, W.A. (1969) Soil factors affecting the control of pace on cricket pitches, in *Proceedings of First International Turfgrass Research Conference*, Harrogate, England, pp. 533–546

Stewart, V.I. and Salih, R.O. (1981) Priorities for soil use in temperate climates, in *Biological Husbandry* (ed. B. Stonehouse) Butterworths, London, pp. 19–37.

Stewart, V.I., Salih R.O., Al-Bakri, K.H. and Strong, J. (1980) Earthworms and Soil Structure, Report No. 21, Welsh Soils Discussion Group, pp. 103–114.

Stewart, V.I. and Scullion, J. (1989) Principles of managing man-made soils. *Soils and Management*, 5, 109–116.

Stewart. V.I., Scullion J., Salih, R.O. and Al-Bakri, K.H. (1988) Earthworms and structure rehabilitation in subsoils and topsoils affected by opencast mining for coal. *Biological Agriculture and Horticulture*, 5, 325–338.

Thornton, D.J. (1978) *The Construction and Drainage of some Specified Sports Field Playing Surfaces*. Ph.D. Thesis, University College of Wales, Aberystwyth.

Vaughan, D, Wheatley, R.E. and Ord, B.G. (1984) Removal of ferrous iron from field drainage waters by conifer bark. *Journal of Soil Science*, 35, 149–153.

Index

Index